OPEN BORDE

OPEN BORDERS
The Case Against Immigration Controls

Second Edition

TERESA HAYTER

Pluto Press
LONDON • ANN ARBOR, MI

First published 2004 by PLUTO PRESS
345 Archway Road, London N6 5AA
and 839 Greene Street, Ann Arbor, MI 48106

Second edition 2004

www.plutobooks.com

British Library Cataloguing in Publication Data
A catalogue record for this book is available from
the British Library

Library of Congress Cataloging in Publication Data
Hayter, Teresa.
  Open borders : the case against immigration controls / Teresa Hayter.
    p. cm.
  ISBN 0–7453–2245–X (hard) — ISBN 0–7453–2244–1 (pbk.)
  1. Europe—Emigration and immigration—Government policy. 2.
Immigrants—Government policy—Europe. I. Title.
  JV7590 .H39 2000
  325.4—dc21
                                                      00–009580

ISBN 0 7453 2245 X hardback
ISBN 0 7453 2244 1 paperback

10   9   8   7   6   5   4   3   2   1

Designed and produced for Pluto Press by
Chase Publishing Services, Fortescue, Sidmouth, EX10 9QG, England
Typeset from disk by Stanford DTP Services, Northampton, England
Printed and bound in the European Union by
Antony Rowe, Chippenham and Eastbourne, England

CONTENTS

TABLES

PREFACE TO THE FIRST EDITION

This book was written thanks to a grant from the Joseph Rowntree Charitable Trust, for which I am extremely grateful. The trust accepted my proposal to take a radical look at immigration controls. The Joint Council for the Welfare of Immigrants (JCWI) very kindly supported my application and gave me freedom to express my opinions. I am particularly grateful for the help and support of Don Flynn.

The book is also based on over six years of campaigning against Campsfield immigration detention centre, as a member of the Campaign to Close Campsfield. A good many of my examples of the mistreatment of refugees are taken from the experiences of those who are or have been locked up in Campsfield. I believe that Campsfield exemplifies this mistreatment, and that it is not extreme or untypical. I can report on it from first-hand experience. Nine of us were outside Campsfield with placards when it opened on 26 November 1993, and I have been to nearly all the monthly demonstrations ever since. I have had the great good fortune to meet many refugees, both inside and outside Campsfield, and of course am indebted to them for much that is in this book. I hope they approve. I have visited refugees not just in Campsfield but also in Winson Green, Rochester, Blakenhurst and Bullingdon prisons and at Harmondsworth detention centre. I have been to several appeals and bail hearings in Birmingham and London and talked to many lawyers. Eleven asylum seekers have stayed in our East Oxford house, for periods ranging from a few days to over two years, and have been unfailingly considerate and good to have around. I do not accept the moral distinction between political refugees and those who cross frontiers in search of work. But, for what it is worth, my experience is the reverse of that of the Home Secretary Jack Straw, who told *The Economist*, as it reported on 14 February 1998, that 'Of all the asylum applications I have dealt with in my constituency, only one was genuine.' Of the many asylum seekers I have met, only two were not refugees in the narrow political sense. One, who entertained us in our house for several months, was straightforwardly trying to improve his life. The other was a young and very distressed Peruvian. As soon as he started talking to us in Campsfield, he told us he was not in fact a member of Sendero Luminoso, but the oldest of six children looked after by their mother. She had raised the money to send him to Britain

vii

by mortgaging their house, in the hope he could send back money to support them. He had got through immigration and found some cousins, who advised him to go to Croydon and apply for asylum. He did so, and was arrested and sent to Campsfield.

I am grateful for the generous encouragement of Bob Sutcliffe, who urged me to use whatever I wanted to from his book *Nacido en otra parte*, which advocates 'the right to total worldwide freedom of movement and residence', which unfortunately is still only in Spanish but from which I have plundered many ideas and facts. Nearly all the quotations of politicians in Chapter 2 are from Paul Foot's extensive research in Hansard for his book *Immigration and Race in British Politics*, with his kind agreement. The section on Fortress Europe is mainly based on a much more detailed document which Don Flynn has written, and is available from him at the JCWI. The section on the trial of the Campsfield Nine is mostly based on an article I wrote for *Red Pepper*. I am very grateful for comments on the first draft from Frances Webber, Bob Sutcliffe, Bill MacKeith, Pritam Singh, Steve Cohen, Robin Cohen, Rohini Hensman, Ann Dummett, Meena Singh, Tony Richardson and Don Flynn. I hope I have done some justice to them. Thanks also to Anne Beech and Pluto Press for commissioning the book and to Bill MacKeith for his copy-editing.

Note on translation: The translation of the proceedings of the FASTI conference is by Bill MacKeith. The rest, from French and Spanish, are by the author.

Bibliographical note: The figures in Chapter 1 are mostly from Sutcliffe. The quotations of politicians in Chapter 2 are from Hansard, nearly all of them from Foot; a few are from Spencer (see Bibliography).

PREFACE TO THE SECOND EDITION

The following is a description of some of the changes that have taken place in the treatment of refugees and migrants since I wrote this book in 2000. Because any attempt to describe in detail the latest changes would be out of date by the time this edition was published, I have not changed the main text. But I have made some additions to the list of organisations, the bibliography and the index. I have also added as an appendix our 'Manifesto of the No One Is Illegal group', which we produced in Manchester in September 2003. We hope it will help to win campaigners for migrants and refugees to the view that freedom of movement is an elementary human right, a view that is so far more widespread in other parts of Europe than it is in Britain (see pp. 146–8), and that groups will be set up in Britain to campaign for this right.

Since 2000 the application of immigration controls has become progressively more vicious. There has been virtually nothing in the way of improvement or reform. Everything has been done to make the suffering of refugees and migrants worse, in the largely mistaken belief that this will cut their numbers. The government is conducting what has become known as a 'war on asylum'. It attacks asylum seekers for their supposed abuse of the system and singles them out for harsh treatment. It drives them into illegality, locks them up, does not allow them to work, reduces them to destitution, splits up their families, labels them 'illegal immigrants' and promises to deport more of them if it can't stop them coming in the first place. It also increasingly rounds up others, mostly Caribbean, South Asian and African, who are sometimes described as 'over-stayers' and who may have lived for years in this country and have jobs, houses and families, for sometimes minor infringements of the immigration rules. The government thus bears heavy responsibility for the growth of the hysteria against asylum seekers and so-called 'illegal immigrants' (the terms are often used interchangeably; so much so that the Press Complaints Commission was moved to pronounce that the phrase 'illegal asylum seekers' should not be used, since there is no such thing).

In the process the position of asylum seekers as the new object of race hate campaigns has become entrenched. Their demonisation has no obvious justification. Such increases as there have been in their numbers are, more than ever, related to the wars perpetrated by the major powers: first Kosovans and then Iraqis (in the months before the US/British invasion of Iraq in March 2003) accounted for almost the entire increase. In 2002 the largest numbers of applicants were from Iraq, Zimbabwe, Somalia, Afghanistan and China, in that order. As before, the overwhelming majority come from areas in which there is severe political persecution or conflict, for which, again, the West bears much responsibility (see pp. 5–6). If such conditions arise, governments impose visa requirements on their nationals, as they have done recently for Zimbabweans, thus making it virtually impossible for refugees to travel legally to Britain (see pp. 95–105). They are nevertheless fully entitled to claim asylum under international treaties, and in the last few years around half of all asylum seekers eventually got refugee status or exceptional leave to remain (ELR – now replaced by the more restrictive 'humanitarian protection'). Many more of them ought to do so, but fall foul of the cruelly unjust and arbitrary system for determining whether they are 'genuine refugees' (see pp. 89–95). Those who have, with exceptional enterprise and courage, managed to flee poverty rather than wars or political persecution are likely to be similarly the victims of the actions of major Western powers. The reality is that most asylum seekers, whatever their reason for migrating, are highly educated and are often dissident members of the elite. Many take a large drop in their standard of living. They cost public money almost entirely because of the escalation of the repressive apparatus which is supposed to stop them coming here, and because they are no longer allowed to work (see below). If they do work, they are forced to work long hours for low wages in jobs that do not require their qualifications. The British are lucky that they come here.

Moreover, whatever the scaremongers may say, the number of asylum seekers migrating to Britain is relatively small, both compared to refugees elsewhere in the world and compared to other types of migration to Britain. Less than 2 per cent of refugees in the world as a whole are in Britain, although a recent poll showed that people believe the figure is 25 per cent. According to Home Office statistics on Control of Immigration, there were 84,130 asylum applications in Britain in 2002, which was the peak year. In the same year, and in each of the preceding five years, there were around 8 million visitors from abroad. There were 1.3 million returning British and other nationals. 369,000 foreign students were given leave to enter. 235,805 people were given official permission to work in Britain. Yet the Labour government constantly reiterates that it is doing its best to reduce the numbers, not of visitors, students, employees of multinational corporations, workers and so on, but of people applying for asylum. On 7 February 2003, in an interview on BBC's *Newsnight*, the prime minister Tony Blair announced that the government would halve the number of asylum applications, from its peak of 8,900 a month in October 2002, by September 2003. It claims credit for a recent decline in applications (although this is likely to have more to do with the situation in Iraq).

The government says its actions are necessary to defeat racism and the far right. But they both pander to and feed the sections of the media whose political agenda it is to stir up racism. The *Daily Mail*, the *Daily Express*, the *Sun* have almost daily headlines disseminating lies and slander about asylum seekers and 'illegals', some of them using language and information which appear to have come from official sources, attacking refugees for supposed crimes, scrounging and ill health, for being too many, or for resorting to catching and eating swans. The government only very rarely seeks to counter the media's lies and distortions with the truth. Its policies encourage the Tories to outbid it. Occasionally even the Tories are moved to criticise some particularly illiberal government measure; Oliver Letwin, shadow home secretary, for example, said that children should not be confined in 'accommodation centres' (see below) for six months; there should be a maximum ten-week limit. More often, the Tories make half-baked proposals such as that all incoming asylum seekers should be confined to an unspecified off-shore island. The British National Party (BNP) has made full use of the growth of prejudice against asylum seekers in its sometimes successful local election campaigns, especially in areas where no asylum seekers or refugees live. Asylum seekers themselves, especially those who are being dispersed outside London and the South East where their communities are strong, are being subjected to increasing levels of violence, such that many fear to leave their accommodation. The Institute of Race Relations has recorded on its website 24 deaths in racist attacks since 1999, including four murders of asylum seekers in the last two years, and ten major violent attacks, including, for example, systematic attacks on Iraqi Kurds in Hull, resulting in injuries to at least 13 of them; they held a demonstration in July 2003 to protest against failure by the police to protect them. The government's policies have also helped bring a small organisation called Migration Watch, now widely quoted as an authority on immigration and the supposed dangers of 'over-population', out of the woodwork. Its chair, Sir Andrew Green, former ambassador to Saudi Arabia, testified to the House of Commons Home Affairs Committee on Asylum Removals in September 2002 as one of three main 'experts'. Yet its chief researcher is Professor David Coleman, of Oxford university, who has held office in the Eugenics Society and its successor the Galton Institute, bodies which promote the notion that the purity of the white race should be preserved.

It is hard to see why the government aids and abets the racists, unless it is that it is so unpopular on most issues that it believes it can regain a little popularity by appearing to be stemming a 'flood' of asylum seekers who might otherwise 'swamp' British schools and the welfare state. The detention of asylum seekers, for example, which is one of the harshest consequences of immigration controls and causes great suffering for migrants and refugees, is little more than window-dressing. It does not serve its main function of deterring potential immigrants, and it does not even make it easy to deport people. In the end the government seems to be doing little other than trying to convince the opponents of immigration that it is keeping people out of Britain. On 18 September 2003 *The Times* reported as follows:

A 'short, sharp Bill' to curtail the appeals process for asylum-seekers and deter the growing number of people who destroy their papers in transit will be announced in the Queen's Speech.

The Times has learnt that the Bill will be rushed through Parliament early in the next session to make sure that it can have an impact on the number of asylum-seekers arriving in Britain before the next general election.

Tony Blair hinted at the measures in a meeting with his MPs yesterday, warning them that 'some people will not like it'. However, he said that he was aware that it was an issue in many constituencies and could cost Labour votes if more progress was not made.

Polling research suggests that many voters do not believe government statistics which show that applications have fallen, and need more reassurance. 'The Bill will certainly cut down on the legal gravy train and stop people playing the system,' a Whitehall source said.

Governments are constantly introducing changes in immigration laws. The changes are themselves a reflection of their inability to control the movement of people. The Tories' Asylum and Immigration Appeals Act of 1993 and its Asylum and Immigration Act of 1996 were followed by Labour's Immigration and Asylum Act of 1999 (which is described in some detail in this book). In November 2002 Labour passed another act, the Nationality, Immigration and Asylum Act. Yet another is apparently due in 2004.

The 2002 Act was preceded by a White Paper entitled 'Secure Borders, Safe Haven: Integration with Diversity', published in February 2002. This is a curious document. Its first half is devoted to arguing that immigrants make a large contribution to British prosperity and to meeting shortages of skills, and that Britain needs more of them. The second half is about how the government will stop them coming. The explanation, it seems, is that the government wants 'managed' immigration. By this it means that it hopes to be able to select the immigrants it wants, in the numbers and types that it wants, and to bar entry to anybody else. This is an idea that is becoming quite widespread, including among those who believe that immigration controls can somehow be made more humane and fair. The argument is that if legal channels of entry are broadened, then there will be less incentive for people, including asylum seekers who are supposedly not really asylum seekers, to come to Britain without permission. But of course such a policy leaves the whole repressive apparatus of immigration controls intact, and there is no sign that they will do anything other than continue to become more vicious. If the government's renewed interest in attracting immigrants satisfied the demand for asylum or work in Britain, there would be no need for immigration controls. The reality is that, while the government sends out recruiting teams to pillage the skills of trained Third World professionals, it simultaneously spends millions on making skilled people suffer, and perhaps deporting them, if they come to this country on their own initiative to seek asylum or to work. It recruits nurses in Zimbabwe, but imprisons Zimbabwean nurses who flee persecution.

Like other European governments, the Labour government is worried about skills and labour shortages, declining birth rates and an ageing population. Reports by Ceri Gott, Stephen Glover and others, published by the research directorate of the Home Office in 2001 and 2002, argue that immigrants not only contribute to prosperity and economic growth, but make a net contribution of approximately £2.5 billion a year to public finances, since they are mostly young, fit and have been educated at others' expense. A *Guardian* leader on 17 November 2003 reported that the home secretary David Blunkett, in response to the appointment of David Davis as his new hard-line shadow, 'rightly noted that legal migrants made up 8% of the UK population, but generated 10% of the nation's wealth'. The work permit system, under which employers can apply to the government for permission to employ foreigners in specific jobs, has been expanded; work permits have nearly doubled, from 68,400 in 1998 to 120,115 in 2002. The government has launched a Highly Skilled Migrant Programme, under which certain 'highly skilled' people can enter without specific job permits. Foreign students, in demand because they pay higher fees, can stay in Britain if they complete their courses and find a job. The scheme for importing casual labour on short term contracts has been extended from agriculture into other sectors with labour shortages, such as construction and catering.

In most cases the chosen immigrants will be admitted on short term contracts for specific jobs. This constitutes a radical break with previous, pre-immigration controls policies, when people who came to meet labour shortages in Britain from the Caribbean and South Asia before 1962 had the same rights as British subjects born in Britain (see pp. 43ff). It will mean not only, as the government intends, that the new contract workers will in theory have to leave when their contracts end, but that, as the government may also intend, they will be highly exploitable even while they are working in Britain legally. Their position will be little better than the position of 'illegal' workers. Attempts by the new legal immigrants to win better wages and conditions or join trade unions could lead to the sack and therefore to deportation. The government's intention may be that this will contribute to its drive for greater 'flexibility', in other words casualisation and insecurity, and to driving down wages and conditions, both in the sectors in which immigrants are concentrated and in the workforce as a whole. There are signs that trade unions and others are beginning to realise that the only way to counter this is to argue, not for zero immigration because it will not happen, but for full and equal rights for all workers and residents, including the right to join trade unions and struggle for better wages and conditions without the threat of deportation. In particular in the United States the AFL-CIO now argues not for stopping immigration, but for the legalisation of so-called 'illegals'. The British Trades Union Congress may yet follow. In July 2003 the TUC's international department published a report, entitled *Overworked, Underpaid and*

Over Here: Migrant Workers in Britain, which says that the lack of legal protection for migrant workers is 'giving the green light to unscrupulous gang-masters, agencies and employers to exploit foreign workers on a massive scale', and shows that the problem applies to both illegal and legal migrants; TUC general secretary Brendan Barber was quoted in a press release to launch the report as saying that: 'If every illegal worker was removed from the UK, parts of the economy would collapse overnight ... Everyone working in the UK deserves basic rights at work ...' In France the *sans-papiers* (see pp. 142ff) are now arguing that the sudden deprivation of rights for long-term immigrant residents and workers has created a new form of slavery, and argue for solidarity from other workers not out of pity, but to prevent the contagion spreading in European countries which have up to now had relatively strong employment rights. In their joint declaration to the European Social Forum in November 2003, calling for a European day of action in support of migrants on 31 January 2004, the *sans-papiers* argued for 'citizenship rights for all, based on residence', since 'the undocumented are only the visible tip of an iceberg of job insecurity and casualisation spreading to other migrants and then to workers in general', and because of 'the special position held by the undoc-umented in the process of restructuring the work environment through generalised casualisation', and the resulting 'centrality of the struggles of the undocumented'.

At the same time as promoting an increase in the number of insecure or 'managed' immigrants, the government appears intent on making it harder for others to work without legal permission. This too appears contradictory, since illegal workers, as the *sans-papiers* recognise, are the ultimately exploitable workforce. It is presumably based on political rather than economic calcu-lations. The government believes, probably correctly, that the fact that it has up to now been relatively easy to get work in Britain without papers is one reason why some refugees are desperate to cross the Channel. It also wishes to curry favour with the racists by showing that Britain is not a 'soft touch' and is not an attractive destination for asylum seekers or other migrants, but is, on the contrary, as the home secretary David Blunkett has put it, 'tough as old boots'. The 2002 Act introduced provisions designed to make it harder for new immigrants, including refugees, to obtain British citizenship, including the requirement that they should speak English, and have more knowledge about, and allegiance to, British institutions than most of the rest of us. It also introduced severer penalties and checks on employers. In July 2002, the government removed the 'concession' which in theory allowed asylum seekers to work if their claims were not determined within six months (see p. 106). Asylum seekers have been issued with 'smart' cards which carry their photograph, finger-prints, and a statement on whether or not they are allowed to work. Identity cards, on whose absence in Britain politicians have long prided themselves, are to be introduced, at first, in 2005, for foreigners. As the *Guardian* of 12 November 2003 reported, David Blunkett stated that:

An ID card scheme will help tackle crime and serious issues facing the UK, particularly illegal working, immigration abuse, ID fraud, terrorism and organised crime.

Identity cards would also make clear who is and is not entitled to health care and other public services, as well as to work, and thus facilitate the incorporation of health workers and other public officials as agents of immigration controls. They are no doubt intended to facilitate an increase in random immigration checks on people who look foreign, such as have existed in France and elsewhere for many years.

In November 2003, according to the *Guardian* of 14 November 2003, David Blunkett announced that the government was considering a scheme called 'earned regularisation'. This was intended to deal with the 'emotive' situation of valued but illegal immigrants who would not obtain identity cards when they were made compulsory for foreigners. They would have to demonstrate that 'they had not abused the system and could not be removed', that they were making a valuable 'contribution to the labour market' and had not engaged in 'welfare benefit abuse' or 'entered the country illegally' (which would exclude the majority of asylum seekers – see below). Those who qualified would be given a one-year legal work permit. Sarah Spencer, a researcher who has been influential with New Labour, apparently suggested the 'earned regularisation' idea to Mr Blunkett and was quoted as saying that the scheme 'would need to be selective to avoid the evident problems with the kind of general amnesty that has happened in other parts of Europe that have encouraged other people to come'. The Home Office apparently rapidly back-tracked from even this proposal. But Blunkett's chilling statement that he wanted 'to deal sensibly with people who are prepared to put their hands up' demonstrates the dangers of such 'regularisation' or amnesty schemes. Like the schemes in Britain in 1974, and in France in 1997 (see p. 145), they are likely to turn out to be a trap rather than a means of escape for many thousands of people, who risk putting their heads above the parapet and finding they are not among the chosen few.

As part of its policy of making asylum seekers suffer in the hope that this will deter others (see p. 74, and pp. 105ff), the government has introduced some measures of extreme severity. Food vouchers, introduced under the 1999 Act (see pp. 109–10), led, as predicted, to the stigmatisation of asylum seekers who held up check-out queues in their attempt to buy food up to the exact amount of their £30 per week vouchers. Vouchers were supplied late or not at all. Asylum seekers were, and are, dispersed (see p. 111) to one 'no-choice' offer of accommodation, sometimes in sub-standard housing, sometimes with unscrupulous private landlords, sometimes in hard-to-let council housing on estates where they are subjected to racist violence, including in Glasgow's Sighthill estate a murder. A parallel administrative system, National Asylum Support Service (NASS), was set up, paying asylum seekers much less than normal state benefits at much greater cost to the state. After widespread criticism, including by Bill Morris who was then general secretary of the Transport and General Workers Union, the government did a volte-face on

the food voucher system, substituting equally low cash payments. But worse
was to follow. Section 55 of the 2002 Act provided that, from January 2003,
asylum seekers who had failed to apply for asylum at ports of entry, or immediately after their arrival ('in-country' applicants), and others who had had
their claims turned down (but who might still be trying to exercise their legal
rights to oppose removal) would be denied access to even the poor-law support
provided by NASS. Home Office figures show that around two thirds not
only of all asylum seekers, but also of the people who are accepted as refugees,
have applied for asylum 'in-country'. In 1996 (see pp. 106–7) the Conservative
government had tried to remove all forms of public support from 'in-country'
and 'failed' applicants, and been prevented from doing so by the courts. Now
that Labour is trying to do much the same, they too are having trouble with
the courts. In February 2003 the High Court condemned the whole scheme
of the Act as inhuman, and also said that the Home Office had failed to prove
that the apellants had not applied for asylum as soon as they could. The
Home Office subsequently got the courts to accept that section 55 would only
constitute inhuman treatment if asylum seekers could be proved to be
destitute. In September 2003 the first case was won by the Home Office; the
court considered that a Malaysian asylum seeker who was sleeping rough
in Heathrow airport was not really destitute, since he had access to shelter
and some food. A further 200 cases are pending. Meanwhile, increasing
numbers of asylum seekers, currently around 5,000, were and are in fact being
reduced to destitution. They are not allowed to work, and they receive nothing
from the state. The government may find that, for the first time in Britain,
there is open and widespread revolt by the undocumented, such as has existed
for some years in other European countries (see Chapter 4).

Some of those made destitute, notably Iraqi Kurds and Somalis, are people
who have had their claims for asylum rejected but cannot be returned to their
own countries because they are unsafe, because their governments will not
accept them, because they have no documents, or because air travel to their
region is unavailable. Some have been denied support because, as is the case
with many refugees, they have been forced by government policies to travel
in the backs of lorries (see pp. 95–105), have been unaware that they are
crossing frontiers, and are deemed not to have found out how to claim asylum
quickly enough. An Iraqi Kurd, for example, who was perhaps fortunate to
have arrived before the new provisions on destitution, spent 24 hours in the
tyre compartment underneath a lorry, hoping he was being taken to Sweden.
He was deposited on a dual carriageway, realised he was in England not
Sweden, approached the nearest lights, asked for a police station, was collected
by the police and provided with their hospitality for the night. In the morning
he was told to go to Croydon. When he asked how to get there without
money, he was advised to go to Asylum Welcome, a charity in Oxford. Asylum
Welcome found him accommodation for the weekend and a lawyer who
claimed asylum for him. Two years later he got refugee status.

The government claims that it is taking strong measures to deport (or 'remove') the people who fail to get refugee status. One of the cruel ironies of the current system is that asylum seekers are put through the misery (and heavy public costs) of detention, destitution and continuing threats of deportation to the dangers they have fled from, sometimes over a period of years, but then when their claims are finally turned down they are not deported. Unsurprisingly this is one of the major complaints of the tabloids and the rest of the racists. The government's response is not to abandon the whole pointless exercise, but to promise to deport more asylum seekers. Removals have increased steadily under the Labour government, from 6,990 in 1998 to 10,740 in 2002, but apparently this is not enough. In 2000 the government set a target of 30,000 removals of 'failed asylum seekers' a year. It had to abandon this target as unworkable, even though it would have been less than the recent annual number of asylum claims rejected, let alone the number of people turned down and not removed in previous years. In 2002 it 'removed' 65,460 people, but only 10,740 of them were 'failed asylum seekers'. In an attempt to speed up deportations, the Home Office has been going for soft targets, especially families and people with long associations and commitments in Britain who are easier to find and deport than single men. People may be picked up in the street, on the underground or at work, or their houses may be raided in the early hours. Fathers who are breadwinners are deported, leaving their families dependent on public support. The charity Bail for Immigration Detainees (BID) has on occasion succeeded in persuading the courts to release people on the grounds that the government is violating the human right to family life. There are horror stories of people losing contact with their children, being unable to meet commitments to collect them from school, losing their houses, jobs and even their personal possessions, being deported at short notice without the chance to contact either their families or their solicitors. The Immigration Law Practitioners' Association (ILPA), in its submission to the Home Affairs Committee (see above) gave some examples among the many, including the case of:

A Lithuanian minor arrested for a driving offence who was then detained under Immigration Act powers overnight and removed the next day. He had been unable to telephone his mother who was awaiting consideration by the Home Office of her human rights claim; the minor was dependent on his mother's claim yet not only was there no contact between mother and son, but she was left not knowing what had happened to her son for two to three days.

Detainees are sometimes removed from detention with extreme violence, pinned to the floor and made unconscious. Some resist, for example by stripping at airport check-outs, and are returned to detention because pilots refuse to carry them. Others make the journey in handcuffs, surrounded by guards. Even Wackenhut, a private security firm used to 'escort' people to airports, was moved to express its disquiet at the way they were treated in evidence to the Home Affairs Committee on Asylum Removals, describing for example:

An incident where a child, who had recently undergone a splenectomy and was under continual medical supervision with tubes and wires coming out of various parts of his body, was subjected to the ignominy of initial moves towards deportation.

The Chief Executive of another company, Loss Prevention International Ltd, which provides guards on flights, told the committee how they hand over their charges to the authorities they may have fled from:

Some countries insist on us handing the individual over to their own authorities, which we do ... In China, for instance, in Beijing, we are always met by their own immigration authorities, the individual is handed over to them, we are asked a number of questions and they are taken away. Down in Lagos, for instance, the agreement that we have there is that we actually hand the returnee over to the ground staff of either British Airways or Virgin Atlantic ... Standing right next to them are the Nigerian immigration officers who watch that process and then we walk away from it ... The Turks actually take them away so I cannot comment about seeing people out on the airport at Istanbul ... Last year, sir, it was our top destination! ... [they were] Turkish Kurds in general.

To facilitate removals the government has announced its intention to set up a smooth process under which asylum seekers are first to be sent to 'induction centres', then moved on to 'accommodation centres' or, failing that, made to report to 'reporting centres' from the accommodation to which they have been dispersed (see p. 111), and then, if their claims are rejected (but sometimes in practice before they are rejected, see below), to 'removal centres'. One induction centre exists at Margate; in June 2003 some of its enforced occupants went on hunger strike. The government is having trouble with its accommodation centres. It proposed four sites, each to accommodate 750 asylum seekers, including women and children, in isolated rural areas. After vociferous and often racist local objections, it had to abandon its plans for two of them. Although the government's planning inspector turned down the application for a third accommodation centre on a military site near Bicester, the Bicester centre is to open in 2005. The induction centres and accommodation centres are not to be locked, but they are prisons in effect, with strong inducements (and penalties) for the people assigned to them not to leave, and they will operate a kind of curfew. The Home Office has stated that if people fail to obey 'clear rules' then not only will they lose all future public support, but 'breaking the rules may also affect their claims for asylum' (which must be unlawful under the rules of the refugee conventions). The centres will be built and run by private contractors. According to the *Oxford Mail* of 1 October 2003, three companies are bidding to operate the Bicester accommodation prison: United Kingdom Detention Services, Group 4 and Premier Prisons. There are to be medical, legal and educational facilities and meals provided within the centres, but no self-catering facilities and probably little transport to local towns. Children will not be allowed to go to local schools, so the chances of them learning English, let alone getting an adequate education and having the chance to integrate, will be minimal. The home secretary David Blunkett, outdoing his predecessor Jack Straw, said that schools were in danger of being 'swamped' by asylum seekers' children.

The existing immigration detention centres (see pp. 116–23) have been renamed 'removal centres'. The Labour government announced that it would more than quadruple the numbers detained under immigration laws to 4,000; the numbers initially more than doubled but then declined to 1,690, including 1,355 people who had claimed asylum, at the end of June 2003. The reason for the recent decline is loss of capacity. The government announced at the beginning of 2002 that it would no longer detain asylum seekers in ordinary prisons (although by the end of 2002 the numbers in prisons were up again, to 19 per cent of immigration detainees). The two big new detention centres at Harmondsworth, near Heathrow, and Yarl's Wood, near Bedford, opened in 2001, were meant to replace this loss of capacity and expand the 'detention estate'. But half of the 550 spaces at Harmondsworth are no longer in use. The Home Office claimed this was to enable fire sprinklers to be fitted (see below), but it seems the real reason was that the private contractors UK Detention Services Ltd (UKDS) could not prevent widespread violence within Harmondsworth, involving both guards and detainees, at least one suicide and several attempted suicides. And in February 2002 the occupied half of Yarl's Wood, which was supposed to contain 900 asylum seekers, was burnt down (see below). Yarl's Wood remained closed until September 2003. Meanwhile, a Young Offenders' Institution at Dover, a prison at Dungavel near Glasgow and part of Lindholme prison near Doncaster have been redesignated as immigration prisons. In October 2003 20 people escaped from Lindholme, 8 or 9 people escaped from Dover, and there was a big protest at Haslar which closed one of the dormitories. And so on. The Institute of Race Relations has recorded on its website 14 suicides of 'victims of the asylum system' in the last five years, three of them in immigration prisons.

The government says that the purpose of removal centres is to detain for short periods people who have had their asylum claims rejected. But only a small proportion of the people detained have exhausted their rights to appeal against refusal, some have not been given an initial decision by the Home Office, and some are detained, in continuing arbitrary fashion, when they apply for asylum at ports and airports. The government will not give figures on what the proportions are. But after Yarl's Wood prison was opened in November 2001, and the home secretary David Blunkett had said on local radio that it was a 'removal centre' where 'failed' asylum seekers would be held for 24 hours prior to their removal, Lord Rooker, then immigration minister, announced that of the 385 people imprisoned there, only 46 had dated removal notices. Many had already been detained for many months. According to Home Office statistics, of the total numbers detained at the end of 2002, 28 per cent had been so for more than four months, including 35 for over a year, 105 for over six months, and 100 for between four and six months. People who flee death, prison or torture can find themselves taken to a place called a 'removal centre' before they have even entered the country. Others are picked up for not having their immigration papers in order. Such people, who are threatened with immediate deportation, now form a growing proportion of those detained.

The 2002 Act repealed the provision for automatic bail hearings for immigration detainees which had been in the 1999 Act but had not been implemented. It thus removed the government's one response to repeated criticisms of the lack of judicial supervision of detention. The Home Office now moves people around from centre to centre at frequent intervals without notice or reason; it is hard to escape the conclusion that this is to deny them contact with their lawyers, families and supporters, and to reduce further the possibility of bail. Possibly because the private security companies running the prisons cannot process the paperwork fast enough, some detainees have been kept in vans for more than 24 hours, deprived of food, water and even toilet facilities. There are well documented examples of detainees being treated with violence by the private companies transferring them.

Perhaps the worst innovation of the current Labour government is that, unlike any other government in Europe, it now detains whole families, including young children and babies, and pregnant women. At the end of 2002 115 women were detained. The Home Office gives no figures on the number of children, apparently considered non-persons, detained. Because of the inability of UKDS to protect the women and families detained in Harmondsworth, they have been moved elsewhere. Yarl's Wood was reopened in September 2003 for women and apparently, in future, children. Children and their mothers are detained at Dungavel, Tinsley and Oakington. Some children have been moved from mainstream schools, where they were much appreciated by their friends and teachers, and have been locked up in prison-like conditions, at Dungavel for example, for months on end, in spite of numerous protests, in the House of Lords and elsewhere. Pregnant women have inadequate medical attention. Mothers have to queue for hours to receive powdered milk or nappies, which are allocated one at a time. A report by Bail for Immigration Detainees, *A Crying Shame: Pregnant Asylum Seekers and their Babies in Detention*, gives a harrowing account based on interviews with some of these women.

Most of the immigration prisons continue to be run by private security firms. Group 4 in particular continues to display its brutal incompetence, and continues to be hired by the government. It won the contract to build and run the new Yarl's Wood prison. On 14 February 2002, a few months after it was opened, the occupied half of it was destroyed in a fire. The best the police could say was that 'we can categorically say it is unlikely' that anyone died. As had happened at Campsfield (see pp. 128–33), some of the detainees were arbitrarily picked out by Group 4 and prosecuted, in this case for arson, violent disorder and affray. It remains unclear why and how the fire was started; there were no convictions for arson, and the defendants themselves were appalled by the fire and spent much of their time helping other detainees, nurses and even Group 4 employees to escape from it. At their trial in 2003 much of Group 4's evidence was thrown out; charges were dropped during and before the trial; Henry Momadou and Behar Limani were convicted of violent disorder, were given four years, are incarcerated in Wormwood Scrubs, and are appealing; Ahmed Aliane pleaded guilty to violent disorder, was deemed to have already served his time but is still in Wormwood Scrubs, after 29 months in various prisons and numerous suicide attempts; Nasseem Mosstaffa pleaded guilty to affray, having thrown a half-empty plastic bottle at a distant line of officers in riot gear, was deemed to have spent his three-month sentence but, having spent time in five different prisons, decided to accept 'voluntary' removal. The very active local Campaign to Stop Arbitrary Detentions at Yarl's Wood, SADY, has commented as follows:

The Home Office showed a total disregard for human life by detaining people at Yarl's Wood in unsafe conditions operated for private profit by Group4, described by the prosecution in court as a 'national laughing stock ever since they first blundered into the field of private custodial services'. It is the Home Office and Group4 who should be prosecuted for Unlawful Imprisonment and Recklessly Endangering Lives. Their responsibility for what happened at Yarl's Wood is significant. Firstly the Home Office arbitrarily detained men, women and children who are not accused of a crime, indefinitely – in a wooden framed building they decided not to fit sprinklers to. Then Group4 pinning a 51 year old woman to the ground, dragging her along the floor, triggering the whole incident, which they went on to grossly and negligently mis-manage – including delaying access to fire fighters and police, and locking detainees into the burning building. Not enough, they went on to hinder the defence of those picked for prosecution – Group4 subverted the investigation process by a series of 'wholly improper' actions and the Home Office deported most of the detainee eye witnesses.

Group4 were under investigation for Corporate Manslaughter, and under threat by police of being interviewed about obstruction ...

The Fire Brigades Union, from the start, stated publicly that their members had been prevented from entering the burning building for over an hour, confirming what detainees, who desperately wanted them to come and rescue them, had told us. At a public meeting in London in September 2003, a fire controller confirmed this and stated that her colleagues had also asked to be allowed at least to break ground-floor windows so that detainees could escape the fire, and been refused. According to Nigel Leskin, one of the defence lawyers, there was also clear police video evidence that detainees, who were kept outside in below zero temperatures with children and babies for many hours, desperately appealed to the lines of uniformed officers to help people they could see trapped inside, and were told to 'go and get them yourselves'. Andy Gilchrist, general secretary of the Fire Brigades Union, commented as follows at the Trades Union Conference Annual Congress in Brighton in September 2003:

Of course the main conclusion to be drawn from this incident is that asylum seekers were treated as sub-humans. So the building was put up on the cheap, the staff supervising the inmates (for that is how they were treated) were untrained and poorly paid, and the exigencies of so-called Riot Control overrode those of firefighting. At every stage fire safety took a back seat.

Campaigns against detention continue, and new active campaigns have started, especially against Yarl's Wood and the Dover removal centre. In September 2003 there was a demonstration of 2,000 people against the refugee prison at Dungavel. Most of these campaigns have joined together and set up Barbed Wire Britain, a network to end refugee and migrant detention. The Campaign to Close Campsfield won a victory when, in the House of Commons on 7 February 2002, David Blunkett announced that:

I can also confirm that I intend to close Campsfield House. This outdated centre is no longer appropriate to the 21st century. These places will be transferred to the new high-standard removal centres.

Campsfield was refurbished in 1993, at a cost of £20 million, from buildings much newer than some of the buildings in which refugees are locked up. The only possible explanation for the decision to close it was the protests, inside and outside it (see pp. 127–33). As I wrote in 2000, such protests had not occurred at other detention centres. Since then the government has had troubles at both its 'new high-standard removal centres', and in others too (see above). This presumably explains why, on 22 October 2003, the immigration minister Beverley Hughes announced that the government would keep Campsfield open and, shamefully, expand it to 290 places.

Campaigners for the rights of refugees frequently point to the injustice of the procedures for determining asylum claims, which means that many who need protection are removed to possible death, persecution and extreme hardship, and argue for greater fairness. The government moves steadily in the other direction. The White List of supposedly safe countries, attacked by Labour and formally abolished by them, has reappeared. People coming from countries which the Home Secretary designates 'safe' are considered to have 'clearly unfounded' cases and are subject to accelerated procedures, unless the Home Office decides otherwise. They have only 'non-suspensive' rights of appeal, which means they can only appeal from abroad. The current list includes all the countries which are to join the European Union. Therefore, for example, Roma who have fled severe persecution in Poland or Hungary, from which the state authorities do little or nothing to protect them, can be returned to those countries without the right to appeal in Britain. However it now appears that deporting them will be a quite unnecessary act of cruelty, since accession to the EU will imply free movement in May 2004. The 2002 Act introduced new curtailments of rights to judicial review. Since then the government has announced, in a further twist of the screw, that legal aid will be limited to five hours for initial advice, including solicitors' travel time to remote detention centres and everything else, and four hours to prepare an appeal. In most cases conscientious solicitors know that they cannot remotely stay within these limits. So many have withdrawn from the work, leaving what the government calls the 'legal aid gravy train' in the hands of the charlatans. Blair, in his speech to the Labour Party's October 2003 conference, said the following:

> We should cut back the ludicrously complicated appeal process, we should derail the gravy train of legal aid, fast-track those from democratic countries, and remove those who fail in their claims without further judicial interference.

So much for the rule of law.

Refugees and migrants are being further penalised by their supposed association with terrorism, both in government actions and in public perceptions. In 2000 the government passed a Terrorism Act. The act criminalised members and supporters of 'terrorist organisations' including, for example, the PKK (Kurdistan Workers Party). Kurdish refugees from Turkey are put in a double bind. If they fail to tell immigration officials that they are members of the PKK, they diminish their chances of refugee status. But if they confess to their membership, they are liable to prosecution under the Terrorism Act. The act has been used against British protestors as well, for example in 2003 against people expressing solidarity with 'terrorist organisations' and people protesting against the Fairford Air Force base and the arms fair at Canary Wharf, demonstrating that the repressive powers acquired against foreigners are liable to spread and poison society as a whole. In 2001, shortly after the attack on the World Trade Center on 11 September 2001, the government passed another act, the Anti-Terrorism, Crime and Security Act. This act gave the government powers to detain without trial and indefinitely non-British citizens whom it suspected of terrorist links but did not have enough evidence to prosecute, claiming that a national emergency existed which warranted derogation from the European Convention on Human Rights. The government took these special powers because some of those whom it wished to detain could not be deported to their countries of origin, and its existing powers of indefinite detention without trial enable it to detain only those who are liable to deportation. But in other respects the situation of those who are suspected of terrorism differs little from those who are suspected, often wrongly, of not really being refugees. The differences between migrants and refugees and 'terrorists' is blurred in other ways by the act, which tends to intimidate refugees and migrants and to deter solidarity with resistance against repressive regimes abroad, many of which are supported by the British government. One of the goals of the new Campaign Against Criminalising Communities (CAMPACC) is to 'defend the democratic freedom to dissent and to resist oppression, nationally and internationally', both for British and non-British citizens.

The government seems anxious to escape its legal obligations under the Geneva Refugee Convention (see p. 71) without formally repudiating the convention. Its opponents have attacked many of its new measures on the grounds that they fail to comply with these obligations; 'death of asylum by a thousand cuts', Amnesty International calls it. Most blatantly, in February

2002, the government made a proposal to the European Union, entitled *New Vision*, that asylum seekers who make it to Britain and other EU countries should be transferred, before their cases are considered, to two categories of camp: 'transit processing centres' in states bordering, but outside, the European Union, and, apparently for people whose claims had been rejected but who could not be returned to their own countries, 'regional protection areas' in 'refugee-producing' regions. Both types of camp would be in effect prisons. In the transit processing centres claims would be processed by the UNHCR. The British government's *New Vision* report states that: 'As UNHCR would be an independent body the only remedy would be an administrative review of the decision, perhaps by a senior board on the papers only.' These centres would be designed, the British report stated, to act as a deterrent to persons abusing the asylum system. As Amnesty International commented in a mimeo document entitled 'Unlawful and Unworkable – Extra-territorial Processing of Asylum Claims', dated June 2003:

The real goal behind the proposals appears to be to reduce the number of spontaneous arrivals in the UK and EU states by denying access to territory and shifting the asylum-seekers to processing zones outside the EU, where responsibility, enforceability and accountability for refugee protection would be weak and unclear.

The United Nations High Commission for Refugees (UNHCR) made an almost equally shocking 'counter-proposal'. This included the immediate transfer of asylum seekers whose claims were considered 'manifestly unfounded', on the grounds of their national origins, to closed 'common processing centres', or in effect prisons, within the EU but near its borders, where their claims would be processed with even fewer rights of appeal than exist within most European countries. 'No Borders' and other protest groups in Europe, which have already started a campaign against the Organisation for International Migration, are now considering extending it to the UNHCR. A Communication adopted by the EU Commission on 3 June 2003 was cautious about the proposals, and the EU summit at Thessaloniki in Greece in June 2003 rejected them. But they remain on the table.

The Amnesty International report makes clear that the proposals for transferring asylum seekers to closed camps outside the countries in which they have applied for asylum are likely to violate several international treaties. It also comments that these are not the first attempts to 'extra-territorialize' asylum procedures, referring for example to the treatment of Vietnamese refugees in the 1980s and 1990s. The false assumption was made that they were economic migrants and resulted in arbitrary, long term detention of Vietnamese refugees who arrived in Hong Kong and elsewhere, and the forced repatriation of many hundreds of them. Some, at least, had escaped torture and long prison sentences for supposed anti-state activities in Vietnam (a novel called *The Ghost Locust* by Heather Stroud, who spent six years working in the refugee camps in Hong Kong and did research in Vietnam, gives a gripping fictionalised account of some of their stories).

The more governments cast around for ever more brutal and repressive ways of trying to keep people out, the clearer it becomes that it is impossible to win any particular improvements in immigration controls, important though it is to expose and campaign against their harshest consequences. The suffering imposed on asylum seekers and other migrants is not some random or unintended consequence of immigration controls. It is deliberate government policy. Governments believe in deterrence, or the potential for reducing the number of people applying for asylum by making conditions harsh. Even supposing there was any prospect that governments might abandon this belief, suffering is an inevitable consequence of immigration controls, which give to the state the right to choose between the deserving and the undeserving. The people best able to decide whether they need to migrate, or to seek refuge, are migrants themselves.

It is also not enough to argue, as some do, including Nigel Harris in his new book *Thinking The Unthinkable*, that people should be free to migrate for work, just as capital and goods are supposedly free, and that decisions on whom to employ should be left to employers rather than determined by the state. If migrant workers do not have citizenship rights, they will constitute, as they now do, a threatened and precarious underclass, and they will be open to extreme forms of exploitation. Trade unions and all workers have an interest in supporting the rights of migrants, in order to prevent their own rights and working conditions being undermined (see above). New migrants need to have exactly the same rights as all others who are living and working in a particular country or area, whatever their nationality. A demand which is now widespread in France and other European countries is for citizenship based on residency, rather than on nationality. New migrants must have not only the right to work, but the right to join trade unions, to employment protection, to go on strike and to vote, and they must have full access to all the benefits enjoyed by other citizens, including health care, education, unemployment benefits and social security. They must not be threatened with deportation if they attempt to assert their rights.

Finally, it remains true that whatever the economic rationale for securing a cheap and compliant workforce through 'managed immigration', ultimately immigration controls are explicable only by racism. If governments merely wanted a compliant workforce they could allow employers to make free use of the vast reservoir of labour which now exists in the world because of centuries of imperialist theft, as many employers in the United States and elsewhere urge. It is perhaps conceivable that immigration controls could disappear under capitalism (see for example pp. 152–5). Many disagree, believing that free movement of people will only become a political possibility once the capitalist expropriation of the wealth of the Third World, and the wars to enable this, end. But while the abolition of immigration controls may require a revolution, what is clear is that, as we said in our manifesto *No One Is Illegal*, to render them fair would require a miracle. There can be no such thing as fair or non-racist immigration controls. Immigration controls have their origins in racism, and they legitimate and breed racism (see Chapter 2 of this book). They are inherently discriminatory, since they exclude foreigners or outsiders. They need to be opposed in their totality.

Teresa Hayter
October 2003

INTRODUCTION

Human beings have migrated throughout their history. People and their rulers have at various times and in different ways tried to exclude others from their territories, or to expel them once they are there. Most people now appear to take immigration controls for granted, at least in the rich industrialised countries of the West. But comprehensive controls to stop immigration are a recent phenomenon. A hundred years ago they did not exist; it was the people who advocated them who were condemned as extremist. Immigration controls are a function of nation states which themselves have existed for not much longer, and which are now said to be in decline. Unlike nations, border controls are flourishing, and they are becoming ever more extensive and oppressive. The state powers to which the governments of industrialised countries most tenaciously cling are their powers to keep people out of their territories. Their object, though not always achieved, is to exclude poor people, and especially black people.

The right of free movement across frontiers is not a right enshrined in any declaration on human rights. Its denial, on the other hand, gives rise to some of the worst and most vicious abuses of human rights, and provides perhaps the most fertile terrain for the agitation of the far right. Governments make use of whatever measures they choose to deter, punish and eject the people they do not wish to receive in their territories. Frequently they treat them in ways in which they would not treat their own citizens, and which undermine accepted norms of liberal democracy, the rule of law and human rights.

On 10 December 1948 the General Assembly of the United Nations proclaimed the Universal Declaration of Human Rights. Article 13–1 of the declaration states that 'Everyone has the right to freedom of movement and residence within the borders of each state', and article 13–2 states that 'Everyone has the right to leave any country, including his own, and to return to his country.' This freedom is qualified by ommission. People may leave their own country, but the declaration is silent on their right to enter another one. Unless they can prove they are refugees: article 14 states that 'Everyone has the right to seek and to enjoy in other countries asylum from persecution.' These asylum rights were incorporated, and given a restrictive definition, in the 1951 United Nations Geneva Convention on Refugees and in its 1967 Protocol. They are in theory still operative. But the governments

1

of the rich Western countries, more and more, do their utmost to stop refugees coming to their countries to apply for asylum. They are now talking of revising the convention to formally curtail those rights. They impose increasingly harsh suffering on innocent refugees, who have often been traumatised and tortured, in a partly vain attempt to deter others. In the process they are flouting other rights enshrined in the Universal Declaration and in other international agreements on human rights, such as the right not to be arbitrarily arrested and imprisoned and the right not to be subjected to cruel, inhuman or degrading treatment or punishment (see Chapter 3).

For the rest of humanity, those who are fleeing poverty rather than political persecution, or who simply want to migrate to improve their lives, entry into the rich Western countries to settle and to work has since the 1970s become possible only in exceptional circumstances. If they are highly qualified, and going to particular jobs, and if they are wealthy, they may be allowed in. If they belong to the immediate family of people already settled in these countries they may also be allowed in, providing they can surmount the often brutal obstacles put in their way. If they are citizens of the European Union they can go and work in another EU country. Within their own countries they are actively encouraged to move around in search of work. As Bob Sutcliffe comments in an article in *Index on Censorship*:

> On your bike, as Margaret Thatcher's minister Norman Tebbitt said, and you are a saint shining with neo-liberal virtues. On your ferry, and you are a demon against whom great European democracies change their constitutions in panic.

People trying to cross frontiers in search of work are branded 'illegal immigrants', persecuted and vilified. Sometimes they are simply called 'illegals', as if a human being could be categorised as an illegal human being. The term of abuse most frequently used against refugees themselves is that they are in reality 'economic refugees' rather than political ones and therefore 'bogus', 'abusing the system'. There is no such thing as the free movement of labour internationally.

This lack of freedom of movement may be one of the reasons why vast international inequalities of wealth persist and are growing. The wealth of Europe and other industrialised countries was built, from the sixteenth century onwards, through the exploitation of the natural resources and peoples of the rest of the world. Europeans used the labour of conquered peoples to produce raw materials and primary products for consumption in Europe, and they destroyed the industries of the more advanced civilisations they encountered in their imperial expansion. They then embarked on their own industrialisation and they protected their new industries through quotas, tariffs and prohibitions. Once they had established their dominance, they advocated free trade. The methods they used, and use, to prise open markets and secure raw materials throughout the world range from military force to the more obfuscated pressures of the World Bank and the International Monetary Fund. Since the 1980s the major powers have embarked on an orgy of 'liberalisation'. They demand and have to a great extent achieved the removal of controls not only on imports and exports of goods, but also on capital flows (especially outflows) and investment. According to the economic theories used to justify these policies, economic liberalisation is supposed to lead to greater welfare for all. In reality it has led to polarisation and crisis, as is the normal observable reality of markets. Although some countries, especially in East Asia, grew fast in the last 20 years, others have become poorer. The gap between them and the richer countries is growing wider.

Integration into the world market, together with continuing high levels of inequality and exploitation, have caused some enterprising people to attempt to migrate in search of work, as market economics would predict. But the logic of economic liberalisation has not been applied to the movement of people. According to this logic, economic liberalisation should of course include the free movement of labour as well as of goods and capital, and this in turn, according to market theory, should lead to an equalisation of wage levels internationally. This might or, more likely, might not turn out to be the case in reality, just as within countries inequalities persist and often grow in the so-called 'free market' (as a result, free marketeers would say, of 'market imperfections'). But it is likely that polarisation is aggravated by the denial of people's right to move around the world in search of employment and a better life. The aim of immigration controls is to ensure that there is no such possibility. They are a market imperfection of an extreme variety, and one more demonstration that the so-called free market does not in reality exist. Samir Amin, the celebrated Marxist economist, argued in a lecture at Wolfson College in Oxford on 23 February 1999 that it is no mere chance that 'globalisation' has not resulted in the peoples of Asia, Africa and Latin America 'catching up':

I advance the thesis that polarisation is immanent to the global expansion of capital. This is because the 'world market' in question remains deeply unbalanced by the single fact that it remains truncated; constantly widening its commercial dimension (trade in goods and services) and in the domain of international transfer of capital, this market remains segmented with regard both to labour and to international migrations of workers which remain subject to controls. ... A real coherent liberal should insist on the opening of borders in every direction. ... The end result was ... a globalisation of capital and not of the economy, which, on the contrary, differentiates itself in the centre/periphery dichotomy that continues to worsen. (mimeo copy of speech)

Yet obtaining labour for the growing needs of capitalist expansion has been a continuing preoccupation of employers and governments. In their colonies, though not in the metropolis, they resorted to force to obtain workers, from the slave trade to indentured labour and forced labour in Africa and India. After the Second World War, European governments set up recruitment agencies to obtain foreign workers to work in their own industries and services. The fact that for most of this period there was net emigration from

Britain has sometimes been seen as the explanation for slow British growth compared to, for example, French and German. Employers at times put pressure on governments to relax immigration controls, especially in the United States. The reasons why these capitalist pressures are not more successful, or more determined, have little to do with the material interests of capitalism. Thus for example the London *Financial Times*, a strong proponent of the 'free' market, has acknowledged that it is inconsistent to exclude labour from such freedom, but argued that increased immigration would cause, not economic problems, but social problems, or problems of 'assimilation'.

Immigration 'problems' are not a problem of excessive numbers of immigrants. They are a problem of the racism of Europeans, North Americans and white majorities elsewhere, who more or less explicitly harbour notions of the superiority of the white 'race', whatever that may mean, and the undesirability of destroying the supposed homogeneity of their nation. In the past these notions have been applied to virtually all new immigrants, whatever their nationality or race. In the last forty years the main objects of anti-immigrant racism in Britain and elsewhere have been, and are, people of African and Asian origin. In the 1950s and 1960s British politicians tried to work out how to exclude 'coloured' Commonwealth citizens without excluding white Commonwealth citizens and the much larger numbers of Irish immigrants, without giving an appearance of discrimination and without causing offence to the governments and peoples of the 'multiracial Commonwealth'. Eventually they abandoned the attempt, and immigration controls, from 1962 onwards, were at first covertly and then blatantly based on racist discrimination not only against foreigners in general, but against particular types of foreigners (see Chapter 2).

The currently dominant form of anti-immigrant racism, that which is directed against black and Asian people, and most recently Romany people, is sometimes 'explained' by the assertion that they are more easily identifiable as immigrants, or the children of immigrants, than most of the other waves of migrants to Britain over the centuries. But similar things have been said about the supposed 'non-assimilability' of other immigrants, and in any case it is unclear why such distinctions should matter. The most convincing explanation for the strength and persistence of anti-black racism is to be found in the myths which the imperialists invented to justify to themselves the extreme forms of suffering they imposed on their colonial subjects. These myths survive, permeate British people's consciousness, and infect the way all of us think and act. It would nevertheless be surprising if prejudice against black people did not diminish in the same way as prejudice against earlier immigrants has. Meanwhile, anti-immigrant hysteria is whipped up not only against black, Asian and Romany refugees but also against other recent groups of refugees and migrants: Kosovans and other white east Europeans.

The primary targets of racism and xenophobia are now refugees. Since the 1980s there have been rapid increases, from a low level, in the number of people coming from the Third World and eastern Europe to Britain and other rich countries to seek asylum. The increase in asylum seekers followed the closing of borders against people coming to seek work in the 1960s and 1970s. The government and others have made the false logical leap that this means that asylum seekers are actually economic migrants trying to exploit a loophole in immigration controls. A few are. But to claim that most asylum seekers are 'bogus', as government ministers and the media often do, is false and unjust. They come overwhelmingly from countries and regions in which there are repressive regimes, civil wars and violent conflicts. Most of these are not the areas from which people had previously migrated to work. There is in fact a connection between the two types of migration, but not in the way in which those opposed to immigration see it. This is that imperialism bears much responsibility for both of them. Imperialism created links between the colonies and the metropolis. While war, conflicts and repression are often the product of many internal factors, including the chauvinism of religious and ethnic majorities, various forms of nationalism and more straightforward struggles for domination and wealth, it can be argued that some arise from centuries of imperialist control, and in particular the imperialists' divide-and-rule tactics and the boundaries they drew on maps. Imperialism in its modern guise has created new forms of impoverishment, which may exacerbate existing nationalist and ethnic tensions. When the long postwar capitalist boom ended in the late 1970s, the rich countries succeeded in transferring much of the burden of their own crisis to the Third World. The prices of Third World countries' exports of primary commodities and raw materials collapsed. When at the beginning of the 1980s first the Reagan government in the United States and then European governments raised interest rates to unprecedented heights, they massively increased the cost of servicing foreign debt for governments in the Third World (which had been pressed to borrow at low or even negative interest rates from Western banks seeking a 'sinkhole' for the money deposited by oil-exporters in the 1970s). In order to force governments to continue to service their debt at these new extortionate rates of interest, a cartel of the World Bank, the IMF, Western governments and banks and Third World elites imposed cuts in public expenditure on social services, wages and employment in Third World countries which bore most heavily on the poor and urban wage earners. In Algeria the massacres started when the military denied election victory to the FIS, an Islamic party, whose strength was built especially among the poor in urban areas impoverished by the government's turn to more orthodox pro-Western economic policies. The imposition of IMF/World Bank 'liberalisation' in Yugoslavia led to severe poverty and unemployment and heavy indebtedness to Western banks and financial institutions. In their attempt to get Yugoslavia to service this debt, the IMF/World Bank forced the federal government to cut investment and transfers to the regions. Michel Chossudovsky in a detailed article on this issue says: 'Secessionist tendencies feeding on social and ethnic divisions gained impetus precisely during a period of brutal impoverishment of the Yugoslav population. ... The "economic therapy" (launched in January 1990) contributed to crippling the federal State system. State revenues which should have gone as transfer payments to the republics and autonomous provinces were instead funnelled towards servicing Belgrade's debt ... .' This in turn fuelled the populist nationalism which led to the break-up of Yugoslavia and war.

In a more direct sense, repression and wars in the Third World are largely made possible because both the regimes and those who fight them obtain weapons from the industrialised countries, frequently with the help of official loans. Many of the world's most repressive regimes are supported, with aid for example, by European governments and the United States. Both the Nigerian and the Zairean governments, as well as many governments in Latin America and Asia, were supported for years while they oppressed and tortured their peoples and stole their wealth. When right-wing governments are thrown out or voted out by liberation movements or left-wing political parties and attempt to carry out reforms and to redistribute wealth to the poor, the West intervenes by cutting aid, boycotting trade and sometimes by military intervention, directly or through its surrogates. It thus has direct responsibility, for example, for refugees from Chile and from Angola, among others. The recent flow of refugees from eastern Europe follows the introduction of capitalism and market systems and the break-up of Yugoslavia and the Soviet Union, most of which was welcomed and supported by the West. In 1999 more than half of all asylum seekers in Europe were from the Federal Republic of Yugoslavia, nearly all of them Kosovans. Those who assert that refugees and migrants are a problem should examine the causes of forced migration, rather than blaming and punishing refugees.

In Britain there have been three main historical phases of anti-immigrant agitation, leading in the first two cases to the abandonment of what were thought to be inviolable principles of free movement, and potentially doing so in the third, current, phase. In the first phase controls were introduced in 1905 to restrict the entry of 'aliens', mainly Jewish refugees from eastern Europe and Russia. In the second controls were introduced in 1962 to stop the entry of 'coloured' British Commonwealth citizens. In the third, while entry for political refugees is still in theory allowed, this principle is being undermined. There are distinct parallels between the first two of these phases. In both cases immigration controls were initially demanded by an extreme right-wing racist minority, following a larger influx of immigrants than previously. The demands for controls were not the result of any economic imperatives or problems. They fed, and were fed by, a growth of irrational prejudice against outsiders. Controls on the free movement of people were at first opposed by high-minded rhetoric from mainstream politicians of all parties, who eventually succumbed to racist pressures, or allowed their own prejudices to prevail, and introduced controls. As each measure of control was introduced, this, rather than appeasing the racists, merely led to demands for more. The fate of the political refugees who are now attempting to flee to Britain could turn out to be similar.

By far the most important reason for opposing immigration controls is that they impose harsh suffering and injustice on those who attempt to migrate, or to flee for their lives and liberty. The issue is whether the purposes immigration controls are intended to serve justify the imposition of such suffering. Controls are supposed to stop people migrating to the countries which enforce them. They are supposed to preserve and enhance the wealth of those countries against the perceived threats posed by immigration, and so to reassure people who believe that uncontrolled immigration might reduce them to Third World conditions. They are supposed to meet the concerns of racists and so reduce racism. They are supposed to control cross-border crime. In none of these objectives are they very effective or useful. In reality they increase, rather than decrease, both racism and crime, and they threaten to undermine the human rights not just of migrants and refugees, but of the existing inhabitants of the rich countries which are trying to exclude them. Immigration controls should be abandoned.

1   MIGRATION, AND MIGRATORY MYTHS

Current opinion is that human beings originated in East Africa. From East Africa they migrated throughout the world. Everywhere else in the world, therefore, people are either immigrants or descended from immigrants. People migrate for a variety of reasons. Some migrations are voluntary, in the sense that people migrate to conquer and colonise new territories, to improve their economic well-being and prospects of employment, or simply to see the world. Many migrations are involuntary. People have been forced to migrate as slaves or indentured labour. Or they are forced to flee famines, wars or political persecution. Usually the very poor cannot migrate, except perhaps to neighbouring countries. Currently the vast majority of the world's refugees are in countries where poverty is as great as it is in the countries they have been forced to flee from. On the other hand many of the most recent economic migrants, to the United States in particular, are from Asian countries where there has been rapid industrialisation, and where private foreign investment has both created links with industrialised countries and broken links with traditional methods of making a living.

Current nation states are the result of successive waves of immigration, most of which took place before the twentieth century. Although migrants are currently vilified and subjected to unprecedented levels of restriction, to deny the validity of migration is to deny part of the social nature of human beings. But the rate of migration in relation to total population is now lower than it has been at times in the past. In spite of scaremongering about the supposed threat of 'swamping' by immigrants and refugees, there is in fact little evidence that migration is increasing significantly, or likely to do so. The numbers about which so much fuss is made are in reality rather small.

Since the beginning of the industrial revolution and the imperialist expansion of Europe, the main migratory movements (apart from emigrations from Europe) have resulted from the requirements for labour of capitalist industry, mines and plantations. In the conquered territories these were often satisfied by the more or less overt use of force. In *The New Helots* Robin Cohen describes a spectrum of labour recruitment which ranges from total compulsion, as in the slave trade, through situations where people are

8

forced into wage labour by regimes which deprive them of their land and/or force them to raise money to pay taxes and where once recruited they are virtually deprived of their liberty, to situations where the dislocations caused by imperialism and war more or less force people to seek work and safety abroad. After the Second World War European governments sent agencies to recruit workers from, for example, southern Europe, North Africa, Turkey and the Caribbean. Especially in Germany and Switzerland, workers were recruited on contracts which denied them the right to change employment or to settle and gave them few of the other rights enjoyed by native workers.

There have been four periods of major migrations from the beginning of the capitalist period in the sixteenth century until now. The first was entirely forced, the second partially so, the third was mainly voluntary, and the fourth has been more mixed. The first major migration was the forced transportation of between 10 and 20 million people as slaves from Africa to America. This took place from the sixteenth to the nineteenth centuries, after European colonisers had decimated local populations in the Americas and needed new labour for their mines and plantations. The second major migration was of indentured or bonded labour, or temporary slaves, from India and China, again to remedy the lack of cheap or available labour in the places of destination. In theory the indentured workers signed a contract with employers and labour agencies of their own free will. In practice for most of them the choice was little greater than that presented to slaves transported from Africa, and their contracts provided them with no political or human rights. Thirty million indentured workers left India during the colonial period and up to the First World War. They provided a workforce for the mines and plantations of Burma, Sri Lanka, Malaysia, Singapore, Mauritius, South Africa, Guyana and Jamaica. Several million Chinese people migrated in this way to South-east Asia, the Pacific Islands, the Caribbean and South Africa. After the period of the contract, which was of at least ten years, the migrants were meant to return to their country of origin. Some 24 million Indians did return. Many did not, for lack of money or sometimes from personal choice.

The third major world migration was of Europeans to America and Australia, which began in the eighteenth century and reached its peak in the first decade of the twentieth century. According to Sutcliffe in *Nacido en otra parte* it is estimated that, from the early nineteenth century to the 1920s, more than 60 million Europeans migrated to America and Australasia, of whom 5.7 million went to Argentina, 5.6 million to Brazil, 6.6 million to Canada, and 36 million to the United States. Other Europeans migrated to parts of Central and southern Africa. They did so for a variety of reasons, ranging from destitution to a desire for adventure. The experience was in many ways a positive one for the migrants, although its positive aspects have sometimes been exaggerated, for example in the mythology of enterprise, freedom and prosperity in the United States. Its counterpart was the destruction or subjugation of native peoples, and the occupation by the colonisers of much of the most fertile land.

POSTWAR MIGRATION TO INDUSTRIALISED COUNTRIES

The fourth major migration, which began in the 1950s, was a reverse flow from the South to the North. A few people had migrated in earlier periods to countries such as Britain and France from those countries' colonial empires. But there was a large increase in migration after 1945. According to estimates by the United Nations Development Programme (UNDP) around 35 million people from the Third World, including 6 million 'illegal immigrants', came to settle in the industrialised countries between 1960 and 1990. In addition, by the 1990s, there were some 3–4 million refugees in the industrialised countries, according to UNHCR figures.

For most of this period, according to figures quoted by Sutcliffe in *Nacido en otra parte*, immigrants from the Third World were less than half of total immigrants to industrialised countries, though slightly over half in Britain's case and a much higher percentage for the United States in the 1970s and 1980s (76 per cent and 87 per cent). Between 1960 and 1990 about 1 per cent of the population of the Third World migrated to the industrialised countries, or 0.0375 per cent of it per year. The migrants corresponded to an increase in the population of receiving countries of about 0.2 per cent per year. In most countries, including the United States, Canada and Australia which are traditional countries of immigration, there was emigration as well as immigration. Among European countries, there was net immigration during the last four decades to Germany and France; in Britain there were fluctuations, but generally there was net emigration (see p. 20); Italy and Spain were initially countries of emigration but have become countries of immigration as well. Statistics on immigrant populations in Europe are partial and often misleading. They tend to include immigrants from all parts of the world but to exclude 'illegal' immigrants and people born abroad who have become citizens of the country they have migrated to. According to figures published by the Organisation for Economic Co-operation and Development (OECD) foreign population as a percentage of total resident population in 1997 in some European countries was as shown in Table 1.1.

Table 1.1 Foreign population as a percentage of total resident population in European countries, 1997

Austria	9.1	Luxemburg	34.9
Belgium	8.9	Netherlands	4.4
France	6.3	Sweden	6.0
Germany	9.0	Switzerland	19.0
Italy	2.2	UK	3.6

Source: OECD

In most countries, where data exist, it seems that about half of these foreigners are of Third World origin. In Britain the proportion is about 20 per cent, but this is an underestimate of the total number of people of Third World origins who have settled in Britain because many of them have British nationality. Sutcliffe notes that 'the demographic effect of immigration and emigration as a whole appears to be almost insignificant, which makes its apparent political importance the more striking. The latter results partly from the fact that immigration is an issue which the extreme right uses opportunistically ...'.

The new immigrants were drawn to Europe because, in the postwar capitalist boom from the late 1940s to the early 1970s, its industries were expanding and they needed labour. At first workers came from the less prosperous European periphery or were Europeans who had been displaced by the war. Gradually they were supplemented by workers from the Third World, mainly from Africa and Asia. All the highly industrialised countries of Europe made use of temporary labour recruitment schemes, although in some countries, in particular Britain, such schemes were small, and spontaneous migration from colonies and former colonies predominated. Migration of workers to Britain virtually stopped in 1962 because of the introduction of immigration controls (see Chapter 2) and because of the early onset of economic stagnation in Britain. Migration from the Third World to other European countries more or less ended by the mid-1970s. At the same time workers migrated to North America and Australia, initially from Europe and then, when racial prohibitions and quotas ended, from Asia and Latin America.

The main case of temporary foreign worker recruitment, or the 'guestworker' system, was in the Federal Republic of Germany (FRG). Castles and Miller in *The Age of Migration* describe it as follows:

The German government started recruiting foreign workers in the late 1950s. The Federal Labour Office (Bundesrat für Arbeit – BfA) set up recruitment offices in the Mediterranean countries. Employers requiring foreign workers paid a fee to the BfA, which selected workers, testing occupational skills, providing medical examination and screening police records. The workers were brought in groups to Germany, where employers had to provide initial accommodation. Recruitment, working conditions and social security were regulated by bilateral agreements between the FRG and sending countries: first Italy, then Greece, Turkey, Morocco, Portugal, Tunisia and Yugoslavia.

The number of foreign workers in the FRG rose from 95,000 in 1956 to ... 2.6 million in 1973 ...

German policies conceived migrant workers as temporary labour units, which could be recruited, utilised and sent away as employers required. To enter and remain in the FRG, a migrant needed a residence permit and a labour permit. These were granted for restricted periods, and were often valid only for specific jobs and areas. Entry of dependants was discouraged. A worker could be deprived of his or her permit for a variety of reasons, leading to deportation.

The system established a clear distinction between the civil rights of foreigners and those of citizens. Foreigners had no voting rights and, because their work and residence permits usually tied them to a particular employer, they were forced to work in the worst jobs in the worst conditions and could do little to improve these conditions.

The guestworker system was most highly developed in Germany, but, as Castles and Miller relate, it existed to some extent throughout Europe. Switzerland imported labour on a large scale from 1945 to 1974. Swiss industry became highly dependent on foreign workers, who were recruited abroad by employers, while admisssion and residence were controlled by the government; there were severe prohibitions on job changing, permanent settlement and family reunion. Belgium brought in foreign workers, mainly Italians and mainly for the coal mines and the iron and steel industries, immediately after the war. The Netherlands brought in 'guestworkers' in the 1960s and early 1970s. France established an Office Nationale d'Immigration (ONI) in 1945 to recruit workers from southern Europe. Employers had to apply to ONI for labour and pay a fee per head. ONI vetted the applicants and ensured they were healthy and suited to manual labour (examining their hands to make sure they had calluses, according to one report). By 1970, 2 million foreign workers and 690,000 dependants had entered France. The British government brought in some 90,000 European workers under various schemes.

Mainly in France, the Netherlands and Britain, there was in addition immigration for work from colonies and former colonies. Immigration of workers to France from its former colonies was the largest. By 1970, according to Castles and Miller, there were over 600,000 Algerians, 140,000 Moroccans and 90,000 Tunisians in France, as well as many Senegalese, Maliens, Mauritanians and others from former African colonies. Some came as citizens of Overseas Departments, including Algerians before 1962, and an estimated 250,000–300,000 from Guadeloupe, Martinique and Réunion. In the Netherlands, between 1945 and the early 1960s, nearly 300,000 'repatriates' came from Indonesia, as Dutch citizens. By the late 1970s there were also about 160,000 Surinamese, who had Dutch citizenship up to 1975. In Britain 541,000 people had migrated from the 'New Commonwealth' by 1962, when immigration controls stopped most 'primary' immigration for work.

In the United States postwar immigration was lower than it had been at the beginning of the twentieth century, when it was 880,000 per year; in the 1950s there were 250,000 immigrants per year and in the 1980s 600,000. In 1965 the discriminatory national-origins quota restrictions, which had restricted immigration from non-European countries, were abolished under the Immigration and Nationality Act, and there was then a big increase in immigration from Asia and Latin America. There was also widespread use of temporary migrant worker schemes in agriculture which involved especially Mexicans, who lived in extremely harsh conditions. Periodically these schemes were prohibited but they tended to continue illegally, so that large numbers of 'illegals' were and are routinely employed in low-paid work in agriculture and services; one estimate is that in the 1990s there were 10 million 'illegal' workers in the United States. Both Canada and Australia had programmes of large-scale immigration after 1945. In both countries non-Europeans (and at first even southern Europeans) were systematically discriminated against, until the 1960s when Canada changed its criteria to allow immigration of non-Europeans and Australia formally abolished its White Australia policy. There has also been migration within the Third World in search of work. The biggest has been migration to work in the oil-producing states of the Middle East, at first from other countries in the region and then, after 1973 and the increase in the price of oil, from the Indian subcontinent as well. The new workers were mainly on temporary contracts, and had none of the rights of native inhabitants. They formed from 53 per cent to 80 per cent of the workforce in some of the oil-producing states. In addition, workers migrated from less successful economies to faster growing ones within Latin America, South-east Asia and Africa.

MIGRATION TO BRITAIN

Britain, like other countries, is the product of immigration from many different places, and was far from being a homogeneous 'white' nation even before the twentieth century. A poem in the *Pall Mall Gazette* in 1909, quoted by Robin Cohen in *The Frontiers of Identity*, puts it thus:

> The Paleolithic, Stone and Bronze Age races
> The Celt, the Roman, Teutons not a few
> Diverse in dialects and hair and faces –
> The Fleming, Dutchman, Huguenot and Jew
> 'Tis hard to prove by means authoritative
> Which is the alien and which the native.

Migrants to Britain came first as hunters, then as cultivators in search of land, as conquerors, as refugees fleeing persecution, as workers in industries and public services. The first humans are said to have reached Britain during the Ice Age, before the sea cut it off from the continent of Europe, but Britain was not continuously inhabited until about 15,000 years ago, when the climate improved and vegetation and animals could survive. In AD 43, the Romans invaded Britain; their soldiers and administrators were followed by tradespeople and others from Italy and elsewhere in Europe. The Romans were followed by Saxon, Viking and Norman invaders. The Anglo-Saxons were mainly farming people, who came for cultivable land. By the early 600s, London became a trading centre for people from many parts of Europe. From the 800s there were large Danish invasions and settlements, followed by the Norman invasion of 1066. Jewish people migrated to Britain soon after and were confined by restrictive laws to occupations such as medicine and money-lending, in which they became useful to their rulers as a source of finance for their military adventures.

When manufacturing industry began to develop in Britain its labour needs were supplied mainly through migration from rural areas within Britain. From the fifteenth century onwards, 'enclosures' of common land and peasant evictions carried out by landlords created large numbers of landless people who had, as Karl Marx put it, nothing to sell but their labour power. The existence of a displaced rural population was one factor which accounted for the early success of the industrial revolution in Britain. A large pool of workers was available for the new urban factories, as well as to build railways, power plants and other infrastructure. Some migration within Britain from rural areas into urban employment continued in the twentieth century. For example, Welsh people moved to Slough in the 1930s, forming a quarter of its population. Others travelled, sometimes on foot, to work in the car factories in Oxford, and were followed by their relatives once they became established there. The 1980s recessions and industrial closures produced a new group of internal migrants who have followed the advice of the Conservative former minister Lord Tebbitt to 'get on their bikes' in search of work, travelling in most cases from the north of Britain to cities in the south.

The practice of inviting or compelling workers and craftspeople from overseas to remedy the absence of British labour and skills has a long history. Some early immigrants came in response to the desires of kings and noblemen for weapons, artefacts and adornments; from the sixteenth century onwards black slaves were imported as servants. In the sixteenth and seventeenth centuries, Dutch people came to Britain and set up textile, pottery and brewing industries, partly to escape the persecution of Protestants on the continent. From the late seventeenth to the mid-eighteenth centuries, many Protestants, known as Huguenots, fled persecution in France; between 40,000 and 50,000 settled in England. In a work edited by H. E. Malden and published in 1905, *A History of Surrey*, the contribution to manufacturing industry in Lambeth made by the 'huge immigrations' of Dutch, French and Scots is described:

the later extension of this district, the multiplication of the industries carried on within it, and the various degrees of excellence which many of them ultimately attained, have been largely due to the influence of the foreign workmen who at successive stages of our history came to settle within our country.

From the early nineteenth century, people also migrated to Britain from rural poverty in Italy and Ireland. Migration from Ireland on a large scale started with the potato famine under British rule, and grew with the continuing underdevelopment of Ireland by the English. By 1861 there were over 600,000 Irish-born people in England and Wales, about 3 per cent of the population, and a further 200,000 in Scotland, about 7 per cent of the population. After Irish independence and partition in 1921 migration continued. Irish people have not been treated as aliens under immigration rules and they have full citizenship rights.

During the Second World War the British government recruited colonial labour to work in forestry, munitions factories and the services. According to Zig Layton-Henry in his book *The Politics of Immigration*, a group of 1,200 British Hondurans were recruited to fell timber in Scotland and about 1,000 Caribbean technicians and trainees were recruited to work in munitions factories in Merseyside and Lancashire. Although during the Second World War the army and navy exercised a colour bar, turning down volunteers from the empire and attempting to confine recruitment to people 'of pure European descent', many Caribbeans, Asians and Africans did fight in the British armed forces, and the air force was forced by shortages to recruit around 13,500 Caribbeans to work in Britain as ground crews. In addition, thousands of seamen from the colonies were either recruited or enlisted voluntarily in the merchant navy. This war-time experience introduced people to Britain who had previously had no contacts with the 'mother country'. When they were demobilised or their employment ended the government attempted to repatriate them. But some stayed in Britain and others, when they returned to the Caribbean, found there were no jobs.

After the war the British Labour government initially saw unemployment as a continuing problem and a justification for restrictionist immigration policies. It came to realise that a 'labour shortage' was imminent which might cause breakdowns in public transport and the health services. Nevertheless, after setting up a working party in 1948 to consider, among other things, the question of Jamaican unemployment and British labour shortages, the government decided not to organise large-scale immigration of non-white colonial workers on the grounds that they would be difficult to 'assimilate'. Recruitment from British colonies and ex-colonies took place on a small scale. The London Transport Executive made an agreement with the Barbadian Immigrants' Liaison Service, and several thousand Barbadians were given loans to cover their fares to Britain. As late as 1966 London Transport recruited workers in Trinidad and Jamaica. The British Hotels and Restaurants Association recruited workers from Barbados. Woolf's rubber factory in Southall recruited workers from Punjab, and northern textile companies advertised for workers in the Indian and Pakistani press. Before the war the Ministry of Health had recruited nurses and hospital domestic workers from the Caribbean; this practice continued after the war. Enoch Powell, when he was Conservative health minister from 1960 to 1963, continued to recruit doctors and nurses from the Caribbean, India and Pakistan, thus benefiting from the resources devoted by those countries to their training. In the House of Commons on 8 May 1963 Powell commented on:

the large numbers of doctors from overseas who come to add to their experience in our hospitals, who provide a useful and substantial reinforcement of the staffing of our hospitals and who are an advertisement to the world of British medicine and British hospitals.

In the early 1960s employers, especially in hotels and catering, obtained work permits from the government and handed them to agencies, who then sold them to foreign workers already in Britain who recruited their relatives and friends from home.

But initially the main way in which British governments and employers attempted to resolve the problems of labour shortages after 1945 was to recruit Europeans. They turned to Polish people, Italians and other 'displaced people', housed in camps around Europe. According to Castles and Kosack, in their book *Immigrant Workers and Class Structures in Western Europe*, about 460,000 Europeans are estimated to have entered Britain in search of work between 1946 and 1951, although not all of them settled permanently. 115,000 of these were Poles who had fought for the British in France and Italy. They were helped by the government to find work and housing, and to learn English, under the Polish Resettlement Scheme. Some former prisoners of war, including Germans, Italians and Ukrainians, also settled in Britain. In addition the government organised the recruitment of 90,000 European voluntary workers (EVWs), first from refugee camps and then from Italy; they included Ukrainians, Poles, Latvians and Yugoslavs. The EVWs were bound for three years to a specific job chosen by the Ministry of Labour and could be expelled for 'misconduct' and even for accidents or ill health; a boy who lost his sight through falling off a farm vehicle was deported to Germany. They were mainly single men and women; about 4,000 'distressed relatives' were admitted, but families were often split up and wives and husbands sent to jobs in different parts of the country. Most of the male EVWs were directed to agriculture, heavy industry or mining. A further 100,000 foreigners, mainly Europeans, came into Britain with labour permits between 1946 and 1951, most of them for domestic service and catering. Organised recruitment of foreign workers ended in 1951.

During the war the Ministry of Labour also recruited in Ireland, and recruitment continued after the war, especially for the construction industry, the National Health Service and the transport systems. It is estimated that there was a net inflow of Irish people between 1946 and 1959 of around 350,000. Irish people are the largest single immigrant nationality in Britain. At a time when behind-the-scenes worries were being expressed about the 'problem' of 'coloured immigration' (see Chapter 2), Layton-Henry in *The Politics of Immigration* records that Irish people entering Britain outnumbered black and Asian people then entering Britain by about 20 to 1. Irish immigration fell steeply during the 1960s, although there were no legal restrictions on it, because of the lack of jobs.

Most of the migration to Britain of people from the Third World, which began on a substantial scale after 1948, at first from the Caribbean and then from the Asian subcontinent, occurred spontaneously. Unlike 'guestworkers' in other European countries, the great bulk of the migrants organised their own journeys and paid their fares. Until the Commonwealth Immigrants Act in 1962 (see Chapter 2) they could enter Britain to settle and work without restrictions. As a slogan of the 1970s Asian Youth Movement pointed out, 'We are here because you were there.' The initial movement of Caribbean people to Britain after the Second World War was prompted by their wartime experiences in Britain. After the war they came, or returned, in boats, mostly returning troop ships, dressed in their best clothes, some of them still in uniform. On the most famous of these boats, the *Windrush*, which arrived in June 1948, about two-thirds of the migrants had served in Britain during the war. The majority were skilled, with some vocational training; they came mainly from towns rather than rural areas. According to an Economist Intelligence Unit Survey published in 1961 and cited in Nicholas Deakin's *Colour, Citizenship and British Society*, only 12 per cent of a sample of 603 West Indians had been unemployed before leaving the West Indies. On the other hand little had been done to resettle West Indians who were repatriated to the Caribbean after the war, and British rule had created a large amount of unemployment in the population as a whole. A pamphlet published by Lambeth Council, *Forty Winters On: Memories of Britain's Post War Caribbean Immigrants*, quotes Sam King, a former RAF leading aircraftman, as follows:

Many of us were unemployed and we decided to take the first ship back to England.

My family were farmers with a bit of land in Portland, Jamaica, and if I hadn't left I'd be a peasant farmer today. But having been in England and read a few books I decided I could not live in a colony ...

Only one man in ten had the vote and 85 per cent of the land belonged to big English landowners ...

The fare was £28.10s and my family had to sell three cows to raise the money ...

We heard there was consternation in parliament and that newspapers like the Daily Graphic and the Express were saying we should be turned back. It was a Labour Government and the Colonial Secretary Creech Jones said, 'These people have British passports and they must be allowed to land.'

But then he added on, 'There's nothing to worry about because they won't last one winter in England.' It gives me some satisfaction to be able to repeat his words 40 winters later ...

... For those who had nowhere to go the deep air raid shelter at Clapham Common was made available for accommodation and the authorities helped in finding work. Within three weeks each person had a job ...

Immigration from the Indian subcontinent followed. It too had some of its origins in war-time recruitment, especially of seamen from Punjab, Kashmir and Sylhet who had replaced merchant sailors recruited into the army. Some seamen were stranded in Britain during the war and found work in factories. As Ian Spencer comments in his book *British Immigration Policy since 1939*,

There is little doubt that the sailors who settled in ports and moved inland during the war provided the basis for the post-war development of the Bangladeshi and Pakistani communities in Britain. As they developed in the 1950s and 1960s, Bangladeshi and

Pakistani communities often owed their origins to a tiny number of early pioneers. So strong was the process of chain migration that a population of several thousand could be derived from a very small number of kinship groups related to perhaps only a handful of villages. The original migrant would invariably have been financed by a group of close kin and when successful that migrant would have used his savings to help one of his close relatives to join him. They would soon be in a position to sponsor other members of their kinship group whom they would also help with jobs and accommodation on arrival. A study of the 2,000-strong Pakistani community in Oxford reveals that almost all the migrants there can be accounted for by just two chains, one of which began with a man who had settled in Glasgow during the Second World War.

Asian immigration has been almost entirely from the Punjab and Gujarat in India and from half a dozen areas in Pakistan and Bangladesh. Four-fifths of the Indian migrants to Britain were Sikhs, mainly from two districts in East Punjab, Jullundur and Hoshiarpur. Sikhs have traditionally been highly mobile and form about a quarter of the Indian army. Some pressures to migrate resulted from partition, which meant that Sikhs and Hindus were driven out of the the the rich wheat-producing farmland they had opened up in what became West Pakistan, and were forced to subsist on much smaller farms in East Punjab. Similarly, Gujaratis had a tradition of migration, in particular to East Africa; virtually all of the Gujarati migrants were literate and some were highly educated. The Pakistanis and Bangladeshis came mainly from relatively poor hill districts, from Mirpur and Sylhet respectively, and tended to be less literate. Communities originating in other parts of the world were built in similar ways. For example, over 90 per cent of the Moroccan community in Notting Hill in London, which is as large as the Caribbean community in this part of London, is from Larache, a small town in Morocco.

Layton-Henry in *The Politics of Immigration* gives figures on immigration, derived from a House of Commons Library research paper published in 1976 (see Table 1.2). Adding up the totals in the last column gives estimated net immigration from the new (or non-white) Commonwealth from 1953 to mid-1962 of nearly half a million people. The numbers dipped in the late 1950s, when there were fewer jobs, and rose dramatically in the early 1960s to beat the expected immigration controls (see Chapter 2). After the 1962 Commonwealth Immigrants Act, the numbers settling in Britain from the Caribbean and South Asia continued to rise, both because workers were at first admitted in larger numbers than had arrived spontaneously before the 1961–62 bulge, and because family reunion was with difficulty allowed. By the late 1960s the black and Asian population had doubled to around 1 million. The 1991 Population Census records that the 'ethnic minority' population (which it defines as non-Europeans, in other words people who, while constituting a majority worldwide, are mostly not white) was about 3 million, or 5.5 per cent of the total population.

Table 1.2 Estimated net immigration from the new Commonwealth from 1953 to the introduction of controls in mid-1962

	West Indies	India	Pakistan	Others	Total
1953	2,000	–	–	–	2,000
1954	11,000	–	–	–	11,000
1955	27,500	5,800	1,850	7,500	42,650
1956	29,800	5,600	2,050	9,350	46,800
1957	23,000	6,600	5,200	7,600	42,400
1958	15,000	6,200	4,700	3,950	29,850
1959	16,400	2,950	850	1,400	21,600
1960	49,650	5,900	2,500	−350	57,700
1961	66,300	23,750	25,100	21,250	136,400
1962	31,800	19,050	25,080	18,970	94,900

Source: Zig Layton-Henry *The Politics of Immigration*

The migrants, even when they had qualifications and skills, were employed mainly in low-paid jobs and often in harsh conditions which, especially during the period of labour shortages, were shunned by the natives. They tended to be excluded both from the professional jobs for which many of them were qualified, and from better-paid manual jobs. The print industry, the docks, for a time factories such as those in Oxford producing cars remained white male preserves. But in Bradford, Leicester, Coventry, East London and other places, a large part of the textile and clothing industry is dependent on workers from south Asia, as are numerous small engineering firms, in Birmingham for example, and large sections of the catering and other service industries. Many car-workers at Ford's plant at Dagenham in East London are from the Caribbean. The transport system and large parts of the health service would not function without black workers. Many Asians, discriminated against in employment, became self-employed, and some became wealthy. There was in addition a brain drain of skilled people from the Third World, in particular from the Indian subcontinent, whose training was provided by their countries of origin but benefits Britain: doctors, nurses, accountants, computer operators and academics.

More recently, Third World refugees have come to Britain attempting to escape persecution and wars. There is a myth which has a diminishing relation to reality that Britain is a country which welcomes refugees. Refugees were quite freely admitted in the nineteenth century, until Jewish refugees arrived in larger numbers at the end of the century. But most of the new Third World political refugees are refused asylum, and their treatment in Britain has become increasingly harsh. Most refugees go elsewhere. The numbers coming to Britain are small compared to those travelling to Germany, the United States, Canada or some other European countries, let alone to other countries in the Third World (see Chapter 3).

In all the fuss about migration into Britain and Europe, it is often forgotten that migration in the other direction is larger. Since the beginnings of European imperialist expansion in the sixteenth century, almost twice as many Europeans have migrated to the Americas, Africa and Asia as people from these areas have migrated to Europe. According to a recent letter to the *Guardian* by Marika Sherwood of the Institute of Commonwealth Studies, a total of some 21 million people left Britain to settle elsewhere in the period 1815–1912, most of them economic migrants rather than refugees. In the process, 'the Tasmanian aborigines and most of the indigenous peoples of the Caribbean were extinguished; the population of Australian aborigines was reduced by some 80 per cent; that of the Americas, North and South, was reduced by between 33 and 80 per cent'. Net emigration from Britain continued for most of the period after the Second World War; official British figures for net migration reported by Zig Layton-Henry in *The Politics of Immigration* are as in Table 1.3.

Table 1.3 Net migration to/from Britain, 1871–1991

1871–80	– 257,000
1881–90	– 817,000
1891–1900	– 122,000
1901–10	– 756,000
1911–20	– 857,000
1921–30	– 565,000
1931–40	+ 650,000
1951–61	+ 12,000
1961–71	– 320,000
1971–81	– 699,000
1981–91	– 6,000

Source: Zig Layton-Henry, *The Politics of Immigration*

The net immigration to Britain in the 1930s is mainly the result of British migrants returning to Britain having failed to prosper abroad during the depression. Unlike other more economically successful European countries, Britain did not have a substantial net addition to its population after the Second World War. As Robin Cohen comments in his book *Frontiers of Identity: The British and the Others*:

The xenophobic right is prone to describe the British Isles as under siege from a horde of restless foreigners about to invade their historically undisturbed homeland. This is a curious myopia as it takes little account of the many early invasions of Britain by the Vikings, the Normans, the Romans and others, or the fact that the British themselves have been highly energetic colonisers of other people's lands. Many of the population invasions of the last 250 years started, not ended, in Britain.

2 BORDER CONTROLS

RACISM

Many, probably most, of those who now believe that immigration controls are an obvious necessity would not see themselves as racist. Many liberal-minded people also say they are opposed to racist immigration controls, or controls which discriminate, as they now do, between different categories of immigrants. The current situation in Britain is that the many millions of foreigners who are nationals of the European Union or who have British parents or grandparents are free to enter and settle in Britain. Others are not. The former are mainly white, the latter often black. Non-discrimination would imply either imposing the same restrictions on Europeans and white British Commonwealth citizens as are imposed on other foreigners, or allowing virtually free entry to all. But even on the unlikely supposition that immigration controls ceased to discriminate on mainly racist grounds between foreigners, they would still discriminate against foreigners in general, as opposed to natives. They are therefore, many believe, inherently racist. Immigration controls embody, legitimate and institutionalise racism. They have both been caused by and caused a racism which has become deeply embedded and widely manifest in the rich nation states of the West, and especially so in their apparatus of control, including the police, the immigration authorities and private security guards.

Immigration controls have their origins in racism. Time and again, in the history of controls, it becomes clear that the reason for them is not excessive numbers of immigrants, or any realistic assessment of immigrants' effects on jobs, housing, crime or health, but the supposed 'non-assimilability' or 'inferior stock' of certain immigrants. Historically the main impetus for the introduction of immigration controls has come from open racists. The racist right has been remarkably successful in winning its demands. In 1905 and in 1962 immigration controls, first against 'aliens' or Jews and then against 'coloured' Commonwealth citizens, were introduced in Britain as the culmination of campaigns of anti-immigration agitation by racists and the far right, who were initially dismissed as extremists by mainstream opinion. The main platform of neo-fascist groups has been opposition to immigration and demands for controls and expulsions of non-Aryan or non-white people.

21

As Steve Cohen puts it in *Workers' Control not Immigration Controls*, 'It is politically naive to imagine that immigration controls which were brought into being through organised fascist activity can now somehow be cleansed and made "non-racist".'

Fascist and right-wing racist groups have existed, with fluctuating fortunes, throughout the twentieth century. In 1886, in response to the arrival of Jewish refugees, possibly the first anti-immigrant group, the Society for the Suppression of the Immigration of Destitute Aliens, was set up. It was followed by the Association for Preventing the Immigration of Destitute Aliens and the British Brothers League, the latter set up for similar purposes in 1901 by the Conservative MP for Stepney in East London, Major William Evans-Gordon, and others. After the First World War anti-semitism became more viciously explicit. The 'Britons' were set up in 1918, followed by the Imperial Fascist League in 1928, which favoured killing, sterilising, segregating or expelling Jews. Oswald Mosley founded the British Union of Fascists in 1932, which intimidated Jews especially in the East End of London and reached a membership of possibly 50,000 in 1934. There were a number of smaller fascist groups. Most were extinguished by the Second World War. Mosley was interned, failed to rebuild his Union Movement after the war and went into exile in 1951. The League of Empire Loyalists was formed in 1954 to oppose the end of empire, but lost members to the White Defence League and the National Labour Party, which merged to set up the British National Party in 1960. The 1958 Notting Hill anti-black riots were the product partly of fascist organisation and incitement. In the 1960s a series of anti-immigrant organisations in the Midlands, the most powerful of which was the Birmingham Immigration Control Association, campaigned for immigration controls, while avoiding the tag of fascism, and provided the climate in which the anti-immigrant Tory candidate Peter Griffiths won in Smethwick. The Southall Residents Association was set up in 1963 with similar aims.

The National Front, founded in 1966, was the product of a merger between the League of Empire Loyalists and the British National Party. After the Tory Minister Enoch Powell's 1968 speech, threatening 'rivers of blood' if immigration was not stopped (see p. 53–4), the National Front gained some respectability and recruits. In the 1970s it both pursued electoral politics and organised violent marches and attacks in immigrant areas, notably Brick Lane and Lewisham, draping itself in the Union Jack. Other right-wing groups, including Column 88 and the British Movement, engaged in para-military activities; in January 1981 Roderick Roberts, a leading British Movement official in the West Midlands, was jailed for seven years on conviction of arson, the possession of firearms and explosives, and conspiracy to incite racial hatred. This influence was countered by large-scale and effective campaigning by far left and liberal opponents, and especially by the Anti-Nazi League, in numerous demonstrations, meetings, rock concerts and other anti-racist events.

Mrs Thatcher's notorious 1978 speech on the threat of 'swamping' by immigrants was part of a successful bid to win votes from the National Front (see p. 55–6). With the growth of unemployment, poverty and extremes of inequality during the 1980s and 1990s, and the rightward movement of the Tory Party and much opinion, neo-fascist organisations had a revival. The British National Party (BNP) and the British Movement engaged in, or stimulated, violent attacks against black people. In 1993 a BNP candidate, Derek Beackon, was elected in a by-election as a local councillor in Tower Hamlets; after the BNP election victory racist attacks in Tower Hamlets quadrupled, but Beackon was ousted in the next council elections when local people mobilised against him. The BNP and the National Front have tried, not very successfully, to exploit hostility towards Roma asylum seekers in Dover; the National Front's first attempt to march in Dover was routed by a counter-demonstration by left-wing, anarchist and green activists.

Fascist and right-wing groups consciously exploit long-standing and widespread prejudice against outsiders. Prejudice against the 'other', the stranger, the foreigner, and especially the recent immigrant, has a long, shameful and largely inexplicable history. Peculiarly vague and nebulous arguments are advanced in favour of the virtues of 'national homogeneity', as if diversity was in some unexplained way undesirable. Two examples of such opinions are quoted by Nigel Harris in his book *The New Untouchables*:

Biologically and cybernetically, nations are living streams of a higher order, with different systemic qualities that are transmitted genetically and by tradition. The integration of large masses of non-German foreigners and the preservation of our nation thus cannot be achieved simultaneously; it will lead to the well-known ethnic catastrophe of multi-cultural societies.

– an 'association of German professors' in 1982
(*Population and Development Review*, vol. viii, no. 3, 1982)

Japan's racial homogeneity has helped us become a more 'intelligent society' than the United States, where there are blacks, Mexicans and Puerto Ricans and the level is still quite low.

– the then Japanese prime minister Nakasone in 1986
(*Wall Street Journal*, 13 November 1986)

Yet most countries contain a great variety of people, from whom they have derived great benefits. It is hard to see why or where any line should be drawn between natives and foreigners, or from what date it should be fixed. Arguments on the 'non-assimilability' of certain categories of immigrants have been repeated over the centuries, but their targets vary. In 1924 an immigration official, quoted in Robin Cohen's book *Frontiers of Identity*, provided the following explanation for processing some applications faster than others:

different races display very different qualities and capabilities for identifying themselves with this country. Speaking roughly, the Latin, Teuton and Scandinavian races, starting some of them, with a certain kinship with British races, [are] prompt and eager to identify themselves with the life and habits of this country and are easily assimilated. On the other hand, Slavs, Jews and other races from central and Eastern parts of Europe stand in quite a different position. They do not want to be assimilated in the same way and do not readily identify themselves with this country.

Twenty years later a Royal Commission on Population, appointed in 1944 and reporting in 1949, concluded that the economy required an additional 140,000 people per year to make up for the shortfall in people of working age. But, it said,

immigration on a large scale into a fully established society like ours could only be welcomed without reserve if the immigrants were of good human stock and were not prevented by their religion or race from intermarrying with the host population and becoming merged with it.

A report by the 'independent' research institute, Political and Economic Planning, published in 1949, reached similar conclusions and stated that 'the absorption of large numbers of non-white immigrants would be extremely difficult'. When Caribbeans and Asians nevertheless began to arrive of their own accord in the 1950s in response to labour shortages, first Labour and then Tory governments tried to stop them, preferring the Irish and the previously (and currently) reviled east Europeans.

Over long periods Jews have been the main target of racists, in Britain and elsewhere. From the 1950s onwards, blacks became the targets. But others have been vilified in similar ways and in similar language. In general, it is the newest immigrants who are the main targets of prejudice; previous generations of migrants are often idealised as valuable and different from the current ones. In Britain the fear now appears to be that the country will be swamped by refugees and migrants from eastern Europe, most of whom are white. The *Daily Mail* of 24 November 1998 carried an article by Monica Porter, herself a daughter of refugees from Hungary in 1956, in which she says:

The cynicism and greed of those who come here expecting to be fed, housed and catered for, courtesy of the hard-pressed British – despite the absence of any historical obligations to do so – is quite sickening. ...

To class these opportunistic migrants as refugees is an insult to those genuine victims of tyranny who have sought asylum in the West, gratefully received it and, in return, enriched the cultural and social fabric of their adoptive country.

Prejudice and violent attacks on foreigners are nothing new. In the Middle Ages members of the Flemish colony in Southwark were made to pronounce the words 'bread and cheese' in the London manner; those who failed this test were executed. Among many violent expressions of prejudice, in 1517 in what became known as 'Evil May Day', hostility towards French, Italian and Spanish merchants and financiers took the form of mass indiscriminate attacks against foreigners in the streets by a large mob of people who broke into and ransacked houses and workshops. When there was an influx of some 80,000 Protestant Huguenots from France in the seventeenth and eighteenth centuries, some of the locals described them as 'the very offal of the earth'. Riots against Protestant refugees occurred in London in 1586, 1593, 1595 and 1599. There were anti-black riots in 1919.

The Irish, millions of whom migrated to Britain from the nineteenth century onwards and now form the largest immigrant group in Britain, were initially stereotyped as lazy, idolatrous, diseased and criminal, subjects of an alien Catholic church. They moved into areas, in Liverpool and Glasgow for example, where living conditions were already wretched and they were accused of making them worse. They were forced to live in filthy, cramped cellars and in streets with open sewers and to work in harsh conditions. In the nineteenth century English and Scots workers reacted with pitched battles and riots. In the 1950s landlords put up notices saying 'No paddies, no wogs, no dogs'. Irish people continue to be subjected to discrimination in employment, policing and criminal proceedings. The Birmingham Six, from whom confessions to a pub bombing were extracted in what amounted to torture, spent years in prison before their convictions were quashed.

Jewish people fared even worse. Panikos Panayi in his book *Immigration, Ethnicity and Racism in Britain*, describing the official expulsion of Jews in 1290, comments that 'popular antisemitism' manifested itself partly in 'the idea that Jews killed Christian children in order to use their blood either as part of the passover ritual or for medical purposes', and also in violence:

Violence against Jews occurred with greater regularity and brutality than racial attacks at any other time in British history. ... The worst pogroms occurred in 1190 in York, resulting in 150 deaths. However, anti-Jewish riots broke out elsewhere at the same time, including Dunstable, Lynn, Stamford and Bury St Edmunds. In the last of these fifty-seven Jews died. Between 1262 and 1266 further murders of Jews occurred in Worcester, Northampton, Canterbury, Lincoln and Ely.

At the end of the nineteenth century, mainly as a result of pogroms in Romania and Russia, Jews overtook Germans to become the second largest immigrant group in Britain after the Irish. They then became the main object of anti-immigrant prejudice and right-wing agitation. The term 'alien' became synonymous with Jew, just as the term 'immigrant' subsequently became synonymous with Caribbean or Asian. Some Jews were financiers or professionals, but most lived in great poverty, in particular in the East End of London. As many as half worked in the clothing trade, often under extreme forms of exploitation, for which they were held responsible. They were vilified, contradictorily, both for their poverty and for their wealth. Jews were accused of being 'insanitary', prone to crime and living in overcrowded and wretched conditions. According to the *Manchester City News* of 2 April 1887, Jews were also 'advanced socialists who sympathise with the Paris Commune and Chicago martyrs'. On the other hand trade unionists professed to believe that they could not combine together in unions because of their individualistic nature, and were inclined to represent all Jews as wicked capitalists, the role in which they were stereotyped in much literature. In the population as a whole, some people both on the left and on the right perceived Jews as engaged in capitalist conspiracies to control British society. In a book by Joseph Banister, *England under the Jews* (1901), quoted by Panikos Panayi, the following statement is to be found:

The Jews not only comprise the most numerous and undesirable element among our foreign invaders, but are at the head of the various movements for bringing other obnoxious aliens into this country. The vile looking Italians one sees laying asphalt in our streets are imported by a conspiracy composed of Jews. The introduction of foreign women for immoral purposes is carried on, as is the white slave traffic everywhere, chiefly, if not entirely, by Jews. ... The attempt to introduce swarms of Chinese laundrymen into England was made by Jews ... The German waiters who cringe for tips at so many of our principal hotels, and the cheap German clerks we hear so much about, are imported and nowadays employed almost entirely by Jew firms.

The *Daily Telegraph* of 11 February 1909 reported the opinions of Judge Rentoul at the Old Bailey, who had before him 'aliens of the very worst type in their own country ... the Russian burglar, the Polish thief, the Italian stabber, and the German swindler ... people whom this country would be glad to get rid of ...'. Such aliens were commonly perceived to be Jews. When Lewis Namier applied for a fellowship of All Souls College, Oxford in 1911, the fellows agreed he was by far the cleverest of the applicants, but turned him down because of his (Jewish) 'race'. During the First World War prejudice against Jews intensified on the grounds they were supposedly associated with Germany; anti-Jewish riots took place in Leeds and London in 1917. After the war Jews were linked with the Bolsheviks and the Russian revolution, and blamed for the spread of communism, and Jewish members of the British Communist Party were deported. When Jews were subjected to Nazi persecution from 1933 onwards, Fleet Street newspapers and racist opponents of immigration campaigned successfully to stop the entry of many refugees (see Steve Cohen, *From the Jews to the Tamils: Britain's Mistreatment of Refugees*, and below).

From the 1950s onwards black people became overwhelmingly the main targets of anti-immigrant prejudice. The term 'immigrant' became virtually synonymous with black (or 'coloured', as people from Africa, the Caribbean and the Indian subcontinent were called in the 1950s and 1960s). This was so even though they were usually not a majority of immigrants. Not all blacks were recent immigrants, although until the 1950s there were relatively few black people in Britain. The usual prejudice against outsiders was augmented by the legacy of colonialism. Imperialists had felt the need to prove to themselves and others that the horrors they perpetrated against conquered peoples, and the denial of their freedom, could be excused by the assumption that the latter were in some way inferior. Especially during the slave trade, numerous texts refer to the supposed lesser sensibilities of Africans, who were said to be barely human. Europeans thought that it must be a blessing for African slaves to be provided with masters and regular work and consoled themselves with the idea that 'Negroes have far duller nerves and are less susceptible to pain than Europeans.' Poverty in Africa and the Indian subcontinent was ascribed to the supposed laziness and incompetence of the natives. An Englishman in 1820 found the cause of Indian poverty 'in a natural debility of mind, and in an entire aversion to labour'. Africans were thought to possess a 'worse than Asiatic idleness'. Thus the imperialists, who at first admired and were even overawed by the more advanced forms of civilisation they found in Asia, Africa and Latin America, gradually built up theories of racial superiority (see Teresa Hayter, *The Creation of World Poverty*). They came to convince themselves that they were on a civilising mission, bringing the Bible and other gifts of civilisation to benighted natives.

Hostility towards non-white immigrants was at times expressed with brutal clarity. A leading right-wing campaigner for Commonwealth immigration controls, the Tory MP Sir Cyril Osborne, is quoted as follows by Paul Foot in *Immigration and Race in British Politics*:

This is a white man's country, and I want it to remain so.

Daily Mail, 7 February 1961

Those who so vehemently denounce the slogan 'Keep Britain White' should answer the question, do they want to turn it black? If unlimited immigration were allowed, we should ultimately become a chocolate-coloured, Afro-Asian mixed society. That I do not want.

Spectator, 4 December 1964

I do not like to regard the Irish as immigrants. I regard the Irish as British as I am. When I fought in the First World War, I was glad to have a good Irishman by my side.

House of Commons, 23 March 1965

Another Tory MP, Sir Martin Lindsay, referrring to 'coloured immigration', said in the House of Commons on 5 December 1958 that: 'A question which affects the future of our own race and breed is not one we should merely leave to chance.' Mainstream politicians at times adopted the crude racist language of the extremists. Mr Angus Maude, a Tory MP reputed to be an intellectual and a liberal, said in a speech in February 1965 that: 'It is not unreasonable for a white people in a white country to want to stay a white country.' Sir Winston Churchill, quoted in *The Times* of 20 March 1978, explained his concern about immigration to Sir Hugh Foot, governor of Jamaica, as follows: 'We would have a magpie society: that would never do.' In 1954 Lord Salisbury, an advocate of immigration controls and Conservative leader in the House of Lords, thought that an address sent to him by the Conservative Commonwealth Association (Liverpool Group) was 'extremely moderate and sensible'. The address (quoted by Spencer in *British Immigration Policy*) read in part as follows:

Rooms in large dilapidated houses are sub-let at high rentals to coloured immigrants who exist in conditions of the utmost squalor. Vice and crime are rampant and social responsibilities are largely ignored. Hundreds of children of negroid or mixed parentage eventually find their way to the various homes maintained by the Corporation, to be reared to unhappy maturity at great public expense. Large numbers of the adults are in receipt of unemployment benefit or National Assistance and many are engaged in the drug traffic or supplement their incomes by running illicit drinking dens or by prostitution.

This, the writers opined, was creating a 'new Harlem', and any attempt to improve conditions would only encourage others to come. Labour's representative at a confidential meeting in the Colonial Office in 1954 (reported by Layton-Henry in *The Politics of Immigration*) blamed immigrants for 'overcrowding, ghettos, crime, disease, dependence on National Assistance and the creation of racial friction'. The Labour MP for North Kensington, Mr George Rogers, after the Notting Hill anti-black riots in 1958, made the following comments to the *Daily Sketch* on the effect of the 'tremendous influx of coloured people from the Commonwealth':

Overcrowding has fostered vice, drugs, prostitution and the use of knives. For years the white people have been tolerant. Now their tempers are up.

Racism among the population as a whole was, as before, fuelled by the fact that the new immigrants were forced to live in poor conditions and to work in the worst jobs. Expanding industry and services needed workers, and got them from the British former empire. But it was hard for the new immigrants to find housing. There was no programme to build council housing to house the new workers, and in many areas it was initially almost impossible for immigrants to obtain accommodation on existing council estates, as a result of prejudice both from council officers and from tenants. Prejudice against 'coloured' tenants and neighbours was extreme. As Sam King (see p. 17) put it:

In those days I wouldn't even try to get a room for myself. There were advertisements for rooms all over the place but when you went there it had gone. ...
We were the second black family to buy a house in Camberwell. ...
Because we couldn't get mortgages we pooled all our money to help others.

Immigrants were forced to find accommodation in run-down areas, and were then, as the Irish had been, blamed for the state of these areas. In addition, once an immigrant or group of immigrants had obtained a house, this house was of necessity used to house large numbers of people, which in turn caused neighbours to complain about squalor and overcrowding.

   Commonwealth immigrants came to Britain because there were jobs, and usually found them immediately. But when unemployment rose black people were the first to be sacked. Today their children suffer disproportionately from unemployment. Unemployment for blacks is now two or three times higher than it is for whites; in some inner-city areas as many as 70 per cent of young black men are unemployed. With brutal inconsistency, they are therefore accused both of taking 'British' jobs and of scrounging off the state. Unemployment for blacks is the result of discrimination rather than lower abilities or skills. This situation was documented in particular in a series of reports by Political and Economic Planning (PEP) in the 1960s and 1970s, based partly on sending people of similar qualifications but different national origins to interviews, and has been confirmed in numerous surveys ever since. Virtually no black workers were promoted to supervisory positions, except over other black workers. Few got white-collar jobs. An employer, quoted in a 1966–67 study by Julia Gaitskell cited in Deakin's *Colour, Citizenship and British Society*, thought, for example, that they might get 'wildly excited', in which case their English might 'fall down'. Although the official policy of the Trades Union Congress (TUC) was against discrimination, trade unions often failed to support black workers against discrimination or even to support them when they took strike action, although immigrant workers had a high rate of union membership, were encouraged by their own organisations to join unions, and did not allow themselves to be used as strike-breakers.

Blacks are widely blamed for crime, violence and riots. In reality they are more likely to be victims than perpetrators. By cruel irony this does little to affect the prejudice against them: the view seems to be that if there were no blacks in Britain there would be no attacks against them, therefore blacks cause crime. It would be truer to say that blacks are scapegoats for people's anger, and that in their absence this anger would be expressed in other ways. There was racist violence on a large scale against blacks in Liverpool, Deptford and Birmingham in 1948, and in Notting Hill and Nottingham in 1958. There have been and continue to a shocking number of individual attacks on black people, especially against Asian people, some of which have resulted in deaths. In 1978 the Bethnal Green and Stepney Trades Council published a report entitled *Blood on the Streets: A Report on Racial Attacks in East London*, which listed over a hundred separate racist attacks in Tower Hamlets between January 1976 and August 1978, including two murders and numerous serious assaults. In 1981, 13 people died and 29 were injured in a probably deliberate, racist and National-Front inspired fire at a Caribbean party in Deptford (the New Cross fire). In 1981 the all-party Joint Committee Against Racialism (JCAR) presented to the Home Secretary a dossier of over 1,000 racist attacks. A major report by the Home Office, entitled *Racial Attacks* and published in 1981, listed 2,630 'racial incidents' in the major conurbations from May to July 1981. Since then, the number of racist attacks has risen. In 1999 a flurry of publicity followed publication of the Macpherson report after a long struggle by Doreen and Neville Lawrence to get some justice for the murder of their son Stephen, almost certainly by white racists. A *Mirror* reporter, Brian Reade, went to the South London estate 'where Stephen's killers grew up'; his report on 24 February 1999, which covered several pages of the *Mirror*, says that he found a 'state of hate': 'racism seeping from every pore', swastikas and graffiti saying 'pure Nazi', 'NF', 'I hate niggers like Aaron opposite', 'Kill coons at birth', 'Niggers should be hanged by the balls', and

If there [sic] brown knock them down.
If there black send them back.

Other persistent public campaigns by parents and relatives, for example over the murders of Ricky Reel and Michael Menson, have forced the police to reopen cases which they had dismissed as suicide or accidents. Many more certainly go unreported, and uninvestigated, partly because victims of racist attacks have found they are more likely to be arrested than helped by the police. Roma refugees in Dover have been particularly under attack: among many recent incidents, a woman was assaulted by her next-door neighbour; a 14-year-old asylum seeker was in intensive care after an attack by four young men who kicked his head 'like a football' when he was travelling on the Ramsgate to Dover train with his ten-year-old brother; and so on.

The media, however, more typically report crime committed by black people than crimes committed against them. Even the *Guardian*, on 28 September 1999, put prominently on its front page a story about a black rapist which blamed the Home Office for failing to deport him after a previous offence. Some newspapers consciously use the reporting of crime to promote opposition to immigration. The *Daily Mail* of November 1998 under a front-page banner headline 'BRUTAL CRIMES OF THE ASYLUM SEEKERS', claimed to have uncovered 'the devastating impact of serious crime by asylum seekers', and produced photographs of assorted black criminals, some of whom were asylum seekers. In October 1998 the *Daily Mail* published an article entitled 'The Good Life on Asylum Alley: The *Mail'* s investigation into Britain's immigration crisis reveals the shocking ease with which refugees play the benefit system'. In a three-day period in September 1998, the November 1998 issue of the Refugee Council's magazine *iNexile* picked up the following headlines:

Refugees in Hospital Riot.
Refugee Crime Wave in London.
Refugee Disaster.
Asylum Seekers 'Threat to System'.
We're Being Swamped by Crimewaves of Migrants.
Refugee Flood Looks Set to Hit a New High.
Why Britain is Still a Soft Touch.

Nick Hudson, former editor of *Sunday Sport* and then (later sacked) editor of the *Folkestone Herald and Dover Express*, wrote an editorial in October 1998 in the latter bemoaning the invasion of 'illegal immigrants, asylum-seekers, bootleggers, drug-dealers, the scum of the Earth ... We are left with the backdraft of a nation of human sewage, and no cash to wash it down the drain.' Later the paper claimed that a Roma woman sold herself for a potato, thus undercutting local business, that people were terrified to walk in the streets for fear of attack by asylum seekers, and that Dover Marks & Spencer had to close at midday because of a spate of shoplifting by asylum seekers.

Even the police worried about the provocation caused by such reports. According to an article in the *Observer* of 22 August 1999, 'Kent police asked Hudson to correct his newspaper's impression that the refugees were responsible for a crime wave.' The *Guardian* of February 20 1999 reported that John Grieve, the policeman appointed to deal with racism in the Metropolitan Police after the Lawrence Inquiry, had said that: 'Some press coverage of asylum-seekers, portraying them as ungrateful scroungers at the least and violent criminals at worst, was "dangerous, risky stuff".'

Politicians who wanted ammunition for immigration controls sought support from various committees and reports on the supposed proneness of immigrants to crime. They did not get far. An Interdepartmental Working Party on Coloured Immigration to the UK, re-established in 1953, asked the police for information on immigrant crime and was informed that black immigrants were not responsible for a disproportionate amount of crime, although 56 black men had been convicted for the possession of hemp, and some were living off the 'immoral earnings' of white women. In 1971 an investigation into police–immigrant relations was carried out by the House of Commons Select Committee on Race Relations and Immigration; its report, published in 1972, stated that: 'Of all the police forces from whom we took evidence not one had found that crime committed by black people was proportionately greater than that by the rest of the population. Indeed in many places it was somewhat less.' But, the report said, police officers often believed that black people were more involved in crime, possibly because they are forced to live in high crime areas. In 1994 an international study on youth and crime, the British research for which was carried out by the Home Office research department, published in the Netherlands but not in Britain (but reported in the *Guardian* of 6 July 1994), concluded that, 'contrary to the over-representation in police statistics of young black offenders, the English research showed that there was either no difference or lower offending rates for ethnic minorities with [sic] their white counterparts in property crimes or violent offences'; and 'The English study found one drug user in four among white youth, one in eight amongst blacks and one in 12 among Asians.' Although black people are over-represented in prisons, this is evidence of racial discrimination in arrests and sentencing rather than of high participation in crime.

Most unjustly, black people were blamed for the riots of the Thatcher years. The age of Thatcherism was the age of the riot. In the succession of uprisings or 'riots' which took place in London, Liverpool, Manchester, Bristol, Birmingham, Newcastle and elsewhere in the 1980s and early 1990s there was no general racial pattern or cause, although the riots were sometimes triggered by or developed into racial attacks, for example by white youths against Asian shopkeepers, or by the police against Caribbeans. The main generalisations to be made about the participants are that they lived in deprived urban areas and that they were young unemployed men. Sometimes, in areas of high immigration, the young men were black. Elsewhere, for example in Newcastle's Meadowell estate in 1991, which was among the most violent of all the riots, they were overwhelmingly white. Usually they were a mixture. According to Home Office statistics in their *Bulletin* of autumn 1982, of the 4,000 people arrested in the July 1981 riots, 2,762, or 70 per cent, were white; the others were described as West Indian/African (766), Asian (180), and other non-white (282) (see Teresa Hayter, *Urban Politics*). Nevertheless Kenneth Oxford, chief constable of Merseyside at the time of the 1981 Toxteth riots, blamed the violence on 'young black hooligans', whose 'fight was with us, the police, a symbol of authority and discipline which is anathema to these people'. After the Brixton riots in 1981 Sir Kenneth Newman, then commissioner of the Metropolitan Police and one of the founders of Scotland Yard's community relations branch, was quoted in the US *Police Magazine* as follows:

In the Jamaicans, you have a people who are constitutionally disorderly. It's simply in their make-up. They are constitutionally disposed to be anti-authority.

However the official report by Lord Scarman, *The Brixton Disorders 10–12 April 1981: Report of an Inquiry*, attached considerable blame to the police themselves. And after the riots in Manchester in 1981, according to a shocked letter to the *Guardian* of 9 December 1981 from a group of community workers, some police officers careered through the streets in their vans, beating their truncheons against the sides of the vans and chanting slogans such as 'Nigger, nigger, nigger, oi, oi, oi!'.

Racism is frequently fuelled by, or helps to create, a distorted view of the numbers of immigrants. People say they are afraid Britain is becoming 'swamped' by immigrants. Their fears are partly based on ignorance about actual numbers. For example in surveys carried out in 1967 and reported in Deakin's book *Colour, Citizenship and British Society*, three-quarters of the respondents guessed at figures for the 'coloured population' at least double the true ones, and a quarter estimated that there were more than 5 million 'coloured' people in Britain, at a time when the actual number of black and Asian people in Britain was about 1 million. Figures are inflated by newspapers, which publicise, for example, the landing of a few Asians on beaches in 1967 or the discovery of a few refugees in the backs of lorries in the 1990s as if they were mass invasions. In the summer of 1999 there were approximately 600 asylum seekers in Dover, but figures of 6,000, or alternatively 1,000 a month, were bandied around, while the total population of Dover was thought to be a quarter of its actual figure of over 100,000. Shamefully, politicians as well as newspapers exaggerated the numbers of refugees in Dover. According to information collected by David Turner of Dover Residents Against Racism (reported by Tony Goldman in the October–December 1999 issue of the newsletter of the National Coalition of Anti-Deportation Campaigns), the *Sunday Times* reported that the Labour

MP for Dover had 'said he was concerned about the creation of a "ghetto" of 1,000–2,000 asylum seekers, mainly from Eastern Europe and the Balkans, in a small town unused to ethnic minorities'. Ann Widdecombe, shadow Home Secretary, was quoted by the *Daily Express* as saying that 'more than 5,000 asylum seekers are thought to be living in the area, with more arriving each week', creating 'a tinder box atmosphere'. According to the *Daily Telegraph*, Sandy Bruce-Lockhart, the Conservative leader of Kent County Council, 'put the influx at around 1,000 a month', supposedly outnumbering holidaymakers and driving them out of bed and breakfast hotels.

Both Tory and Labour politicians have nevertheless at times taken strong stands against immigration controls, in particular in the periods before they were introduced and, in Labour's case, in opposition. The Labour Party's internationalist origins predisposed it to oppose controls. In opposition in 1905, 1919 and 1961–62, the Labour Party vehemently opposed them as a 'fraudulent remedy' for social ills, and in the 1980s it advocated the repeal of immigration laws. Some Labour and Liberal politicians recognised that the problem was not immigration itself, but the failure to provide adequate services and housing, at first for the growing workforce required for expanding industry, and later to deal with the consequences of capitalist slump and unemployment. On the few occasions when Labour attempted to counter the prejudices against immigrants and refugees, it had some success. When in 1999 the Labour government accepted some Kosovan refugees, they were made welcome in the areas they were sent to. This may have had something to do with the nature of the publicity put out by the government. The *Guardian* of 18 May 1999 quotes 'confidential minutes of the home office strategy group handling the crisis' of Balkan refugees, and said that:

The document also reveals that the government has drawn up plans for publicity which will 'focus on the human interests of asylum seekers' in order to 'avoid scare stories' about the arrival of the refugees.

Similarly, Labour's strong opposition to the introduction of controls on Commonwealth immigration in 1962 was followed by a sharp reduction in the majorities supporting controls in national opinion polls.

But in general Labour, like the Tories, has done little to counter irrational xenophobic pressures. Racism seems to be a powerful force, difficult to counter with rational argument. More inexcusably, the Labour Party, in its eagerness to beat the Tories at what is perceived to be their game, panders to racism. For much of its history and especially when it has been in government, Labour has appeared to believe that electoral advantage is to be gained by claiming to be tough on immigrants, and now on asylum seekers. Labour politicians clearly fear that any 'softness' on their part will be exploited by the Tories. Thus the major political parties compete with one another to demonstrate their commitment to the idea that the problem is not the racism of white people, but how best to 'crack down' on migrants and refugees. The response of both Tory and Labour governments has, on the whole, been not to confront the racists and refute their arguments and distortions, but to promise to stop or reduce immigration, and thus to legitimate the appeals of the far right to irrational fear and aggression.

From 1962 onwards a justificatory myth began to develop. This was the contradictory argument that immigration controls, rather than legitimising racism, were necessary for good race relations. An article in the *Guardian* of 23 January 1966 by Philip Mason defined the aim of official policy as follows:

We are determined to treat those immigrants who are here as kindly as we treat our older citizens; we are determined to cut down sharply the number of fresh entries until this mouthful has been digested.

This prescription has become the political orthodoxy. By 1987, in a Tory booklet entitled *Our First Eight Years: The Achievements of the Conservative Government Since May 1979*, a short paragraph under the heading 'Better race relations' had only the following to say:

Firm but fair immigration controls have been applied in the interests of harmonious race relations. Last year fewer people were accepted for settlement in the United Kingdom than at any time since the control of Commonwealth immigration began in 1962.

In the House of Commons on 20 April 1995, the Conservative home secretary, Michael Howard, asked whether 'in the interests of good race relations' he would ensure that 'both bogus asylum seekers and illegal immigrants are pursued both fairly and firmly', replied:

I entirely agree with my hon. Friend. It is an inseparable part of the good race relations record, of which we can be proud, that we have a firm but fair immigration control. Our procedures are being abused both by illegal immigrants and by bogus asylum seekers.

Increasingly, Labour promises to provide help for integration and good race relations were coupled with promises to make sure no more immigrants came to add to the 'problems' immigration was supposed to have created. Even those people who accepted that social and economic problems were not the result of immigration, and that immigration controls were not intended to reduce the overall numbers of immigrants, but only to reduce the numbers of certain types of immigrants, nevertheless argued that British people needed some reassurance that immigration was being restricted. Yet accepting that controls of 'coloured' immigration were required implied accepting that coloured immigrants caused problems. It therefore made the task of countering prejudice against them harder. The progressive tightening of immigration controls did not end prejudice and racism; it increased and strengthened them. Each new concession to racist pressures for controls was followed by demands for more.

From the early 1960s Labour Party members, in particular Fenner Brockway MP, began to call for legislation to counter discrimination against black people and immigrants. In 1965, a watered down Race Relations Act was passed which set up a Race Relations Board providing for a conciliation process to avert discrimination in public places, without criminal sanctions, and without addressing the more important problem of discrimination in housing and employment. The first person to be charged under this act was Michael X, a black militant. When Duncan Sandys, a prominent Tory MP, attacked a government report on education by stating that 'The breeding of millions of half-caste children will merely produce a generation of misfits and increase social tension', the Race Relations Board was unable or unwilling to prosecute him. In 1968 a further Race Relations Act was passed which, although it too was watered down, did include provisions against discrimination in employment and housing. The act introduced fines on employers who were found to discriminate on the grounds of race, and compensation, but not reinstatement, for the people discriminated against. It has probably had some effect in stopping the more blatant forms of discrimination, but the enforcement powers of the Race Relations Board remained weak. Its existence was used by the right-wing and the racists to claim, falsely, that black people have 'unfair advantages'.

Immigration controls, in addition, sanction racist behaviour by the authorities. They do so in a direct sense for immigration officials, whose task is to prevent the entry to Britain of undesired foreigners, most of whom in the last 40 years have been black; their Immigration Service Union has openly campaigned for tougher immigration laws. Other sections of the public sector and employers are increasingly expected to check the immigration status of, usually black, people. Arguably, and more indirectly, the existence of immigration controls has contributed to the attitude of the police towards black people, officially recognised since the Stephen Lawrence Inquiry as 'institutional racism'. Some of the police violence against black people has been directly related to attempts to deport them. Racism in the police, as they like to point out, is a reflection of racism in society as a whole. It certainly, itself, contributes to general racist attitudes. A report by J. A. Hunte for the West Indian Standing Conference published in 1966, entitled *Nigger Hunting in England?*, claimed that police officers leaving their stations were heard to say they were going 'nigger-hunting'. A Home Office research study in 1979 found that a black person was 15 times more likely to be arrested under the 'sus' laws than a white person. The 'sus' laws have since been repealed, but the harassment continues. In 1998 over a million people were stopped and searched; the proportions were 37 per 1,000 for whites, 66 per 1,000 for Asians, and 180 per 1,000 for Caribbeans and Africans. In Oxford in 1998 campaigners in defence of a young black man, who had been stopped 22 times for driving his car and had finally lost patience and been charged with threatening behaviour, was told by a black police officer sent to placate them that he had himself been stopped; the officer suggested that Thames Valley police considered it an offence for a black person to drive a car. It is possible to be stopped and accused of stealing one's car simply for having black passengers. Layton-Henry quotes Inspector Basil Griffiths, deputy chairman of the Police Federation, saying in 1982 at a fringe meeting organised by the Monday Club at the Conservative Party conference that:

> There is in our inner cities a very large minority of people who are not fit for salvage ... the only way in which the police can protect society is quite simply by harassing these people and frightening them so they are afraid to commit crimes.

In the last few years several black people have died in police cells and as a result of police actions. Shiji Lapite died of a crushed voice-box after he was held in an armlock by police. Ibrahim Sey died after being sprayed in the face with CS gas. Peter San Pedro died shortly after CS spray gas was used during his arrest on suspicion of being an illegal immigrant; after his release he wandered into the path of a lorry and later died from his injuries. Brian Douglas died after being struck with a police baton. Roger Sylvester died after he was restrained by eight officers. Dennis Stevens, a 'model prisoner', died of 'acute renal failure and extensive muscle necrosis' in Dartmoor prison after being held in a leather body belt for 24 hours in a special cell. Ziya Mustafa Bitirim died after a police officer had knelt on his back to restrain him; a post mortem showed he had died from asphyxia. Oscar Okoye died in prison after he had been arrested on suspicion (later dismissed) that he was drunk when driving; he collapsed with a brain haemorrhage and later died; he told his wife he had been beaten by police officers. Sarah Thomas was arrested and restrained after a minor public order offence; by the time she reached hospital she was in a coma, and she later died. Ahmed El Gammai, Donovan Williams, Lytton Shannon, Wayne Douglas, Christopher Alder are other names in the shameful roll-call of police-associated black deaths. Many others have accounts of being beaten up in police cells and police vans. In 1993 Joy Gardner, a 40-year-old Jamaican woman, died in front of her five-year-old son when three police officers from the Alien Deportation Group broke into her flat, forced her face down on the floor, sat on her body, bound her hands to her sides with a leather belt and manacles, strapped her legs together and wound yards of surgical tape round her head. They had arrived at her flat with specially designed restraining belts, made of thick leather, with a buckle at the back and two manacles at the front to pinion the arms. There has been no inquest and no public inquiry into her death. The police officers were tried for manslaughter but were acquitted by a jury; they said the treatment she received was standard practice. After the trial they were reinstated and not disciplined. There was an investigation by the Police Complaints Commission but it remains a secret. Joy Gardner had come to Britain in 1987 to be with her mother; her son Graeme was born in Britain.

EARLY HISTORY OF BRITISH IMMIGRATION CONTROLS

William the Conqueror, having invaded Britain himself, built castles along the south coast of Britain to stop others following his example. Subsequently efforts to control the presence of aliens mainly took the form of excluding those who were considered undesirable after they had entered. King Henry II banished all 'aliens' on the grounds they were 'becoming too numerous'. In 1290 all Jews were banished. More foreigners were expelled by Queen Mary; some were readmitted, and others expelled, by Queen Elizabeth. These expulsions followed the switches in the rulers' religious preferences between Catholicism and Protestantism. In the seventeenth century the power to deport became the prerogative mainly of the Privy Council rather than of monarchs. In 1793, in reaction to the French revolution, an Aliens Act was passed by parliament which sanctioned expulsion, and capital punishment for expellees who tried to return. It resulted in the deporting of Talleyrand to the United States but was otherwise not much used, though re-enacted from time to time in response to fears that anarchy and atheism might be imported from the continent. In 1848, to counter the perceived menace of revolutionaries coming to Britain after the Paris Commune, a Removal of Aliens Act was passed. Palmerston later repealed it on the grounds it might lead to an abuse of power. Later convicts and trade unionists were transported to Australasia. These Acts, like the expulsions which preceded them, were an assertion of the power to deport people who were considered undesirable, but did not provide for controls on entry.

Erskine May, whose *Constitutional History*, first published in the late nineteenth century, is the most widely accepted authority on British constitutional matters, is quoted by Paul Foot in *Immigration and Race in British Politics* as follows:

It has been a proud tradition for England to afford an inviolable asylum to men of every rank and condition, seeking refuge on her shores, from persecution and danger in their own lands. ... Through civil wars and revolutions, a disputed succession and treasonable plots against the State, no foreigners had been disturbed. If guilty of crimes, they were punished: but otherwise enjoyed the full protection of the law.

In the heyday of liberalism and British industrial supremacy in the nineteenth century this claim was largely justified. Refugees and revolutionaries from political struggles in Europe and elsewhere came to Britain, which was then known as a more liberal country than others in Europe. They could enter freely, stay in Britain and campaign there without fear of expulsion. They included Giuseppe Mazzini, Sun Yat Sen and Karl Marx. Workers too were welcomed, at least by capitalists and politicians. The British espousal of free trade, a result of its dominant position in world markets, was, unlike today, accompanied by the free movement of labour. In particular Irish immigration took place on a large scale to meet the needs of employers in industry and in agriculture, in spite of a good deal of popular hostility towards the Irish. As Paul Foot puts it, 'immigration control, like protection, was irrelevant, unnecessary – a symbol of national decline'.

But from the 1880s onwards there began to be talk of the possible need for immigration control. Anti-immigrant sentiment grew in response not only to relative industrial decline, but also to the arrival of some 120,000 Jewish people who came to Britain between 1875 and 1914 to escape pogroms in Russia and eastern Europe. The Marquess of Salisbury introduced a bill in the House of Lords in 1894 to control immigration. Lord Hardwicke, quoted by Paul Foot, reintroducing the bill four years later, argued that:

It would be a very serious matter if the type of population which is now to be found in many districts of the East End, where there is a strong alien element, were to become at all a common type in the poorer districts of our large cities. It would mean, my Lords, that these classes would become to a great extent non-English in character, and that, both in physique and in moral and social customs, they had fallen below our present by no means elevated standard.

The bill got no further than the House of Lords. But it had support especially from two Tory MPs in the House of Commons, Sir Howard Vincent and Major William Evans-Gordon, one of the founders of the British Brothers League. In 1902 in the House of Commons Evans-Gordon demanded immediate immigration controls. His speech sounded much like the speeches vilifying blacks and demanding immigration controls 50 years later. He accused immigrants of living four or five families to a house once they had turned out its proper occupants, threatening to turn the population 'entirely foreign', engaging in criminal activities and prostitution, carrying knives, causing overcrowding in schools and undermining Sundays; 'A storm is brewing', he said, sounding like a less eloquent version of Enoch Powell, 'which if it be allowed to burst, will have deplorable results'. He proceeded, like Powell, to do his best to stoke up that storm. He compared Jewish immigration to the entry of diseased store cattle from Canada. Mr Cathcart Watson, a Liberal MP, supported him, asking in the House of Commons in February 1903:

What is the use of spending thousands of pounds on building beautiful workmen's dwellings if the places of our own workpeople, the backbone of the country, are to be taken over by the refuse and scum of other nations?

In 1903 a Royal Commission on Alien Immigration reported. It found that, as is the case now, the number of immigrants in Britain was small compared to the numbers in other European countries. It stated that 'alien labour is only or chiefly employed in doing work for which the native workman is unsuited or which he is unwilling to perform' and that it was much less of a charge on poor relief than the natives, though aliens did have slightly higher crime rates. The commission found no evidence to support racist arguments that the immigrants were unclean or diseased, or that they had caused or even augmented overcrowding. Nevertheless it regarded it as an 'evil' that 'immigrants of the Jewish faith do not assimilate and intermarry with the native race'. Its remit was to consider whether or not controls were needed, and it plumped for stringent controls, including the exclusion of undesirable aliens, who were defined as criminals, the diseased (even though the commission had found them to be a tiny proportion of immigrants) and, more crucially, people without ready means of support. All this was followed by racist agitation in the East End, where most Jewish immigrants lived, and scurrilous press reports referring to 'the scum washed on our shores from dirty water coming from foreign drain-pipes', and so forth.

The next attempt to introduce immigration control legislation in Parliament was in 1904, under the Tories. Their bill contained powers not just to deport, but to refuse admission. A Liberal amendment, saying the accusations of sweating by immigrants should be opposed by legislation against sweating rather than the exclusion of immigrants, and that the principle of asylum should be retained, was proposed by the Liberal MP Sir Charles Dilke, who said the Tories had 'raised a devil which they will find it difficult to lay', that immigration was declining, that sweating existed in trades in which there were no immigrants, that the cheap labour of women and girls was a far more serious matter for the trade unions than was the influx of immigrant labour, and that in the past immigrants had usually met with hostility and subsequently been accepted and even praised. Other Liberals strongly opposed the bill, continuing the argument that the remedy for any supposed ills was to build houses for the workers, who were needed for industry, and to improve social and working conditions in general. The bill was withdrawn.

It was replaced by a watered-down version in the next session of parliament. This bill retained the principle of asylum and limited the powers of expulsion by immigration officers to 'undesirable aliens', defined as previous deportees, fugitive offenders, and the destitute who came to Britain on 'immigrant ships' containing more than 20 third-class passengers. Thus 'Potential "undesirables"', Robin Cohen comments in *Frontiers of Identity*, 'were thought to be exclusively found among the steerage passengers ...', a 'stunning demonstration of class justice that allowed those who could afford cabin fares to escape examination'. The bill provided for a right to appeal to an immigration board. The Liberals again opposed the bill. Labour members, none of whom had spoken against the 1904 bill and some of whom had abstained rather than voting against it, did speak and vote against the 1905 bill. Tories resorted to grotesque accusations in its support, such as the remark by W. Hayes Fisher MP:

Just as one river could carry a certain amount of sewage, but not the sewage of the whole Kingdom, so one portion of London cannot carry the whole of the pauper and diseased alien immigrants who come into the country.

The Aliens Act became law in August 1905. The new entry controls required the setting up of an Immigration Service and the recruitment of immigration officials at the ports to determine whether immigrants were to be allowed in. Its chief inspector, W. Haldane Porter, said to be the 'founding father' of the Immigration Service, was a close associate of Major Evans-Gordon, the first in a tradition of immigration officials with links to the far right.

The Tories lost heavily in the 1906 elections, but their Liberal successors failed to repeal the act. The chauvinism stirred up by the First World War led to the passing of a much more draconian Aliens Restriction Act in 1914 with virtually no opposition. This act empowered the Home Secretary 'in time of war or imminent national danger or great emergency' to prohibit all immigrants from landing and to deport them. During the war 21,000 aliens were repatriated and 32,000 were interned. German wives could not buy food in the shops and dachshunds were disembowelled in the streets.

The anti-alien fever continued after the war and led to the passing, accompanied by yet more racist babble accusing foreigners, especially Germans and Jews, of all kinds of iniquity, of another and even more restrictive Aliens Restriction Act in 1919, in spite of the fact that the first one was supposed to apply only in times of national emergency. The provisions of this act were that any alien could be refused entry into Britain at the discretion of an immigration officer; that in general he or she would not be allowed in for more than three months without a work permit or visible means of financial support; and that any alien could be deported either by the home secretary or by the courts if his or her presence was considered 'not conducive to the public good'. Until 1956 there was no right of appeal. But anyone likely to be persecuted if returned was to be granted political asylum. In 1920 a new Aliens Order was passed. This supposedly temporary measure was then renewed under the Expiring Laws Continuance Act every year, by Labour as well as Tory governments, until it was superseded by the 1971 Immigration Act. Some 100 people per year were deported up to the 1960s under the 1919 act, for no stated reasons and without right of appeal (in 1999 over 30,000 people were deported or removed).

The Labour MP Josiah Wedgewood, quoted by Paul Foot, said in Parliament in October 1919:

Generally speaking, aliens are always hated by the people of this country. Usually speaking, there has been a mob which has been opposed to them, but that mob has always had leaders in high places. The Flemings were persecuted and hunted, and the Lombards were hunted down by the London mob. Then it was the turn of the French Protestants. I think that the same feeling holds good on this subject today. You always have a mob of entirely uneducated people who will hunt down foreigners, and you always have people who will make use of the passions of the mob in order to get their own ends politically. ... Members will come forward and tell the people: 'I voted against these foreigners and I voted to keep them out.'

We believe that the interests of the working classes everywhere are the same, and these gentlemen will find it difficult to spread a spirit of racial hatred amongst these people who realize that the brotherhood of man and the international spirit of the workers is not merely a phrase but a reality. We know that the whole of this Bill is devised in order to satisfy the meanest political spirit of the age.

The 1919 act was opposed only by the Labour Party, all of whose members voted against it.

But Labour's internationalist principles did not survive in government. In the few months of the Labour-Liberal government of 1924, under attack from the Tories, they operated the legislation against aliens more harshly than their predecessors. In spite of these efforts Labour lost the 1924 elections. The Tories argued that this was because Labour put the interests of aliens before those of 'our own people'. In opposition, while stating that they recognised the need for controls, Labour proposed a compromise; the Labour MP John Scurr, proposing the compromise amendment, let slip the comment: 'We are not afraid to say we are internationalists – all of us. ... The boundaries between nations are artificial.' This outburst caused great embarrassment to the Labour leadership, intent on regaining power. Back in government in 1929, according to Paul Foot, 'almost the first act' of John Clynes, Labour Home Secretary, was to refuse asylum 'to the most hunted of all political refugees in this century – Leon Trotsky'. In 1931, in response to Tory criticism, Clynes claimed that:

The restrictions relating to aliens and the general conditions under which they have been permitted to enter this country have not been in any way loosened.

Defending the decision to impose a £10 naturalisation fee, he said that 'British nationality is a possession which ought to be highly prized by anyone receiving it ...', and he announced 'triumphantly' that a Labour Home Secretary had naturalised fewer Russians than his Tory predecessor. Foot comments that Clynes:

was the first in the line of that curious political phenomenon: the Labour Home Secretary. He laid down two basic principles for his successors, who, for the most part, have followed them scrupulously. First, behave in office in direct contrast to your promises and principles when in opposition; second, strive mightily to be less humane than the Tories.

This shameful line continued through Sir Frank Soskice and James Callaghan, among others, and now finds its embodiment in Jack Straw, Labour home secretary in the Blair government. Between the wars the numbers of immigrants declined drastically, largely as a result of the slump and high levels of unemployment in Britain. In spite of this, the ruling classes imported a good many 'highly qualified' domestic servants from other countries in Europe. A large proportion of those who did enter Britain were British citizens who had been refused entry to the white colonies, or forced to leave them, because of depression there, much to the indignation of the British ruling class. Anti-alien propaganda, and complaints for example about French onion-sellers taking trade from the natives, nevertheless continued. The most vicious prejudice was as before against Jewish people, who were cited in demands for even stricter controls to ensure the maintenance of British 'stock' against possible weakening by the 'riff-raff of eastern Europe, the stiffs of the Mediterranean and the dead beats of the world'. From 1933 onwards, pressures mounted to stop any arrival of Jewish refugees from Germany. From 1933 to 1938 only 11,000 Jewish refugees from Germany were admitted to Britain; after the intensification of their persecution 55,000 entered in the next two years. 20,000 of them entered as domestic servants, a fact which casts doubt on any subsequent claims of generosity. The first question asked by an immigration officer, according to the Labour MP Josiah Wedgewood, was 'Are you a Jew?', making a mockery of the provision for political asylum in the Aliens Restriction Act. Thus, shockingly, were Jews driven back to the concentration camps.

During the Second World War, the pressures to intern aliens were at first muted by the obvious circumstances of their presence in Britain as refugees from the fascist governments against whom the war was being fought. Yet in July 1941 the government decided to intern all 'enemy' aliens, including thousands of Jews as well as German trade unionists and socialists who had opposed Hitler. Several thousand aliens, almost all of them Jews, were shipped to Australia and Canada, and on at least one ship were badly mistreated by the sailors transporting them. Most of the internees in Britain were released by the middle of 1942, after many complaints about their treatment in camps.

After the war, the new Labour government, which had been elected on a promise of full employment, was inclined towards a policy of strict enforcement of the Aliens Act. It quickly became clear that the problem was not unemployment, but labour shortages. The government was rebuked by some Tory MPs for their failure to realise this. For example in 1946 the Tory MP Peter Thorneycroft stated:

The fact is that with a shortage of manpower in this country every kind of administrative and bureaucratic difficulty is put in the way of the volunteer who tries to get into this country to work. I find something a little contemptible about a party which preaches internationalism abroad and yet takes every step to prevent free men from coming here to work.

The government's restrictive policy was also opposed by James Callaghan, a former union official and now MP, subsequently Labour Prime Minister, who predicted in 1946:

In a few years we will be faced with a shortage of labour – not with a shortage of jobs. We ought now to become a country where immigrants are welcomed. We should break away from this artificial segregation of nation from nation. ... Who is going to pay for the old age pensions and social services unless we have an addition to our population, which only immigration can provide in the years to come?

The government was eventually forced to agree. Poles, displaced persons and European Voluntary Workers (see Chapter 1) were brought in outside the Aliens Restriction Act.

The yearly renewal of the Aliens Order was opposed by a few Labour MPs and in the early 1960s by the Tory opposition spokesperson on Home Affairs,

Sir Edward Boyle. One of the most persistent Labour critics, Reginald Paget MP, spoke as follows on 17 November 1964:

We, in this House, are for the fiftieth time to deny aliens the most elementary of human rights – the right to live under the rule of law. ... we are renewing emergency wartime provisions given to the Government on 4th August 1914 and renewed again without discussion in 1919 and renewed annually since then. These emergency powers give complete control to the Executive over the liberties of the people who come here. ... Entry to this country is subject to the say-so of immigration officers and from their decision there is not really even an appeal to the Executive. The immigration officer can say 'Back you go'.

CONTROLS ON COMMONWEALTH IMMIGRATION

British imperialism, by a curious accident of history and presumably without thought of the possible consequences, had awarded British citizenship to all the inhabitants of all the colonies and dominions. The Aliens Acts therefore did not apply to them. This position was reaffirmed in the British Nationality Act of 1948. Until 1962, when the first Commonwealth Immigrants Act was passed, British subjects from the Commonwealth and colonies could enter Britain freely without controls.

Before the Second World War few black citizens of British colonies took advantage of this freedom. When from 1948 onwards first Caribbeans and then Asians began arriving to work in Britain in large numbers (see Chapter 1), they provided what should have been a perfect solution to the problems of labour shortages experienced by British capitalism. In 1951 in the first Conservative King's Speech after the war, the King declared on the Tories' behalf that:

My government views with concern the serious shortage of labour, particularly of skilled labour, which has handicapped production in a number of industries.

Not only did the new immigrants, many of whom were skilled, fill vacancies, but, unlike the European workers, who were anyway in short supply, they did not have to be recruited, organised or have their fares paid. While the postwar Labour government did something to help the early arrivals, on the *Windrush* for example, find accommodation and jobs, and Labour-controlled local authorities made varying, and usually inadequate, efforts to help in large cities, the Tory governments of the 1950s did virtually nothing.

When pressure groups and a few Tory and Labour backbenchers nevertheless demanded controls to stop 'coloured' (but not the larger white) immigration, these were resisted, as were demands for deportation powers against Commonwealth citizens. Both the government and the Labour opposition were opposed to any openly discriminatory measures against black Commonwealth immigration. The Commonwealth was held to be indispensable to Britain's status as a world power. Tory and Labour politicians made numerous resounding public statements of support for the principles of a 'multiracial Commonwealth' and respect for the inviolable rights of British citizenship. In the debate on the 1948 Nationality Act Sir David Maxwell Fyfe, Conservative shadow Home Secretary (quoted by Layton-Henry) said the following:

We are proud that we impose no colour bar restrictions making it difficult for them when they come here ... we must maintain our great metropolitan tradition of hospitality to everyone from every part of our Empire.

A Conservative Party policy document stated in 1949 that:

there must be freedom of movement amongst its members within the British Empire and Commonwealth. New opportunities will present themselves not only in the countries overseas but in the Mother Country, and must be open to all citizens.

Henry Hopkinson, Conservative minister of state at the Colonial Office, said in a House of Commons debate in 1954:

As the law stands, any British subject from the colonies is free to enter this country at any time as long as he can produce satisfactory evidence of his British status. This is not something we want to tamper with lightly. ... We still take pride in the fact that a man can say *civis Britannicus sum* whatever his colour may be and we take pride in the fact that he wants to and can come to the mother country.

Harold Macmillan, shortly after he became prime minister in 1957, rebuked Sir Cyril Osborne, a Tory backbencher who campaigned against 'coloured' immigration, as follows: 'I would deprecate any reflection that may be cast on the standard of health and conduct of these immigrants.' Prominent Tory politicians including Lord Home, Alan Lennox-Boyd, Iain Macleod, Duncan Sandys, Sir Edward Boyle and Lord Butler, among others, all at different times and with differing degrees of conviction made statements opposing immigration controls. In 1960 Lord Butler, then home secretary, was still saying: 'It is very unlikely that this country will turn away from her traditional policy of free entry.' In 1961 David Renton, under-secretary at the Home Office, told Sir Cyril Osborne that the government refused 'to contemplate legislation which might restrict the historic right of every British subject, regardless of race or colour, freely to enter and stay in the United Kingdom'. In the same year, according to the *Birmingham Evening Dispatch* of 6 April 1961, Sir Edward Boyle told members of the Birmingham Immigration Control Association that 'it is impossible that the Government will introduce immigration control'.

Labour too were strongly in favour of the Commonwealth, and generally opposed to switching allegiance to Europe. Their attitude to the arrival of West Indians on the *Windrush* in 1948, under a Labour government, had however been decidedly mixed. They thought the West Indians must be let in because they were British citizens, but hoped they would not last the winter (see p. 17). Paul Foot quotes George Isaacs, minister of labour, who, when asked about his attitude to their imminent arrival in 1948, said they would be met and told how to register for work, but that he hoped 'no encouragement is given to others to follow their example'. But from 1951 until controls against Commonwealth immigration were introduced by the Conservatives in 1962, Labour was out of government. During this period, apart from some Labour backbenchers who joined Sir Cyril Osborne and other Tory backbenchers in demanding immigration controls, Labour politicians more or less consistently spoke against them. In September 1958 the Labour Party issued a statement on racial discrimination (quoted by Paul Foot) which said in part:

We are firmly convinced that any form of British legislation limiting Commonwealth immigration into this country would be disastrous to our status in the Commonwealth and to the confidence of Commonwealth peoples.

The statement condemned support for controls as capitulation to the worst excesses of racism. Later in 1958 Arthur Bottomley (quoted by Paul Foot) was able to assert from the Labour front bench that:

We on this side are clear in our attitude towards restricted immigration. ... I think I speak for my Right Honourable and honourable friends by saying that we are categorically against it. We are the most industrialised country in the world and we have a direct responsibility for our colonial subjects when they are poor, badly housed or unemployed. ...

If, by an unfortunate error, [a criminal] gets into this country, it is our duty to deal with him, whatever his race, colour or creed, according to the judicial requirements of the land. The central principle on which our status in the Commonwealth is largely dependent is the 'open door' to all Commonwealth citizens. If we believe in the importance of our great Commonwealth, we should do nothing in the slightest degree to undermine that principle.

Hugh Gaitskell, leader of the opposition until his death in 1963, was a notable opponent of immigration controls. He was on the right wing of the party on issues of public ownership and defence, and was both an economic realist and a convinced anti-racist. He recognised that capitulation on controls would strengthen rather than undermine racists and the far right. It is possible that he would have maintained these principles in government if he had not died before the Labour victory of 1964. In 1961, Gaitskell was asked by Cyril Osborne for a statement on the attitude of the Parliamentary Labour Party to immigration control, and sent the following reply (quoted by Paul Foot):

The Labour Party is opposed to the restriction of immigration as every Commonwealth citizen has the right as a British subject to enter this country at will. This has been the right of subjects of the Crown for many centuries and the Labour Party has always maintained it should be unconditional.

When the Conservatives introduced the Commonwealth Immigrants Bill in 1962, Labour opposed it. In the second reading debate Gaitskell made a powerful speech condemning the bill as cruel and brutal anti-colour legislation. Paul Foot quotes part of his speech as follows:

The rate of immigrants is closely related, and in my view will always be related, to the rate of economic absorption. There has been over the years an almost precise correlation between the movement in the numbers of unfilled vacancies, that is to say employers wanting labour, and the immigration figures. As the number of unfilled vacancies goes down, the immigration figures go down, and as the number of unfilled vacancies rises, the immigration figures go up. It is in my opinion an utter and complete myth that there is the slightest danger or prospect of millions and millions of brown and black people coming into this country. Anyone who is trying to put that across is only trying to frighten people into believing it.

Gaitskell and others pointed out that people in British colonies looked on themselves as British, and on Britain as the 'mother country'. Barbara Castle ended her speech against the bill (quoted by Foot) by saying:

I do not care whether or not fighting this Commonwealth Immigration Bill will lose me my seat, for I am sure that the Bill will lose this country the Commonwealth.

Labour's opposition on the first reading of the bill was total. It introduced successful amendments softening the bill. But its unconditional support for free entry wavered in the course of the debates. By the third reading, from which Gaitskell was absent, Denis Healey was admitting that controls might at some future date be necessary; subsequently he repudiated a statement by John Strachey that Labour would repeal the act. From then onwards, Labour's principled opposition to controls on Commonwealth immigration was in decline.

As Ian Spencer in *British Immigration Policy since 1939* documents in great detail from recently disclosed Cabinet and other internal documents, the reality was that, behind the public statements, most of the politicians, and in particular the Tory leadership, wanted to keep black people out. Their problem was that at the same time they wanted to ensure that white Commonwealth citizens, Irish workers and others of desirable 'stock', badly needed for the functioning of British industry and the public services and for other more sentimental reasons, were not excluded. The delay in introducing controls was caused by the difficulty of doing so without giving the appearance of discrimination. As Lord Swinton of the Commonwealth Relations Office (quoted by Spencer) wrote in 1954 in response to Lord Salisbury's arguments for immigration controls:

If we legislate on immigration, though we can draft it in non-discriminatory terms, *we cannot conceal the obvious fact that the object is to keep out coloured people.* ...

There is, in fact, a continuous stream of persons from the old Dominions to the United Kingdom who come here, with no clear plans, in order to try their luck; and it would be a great pity to interfere with this freedom of movement. ...

[A large coloured community] is certainly no part of the concept of England or Britain to which people of British stock throughout the Commonwealth are attached. (Italics added)

Even, it was argued, if restrictions were applied to all citizens of the Commonwealth, black or white, this would still leave the problem of how to justify not excluding the Irish, who were considered to be a desirable and 'assimilable' supply of much needed labour.

The politicians' early efforts to stop the arrival of black workers in Britain concentrated on trying to persuade governments in the Caribbean and the Indian subcontinent to stop emigration at source (thus arguably contravening article 13 of the Universal Declaration of Human Rights). These efforts had some success in India and Pakistan. They were hampered even then by a new trade in false documents, and by a decision of the Indian Supreme Court that it was unconstitutional for the Indian government to refuse to issue passports to its citizens. They were mostly unsuccessful in the Caribbean, where both colonial and independent governments refused to make themselves unpopular by blocking attempts by their citizens, when jobs were scarce in the Caribbean, to go and look for them where they were abundant. Official propaganda, including a film showing severe winter conditions and the supposed difficulty of getting jobs in Britain, did not fool Jamaicans who knew that the British were recruiting European voluntary workers. The government resorted to methods such as denying the right to West Indians to travel cheaply on troop ships returning empty to Britain.

When the Commonwealth Immigrants Act was eventually passed in 1962, it excluded the Irish from its provisions, an exclusion which was exploited by Labour in its opposition to the whole principle of the act. But it got round the problem of how not to appear to discriminate between different categories of Commonwealth citizens by making entry into Britain conditional on obtaining work vouchers. These did discriminate, between skilled and unskilled workers, and the expectation was that most of the former would be white. The act created three categories of job vouchers for Commonwealth citizens wishing to enter and settle in Britain. Category A was for people who had a job to come to; category B was for skilled people; and category C for the rest. People born in the United Kingdom or holding passports issued by the British government were deemed to 'belong to' the United Kingdom and therefore not restricted by the act. In the Cabinet Rab Butler, the then home secretary, is recorded in the recently released Cabinet papers of 6 October 1961 (quoted by Ian Spencer) as introducing the concept of work vouchers to his colleagues as follows:

The great merit of this scheme is that it can be presented as making no distinction on grounds of race or colour. ... Although the scheme purports to relate solely to employment and to be non-discriminatory, the aim is primarily social and its restrictive effect is intended to, and would in fact, operate on coloured people almost exclusively.

The scheme was based on proposals put forward by an interdepartmental working party of civil servants set up by the Conservative government in 1959 to report periodically on the need for controls. The working party tended to produce more arguments against controls than for them. It found no evidence for allegations that immigrants were particularly prone to either crime or disease. Housing was recognised to be a problem, but the working party argued that improving it would provide too much of an inducement for more immigrants to come. It found that unemployment among black and Asian immigrants was not rising; during the years 1959 to 1961, in spite of large increases in the numbers coming to Britain, unemployment never rose above 5 per cent; therefore the argument that immigrants were an excessive burden on national assistance was not tenable. The Treasury, asked to give an opinion on whether or not Asian and black immigration benefited the economy, gave the clear advice that on economic grounds there was no justification for introducing immigration controls; most immigrants found employment without creating unemployment for the natives and, in particular by easing labour bottlenecks, they contributed to the productive capacity of the economy as a whole. In its eventual recommendations for controls, the working party's report (quoted by Spencer in *British Immigration Policy*) had to fall back on 'the dangers of social tension inherent in the existence of large unassimilated coloured communities'. It recognised that 'the advocacy of exclusion of stocks deemed to be inferior is presentationally impossible'. It also recognised that the 'curtailment of immigration ostensibly on employment grounds would not be easy to justify'. It nevertheless proposed a labour voucher system in the following terms:

While it would apply equally to all parts of the Commonwealth, without distinction on grounds of race and colour, in practice it would interfere to the minimum extent with the entry of persons from the 'old' Commonwealth countries. ... The control over the entry of the unskilled would be of the most flexible character. Decisions reached in London could at any time increase or decrease the flow by the simple process of sending out more or fewer permits. While any scheme which effectively limits free entry is bound to run into political criticism, the flexibility of operation of this scheme should keep such criticism down to a minimum.

None of this was said publicly or officially. Throughout the debate on the bill ministers continued to deny that the intention of the legislation was to keep out immigrants from Asia and the Caribbean.

The recession beginning in the 1960s and the growth of unemployment would undoubtedly, in the absence of controls, have caused a large drop in immigration to Britain by young people in search of work. But during the two years up to the passing of the act, it had become widely known that restrictions were likely to be introduced. This meant that people who might not otherwise have planned to come immediately to Britain did so. In addition, before controls were introduced, people came often with the intention that their stay would be temporary. They now had to contemplate more permanent settlement, and to try to bring in their families. Although the Caribbean migrants included families and single women workers, migrants from the Indian subcontinent initially came to Britain overwhelmingly as young single men. Their intention was to work and save or remit their wages for a limited period and then return to their countries, perhaps to be replaced by their sons or younger brothers. The introduction of controls put paid to this rotatory system. After the act the composition of migrants changed from men of working age to mainly women, children and older people, since family reunion was in theory allowed. By 1967 over 90 per cent of all Commonwealth immigrants were dependants. Immigration of Asian and black people to settle in Britain continued at the rate of 30,000–50,000 per year up to the early 1990s, a reduction only in relation to the 'bulge' figures of 1960–62, which controls had done much to create (see Table 1.2 on p. 19). According to Nicholas Deakin's study *Colour, Citizenship and British Society*:

In 1961 net inward migration from India increased fourfold and from Pakistan tenfold over the previous year. Before 1961 the migration from India and Pakistan fluctuated at a fairly low level. As late as 1959 the net inward flow from both countries was only 3,800. ... well over half the Indians and approximately three-quarters of the Pakistanis who arrived in Britain before control arrived in the 18-month period January 1961 to June 1962.

The fear of controls also caused a rise in the arrival of Caribbean people, though it was less marked. Figure 1 in *Colour, Citizenship and British Society*, based on a study by Ceri Peach, shows that arrivals from the Caribbean followed almost precisely the rise and fall in job vacancies, but, as Deakin notes, 'The sharp rise in the rate of West Indian migration in 1961 and 1962 was for the first time against the economic indicators.' Irish immigration, uncontrolled by the act, continued to correspond to job opportunities.

The Tories made much of the fact that, following the act, there were 300,000 applications for unskilled labour vouchers. Their attempts to argue that, if it had not been for the act, 300,000 would have come in were initially contradicted by their own Home Secretary, Henry Brooke, who said in the House of Commons in November 1963:

There are over a quarter of a million applications for vouchers which have not yet been granted. Neither I nor anyone else would seek to argue that if control were lifted a quarter of a million people would immediately arrive in this country.

In the first 18 months after the act was passed, a total of 66,000 vouchers were issued for all categories; only 35,000 were used. Only 21 per cent of the vouchers granted to Indians and Pakistanis were used. Part of the explanation for the large number of applications was, again, as an insurance policy against the possible loss of opportunities in the future.

During the 1964 general election campaign, some Tories, especially in the Midlands, adopted openly racist tactics. The Tory candidate for Perry Barr in Birmingham, Dr Wyndham Davies, put out an eve of poll leaflet which said: '300,000 immigrants: This *could* happen if you Vote Labour'. The Tory candidate Peter Griffiths ran a viciously racist campaign in a 'safe'

Labour seat at Smethwick in Birmingham and defeated Patrick Gordon Walker, Labour's shadow foreign minister, against the national trend (this and the events surrounding it are documented in detail in the first part of Paul Foot's book *Immigration and Race in British Politics*). One of the slogans in the Tory campaign, which Griffiths failed to condemn, was 'If you want a nigger neighbour, vote Labour.' Such slogans no doubt ring in the ears of Labour politicians who might otherwise be moved towards any principled opposition to xenophobia. Nevertheless, during the election campaign Harold Wilson, the Labour Party leader, responded to anti-immigrant hecklers in Birmingham Rag Market as follows:

There is a very real problem of overcrowding which the Government has neglected. We are not having this immigrant question used as an alibi for the total Tory failure to handle the problems of housing, slums, schools and education in this country.

Even after the Labour government had won the 1964 election George Brown, then a senior minister, said at a meeting in Sheffield that 'It is mad to talk of restricting immigration' at a time when there was a shortage of labour, and that anti-immigrant resentment was simply a result of the shortage of schools and housing. But other Labour politicians took to blaming the Tories for immigration. For example David Kerr, candidate for the marginal seat of Wandsworth, issued a leaflet (quoted by Foot) which said:

Large scale immigration has occurred only under this Tory Government.
   The Tory Immigration Act has failed to control it – immigrants of all colours and races continue to arrive here.

Richard Crossman, a leading Labour politician, quoted by Foot from an article in *The Times*, is reported to have said to a West Midlands Labour Party rally in 1964:

Two years ago the Conservatives instituted completely ineffective controls and now they blame us because the flood of illegal immigrants is threatening to undermine the efforts which local authorities are making to integrate these new citizens.

By 1963 the Labour leadership had accepted that controls were necessary, though with the proviso that they would try again to persuade Commonwealth governments to limit emigration at source. Paul Foot comments as follows on the Labour Party's change of tactics:

not a single explanation was given for this remarkable transformation. Was it the figures for applications from intending immigrants which changed the Labour party's mind? Was it the declining importance of the Commonwealth in world affairs? Or was it simply that Labour, cock-a-hoop after a glorious conference, smelt victory and decided that no power on earth, much less political principle, could take it away from them?

After it took power in 1964 the Labour government under Harold Wilson proceeded to tighten up the implementation of the 1962 act. The Act had been loosely enforced, with a wide definition of dependent relatives, the free admission of students and a liberal issue of vouchers. From September 1964 the A and B categories of job vouchers, for those with a job offer or skills, took up the whole of the voucher issue and no more category C vouchers were issued. The Labour government formally abolished C vouchers in 1965 and reduced the numbers in the first two categories to a maximum of 8,500 a year. The result of these and subsequent further restrictions was that the people who came in were doctors, dentists, trained nurses and a few other groups of people whose skills were much needed, and, above all, family members. The numbers allowed to enter for employment fell to 4,010 in 1969. The Labour government also announced stricter enforcement of restrictions on the entry of dependants, to exclude children over 18 and other relatives, and set up a system of entry clearance officers who were posted abroad to investigate applications to enter Britain. Under the Immigration Appeals Act of 1969 entry certificates became a legal requirement, students were to be admitted for only a year and visitors for six months, and the government took powers to deport people who evaded these restrictions. As *The Economist* commented, Labour had 'pinched the Tories' white trousers'.

The rights of partners and dependants entering Britain were not entrenched in legislation, but depended on rules set by the Home Office and applied at the discretion of immigration officials. Officials could require different standards of documentation and proof of family relationships, they could process applications more or less slowly and they could increase or decrease refusals in order to let in fewer, or conceivably more, dependants. These types of arbitrary practices at the discretion of officials, which are not subject to any judicial or parliamentary scrutiny, have become typical of the immigration control process as a whole. They were in practice used as a means of reducing the number of family members entering Britain. Thus for example, according to Ian Spencer, refusal rates for applications for family reunion from the Indian subcontinent rose from 30 per cent to 44 per cent between 1981 and 1983. In 1985 the Commission for Racial Equality published a report of a detailed, formal investigation of immigration control procedures, quoting from entry clearance officers' reports, which made it abundantly clear that the purpose of their work was to exclude as many applicants as possible rather than to make fair decisions.

The treatment of families has caused more misery than almost any other aspect of immigration controls. From the end of the 1960s onwards spouses applying to enter Britain from the Indian subcontinent were kept waiting for months and sometimes years by entry clearance officers, who then asked them a litany of intrusive questions apparently designed to prove that they were not who they said they were. This process reached its humiliating apogee when virginity tests were applied to women, without their consent, who wished to enter as fiancées of men in Britain. The practice was exposed by the *Guardian* in 1979. X-ray tests were also used. The tests supposedly 'proved' that nearly half of the people were not related as they claimed to be. Subsequent DNA testing showed that over 90 per cent of the people subjected to tests were who they said they were, but no retrospective permission to enter was given; for some over 18 it was too late to re-apply; the others were put to the back of the queue. Inside Britain, immigration officials went into people's houses to determine whether couples were living together. Children trying to join their parents were subjected to cruel disappointments. Ann Dummett in *A Portrait of English Racism* describes the conduct of interrogations at Heathrow airport in the 1960s. In one long and moving account, which is semi-fictionalised, with invented names, but based on a number of true events, she says that 'Mr Khan', a bus conductor, and his younger brother go to meet the former's 12-year-old son, 'Ajaib', at Heathrow airport. 'Mr Khan' had saved up over a long period to bring Ajaib from Pakistan to Britain first, before his wife and younger son, in case immigration officials would not believe he was under 16. At Heathrow Ajaib did not appear. Eventually an official came and took the brothers through to within sight, but not touch, of Ajaib. They then subjected them to five hours of separate questioning. One brother said their house had four rooms; the other, who counted the kitchen and bathroom, said it had six. The police said seven people were living there; Mr Khan made the 'serious tactical error' of saying the police were 'lying'; he did not realise they were referring to the fact that three friends had stayed there one night, when they came for a wedding. He could not say the exact date of his son's or wife's birth, because birthdays are of little importance in Pakistan. Ajaib, who was dizzy with exhaustion and hunger, was questioned through a retired English businessman who spoke Urdu rather than the boy's local dialect, with a heavy accent that made it hard for the boy to follow. He knew it was important, says Ann Dummett:

if only he could answer the questions these men kept asking, giving them the answers they wanted, he would get the chance to speak to his father. So he tried. But even more than his father, he became confused. The men repeated the same questions over and over; he tried to answer right, but he could not always guess what they were trying to find out. Asked his younger brother's name, he gave the pet family nickname that all the family used at home; how was he to know that when his father was asked the same question he would reply with Abdul's official name? Asked about the number of cattle, he was not sure whether to include the new calf or not; one time he included it, one time not, so that his answers seemed contradictory.

After five hours, 'Ajaib' was refused admission. The immigration officer told his father that 'We don't believe he's really your son. His answers and yours to simple questions about the family are seriously conflicting. Also, we are not satisfied with the accommodation you have, which is already overcrowded.' The father and son were given an hour together; they wept and embraced, and the boy was put on a plane back to Pakistan.

Further milestones in the shameful history of British immigration controls arose from the perceived threat that Asians from East Africa might come to Britain. Colonialism had created a situation in which Indians, mainly from Gujarat, had migrated to East Africa and had formed a relatively prosperous middle class there. Some of them had opted for British rather than local citizenship when the East African colonies became independent. The 1962 Act therefore did not apply to them. When in 1967 the Kenyan government passed legislation restricting Asians with British citizenship to temporary residence, a campaign started, led by Enoch Powell and Duncan Sandys, to ensure that they did not exercise their right to come to Britain. Like the fears aroused by the threat of controls in 1961, this had the effect of speeding up the exodus; 10,000, mainly skilled and middle-class, Kenyan Asians entered Britain in February 1968. This was considered to constitute a crisis. In March 1968 the Labour government rushed a second Commonwealth Immigrants Act through parliament. The act subjected all holders of United Kingdom passports to immigration controls unless they, a parent or a grandparent had been born, adopted or naturalised in the United Kingdom. The 1968 act left about 200,000 Kenyan Asians with largely valueless passports and in effect stateless, in spite of the promises made to them at the time of independence. As a concession the government introduced a voucher scheme which would allow in 1,500 Kenyan Asians and their families per year. But it also introduced new restrictions on the family members of Commonwealth citizens.

The introduction of the act was opposed by the Commonwealth secretary, George Thomson, who is minuted in the Cabinet papers of 15 February 1968 (quoted in the *Newsletter* of the National Coalition of Anti-Deportation Campaigns of October–December 1999) as follows:

Although he recognised the problems that would be created by a continued inflow of a large number of Asians from Kenya, to pass such legislation would be wrong in principle, clearly discriminatory on grounds of colour and contrary to everything we stood for. ... We should effectively deprive large numbers of people of any citizenship at all or, at best, turn them into second class citizens.

Thomson's arguments were overruled by the prime minister, James Callaghan, who concluded in a memo of 21 February 1968 that:

We must bear in mind that the problem is potentially much wider than East Africa. There are another one and a quarter million people not subject to our immigration control. ... At some future time we may be faced with an influx from Aden or Malaysia.

The 1968 Commonwealth Immigrants Act threatened to scupper the government's new Race Relations Act and the efforts to promote legislation against racial discrimination by the Labour Home Secretary Roy Jenkins, who had said in 1966 in a speech to the Institute of Race Relations that he was 'glad that we appear to have put behind us the sterile debate about the precise level of the flow of immigration' (quoted in Deakin; speech reprinted in *Race*, vol. VIII, no. 3, January 1967). Racism had finally become blatant in the operation of immigration controls.

Far from keeping the racists quiet, the act was followed a month later by Enoch Powell's 'rivers of blood' speech. Powell was at the time a member of the Tory shadow cabinet (although he was subsequently sacked by his leader Edward Heath). His earlier speeches against immigration had not had much attention. His third major speech, made on 20 April 1968, was, and remains, notorious. Its scaremongering had probably the most powerful effect of any Tory politician's on the growth of racism and the far right. In his speech he claimed:

We must be mad, literally mad, as a nation, to be permitting the annual inflow of 50,000 dependants who are for the most part the material of the future growth of the immigrant-descended population. It is like watching a nation busily engaged in heaping up its own funeral pyre ...

As I look ahead I am filled with foreboding. Like the Roman, I seem to see 'the River Tiber foaming with much blood!' That tragic and intractable phenomenon which we watch with horror on the other side of the Atlantic ... is coming upon us here by our own volition and our own neglect.

After this speech the National Front gained some respectability and recruits. The Sheffield organiser of the National Front at the time was quoted in a Socialist Workers Party pamphlet, *The Case Against Immigration Controls*, as follows:

We held a march in Huddersfield in support of what Powell had said, and we signed eight people up as members that afternoon. Powell's speech gave our membership and morale a tremendous boost. Before Powell spoke, we were getting only cranks and perverts. After his speeches we began to attract, in a secret sort of way, the right-wing members of the Conservative organisations.

In a Southall factory, where members of the white workforce had, as in some other British factories, campaigned to keep out black workers, fascist sympathisers were emboldened by Powell's speech to carry out violent attacks on shop stewards sympathetic to Asian workers. In East London some dockers organised a march in support of Powell, although others expressed shame at their action.

The Conservatives were re-elected in 1970. In 1971 they introduced a new Immigration Act. The act doubled the number of vouchers to be issued annually to Kenyan Asians to 3,000. But, apart from this, it in effect brought primary immigration from the Caribbean, the Indian subcontinent and Africa to an end by abolishing the distinction between 'aliens' and 'British subjects', making them all subject to controls, and substituting the categories 'patrial' and 'non-patrial'. Patrials were free from restrictions. They were defined as British or Commonwealth citizens who were born in the United Kingdom or had a parent (or grandparent in the case of British citizens) who had been born or naturalised in the United Kingdom; or British and Commonwealth citizens who had lived in the United Kingdom for five years and had applied to register as a British citizen. Category A and B vouchers, allowing residence and family reunion, were finally abolished and replaced by temporary work permits which gave neither the right of permanent residence nor the right for the workers' families to enter, a system similar to the guestworker system in other European countries. The act thus increased the number of people entitled to enter Britain without restriction, but they were nearly all white. Moreover on the day the act became law, on 1 January 1973, Britain joined the European Economic Community. This meant that an additional 200 million people were to have the right freely to enter and to settle in Britain. Although concern was expressed in some quarters that this might lead to an overwhelming invasion of Spanish and Portuguese waiters (which of course did not occur), there was virtually no populist or racist opposition to this innovation.

From 1971 onwards the Ugandan government under Idi Amin put pressure on people of Asian descent to leave Uganda, and in 1972 it expelled most of them. Under the Labour government's 1968 Act the Conservative government of Edward Heath could have kept them all, or virtually all, out of Britain. It decided instead to persuade other governments to take as many as possible and to allow the rest to enter Britain. 23,000 Ugandan Asians, mostly the best qualified, went to Canada and other countries. 29,000 came to Britain, where the government made a mainly unsuccessful attempt to disperse them away from existing areas of Asian settlement. As a result of this and of continuing family reunion, the Asian population in Britain continued to grow. Immigration of Indians from East Africa and from India increased to a peak of 40,000 in 1972 and continued at around 20,000 a year for the rest of the 1970s; immigration from Pakistan was about 10,000 a year in the 1970s. Immigration from the Caribbean, on the other hand, declined from about 5,000 a year in the 1960s to almost nothing by the 1970s. By the 1990s there was net emigration by Caribbeans.

In government in the 1970s Labour introduced no new controls, and it appeared to have some second thoughts on their effects. There was some recognition that the rushed introduction of the 1968 Commonwealth Immigrants Act had set back Labour's attempts to improve race relations, and that its unexpected defeat in the 1970 general election might have had something to do with its failure to counter Enoch Powell. In 1972 a sub-committee of the party's national executive committee produced a green paper which recognised that increasing the severity of immigration controls only led to demands for more of them, or even for complete bans on immigration. In opposition in the 1980s, the Labour Party, influenced by anti-deportation campaigns and believing there would be few immigrants when unemployment was so high, undertook to repeal the various immigration acts.

The Tories' election victory in 1979, on the other hand, followed the espousal by Margaret Thatcher of some of the rhetoric of the neo-fascist National Front, as well as other right-wing and anti-union rhetoric. On 30 January 1978, Mrs Thatcher was interviewed on ITV's *World in Action*. She expressed sympathy with people who felt immigration was too high and who were 'really rather afraid that this country might be rather swamped by people with a different culture'. 'If you want good race relations,' she said, 'you have got to allay peoples' fears about numbers.' Rather than doing so, she proceeded to misreport figures in an upward direction, asserting that:. 'There was a committee which ... said that if we went on as we are then by the end of the century there would be four million people of the New Commonwealth or Pakistan here. ... The moment the minority threatens to become a big one, people get frightened.' The committee in question, the Franks committee, had predicted a population of 3.8 million black people by the year 2,000 and the Centre for Population Studies had revised this figure downwards to 3.3 million, on the basis of a fall in birth rates. The 'minority' threatening to 'become a big one', by which she presumably meant the black population currently living in Britain, was at the time less than 4 per cent of the total British population.

Although the National Front's vote in the 1979 general election collapsed, much of it going to the Tories, its influence continued. Some of its members joined the Tory Party. At least three former members of the National Front attempted to stand as Tory candidates, and they infiltrated the right-wing Monday Club, whose membership was limited to Tory Party members. These activities were exposed in an unpublished, but widely leaked, Young Conservative report produced in 1983, and by a BBC *Panorama* report on 30 January 1984. The former quoted a letter written by Richard Franklin, a past member of the National Front and other right-wing organisations, who had stood as a Conservative councillor but was later expelled; the letter, quoted by Layton-Henry in *The Politics of Immigration*, said the following:

Those of us who have chosen to work quietly through the Conservative party are not altering one iota of our basic ideology. Far from it, the new strategy merely represents a change of style.

After 1979, the Conservatives completed the process of controlling the entry of 'coloured' Commonwealth citizens, although there was little left for them to do. They described their policies as 'tough but fair', language subsequently adopted by the Blair government. The new immigration rules introduced in 1980 were originally intended to include a register of dependants and the withdrawal of the right of entry of husbands and male fiancés of British citizens. In the event they restricted family reunion by instituting the 'primary purpose rule' under which spouses or fiancés could only enter the country if they could prove that the primary purpose of their marriage was not their wish to live in Britain. Elderly relatives had to pass various dependency tests, and entry was made even more difficult for students and visitors. In 1981 the government introduced a new British Nationality Act, to replace the 1948 Nationality Act. The 1981 act re-categorised the rights of peoples of British colonies and former colonies to British citizenship, confining these rights to 'patrials', or the possessors of a British parent or grandparent, thus bringing citizenship rights into line with immigration rights. It abolished the *ius soli* principle, which entitled anyone born on British soil to citizenship there, and replaced it with *ius sanguinii*, which so entitled only those of British blood, whose parents were British or settled in Britain. In 1988 the government introduced yet another Immigration Act. Since there was no scope for reducing primary immigration, which had virtually stopped, the act further reduced the right of entry of dependants and made it easier to deport overstayers and 'illegal immigrants' by restricting their rights of appeal. The European Court of Human Rights had ruled that the right of men settled in Britain to be joined by their families discriminated against women who did not have this right; the government complied with the ruling by abolishing the right of men rather than extending it to women. In addition, families had to show that they would be able to support their members without resort to public funds; the Labour opposition argued that this was contrary to the European Convention on Human Rights, since it undermined family life.

In 1987 the government had made some concessions to Hong Kong residents under the British Nationality (Hong Kong) Act, to 'preserve stability and prosperity in Britain's last colony' by offering citizenship and the right to settle in Britain to 50,000 British Dependant Territories citizens and their families. This provoked a populist anti-immigrant campaign by the Conservative minister Norman Tebbitt, who asked whose cricket team immigrants would cheer for.

This series of immigration and nationality acts has created a situation which is confusing and arbitrary. Thus for example an Indian couple who came to Britain for postgraduate degrees at Oxford University in the 1960s would have retained unconditional entry and unlimited residence rights if they had not moved to India in 1972. Their daughter did retain such rights because she was born before the 1971 act, but their son did not because he was born after it, although both went to school and university in Britain. The parents retain voting rights in Britain. They lost the right to enter without a visa when visas were imposed in 1985/86. Under one of the most outrageous provisions of Labour's 1999 Immigration and Asylum Act, a pilot scheme is to be set up requiring visitors from the Indian subcontinent to put up a 'bond' of £5,000. If protests do not achieve the abandonment of this scheme, the couple will be unable to visit their children in Britain.

By the late 1980s refugees had come to supplant Asian family members in the eyes of racists as the perceived main threat to the British way of life, and the Tories began the process of legislating to make it more difficult for asylum seekers to seek refuge in Britain (see Chapter 3).

FORTRESS EUROPE

Since 1957, when the Treaty of Rome set up the European Economic Community, the institutions and treaties of Europe have had as their objective not only the elimination of trade barriers and the free movement of capital within Europe, but also the free movement of people. In this they differ, for example, from the North American Free Trade Agreement (NAFTA), which excludes labour from its freedoms. The Treaty of Rome contained a chapter entitled 'Freedom of Movement for Workers'. The intention was not only that labour should be treated as one of the commodities traded across frontiers, for the benefit of capital, but that this freedom of movement should be a means of increasing popular support for European integration. Migrants within Europe were to have full social and family rights. When Greece joined the EEC in 1980 and Spain and Portugal in 1986, this meant that people who had traditionally emigrated to northern Europe for work now had freedom to do so. In 1986 the Single Europe Act was adopted. Its article 7a states that:

The internal market shall comprise an area without internal frontiers in which the free movement of goods, persons, services and capital is ensured in accordance with the provisions of this Treaty.

The implication was that, just as there are no controls between regions in national markets, there should be none at frontiers between member states.

However in the 1970s two different sets of immigration rights began to be created. Not only was immigration from outside Europe virtually stopped, but the rights of 'third-country nationals' who were already settled in Europe differed sharply from those of migrants with the nationality of one of the member countries. The prospect of the elimination of border controls at frontiers aroused irrational fears in the authorities of uncontrolled movements of hordes of non-European nationals across frontiers. Although they had been prepared to take the risk that Spaniards, Italians, Portuguese and Greeks might migrate en masse to northern Europe, apparently they were unwilling to contemplate the prospect that, for example, all Turkish people settled in Europe might choose to migrate to Germany, North Africans might all travel to France and Pakistanis to Britain. 'Third country nationals' therefore continued to have severely restricted rights to move around Europe and limited rights to family reunification and social protections if they did move.

In addition, while internal borders were being dismantled, the west European states became more concerned about the joint enforcement of their external borders. There was pressure from northern countries for southern countries to introduce and tighten immigration controls. There had been an almost total absence of immigration controls in Greece, Italy, Spain and Portugal, traditionally countries of emigration rather than immigration, but now more attractive as destinations because of their membership of the European Community. In Italy, for example, a decision was made to stop issuing new labour permits in 1982, but foreign workers continued to work without them; it was not until 1986 that immigration legislation was enacted to prohibit illegal immigration, followed by the 'Martelli law' of 1990 which set annual quotas for admitting immigrants, and established asylum procedures. In Portugal, an Aliens Law was passed in 1992; it established detention centres for migrants and introduced visa requirements. Spain passed an Aliens Act in 1985, with a labour permit scheme. Both Spain and Portugal have regularised large numbers of foreign workers and granted amnesties.

Pressure on these countries to enforce their border controls, and other attempts to coordinate the policing of immigration policies, took place under what was called 'ad hoc' intergovernmental cooperation. This meant that discussions were secret and outside the political arena, not open to questioning by the European Parliament. States were unwilling to hand over any control of their national borders, which they considered a sensitive matter of national sovereignty, to European institutions, believing the latter were too favourably disposed towards migration and the human rights of migrants. But France, Germany, Belgium, the Netherlands and Luxemburg signed an agreement at Schengen in 1985 under which border controls between themselves were to be abolished by 1 January 1990. A further agreement on procedures for people crossing the external frontiers of the Schengen group, and a procedure for determining the country responsible for considering asylum applications, was signed in June 1990, when the agreement became the Schengen Convention. Subsequently all other EU states except Ireland and Britain have joined or stated their intention to ratify the Schengen Convention. The British objection to Schengen was based on its unwillingness to abandon immigration controls on people travelling from the rest of the EU. But the British Home Office was keen to participate in other Schengen activities, such as the exchange of information between immigration authorities and sanctions against airlines and shipping companies carrying undocumented refugees. The British had also been enthusiastic participants and founder members in the earlier Trevi Group, set up in 1975 to formulate policies on terrorism, drugs and illegal immigration.

In 1986 an Ad Hoc Group on Immigration was set up, following a proposal from the British government. It was concerned with the harmonisation of asylum policies, to examine 'the measures to be taken to reach a common policy to put an end to the abusive use of the right to asylum', and also with the harmonisation of visa requirements. In 1987 a list of 50 countries, whose nationals would require visas to enter the EU, was agreed. By 1993 the list had expanded to 73 countries, with a further 92 countries from which visas were required by only some European states. The list now contains virtually all Third World countries, and all the 'refugee-producing' countries. In 1990 the Dublin Convention was signed, following closely an arrangement already agreed by the Schengen countries. This stated that asylum seekers had the right to make only one application in the territory of the European Community. Rather than giving asylum seekers a choice in the matter, the convention laid down that the state responsible for considering an application should be either the one in which the refugee first arrived, or the state which had issued a visa or otherwise facilitated entry. If this was a country other than that in which the applicant had applied for asylum the applicant could be removed to that country. The agreement caused many problems, and was not ratified by all states until 1997. It fails to comply with the UN Convention on Refugees, which states that all signatories are obliged to consider requests for asylum, rather than passing responsibility to another country. It means that someone whose asylum application is turned down by one member state is automatically excluded from the EU as a whole. It also raised questions of 'burden sharing'. Asylum seekers who had entered via southern European countries, for example, in the hope of claiming asylum in other countries where they might have relatives or communities, could be returned to those southern countries. Northern governments then had a tendency to say it was the latter's fault for allowing them in in the first place, ignoring the fact that they were not illegal immigrants, but refugees, who had a right to protection.

In 1992 the Maastricht Treaty, officially the Treaty on European Union, was signed. It came into force in November 1993 and established the European Union. It had three 'pillars' (as in a Greek temple), in which decisions were to be made jointly by governments and the European Commission, and could be adopted on a qualified majority. The 'third pillar' was concerned with justice and home affairs issues, including free movement, asylum policy, immigration controls, drug addition, fraud, and judicial, customs and police cooperation. The treaty failed to secure the goal of a frontier-free Europe by January 1993, set by the Single Europe Act. Member states failed to agree on security measures at external frontiers. The Portuguese, Czech and other governments were reluctant to engage in the expense of a full system of border controls. Harmonisation of visa and asylum procedures and the abolition of controls on the movement of third-country nationals across internal borders were thwarted by governments intent on preserving sovereignty over their borders, of which the British government under John Major was the most vociferous. The Conservative government was supported without qualification by the Labour opposition, whose shadow foreign secretary Robin Cook proclaimed British immigration controls to be 'non-negotiable'. Tory and Labour leaders vied with each other to prove their commitment to the sanctity of British border controls. Thatcher was accused by Labour of having ceded sovereignty on this issue when she signed up to the Single Europe Act, while the Tories maintained that she had won a cast-iron 'opt-out' from any such concession on frontiers. The flavour of the British position is to be found in an article by Kenneth Baker, former Conservative home secretary, in the *Mail on Sunday* of 19 February 1995 headlined 'Fight for Our Frontiers', in which he said that:

In my view, the autonomy of a country in policing its borders is just as vital in preserving national sovereignty as currency or any other matter.

For the first right of any country is who should, and should not, have the privilege of living in that country. Britain is a sovereign nation, not a hotel. ...

Any Colombian, Russian or Nigerian who had legally entered the EU through Rome, Vienna or Paris would be free to waltz into Britain with no checks on them. ...

Thus, the Portuguese consulate in Mozambique, or the German consulate in Colombia, by issuing a visa, could determine who ultimately entered Britain. ...

This was a bombshell. ...

We had never envisaged that freedom of movement within the European Union meant that we would be obliged to admit non-EU citizens without any right to control their numbers.

The British, of course, flattered themselves if they thought that people who had managed to enter Germany or Portugal would then wish to 'waltz' into Britain in any numbers.

The Amsterdam Treaty, negotiated in 1998, stated that within a five-year period there should be agreement on measures with respect to external borders to allow free movement of persons in line with article 7a of the Maastricht Treaty; measures to implement an 'absence of any controls on persons, be they citizens of the Union or nationals of third countries, when crossing internal borders'; and measures to harmonise the treatment of refugees. In an initial three-year period decisions were to be made by the Council of Ministers, acting unanimously; subsequently decisions could be by qualified majority. The Schengen agreements were absorbed into the Maastricht Treaty and became law, with a protocol enabling Britain to opt in to its provisions. In March 1999 the British Home Secretary Jack Straw announced in Brussels that Britain now wished to opt in to aspects of the Schengen Convention which related to police and judicial cooperation and information-gathering, such as the strengthening of Europol, and to participate in the Schengen information system (SIS), set up to provide a computer database on 'criminals, asylum seekers and illegal immigrants'. Europol is a European police organisation originally set up under the Maastricht Treaty as the 'European Drugs Unit', which has recently become involved in the hunting and detention of migrants, including asylum seekers. The SIS is a massive system, which has been condemned by both Amnesty International and the UNHCR, designed to increase internal controls on migration; it has more than 30,000 terminals and contains large amounts of personal information, including fingerprints. Almost 90 per cent of those registered on the SIS are 'unwanted immigrants', including many asylum seekers. The British were also enthusiastic promoters of such control measures at the special EU justice and home affairs summit at Tampere in Finland in October 1999. Straw was said to hope that agreement on asylum criteria at Tampere and afterwards might help to curb what he considered to be the excessive liberalism of British judges. The likelihood was that the search for common procedures and criteria would lead to agreement on the lowest common denominator.

The curbing of migration and asylum seeking, and in particular of what is called in the jargon the 'trafficking' of migrants and refugees, has become an obsession with the authorities of European states. According to John

Morrison, in his report entitled *The Cost of Survival: The Trafficking of Refugees to the UK*, there are currently about 30 intergovernmental fora, groups and subgroups dealing with migration, asylum and refugee issues in a European context, several of which are concerned with migrant trafficking. There are 16 working groups operating under the provisions on justice and home affairs of the Maastricht and Amsterdam treaties, with further 'horizontal' groups combining different aspects of migration, enforcement and anti-trafficking initiatives. These respond to and commission information gathered by the Centre for Information, Discussion and Exchange on Asylum (CIREA) and the Centre for Information, Discussion and Exchange on the Crossing of Borders and Immigration (CIREFI). 'Most of the discussion', says Morrison, 'is highly secretive and not available for scrutiny by any elected assembly at national or European level ... the over-arching agenda is clearly one of enforcement.' The UNHCR has observer status at CIREA but no access to CIREFI. Morrison quotes an article in the April–June 1998 issue of *Race and Class* by the Berlin-based Forschungsgesellschaft Flucht und Migration (FFM) as follows:

In recent years, [European] police forces have emphasized the struggle against so-called organised crime as an overriding and all-embracing theme into which refugee policy, too, is being fitted. Illegal migration is now being construed as an imported crime, so that commercial assistance for refugees is accordingly categorised as 'organised crime'. ... Phenotypical criteria like skin pigmentation, 'alien' behaviour and other visible signs of foreign origin are the triggers for surveillance, monitoring and investigation. ... Ultimately, an 'overall European security zone' will be constructed based on the 'organised crime' scenario and on the criminalisation of migration. ... Using a criminological redefinition of offenders ('smugglers and traffickers') and victims (penniless refugees, women forced into prostitution), police forces and public authorities are trying to use human rights to justify and legitimise their actions.

The European Union is acting to strengthen its external borders both by imposing financial penalties on airlines and other 'carriers' who allow passengers to travel with false or no documents, and also by extending controls beyond its borders. Several European countries are now developing their own equivalent of British pre-embarkation controls, such as airport liaison officers (ALOs), thus moving towards the standardisation of EU extra-territorial enforcement at airports throughout the world, as the first outer defence of Fortress Europe. In addition, European states are attempting to secure the 'soft underbelly' of Europe represented by Italy and the countries on the eastern borders of the EU. The latter are being financially assisted to act as a 'buffer zone' or 'cordon sanitaire' between the EU and the rest of the world. There are now over 100 bilateral arrangements to prevent migrants and refugees entering western Europe from its eastern neighbours and to secure their 'readmission' to the countries they have travelled through. John Morrison in *The Cost of Survival* writes that:

The most substantial of all these arrangements is that between Germany and Poland signed on 7 May 1993. From 1993 to 1996, Germany spent DM 120 million on 'financing material and equipment along Poland's western border and creating a Polish administrative system for refugees and deportation'. Now, the interest of German authorities has spread further eastward to strengthening Poland's border with the Ukraine and Belarus. ...

It is important to note that none of these readmission agreements contain any criteria for dealing with asylum seekers and refugees as opposed to illegal migrants in general, or mention the state's obligation towards refugees under international law. Germany regards all of its neighbours, including Poland and the Czech Republic, as 'safe places' to return refugees interdicted at the border. ... 1,453 of those bounced back to Poland were subsequently deported from Poland to its eastern neighbours (Lithuania, Belarus and the Ukraine) or directly back to countries of origin (such as Sri Lanka), mostly within 48 hours of being arrested. The concern ... is that the 'domino effect' of chain removal can result in refoulement to persecution.

Nevertheless there are signs that, even at semi-official levels, there is greater openness towards the idea of immigration. A group of academics, the Academic Group on [Im]migration – Tampere (AGIT), whose comments were invited by the EU before its summit at Tampere in October 1999, produced a document which recommended that, in response to 'realities', 'new legal channels of immigration based on economic, social and other needs should be created, in line with the European Union Member States' own positive approach to the freedom of movement between them for economic purposes' and talked of 'necessary and useful labour migration'. At a Refugee Studies Programme seminar at Oxford University in 1999, the speaker was Dennis de Jong, who worked for several years in the European Commission and then returned to the Dutch ministry of foreign affairs. He concluded his speech with the comments that, while this 'whole range of restrictive measures' had had a small effect on reducing numbers of asylum applications, the numbers were now rising again. His belief was that governments 'recognise that they won't work', since they go against the grain of globalisation, and they might therefore decide to 'give it all up'. He proposed that governments should 'give some air to immigration' and should not condemn economic migrants. North Africans, he said, had argued that free movement should be permitted; the French government was now willing to engage in discussions on the issue. In answer to the question why not abolish controls altogether, he said that EU governments were fearful of opening their borders to eastern Europe, but North Africa was a different matter; the opening of borders from North Africa was on the agenda, in particular because of the impossibility of returning 'illegals'. 'It will happen', he said. Meanwhile, European officials suggest that there will have to be at least some relaxation of immigration controls in order to take the pressure off the asylum determination system. The Dutch government is discussing the possibility of giving all asylum seekers three-year permits to stay, and examining their cases thereafter. Fortress Europe is not impregnable.

3   REFUGEES: TIGHTENING THE SCREW

Nearly all migrants, apart from refugees, seeking to live in the rich industrialised countries are now excluded. Migration for economic betterment, rather than being considered, as it should be and as it was when Europeans did it, a sign of enterprise and courage, is now regarded as criminal and somehow shameful. European Union nationals can travel to work and settle in other countries of the EU. For the rest, work permits are issued only for specified jobs to people whose skills are desired. In Britain this means they are issued almost entirely to nationals from the United States, Japan and one or two other countries, rather than to nationals of the Third World or eastern Europe. The exceptions are the continued issue of permits for domestic servants, which are available to Filipinas and others as they were to Jewish women fleeing Nazi persecution in the 1930s; the employment of east Europeans and north Africans on seasonal visas to work on farms, mainly in East Anglia; and the association agreements with some east European countries, including the Czech Republic, Poland and Romania, which allow their nationals to set up businesses, including small ones such as window cleaning, provided they are self-supporting. In addition an unknown number of people, some of them asylum seekers whose claims have been rejected, are working in Britain and other industrialised countries illegally. They provide an extremely vulnerable and highly exploitable workforce.

Refugees are increasingly lumped together with 'illegal immigrants' as people whose presence is unwelcome. Nevertheless, in theory, a distinction is made between refugees (or 'asylum seekers', as people who have asked for refugee status but have not yet been granted or refused it are officially termed) and other migrants. The current orthodoxy is that refugees are a good thing and that other migrants, usually defined as economic migrants, are bad. Refugees can still in theory enter European countries legally and they can, if they win refugee status, settle and acquire much the same rights as EU nationals. But because of the existence of immigration controls, they are forced to undergo examination to determine whether they are accepted as refugees. Even now, when the main objective of governments' immigration policy and legislation seems to be to keep refugees out, or at least to reduce their numbers, their *stated* objective is to keep out not refugees, but people who they claim are economic migrants posing as refugees. Thus 'genuine' refugees are okay, but 'bogus' asylum seekers and 'economic migrants' are to be cracked down on.

The claims that most asylum seekers are 'bogus' are grossly unjust. The Home Office, for example, turns down 96 per cent of the initial applications of Sri Lankans. As Rohini Hensman comments in *Journey Without a Destination*, based on many interviews with Sri Lankan refugees:

If there is no fear of persecution, why do hundreds of thousands of Tamils suddenly decide to leave Sri Lanka? The Home Office explanation, apparently, is that they are in search of better jobs and economic prospects. In the case of Sri Lankan refugees, this is really the ultimate irony. Those who have been able to get to Britain are precisely those who come from relatively affluent families in Sri Lanka, most of which own at least their own home, and often additional land as well. ...

The idea that all these people with a comfortable standard of living in Sri Lanka, and sometimes with prestigious, high status jobs too, should come to Britain *voluntarily* in order to be unemployed, or to do unskilled jobs in petrol stations, shops or other workplaces, is grotesque. The media as well as the politicians who repeat this story ad nauseam are either shamefully ignorant ('shamefully' because they ought to make sure they are better informed before making statements in public), or even more shamefully dishonest, spreading untruths which they know will be used as a pretext for vicious attacks on helpless people.

This is not to imply that there is anything wrong in coming to Britain in search of employment or economic security. But the fact is that for Sri Lankan refugees, the very *opposite* is the case: most of them come to Britain *leaving* employment, property, status and economic security because their lives are at risk; and the allegation that they are economic migrants who have left their country voluntarily must be exposed for the contemptible lie that it is.

Who is considered to be a 'genuine' refugee, and who is not, is entirely within the discretion of governments. Governments can vary the numbers of people they accept for settlement without infringing the various conventions on refugees, since these theoretically guarantee the right to seek and enjoy asylum, but not the right to obtain it. The British and other governments' assertions that most asylum seekers are bogus is based simply on the fact that they turn down most of their claims. Thus the Conservative home secretary Michael Howard, asked in the House of Commons on 20 April 1995 for an estimate of the numbers of 'illegal immigrants' and 'bogus asylum seekers' currently in the United Kingdom, replied as follows:

There are no official estimates of the number of illegal immigrants into the United Kingdom. By its very nature, illegal immigration is difficult to measure and any estimates would be highly speculative. It is also difficult to estimate the precise extent of the abuse of asylum, but in 1994, around 80 per cent of asylum decisions, amounting to some 16,000, were outright refusals.

Similarly, Home Office immigration minister Charles Wardle, in a letter to John Patten MP in response to a letter from one of his constituents, dated 15 April 1994, said the following:

The number of asylum seekers entering the United Kingdom rose sharply from some 4,000 in 1988 to a peak of 45,000 in 1991. Following the introduction of new screening procedures, the number of applications fell to about 25,000 in 1992 but this was still some six times higher than in 1988. Significantly, the proportion of applicants found to be genuine refugees as defined by the 1951 UN Convention relating to the Status of Refugees decreased from about 60 per cent in the early 1980s to 25 per cent in 1990; and to only about 5 per cent in 1992. Against this background I am afraid that it would fly in the face of reality to deny that asylum has been claimed by a huge number of individuals in order to circumvent the immigration control and obtain settlement here.

This does not mean that the claims are without foundation, but merely that governments turn down claims which should not be turned down. A Home Office-appointed special adjudicator, charged with determining appeals against refusals, spent the first half of an interview with the author in 1994 asserting that claims were always dealt with on their individual merits; a little later he said that the numbers of asylum claims were increasing so fast that 'something had to be done to bring them down'. The rates at which people are recognised as refugees have declined over time and vary between countries. Thus, according to Danièle Joly's book *Refugees: Asylum in Europe?*, the acceptance rate for applicants in Europe was nearly half in 1984; ten years later it was less than one in ten. The *1998 Statistical Overview* of the UN High Commissioner for Refugees (UNHCR) gives an average recognition rate for asylum applicants in Europe over the period 1989–98 of 9.1 per cent; the lowest rate was 6.1 per cent in 1993. In 1998 the average for Europe was 9.2 per cent. In Britain it was 16.9 per cent, up from 5.7 per cent in 1996; in 1999 the initial recognition rate in the UK increased to 54 per cent. In Germany it was 7.7 per cent, in France 17.5 per cent, in Italy 29.6 per cent, and in Canada 43.8 per cent. In the Czech Republic it was 100 per cent in 1990 and 2.8 per cent in 1998, a pattern common to east European states. In Portugal it was 46.3 per cent in 1989 and 1.6 per cent in 1998. In general, the process of applying for asylum is fraught with arbitrariness and bitter injustice.

Clearly, since virtually all legal possibilities for migrating from the Third World for economic betterment have now been closed off, there is likely to be some increase in migration by clandestine means, and also in claims for political asylum by people who would otherwise have migrated legally as workers. Thus, for example, many of the people claiming asylum in West Germany, after the German government stopped recruiting guestworkers in the 1970s, were Turkish and Kurdish, as were the guestworkers. This may not, however, mean that the refugees were not in reality refugees, but rather that many of the Turkish and Kurdish workers were also refugees. Much the same can be said about workers/asylum seekers from the Indian Punjab. People fleeing persecution in the Punjab came to Britain as workers or dependents while they could, and began to claim asylum when that became the only way of achieving protection. On the other hand most of those who come to Britain to seek asylum come from different parts of the world from those who migrated in search of work in the 1950s and 1960s. Few Africans are in the latter category, and virtually no Caribbeans in the former. Asian workers came to Britain mainly from Gujarat, from what is now Bangladesh, and from the parts of Punjab which are in Pakistan, as well as from the Indian Punjab (see p. 18). The people from the Indian subcontinent who now seek asylum in Britain are nearly all from Sri Lanka, Kashmir, and the Indian Punjab. Thus they, like other refugees, are overwhelmingly from countries and regions with repressive regimes or in which there are civil wars and armed conflicts, for which the governments of the rich industrialised countries moreover bear much responsibility (see Introduction). In the mid-1970s, after the Vietnam war, there were mass flights from Vietnam, Kampuchea and Laos. The United States has allowed free entry for Cubans, while closing its borders against Haitians. The killings and torture by dictatorial regimes in Argentina and Chile (after the socialist government had been overthrown with CIA involvement) created more refugees. In the 1970s people also fled from the Lebanon, Afghanistan, Zaire, Uganda, Namibia and South Africa. Most of the recent refugees are from repressive regimes in Nigeria, Zaire, Ivory Coast (Côte d'Ivoire), Kenya, Iraq, Iran, China, Turkey, Pakistan and eastern Europe, and from civil wars and conflicts in Sri Lanka, Rwanda, Somalia, Algeria, Angola, Sierra Leone, Liberia, Kashmir, Colombia and the former Yugoslavia. The UNHCR records in its *1998 Statistical Overview* that the ten countries from which most asylum seekers came to Europe over the period 1989–98 were, in the following order, the Federal Republic of Yugoslavia, Romania, Turkey, Iraq, Bosnia and Herzegovina, Sri Lanka, Bulgaria, Iran, Somalia and Democratic Republic of the Congo (former Zaire). Between them, these ten accounted for 61 per cent of all asylum applications to 17 European countries.

The treatment and admission of refugees is surrounded by a rhetoric of humanitarianism and altruism. Thus for example a 1967 resolution of the Council of Europe on Asylum to Persons in Danger of Persecution stated that governments should 'act in a particularly liberal and humanitarian spirit in relation to persons who seek asylum on their territory'. This attitude towards refugees is presumably based on some sympathy with the plight of people who are forced to flee from imprisonment, torture or death, as opposed to others who are sometimes referred to as 'economic refugees' but are considered to have more choice. It may also have something to do with class affinities. The political refugees who have succeeded in reaching European countries have tended to be educated, middle-class democrats and liberals, whereas those who migrate in search of work may do so because they are poor, or are assumed to be so. Nearly half of all refugees settling in Britain in the late 1990s already had university or higher education qualifications, and over 80 per cent had completed secondary education. Many of them have given up opportunities for lucrative careers within government elites in order to struggle against corruption and for democracy and more attention to the needs of the poor. Others have had to leave good jobs and comfortable living standards because of wars and conflict. They take a sharp drop in income when they flee to Europe, and have to adapt painfully to levels of deprivation to which they are unaccustomed.

The national origins and political allegiances of refugees, and of the regimes they are fleeing from and to, also play a role. Untypically, in the nineteenth century British governments admitted some individual refugees whose political views they were hostile to, while at the same time admitting bourgeois revolutionaries with whom they presumably had more sympathy. Marx, Engels and Lenin lived in Britain under Tory and Liberal governments. The huge number of refugees in Germany, and the liberal nature of German asylum laws until 1992, are to be explained mainly by Germany's willingness to take in some of the more than 12 million ethnic Germans who were expelled from the areas of eastern Europe occupied by Soviet forces after the Second World War. Some of the estimated 60 million Europeans who were displaced during the war, if they did not return to their countries of origin, were resettled in European countries under various employment schemes. In the days of the Cold War the United States (until the 1980 Refugee Act restricted the definition of a refugee) and other industrialised countries accepted without question anybody fleeing from a communist regime. Since the break-up of the Soviet Union and Yugoslavia, there have been larger flows of refugees from these areas. But Western governments, which had previously expressed outrage at the refusal of communist governments to allow people to escape, are now desperately trying to keep out people who are still trying to escape, but from post-Soviet regimes. In Britain recently, the clearest pattern in an apparently arbitrary decision-making process is that refugees from certain countries, such as Iraq, are mostly accepted, and that refugees from other governments to whom, for example, the British government sells weapons or with whom it has military alliances, such as Nigeria and Turkey, are mostly refused, although Kurds suffer similar levels of persecution in Turkey and in Iraq, and the levels of suffering, torture and arbitrary imprisonment in Nigeria recently have been some of the worst in the world. In France and Germany the Kurdish party PKK has been banned and suspected members have been rounded up and expelled as terrorists. The British Conservative government did not accept left-wing Chilean refugees after the 1973 Pinochet coup; between 1974 and 1979, in one of the few principled reversals of Conservative policies by a Labour government, 3,000 Chilean refugees were admitted; the policy was reversed again by the next Conservative government after its re-election in 1979. Governments are unwilling to accept evidence of persecution by governments with which they wish to remain on good terms. In a 1991 debate in the House of Commons (reported by Pritam Singh in *Economic and Political Weekly*) the Conservative minister of state for foreign and commonwealth affairs, Tristan Garel-Jones, replied as follows to concerns raised about mass torture, killing and persecution of civilians in the Indian Punjab:

... we must judge carefully just how much prominence to give the human rights issues in our relationship with other governments. Sometimes, with a friendly government, that makes for hard choices ...

If we had dealings only with countries with impeccable human rights records our influence in the world would be significantly reduced, and there would almost certainly be a consequent loss of jobs in this country.

India was subsequently put on a 'white list' of countries whose nationals' asylum applications would be summarily dealt with. Refusals of asylum are commonly based on reports by British embassies in the countries concerned. In 1994 the Conservative home secretary Michael Howard told the foreign secretary Douglas Hurd, in response to representations on behalf of a detained Zairean asylum seeker, that the Home Office's refusal of asylum was based on information from 'our embassy in Kinshasa where the chargé d'affaires and her staff are well placed to provide objective assessments of political developments': 'although there are sporadic arrests of political activists', Howard's letter said, 'there are, in fact, very few political prisoners and the widespread opposition to President Mobutu and his government is usually tolerated'. (Even supposing this had been remotely true, it failed of course to justify the refusal of asylum to those who *had* been political prisoners in Zaire, or the wisdom of incarcerating a Zairean who Douglas Hurd's correspondent (a former British ambassador) had described as 'of intelligence and good character, well educated and with excellent manners, just the sort of young man whom African countries now need and whom we ought to be encouraging', whose repatriation might 'perhaps ... condemn him to death'.)

Once refugees start coming in larger numbers, rather than as a few individuals, they are less welcome. The 1905 Aliens Act, the first legislation which gave the British government general powers to refuse entry, arose because of the large numbers of Jewish refugees fleeing persecution in Tsarist Russia, even though asylum seekers were eventually excluded from the Act's provisions. Later the deaths of millions of Jews in Nazi concentration camps was in part a consequence of European governments' refusal to provide refuge. In a letter in the *Daily Telegraph* of 15 April 1994 Maureen Renyort explains why she was at Campsfield immigration detention centre, protesting against the imprisonment of refugees, as follows:

I was there with my husband for two reasons: as refugees from Hitler's Germany in 1939 we are often asked why Jews did not defend themselves from attack and persecution (if there is no place to flee, how is this to be done?); and, when my husband came home he began work as an engineer (helping the war effort) but was interned a year later as an enemy alien! All the arguments used then are being used now and they are the reason people like us are demonstrating against detention.

During his internment my partner, like many of his fellow refugees, was imprisoned with members of the Nazi party, the Home Office policy being, then as now, 'Collar the lot'. ...

Fleeing Hitler's Germany was seen as 'suspect' even in 1939, which is why my husband is the sole survivor of his family, all sent to Auschwitz.

European governments' current frenzied attempts to keep out refugees are a result of a rapid growth in their numbers, but from low levels. According to a 1991 report of the Organisation for Economic Co-operation and Development (OECD), about 13,000 people sought asylum in western Europe in 1972. By 1989, according to UNHCR's *1998 Statistical Overview*, the numbers applying in Europe as a whole had increased to 311,770. By 1992 they had doubled again, to 692,760. 1992, however, was the peak year. They then declined until 1996, and rose again, to 457,600, in 1999. In 1999, asylum applications from the Federal Republic of Yugoslavia were over half of all asylum applications to Europe; 90 per cent of these were Kosovo Albanians. Over the period 1989–98, around half of these asylum applications were in Germany. Applications to Britain were about one-sixth of those to Germany, slightly lower than those to France, and slightly higher than those to the Netherlands, Spain and Sweden. In 1998 Britain was ninth out of 13 European countries in the rate of asylum seekers per 100,000 population, even though its share was higher than it was in the early 1990s. According to the UNHCR, asylum applications in Britain in the 1990s were as shown in Table 3.1.

Table 3.1 Asylum applications in Britain in the 1990s.

1990	26,205
1991	44,840
1992	24,605
1993	22,370
1994	32,830
1995	43,965
1996	29,640
1997	32,500
1998	46,015
1999	89,701

Source: *UNHCR Statistical Overview*

The big increase in 1999, raising Britain's share of applications in Europe from 15.6 per cent to 20 per cent, was partly the result of recalculation by the UNHCR, in a report published in February 2000, to include dependants. But, as in the rest of Europe, it was mainly the result of the war in Kosovo. At the beginning of 2000 the rate of applications was declining. In the world as a whole the 'refugee population', or stock of recognised refugees, the majority of whom are in the poorer parts of the Third World, was 14.9 million in 1989. The numbers peaked in 1992 at 18.2 million, and in 1998 they were down to 11.5 million, the lowest of the last ten years. The decline was mainly due to declines in the numbers of refugees in Africa and Asia. But numbers with refugee status in Europe also declined, from 3.2 million in 1992 to 2.7 million in 1998, in spite of large increases in refugees from eastern Europe. 116,100 refugees, or less than 1 per cent of the 1998 world total and 3 per cent of the European total, were in Britain.

Attempts to organise the treatment of refugees on an international basis began in the 1920s when Fridtjof Nansen was appointed by the League of Nations as 'High Commissioner on behalf of the League in connection with the problem of Russian refugees in Europe'. Some groups of stateless refugees were issued with a 'Nansen passport'. The League of Nations also established a 'High Commission for Refugees (Jewish and other) coming from Germany'. The High Commission was largely unsuccessful in its efforts to help Jews. After the war the United Nations Relief and Rehabilitation Agency (UNRRA) was set up to help resettle refugees; it was replaced by the International Refugee Organisation (IRO) and then in 1951 by the United Nations High Commissioner for Refugees (UNHCR), which had and still has the task of protecting refugees. The UNHCR was set up under the United Nations Convention on the Status of Refugees, adopted at Geneva in 1951 and sometimes known as the Geneva Convention. The 1951 UN convention continues to be the most important legal instrument determining the fate of refugees, although in June 2000 the British home secretary Jack Straw raised the possibility of revising it. It does not, as pre-war international agreements had, provide for protection of national groups. Instead, it provides protection for individual refugees who are defined as follows:

Any person who owing to well founded fear of being persecuted for reasons of race, religion, nationality, membership of a particular social group or political opinion, is outside the country of his nationality and is unable, or owing to such fear, is unwilling to avail himself of the protection of that country; or who, not having a nationality and being outside the country of his former habitual residence, is unable, or owing to such fear, is unwilling to return to it.

Under the convention the events giving rise to such fears had to have occurred before 1951, and most states limited recognition to events which occurred in Europe. The convention was thus set up to deal with the refugee crisis in the aftermath of the Second World War and the effects of the Cold War; the original mandate of the UNHCR was for three years. However in 1967 the Bellagio protocol was adopted and extended the provisions of the convention to events occurring after 1951 and to non-Europeans, reflecting the development of conditions in the Third World which cause people to flee. One hundred and eight states have signed either the convention or the protocol or both, including all the states of western Europe and some in eastern Europe. The convention contains a strong prohibition on *refoulement*, or sending back refugees to places where they face persecution; article 33 states that 'No Contracting State shall expel or return a refugee ... to the frontiers of territories where his life or freedom would be threatened.' In other respects its provisions are quite subjective, especially in relation to the definition of a 'well founded fear of persecution', and leave much flexibility to governments to interpret them so as to admit or exclude particular individuals and groups of people according to the priorities of state policy. Refugees are increasingly expected, against the spirit of the conventions and the guidelines of the UNHCR, to provide 'proof' that their fear of persecution is well founded.

The convention itself provides a narrow definition of refugees, which has excluded people who badly need asylum. People whose persecution is not by governments and their agencies are, according to some governments' inter-pretations of the convention, including the French and German, excluded. People who are not themselves politically active, but have been caught up in generalised conflicts and wars, are usually not recognised as refugees within the definitions of the convention. Women who have, for example, been raped by soldiers or police have had difficulty in having their claims recognised, even though the UNHCR suggested in 1985 that states should grant refugee status to women persecuted as a 'particular social group'. Some lawyers have succeeded in arguing the cases of refugees under the European Convention on Human Rights, which was incorporated into British law in the Human Rights Act of 1998 and is due to become operative in Britain in October 2000. In addition, the 1966 International Covenant on Civil and Political Rights and the 1984 UN Convention against Torture and Other Cruel, Inhuman or Degrading Treatment or Punishment have been used to protect refugees. It has also been argued that refugee status should be determined on the basis of violations of the UN Universal Declaration of Human Rights, which includes prohibitions against torture and cruel, inhuman or degrading treatment or punishment and against arbitrary arrest, detention or imprisonment without independent judicial process, and states that 'Everyone has the right to seek and enjoy in other countries asylum from persecution.'

People who are not recognised as refugees under the terms of the Geneva Convention may nevertheless be allowed to stay for temporary periods for various 'humanitarian' reasons. In Britain they can be given 'Exceptional Leave to Remain', for a limited but renewable period, but without the right to be joined by their families or to travel abroad; in Germany they may be given temporary residence permits.

Some refugees are forced to travel from country to country without their claims being determined; the phenomenon has become so common that they are known as 'refugees in orbit', or even as RIOs. The Dublin Convention, signed by European Union member states in 1990, stipulates that asylum applications should normally be determined in the first EU state in which an applicant arrives. This means for example that, even if refugees have friends or relatives in Britain, the fact that they spent a few hours in transit in another European country entitles the British state to return them to that country without examining their case. In 1992 in London EU interior ministers agreed to extend this principle to states outside the EU which they consider to be 'safe', providing the refugee has passed through such a state. The 'safe' country may, however, be quite unsafe. Danièle Joly in *Refugees: Asylum in Europe?* relates that 'four Iranians were sent to Turkey after being returned to West Germany by Denmark'; and '15 Tamils were sent to India where they faced immediate imprisonment after being returned by Denmark via Finland and Poland.' The European Council on Refugees and Exiles (ECRE), based in London, published a report entitled *Safe Third Country* which gives more examples. A family of Iraqi Kurds asked for asylum in Slovenia, which they had reached via Jordan and Italy. Slovenia returned them to Italy and Italy returned them to Jordan. The UNHCR representative in Jordan was, implausibly, told by the Jordanian authorities that the family 'had decided to go back to Iraq'. Another Iraqi was sent back from Denmark to Italy, accompanied by Danish police, then from Italy to Tunisia where he was imprisoned and interrogated, allegedly beaten and burnt with cigarette ends, threatened with being turned over to the Iraqi embassy, but then returned to Denmark where he was finally given refugee status.

There are, in addition, numerous cases of refugees being imprisoned, tortured and killed after having their asylum applications turned down and being returned to their countries of origin. These include, among many others, the case of five Tamils, who were deported from Britain to Sri Lanka after their appeal was turned down by the House of Lords in 1989; three were detained and tortured and two went into hiding. A Moroccan student who had been active first on the left and then, after a period in prison, in Islamic groups opposed to the Moroccan government, whose father had spent 17 years in Moroccan gaols, and who had travelled to Britain in the hold of a ship, was detained in Britain, spent a year in Campsfield detention centre and was then deported to Morocco, where he was imprisoned again, and only released after the intervention of a Moroccan human rights lawyer who happened to hear about him from his supporters in Britain. In 1997 the Home office rejected 86 per cent of the 765 Algerians who applied for asylum, and in 1998 it was still deporting about 20 a month, even though there was much evidence that Algerians were being tortured with electric shocks, burning, rape and other forms of abuse; some were known to have been immediately arrested on their return and at least two were tortured; eventually the Home Office, faced with this evidence, did stop removals to Algeria. In 1994 Yorkshire TV made a documentary, *Desperately Seeking Asylum*, in which a man returned to Zaire was filmed being detained by officials at Kinshasa airport. A document produced by the London charity Asylum Aid, *Adding Insult to Injury*, provides evidence that imprisonment and torture, or worse, were common for Zaireans returned during this period. A Nigerian who was deported after being detained in Campsfield wrote a letter to his visitor (quoted in the Autumn 1999 *Newsletter* of Asylum Welcome, a charity in Oxford) as follows:

> I was locked up when I arrived in Nigeria until my police friend bailed me out with 40,000 naira after all the beating and torture. ... I try to see if I can go to Cotonou [in Benin] but they have tightened their border ... many of my cousins has been tortured to death, even the so-called conflict is worse now than when I left. ... I am still surviving because of my police friend ... this country is still not safe for me.

Many are simply not heard of again. Their friends in Britain assume the worst.

European governments now attempt to deter refugees from applying in the first place, in particular by locking them up in prisons and detention centres and imposing harsh material conditions, including the denial of welfare benefits. Governments have not formally repudiated international refugee conventions, but they are undermining them, in an underhand way, and they are contravening certainly their spirit, if not their letter. Rather than smoothing refugees' access to a safe haven, they impose harsher and harsher obstacles, in the hope that news will travel back to the countries from which refugees might flee. They are thus, in effect, punishing refugees and asylum seekers not for anything they themselves have done, but in the hope that their treatment will deter others from coming, as *The Economist*, in a leader on 14 February 1998, recognised: 'The illogicality of punishing those who are here in an effort to deter those who might come should always have been obvious.' There is little evidence, moreover, that the competition to be the least attractive destination has much effect, beyond adding to the suffering of many innocent people. Many refugees have little choice or even knowledge of their destination, but are in the hands of agents who may make their decisions on the grounds of convenience and profitability to themselves. The refugees who find themselves confined in prisons and detention centres on arrival in Europe express surprise and shock at having their expectations of humane treatment according to democratic norms dashed. The often-repeated claim that, for example, Britain is a 'soft touch' is a myth: Denmark, Finland, Luxemburg, Norway and Ireland all offer more support than Britain; Germany, Switzerland and Sweden offer only slightly less. The rise and fall in applications in one country tend to mirror those elsewhere. It is likely that numbers are far more affected by political situations abroad than they are by 'deterrence' in receiving countries. The British government admitted as much when, in response to a rise in officially recorded asylum applications to 71,000 in 1999, the *Guardian* reported that:

> Downing Street blamed the rise on the conflict in Kosovo and said the increase in asylum seekers was 'not a problem unique to Britain'.

Barbara Roche, the new immigration minister, nevertheless claimed that 'a move to a "cashless" voucher system would tackle the problem' (see below).

Perhaps in recognition of the ineffectiveness of deterrence, governments also endeavour to stop escape at source. Their main instrument is the requirement of visas. Visas are imposed when conditions in certain countries and areas deteriorate and cause people to flee. Sweden and then Norway imposed visas on Chileans in the late 1980s. Denmark imposed visas on Romanians in 1989. Belgium imposed visas on the main 'refugee-producing' countries in 1986. France has imposed visa requirements on all non-EU nationals apart from the Swiss, and in 1991 it imposed in addition transit visa requirements on eleven 'refugee-producing countries': Albania, Angola, Bangladesh, Ethiopia, Ghana, Haiti, Nigeria, Pakistan, Somalia, Sri Lanka and Zaire. Britain placed visa restrictions on Sri Lankans in 1985 after the persecution of Tamils intensified. It then extended the requirement to India, Bangladesh, Ghana, Nigeria and Pakistan. From 1989, after 4,000 Kurds had applied for asylum on arrival in Britain, Britain required visas for Turkish nationals. Visas were imposed for Sierra Leone and Ivory Coast (Côte d'Ivoire) in 1994, and for Colombia in 1997, again as a result of the increase in refugees from those countries. In August 1999 the British government threatened to reintroduce visas for the Czech Republic, an aspirant EU member, when asylum applications rose from 55 in January 1999 to 150 in June; Lord Bassam, Home Office minister, said many of them were Roma gypsies who, although they might well face discrimination at home, did not fill the criteria for refugees. After 56 Kosovars arrived at London's Heathrow airport as transit passengers in March 1998 and tried to claim asylum there, a new category of transit visa was imposed, the direct airline transit visa (DATV); these are now applied to 14 other countries, including Turkey, Iran, Iraq, Somalia, Sri Lanka and Ethiopia. European Union members are now attempting to coordinate their visa policies.

Having imposed visa requirements, governments enlisted airlines and shipping companies to help them enforce them, imposing fines if they failed to do so, under carriers' liability legislation (see below). The British government employs airport liaison officers as a further aid to the detection of people who lack proper documents, and other European countries are following their example. The result is that it is now virtually impossible for refugees to travel legally to seek asylum in Europe. Article 31 of the 1951 UN Convention on Refugees says the following:

The Contracting States shall not impose penalties, on account of their illegal entry or presence, on refugees who, coming directly from a territory where their life or freedom was threatened in the sense of Article 1, enter or are present in their territory without authorization, provided they present themselves without delay to the authorities and show good cause for their illegal entry or presence.

This article is being flouted by governments, which penalise refugees who arrive with false documents, for example by using this as a 'reason' for locking them up, and which publicly vilify refugees for being 'illegal',

European governments, moreover, find it difficult to deport people whose claims they have rejected, often after years of delayed appeals and sometimes after they have spent months in detention. This may be because the asylum seekers' governments will not provide them with papers, or perhaps because the longer they stay, the more compassionate reasons there are for not deporting them, or sometimes presumably because the difficulty and expense of finding and deporting them is too great. In Britain it is estimated that less than a third of asylum seekers whose claims have been turned down have left. Amnesty International says that between 1992 and 1995, 54,000 asylum seekers in Britain reached the end of the legal process, but in the same period fewer than 8,000 were deported. The Home Office estimates that there are at least 30,000 'illegals' who should have left the country but who have disappeared; others put the number at 100,000. In Germany and the Netherlands officials say, with chagrin, that the great majority of failed asylum seekers cannot be deported.

LEGISLATION AND LEGAL PROCESSES IN BRITAIN

In 1987 the British Conservative Party's general election manifesto said that tackling the 'problem' of 'fraudulent' asylum seekers was one of its main priorities. Conservative governments introduced three new bills aimed mainly at asylum seekers: the Immigration (Carriers' Liability) Act in 1987, the Asylum and Immigration Appeals Act in 1993 and the Asylum and Immigration Act in 1996. The Carriers' Liability Act made airlines and shipping companies act in effect as an arm of British immigration control, imposing fines of £1,000 (increased to £2,000 in 1991) for each passenger carried without the required documentation. By 1999 £75 million had been levied in such charges, although according to the Home Office only £62 million had been collected. The 1993 Asylum and Immigration Appeals Act extended the right of appeal to all asylum seekers but subjected what it called 'vexatious or frivolous cases', and the cases of people who had travelled through third countries, to 'fast-track procedures' with short time scales and no appeal to the Immigration Appeals Tribunal if appeal to an adjudicator failed (see p. 90). Ministers claimed that, by speeding up procedures in cases which were found to be without foundation, they would improve the situation for 'genuine refugees', who had 'nothing to fear' from the new measures. The act was followed by an unprecedented increase in rates of refusal, from 14 per cent in the six months before the act to 72 per cent after it, while the granting of Exceptional Leave to Remain (ELR; temporary status on compassionate grounds) fell from 76 per cent to 22 per cent of decisions. Thus, while the Home Office claimed that it treated all applications on their merits, 2,365 Sri Lankans were granted ELR in the six months before the act and only 55 in the six months after it, even though the situation in Sri Lanka had not improved. Michael Howard, the home secretary, was reported in the

Guardian of 14 March 1995 to be 'considering legislation to "crack down on illegal immigrants"', which, said the *Guardian*, would 'be seen as a victory for right-wing Conservative MPs who have been demanding even tougher controls'. The 1996 Asylum and Immigration Act extended the grounds on which an application could be 'fast-tracked'. It abolished the right of appeal when removal was to another EU country. It introduced a 'white list' of 'safe' countries, which included India, Pakistan and Romania, and also included Nigeria until protests forced its removal from the list. It removed the right to welfare benefits for those who applied for asylum after entry to Britain, or who were pursuing their legal right to appeal against a Home Office refusal of their claim, thus potentially either making them destitute or forcing them to abandon their appeal. It introduced employer sanctions, placing a legal duty on employers to check the status of their employees and making it a criminal offence to employ somebody who did not have permission to work in Britain.

The Labour Party, as usual in opposition, strongly opposed the harshness and illiberality of this legislation. Jack Straw, shadow home secretary, accused Michael Howard of 'playing the race card' before the 1997 general election, and the *Independent on Sunday* of 10 September 1995 quoted Straw as follows:

It is obscene that, of all people, Mr Howard, whose family directly benefited from liberal refugee laws, should allow asylum and immigration to be used in political stunts.

A document produced before the 1997 election by Jack Straw and Doug Henderson, shadow home affairs minister, entitled *Fairer, Faster and Firmer: Labour's Approach to Asylum and Immigration*, castigates the Tory government for the failings of their immigration policy and the 1996 Act and quotes Andrew Lansley, the outgoing head of the Tory Research Department as saying:

Immigration ... an issue we raised successfully in 1992 ... played particularly well in the tabloids and has more potential to hurt [the Labour Party].

'No other act in this Parliament has aroused such justified and widespread opposition as the Asylum and Immigration Act', said Straw and Henderson, and they quoted *The Economist* of 9 January 1996:

... by promoting anti-immigrant policies the government risks encouraging racism and undermining liberty. It deserves contempt, not votes, for proposing this nasty little bill.

They continued:

Labour fought the act every step of the way because it:

1 hits genuine asylum seekers as hard as fraudulent applicants,
2 threatens race relations,
3 places a dangerous and impractical burden on employers,

4   inhumanely denies refugees the means to live,
5   creates the unprincipled and impractical white list,
6   removes the right of appeal to third country decisions.

They then quoted a number of business sources arguing against making it a criminal offence to employ people without entitlement to work in Britain, and pointed out that 'Far from saving money, the withdrawal of benefits may actually lead to an increase in costs', that more people who applied for asylum after entry were granted asylum than those who applied immediately on entry, and that the policy was inhumane.

Once in government Labour proceeded to do the same, and worse. Its promises of clearing up the 'shambles' of Conservative immigration and asylum policy were, wrongly, taken by some to mean that it would institute procedures which would improve the situation of asylum seekers and ameliorate the harshness, arbitrariness and long delays of the system. In July 1998, a year after the Labour government took office and after much delay, it produced a white paper which confirmed fears that in reality the Labour government would be harsher in its treatment of asylum seekers than its predecessor was. The white paper, laughably entitled *Fairer, Faster and Firmer – A Modern Approach to Immigration and Asylum*, included provisions to deny welfare benefits to all asylum seekers rather than to some of them and substitute food vouchers and one 'no choice' offer of accommodation, and other measures to toughen procedures. There was a period of 'consultation', during which a large volume of reasoned objections were put forward by organisations which support refugees, including the Refugee Council, Joint Council for the Welfare of Immigrants (JCWI) and Amnesty International. The Refugee Council, in particular, believed that a public campaign would jeopardise their access to ministers behind closed doors. Their representations went almost completely unheeded. The white paper was turned into a bill which went to the House of Commons early in 1999. No Labour MP voted against the bill at its second reading on 22 February 1999, and only Tony Benn and Jeremy Corbyn abstained; all the Liberal Democrats and two Scottish Nationalists voted against it. Labour MPs were told they could only be on the committee to debate the bill if they voted for it; their criticisms in committee, and those of Liberal Democrats and some Tories from the left, achieved minimal concessions, including an increase in asylum seekers' weekly cash allowance to £10. The concessions were nevertheless said to have mollified the rebels. At the bill's third reading on 16 June 1999 it was passed by 310 votes to 41. The 41 included seven Labour MPs and one Plaid Cymru MP; all the others, and the two tellers, were Liberal Democrats. The major revolt, which some Labour MPs predicted would eclipse the resistance to cuts in welfare benefits, thus failed to materialise. On 20 October 1999 the House of Lords passed an amendment, voted for by 161 peers of whom 104 were Tories, to the effect that normal welfare benefits should be restored until the government had met its own six-month target for processing asylum claims. According to the *Sunday Times* of 31 October 1999, John Tincey, spokesperson for the Immigration Service Union, said the amendment meant that 'It is debatable whether we have any effective immigration controls left.' In addition, said the front-page article, a 'confidential internal Home Office briefing seen by The Sunday Times' claimed the Lords amendment would lead to a doubling of asylum seekers next year, adding a further 40,000 at a cost of £500 million: 'Jack Straw, the home secretary, hoped the bill would curb the rapid increases in asylum applications from migrants simply seeking a better life in Britain.' But, said the the *Sunday Times*, 'A Home Office source said the bill may have to be delayed until the next parliamentary session to overturn the amendment on vouchers', in which case '"You can forget any attempts to keep numbers down next year."' When the bill returned to the House of Commons on 9 November 1999, Ann Widdecombe and William Hague withdrew Tory support for the Lords amendment. On this occasion 60 MPs voted for the amendment, of whom 17 were Labour, three were Conservative, five were Scottish National Party, one was Plaid Cymru, one was Ulster Unionist, and the rest, plus the two tellers, were Liberal Democrats. The Immigration and Asylum Act became law on 6 December 1999.

The Labour Party's actions seemed to many people inexplicable. But the explanation is probably quite simple. Straw's and Blair's attitude towards asylum seekers has many precedents in the behaviour of previous Labour governments, and presumably parallels their attitude to criminals: Labour must demonstrate that it can be tougher towards them than the Tories were, and so remove one of the perceived electoral assets of the Tories. Yet the Labour government is unlikely to be successful in its attempts to outdo the Tories. In the summer of 1999 Ann Widdecombe, Conservative shadow home secretary, and William Hague, leader of the Conservative opposition, embarked on a campaign of attacking Labour – for being soft on asylum seekers. The *Guardian* of 1 September 1999, under the heading 'Hague takes up the battle over asylum seekers', reported that Hague had called a 'crisis summit' on immigration, accusing the government of 'dereliction of duty' for allowing so many people to seek refuge in Britain, and saying that he was 'particularly outraged' to discover that Westminster Council 'had more asylum seekers dependent on social services than "old ladies in nursing homes"'. Straw responded with a letter to Hague 'pointing out that in the past Westminster Council had supported the government's measures to deter abusive asylum seekers' and had said the government's asylum bill was '"a considerable move forward"'. Claiming that 'the Tory party nationally had failed to make any proposals to deal with illegal immigration', Straw, says the *Guardian*, wrote:

You can either support the views of our party colleagues in Westminster and back our moves to crack down on the problem of illegal immigration – or you can side with your frontbench colleague, Ann Widdecombe, and weaken control. It cannot be both.

Similarly, after a spate of tabloid headlines on 'aggressive' begging by a few asylum seekers, Barbara Roche, immigration minister, said their cases would be 'fast-tracked'. Ann Widdecombe said they should be imprisoned and then deported. When, in April 2000, the Conservatives embarked on the base tactic of putting in a by-election manifesto that Britain was 'a soft touch for the organized asylum racketeers who are flooding the country with bogus asylum seekers', and William Hague said that if the flood was not stopped there would be more National Front marches in the streets, Straw, finally, was moved to retort, according to the *Guardian* of 1 May 2000, that:

pandering to the National Front and other such groups is no way to oppose them. Mr Hague has fed the anxieties which can lead to extremism by grossly exaggerating the position on asylum.

He added, however, that Hague was also 'irresponsibly opposing our sensible measures like the new civil penalty on hauliers', which imposes heavy fines on lorry drivers providing one of the few remaining ways for refugees to escape to Britain. For 'sensible' read 'savage'.

The government's white paper did announce measures to clear part of the backlog of 70,000 unresolved asylum cases which were stuck in the chaos of Home Office failure to deal with them. Applications for asylum which dated from before 1995 and which had not received an initial decision from the Home Office were to be dealt with in two categories. Those who first applied before the 1993 Asylum and Immigration Appeals Act came into force in July 1993, about 10,000 people, were to be given indefinite leave to enter or remain, unless they had committed a serious criminal offence or had applied for asylum after a removal or deportation process had started. For a further 20,000 who applied between July 1993 and December 1995, there would be no automatic granting of Exceptional Leave to Remain (ELR), but compassionate or exceptional factors such as the presence of children at school or a record of local community work might weigh in their favour. But these people would be granted only ELR, and possibly lose their right to full refugee status. And the 20,000 who were waiting for appeals to be heard against a Home Office refusal, some of whom had waited for many years, and a further 20,000 who had applied for asylum after 1995 and were waiting for initial decisions by the Home Office, were unaffected by the measures.

The government resisted any use of the word 'amnesty' and was said to be extremely nervous about the effect of such a policy on public opinion and the tabloids. And indeed the *Mail on Sunday* of 15 March 1998 carried a front-page headline saying 'OPEN DOOR FOR BOGUS REFUGEES'; its leader made the following unsubstantiated assertions:

It didn't take long for the Government to throw in the towel.

Less than a year in office and they are allowing 55,000 bogus asylum seekers and illegal immigrants to stay in Britain in what amounts to an outrageous amnesty for lawbreakers.

Instead of ... whingeing that thousands of one-time asylum seekers have vanished without trace ... Home Secretary Jack Straw should be recruiting special task forces to track down the absconders ...

What's wrong with combating the fraudsters and racketeers responsible for the huge inflow of bogus refugees that is still pouring into this country? ...

Mr Straw has many admirers. After this decision he will have fewer.

The *Daily Mail* of 28 July 1998 carried on the theme, with a headline saying 'Straw Opens Door to 30,000 refugees', adding:

But Mr Straw rejected the attacks, pointing to a series of tough new measures to root out fraud and punish bogus asylum seekers and those who help them cheat the system. ... 'We are strengthening immigration controls and there will be no amnesty', he told MPs. ... Shadow Home Secretary Sir Norman Fowler said strict immigration controls were necessary for good race relations in Britain.

Headlines appeared in newspapers telling a different story, possibly at the behest of Labour's spin doctors; in June 1997 the *Daily Telegraph* announced on its front page 'Labour to send back 50,000 migrants', and the *Daily Mail* said 'Straw to kick out thousands of illegals'. Deportations under Labour are, as promised in the Labour Party's 1997 election material, increasing. Since the May 1997 general election the government has deported over 90,000 people; deportations and removals in 1999 were over 9 per cent more than in 1998.

A Guardian/ICM poll, whose results were published in the *Guardian* of 9 February 1999, was said to show that Jack Straw had 'popular backing for his proposal ... to strip asylum seekers of their remaining rights to claim benefits', and, says the article:

The survey also shows majority backing among the electorate, including Labour voters, for further tightening Britain's asylum and immigration laws. This is in spite of the fact that an overwhelming majority of those polled agree that immigration has enriched Britain by making it open to ideas and cultures. ...

The concept of asylum has taken a severe populist battering. Now 49 per cent agree that genuine victims of political persecution should be allowed to stay in Britain, an increase over other recent opinion polls but far below the popular acceptance in other European countries.

Far from attempting to counter such views and build on the 49 per cent support for 'genuine' refugees, the Labour government itself refers to asylum seekers as 'bogus'. Mike O'Brien, Home Office minister in charge of immigration from 1997 until the summer of 1999, was asked in an interview in the November 1998 issue of the Refugee Council's magazine *iNexile* whether the government intended to do anything about the 'misperception about why refugees have to come to the UK'. His response (in full) was as follows:

We decided we should stop using the word 'bogus', to take it out of the lexicon. We don't use it – I think that Jack [Straw] slipped up once – but we are trying not to use it. It had become merely a phrase. So now we are using a different one which is 'abusive asylum seekers', in trying to distinguish them from the genuine. At the moment the word 'asylum seeker' has been linked in the media to 'bogus' and all asylum seekers are not bogus. We recognise that.

Refugees are always genuine, asylum seekers may or may not be. They may be abusive or they may be genuine. Once they are accepted as a refugee they are genuine. But the words will change. A year from now, perhaps, the word 'abusive' will have become a pejorative term. But it is making sure that the issue is kept in focus and that the words don't distort the agenda.

Which didn't stop Mike O'Brien telling demonstrators outside Campsfield immigration detention centre that nearly all the detainees there (some of whom subsequently get refugee status) were bogus. When demonstrators suggested that the government was failing to uphold Labour's principles in its treatment of asylum seekers, O'Brien said 'We are *New* Labour.'

When a few hundred Romany refugees began to arrive in Dover the government, rather than putting the matter in perspective and expressing sympathy with the Romas' plight under the post-communist regimes they were fleeing from, promised to deal with them firmly and to send them back. As Gill Casebourne, of the Kent Refugee Action Network, wrote to the *Guardian* of 21 August 1999,

The local population has been repeatedly assured over three years in all official national and local pronouncements that asylum-seekers are nearly all 'bogus' and will a) be prevented from arriving or b) promptly despatched elsewhere. ...

Despite repeated appeals, no official effort has ever been made to present the facts to the public about real numbers and support levels, to deny racist and inflammatory rumours or to denounce prominently verifiable violent attacks on asylum-seekers including children ...

What is clear is that the igniting of the tinderbox was absolutely inevitable given the failure of the authorities to recognise what effect their persistent negative publicity would be bound to have on baffled and suspicious local people. J'accuse.

A *Guardian* column of 26 June 1999 reported correspondence with Mike O'Brien, who responded to the *Guardian*'s accusation that 'Not one minister has publicly condemned the outpouring of racist filth against Gypsies and Kosovans in local and national newspapers in the last two years' by saying that he 'did precisely that in the House of Commons last Tuesday'. The *Guardian* continued:

I checked. And this is what he said: 'Setting aside the knee-jerk reaction of the appallingly racist Dover Express and the bilious mendacity of the odd leftist journalist, the debate on the bill has been constructive in the national press' ...

Admittedly, the Dover Express was so bad that the editor was interviewed by the police, but it is not alone in spreading prejudice against refugees, and it is not a national newspaper. The Sun ('Kick the gypsies out') and the Mail ('Kosovo on sea') are, regrettably, distributed throughout the country. But I'm sure New Labour finds their support constructive.

In August 1999 Jack Straw, on whom the connections were surely not lost, launched an attack on 'travellers', accusing them of defecating in doorways and suchlike, while saying they were different from 'normal itinerants' (as his spokesperson put it in his defence). Malcolm Imrie, in a letter to the *Guardian* of 21 August 1999, drew parallels. Quoting from an autobiographical book by Otto Rosenberg, *A Gypsy in Auschwitz*, he wrote:

In 1936, Dr Robert Ritter, director of the 'Racial-hygienic and Genetic Research Office' claimed that many so-called Gypsies were 'half-breeds' and should be distinguished from 'racially pure Gypsies'. It was not clear who belonged to the latter category, but the former, having 'inferior genes', were 'highly unstable, unprincipled, unpredictable ... lethargic or restless and irritable ... work-shy and asocial'. Surprisingly, perhaps, he didn't actually claim that they defecated in doorways. The distinction between real and fake Gypsies made little difference in the concentration camps where many thousands of them were murdered indiscriminately.

A letter on the same date from Mita Castle-Kanerova, who works with Roma refugee organisations, suggests Straw's purpose may have been 'to sway popular support for tougher immigration law', in spite of the Romas' 'centuries-long fight against discrimination, marginalisation and outright ostracism'.

The Asylum and Immigration Act included a provision to give powers to marriage registrars to check on 'bogus marriages', to make sure they were not contracted as a means of evading immigration controls. This enabled the *Express* to print, under a front-page headline 'WAR ON SHAM MARRIAGES: Bid to end migrant scandal of 10,000 bogus ceremonies', the following:

Sweeping powers to stop bogus marriages that flout immigration laws are on the way. The crackdown is aimed at halting an estimated 10,000 sham ceremonies every year. ... A team of immigration officers set up to tackle the problem believes that eight out of 10 marriages in London involving foreign nationals are bogus. But Home Secretary Jack Straw's move could hit problems because some registrars resent the idea of being made to police the immigration laws, and some councils fear they could end up being sued by genuine couples forced to scrap reception and honeymoon plans ...

The white paper paid a brief tribute to the contribution which refugees and migrants have made to British society. But it dwelt at length on the 'abuses' which 'false claimants' are supposed to perpetrate. The words 'abuse', 'abusive' or 'abusing' occur on practically every page of the document. 'Racketeers' and 'racketeering', 'fraud' and 'fraudulent' are other favoured words, and 'bogus' is to be found here and there, in phrases such as 'bogus marriages'. There is talk of 'stemming the tide'. Paragraph 11.3 reads as follows:

The Government is determined to stamp out the blatant and often cynical abuse that clogs up the system with hopeless and unnecessary appeals. The existing criminal offences directed at those who seek or obtain leave to enter or remain by deception will be extended and strengthened. Failed asylum seekers whose claims have involved blatant deceit will be liable to prosecution in appropriate cases. The criminal law has a role to play in stamping out abuse of immigration control.

Under the heading 'Multi-agency cooperation', paragraph 11.6 regurgitated the sort of smears to which immigrants are commonly subjected:

Immigration-related crime crosses many barriers – benefit and housing fraud, unlawful employment, illegal activities linked to prostitution, rackets involving asylum claims and marriages, student loan fraud, passport and document abuse. Immigration crime generates huge sums for criminal activities and facilitates other criminal activities, such as drug trafficking and money laundering. It exploits the vulnerable: those who enter clandestinely are unable to defend themselves against further exploitation, and many become victims of extortion. To combat this crime more effectively, the government is developing a more proactive approach to intelligence and inter-agency cooperation.

The four case studies in the white paper were all illustrations, not of the hardship and injustice endured by refugees, but of supposed 'abuse' of the system.

It is of course true that the criminalisation of refugees, making it impossible for them to travel legally to Britain, exposes them to exploitation and suffering. The white paper, and the act, however, were intended to intensify their suffering through a number of proposals to make it harder for refugees to escape. Under the heading 'Pre-entry Controls', the white paper claimed in paragraphs 5.1 and 5.2 that:

As the desire to come to the UK for economic betterment has increased, attempts to circumvent our control, both by individual and by criminal organisations, have grown correspondingly. The large numbers of fraudulent claims and the use of forged and stolen documents are the visible evidence of an increasing awareness of how any loophole or potential loophole in immigration control may be exploited. ...

We rely heavily on an effective pre-entry control, with the use of visa and transit visa requirements ... The entry clearance arrangements must also reflect the wider interests of the UK. We need to ensure that visitors, businessmen, students and others whose activities benefit the UK feel encouraged to come here. The Government is committed to ensuring that all those who have a genuine reason to come to the UK are allowed to do so ...

The white paper referred elsewhere to 'genuine travellers'; this term apparently does not include refugees and asylum seekers. The government is planning a 'bond scheme' for visitors, requiring visitors or their relatives to put up money which would be lost if the visitor failed to leave Britain; it announced early in 2000 that the scheme would be piloted by requiring visitors from the Indian subcontinent to put up bonds of £10,000, reduced after protests to £5,000. The Carriers' Liability Act is to be strengthened, by extending it to cover all road passenger vehicles, shipping, air transport and international railways, and by imposing fines on lorry drivers carrying 'clandestine' migrants and impounding their vehicles to cover the fines. In addition carriers are to be given more training in the detection of forged documents before embarkation. And, say paragraphs 5.15 and 5.16 of the white paper, these measures to 'stem migratory pressures' have become inadequate:

their effectiveness has been undermined in recent years by racketeers and organised crime exploiting and facilitating economic migration by people who are not entitled to enter the UK. More sophisticated forgeries, an increasing trend for people to impersonate others, and increasing numbers of passengers destroying their documents just before their arrival in the UK, are all combining to counter the responsible attitude and diligent efforts by most carriers to prevent the carriage of inadequately documented passengers.

The Government intends to take a tougher approach to deterring and preventing the arrival of inadmissible passengers.

The act therefore makes it a criminal offence for asylum seekers to try to enter or remain Britain using 'deception' and for their representatives to 'knowingly' make false statements on their behalf, although it does also create, in its section 31, an 'Article 31 defence' (see p. 175). In order to catch more of the people who do not have their own documents, the government is to recruit more airlport liaison officers (ALOs). ALOs operate abroad and, according to the white paper, have cooperated successfully with 'authorities, carriers and the Immigration Services of other countries' in stopping 'large groups of inadequately documented passengers from reaching Western Europe and North America'; '120 were returned to their point of departure by the Cambodian authorities, 50 by the authorities in Lesotho'; 'As a result of their work, around 1,800 inadequately documented passengers will have been denied boarding to the UK over the past year', and presumably left to the mercy of the authorities they are fleeing from.

Within Britain, the government apparently intends to move further towards a continental system of internal identity checks. They will affect those who are considered suspicious and look foreign, in other words mainly blacks. The checks on immigration status at work are to remain, in spite of Labour's manifesto commitment to repeal clause 8 of the 1996 act. The 'primary purpose rule' has in theory been abolished, another manifesto commitment, but there are checks for 'bogus marriages' by registrars. Immigration officers are to have increased powers of arrest and forcible restraint. This apparently is to relieve police officers of the damage to community relations incurred from breaking into people's houses and violently removing them from their families and friends. According to Diane Abbott, the local MP, a Hackney police superintendent had said he was unwilling to continue to carry out 'fishing raids' for illegal immigrants. Entrusting such tasks to immigration officials, many of whom appear to relish their job but who have no training and were, before an amendment to the Act, not to be subject to the external checks under which police operate, is likely to result in more injuries and perhaps deaths.

Discussion in the 1998 white paper of further measures to 'stem the tide' come under the heading of 'deterring abusive claimants'. The government is now saying openly that the purpose of its new measures, including the denial of benefits, is to act as a deterrent. Both the white paper and a Home Office manual published in February 1999 made this clear, the latter for example stating that one aim of the new arrangements was 'to minimise the incentive to economic migration, particularly by minimising cash payments to asylum seekers'. In this as in much else it followed in the footsteps of previous Tory governments, to which the white paper refers in paragraph 1.9:

Following the introduction of measures in November 1991 to deter multiple and other fraudulent applications, numbers fell back in 1992 and 1993. However, applications increased substantially in 1994 and again in 1995 (to 44,000), but, after falling back in 1996 (following the reduction in benefit entitlement for asylum seekers), continued rising in 1997 and 1998.

But asylum seekers are unlikely to be acting on precise information on the state of benefit entitlements. The denial of benefits to those who apply after entry produced no change in the proportion of people applying at ports rather than 'in-country', which remained at 51 per cent for the former and 49 per cent for the latter.

The white paper said that 'The real issue is how to run an asylum system which serves the British people's wish to support genuine refugees whilst deterring abusive claimants.' It thus simply took for granted that it is all right to impose hardship on the much vilified 'abusers', whose 'crime', even supposing they really are not refugees, is merely to have travelled abroad in a sometimes desperate attempt to improve their lives and perhaps to support their families. It also admitted implicitly that some of its measures will add to the suffering of 'genuine refugees', however these are defined (while also claiming that its tightening up of procedures will benefit the latter, and impose hardship only on the 'abusers'). It is clear that the government's attempts to stop people with false documents at source will hit randomly, and will in fact hit political refugees hardest, since they have most to lose from being delivered into the hands of the authorities they are fleeing from. The deterrent measures proposed within Britain, primarily detention and destitution (see the following two sections, this chapter), also punish the 'genuine' together with those the British government wishes to get rid of. Many detained asylum seekers subsequently get refugee status. Destitution will hit all asylum seekers without distinction.

The government says that delays are at the heart of the problems in the system, and at times has used the argument that, if the process is speeded up, any suffering caused by these provisions will be short-lived and easily bearable by 'genuine refugees'. The white paper, in paragraph 8.7, said:

The key to restoring effectiveness to our asylum system and to tackling abuse is swifter determination of applications and appeals. The Government has inherited backlogs of over 50,000 cases awaiting decision and over 20,000 queuing for an appeal hearing. Some undecided cases date back to 1990 and appeals can take 15 months to list in London. Delays of this order send a clear message to abusive applicants that the system cannot cope and is ripe for exploitation; while those in genuine need of protection are condemned to a cruel limbo of worry and uncertainty over their future.

This is one of the few recognitions that delays, or any other aspect of the system, cause suffering to refugees. Mostly, however, delays are blamed on 'abuses' by people who, not surprisingly, do whatever they can to avoid being deported. Paragraph 8.9, summing up the reasons for aiming at faster decisions, concludes:

At present economic migrants abuse the system because its inefficiency allows them to remain in the UK for years. A faster system with more certain removal at the end of the process will significantly deter abuse.

So the white paper announced plans to computerise immigration records to 'provide a basis for improvements in identifying fraud and abuse of the immigration and nationality processes'. It proposed to control 'unscrupulous immigration advisers' who are alleged to spin out the process unnecessarily. Although the act ends the scandal of the non-availability of legal aid for representation at appeals, the white paper complained that £26 million is spent on legal aid for immigration cases and proposed to bring its use 'under tighter control' so that 'public funds are not misused in support of deliberate abuse of asylum procedures and immigration controls'.

The reality is that it is refugees who suffer from the activities of unscrupulous lawyers, and are exploited by them, but the white paper did not say so. It is true that some, scrupulous rather than unscrupulous, immigration lawyers work long hours with great dedication and skill and do, as the Home Office accuses them of doing, explore all avenues to save their clients from deportation and removal. But they are probably greatly outnumbered by lawyers who, far from doing too much work, often do little work at all. They may not turn up for appeals, which are then quickly dismissed. They may also be either incompetent or fraudulent or both; some, for example, demand fees from asylum seekers even though they are receiving legal aid. Diane Taylor in the *Big Issue* of 22–28 February 1999 gives an account of the 'blatant corruption' experienced by asylum seekers queuing at the Immigration and Nationality Directorate at Lunar House in Croydon:

'interpreters' employed by unscrupulous firms of solicitors openly tout for business in full view of immigration officials and right next to a notice saying: 'Representatives are prevented from soliciting for business'. ...

Although the Home Office has promised to be 'firmer when dealing with abuse' such as this, there was no evidence of officials mingling with the queuers, and not even a glimmer of interest from the desk-bound officials. ...

Interpreters are paid around £300 a week to recruit as many as 100 other new asylum seekers for firms of solicitors. .... once they're signed up they get little or no such help and are left to flounder in the choppy waters of the system.

If the government does actually protect asylum seekers from the activities of such lawyers this would be welcome. But the fact that the reasons the government gives for controlling 'unscrupulous advisers' are solely that they allegedly waste public funds and string out abusive claims does not inspire confidence.

The 1999 act abolished the so-called white list. But it leaves open the possibility that those whose claims are considered unfounded, and who are likely in practice to come from former 'white list' countries, will be subjected to 'fast-track procedures'. In a move that has not received much attention, it potentially greatly reduces the right of appeal by 'consolidating multiple appeal rights into a single appeal right and strengthening the role of the Immigration Appeal Tribunal': 'The intention is that in most cases the appeal before the adjudicator should produce finality and that the entire process should be completed within six months.' It abolishes the separate right of appeal against deportation. Specific deadlines are to be imposed on asylum seekers, not the Home Office. The period for presenting further material after an initial interview is to be shortened from 28 days to five days. 'While large backlogs remain', says the White Paper, 'abusive applicants will continue to believe that they can exploit the system.'

But the backlogs do remain, and they are growing. By January 2000 the backlog had risen, not fallen, from 70,000 to 103,000. The government's attempts to speed up initially failed, mired in the incompetence of the Home Office which attempted to introduce a new computer system, which failed, at the same time as it was moving its Croydon offices. Only 425 decisions on asylum claims were made in January 1999, compared to nearly 4,000 per month in 1998. (However, in 2000 the government claimed to be exceeding the latter figure.) The £77 million computerisation scheme contracted with Siemens Business Services was investigated by the National Audit Office; by March 1999 it was 14 months behind schedule, and the plans to sack 500 immigration officials had to be abandoned. Siemens also had the contract to computerise the Passport Agency; its failure there caused a flurry of publicity when people missed their holidays. But the problems for refugees are much greater. In January 2000 a report by the House of Commons Public Accounts Committee recognised that delay 'has caused enormous personal distress to hundreds of thousands of applicants and their families'. Lunar House in Croydon had more than 200,000 paper files occupying 14 miles of shelves. Some 150,000 of these files are now partly or totally inaccessible, some of them in underground storage filled with fumes from a car park above. Telephone lines are constantly jammed. Letters are not opened, let alone answered or attached to the relevant file. The Home Office admitted it was holding 22,000 passports of foreign nationals, many of them belonging to businessmen and other supposedly desirable visitors requiring visa extensions, as well as those of refugees. Many refugees wait in detention centres and prisons. Others queue for hours on end outside Lunar House, in a concrete and sunless 'wind tunnel'; once inside, they discover incompetence so extreme that even officials admit the system has collapsed. Lawyers can no longer ring up and speak to case-workers. When files cannot be found no progress can be made with asylum cases. Some accuse immigration officials of deliberately obstructing contact and failing to answer telephones and letters; others accuse them of doing so discriminately to delay granting refugee status to nationals of countries where the situation might improve and so enable them to be sent back. Most agree that the situation is the result of a combination of incompetence, ignorance and malice.

Much the same can be said of the process of determining asylum cases. 'Three small children', says an article in *The Economist* of 14 February 1998, 'were recently on the point of being sent back to Nigeria without their parents. Their deportation was stopped only when a minister asked officials what would happen to the children on arrival at Lagos. He was told: "I suppose social services will look after them."' Who does or does not get refugee status is arbitrary, a lottery, like drawing straws. One African student escaped to Britain when others he associated with were arrested and killed; he had no evidence whatsoever to support his case, but the adjudicator believed him and he now has refugee status. Another from the same country had been imprisoned in a secret gaol and escaped only through family connections with the military elite; his appeal against Home Office refusal has never been heard. Four Nigerians have similar accounts of imprisonment and torture; two have refugee status, one has ELR, and the fourth lives in continuing fear of deportation.

The current system for determining asylum claims is based on the Conservatives' 1993 Asylum and Immigration Appeals Act. It is little changed by Labour's act, apart from the introduction of a 'consolidated', and more restrictive, appeals system, shorter deadlines for asylum seekers, and, on the other hand, the introduction of legal aid for appeal and bail hearings. All applications for asylum are considered and determined by officials in the Asylum Division of the Home Office's Immigration and Nationality Directorate (IND). The union to which most of them belong, the Immigration Service Union (ISU), broke away from the Society of Civil and Public Servants in 1982 because of the latter's support for anti-racist causes; since then the ISU has campaigned for measures to reduce the rights of immigrants and asylum seekers and strengthen controls; as the Greater Manchester Immigration Aid Unit comments in 'The Immigration Service Union: a scab union', immigration officials 'do not merely implement the rules. Through the ISU they help to create the rules.' Asylum applicants who are already legally in Britain are given questionnaires for self-completion within four weeks and are then interviewed by an Asylum Division official. Others apply for asylum at a port or airport before going through immigration control. Over half of all asylum seekers are categorised as 'illegal immigrants' because, often through uncertainty over the best way to proceed, they enter or try to enter on false documents or without documents and only ask for asylum *after* going through immigration; or because they apply for asylum only after they have 'overstayed' their students' or visitors' visas. Those who apply for asylum on entry are usually interviewed by an immigration officer based at the port of entry (a term that includes airports), who will have received minimal training in asylum matters, and who carries out an initial examination, usually without the presence of a lawyer but with interpreters who may or may not be accurate, and passes a transcript of this interview to the Asylum Division for determination. The immigration officials at the ports and airports also have the right to decide, on their own authority, whether asylum applicants should be detained or, alternatively, granted 'temporary admission'; in the latter case they may be required to sign on at police stations at regular intervals. If the Home Office's Asylum Division turns down an application, or decides that the applicant has travelled through a 'safe' country to which he or she should be returned without the application being considered, the asylum seeker has a right to appeal to the Immigration Appeals Authority (IAA). Appeals are heard by a single adjudicator, appointed by the Home Office, who is not always legally trained and may be, for example, a retired colonial officer. Adjudicators accept on average about 10 per cent of the appeals. Legal aid is available for the preparation of appeals but, before January 2000, was not available for representation at appeal hearings. If the appeal is turned down, asylum seekers can ask for leave to appeal, on a point of law only, to a three-member Immigration Appeals Tribunal (IAT), appointed by the Lord Chancellor's office. In 1994 the IAT overturned just over 11 per cent of the adjudicators' decisions. Under Labour's Act, vouchers and accommodation will no longer be provided during this second appeal stage. Sometimes, if the right to appeal is refused, asylum seekers can apply for judicial review in the High Court. There are time limits on putting in appeals at each stage, but the Home Office may delay for months or years before responding to an application or setting an appeal hearing date.

Good legal representation cannot prevent the majority of applications, many of them fully justified, being turned down. But asylum seekers who find themselves with incompetent and perhaps dishonest solicitors, who do no work for the legal aid payments they get and then leave them alone at their appeal hearings, almost invariably lose their appeals. If asylum seekers are themselves extremely articulate and skilled they may possibly succeed in defeating the Home Office and winning their appeal. This was the case for an Ivoirien activist and socialist who, having rapidly learnt English, single-handedly convinced an adjudicator that he was the one in a hundred political fugitives from repression in the Ivory Coast (Côte d'Ivoire) who should have refugee status. Whether or not an asylum seeker has a good lawyer is itself a lottery. Some have the luck to be befriended by determined supporters or visitors to detention centres who succeed in getting better legal representation for them. Their lawyer may then, for example, take the trouble of going to the Medical Foundation for the Care of Victims of Torture and obtaining evidence that they have been tortured, and sometimes appear in court for them unpaid. This happened to a Nigerian Ogoni, who had been imprisoned and tortured three times in Nigeria but had lost his appeal in the absence of legal representation and been removed as far as Belgium; at Brussels airport he contacted a UN representative and was returned to Britain; his visitor persuaded a good lawyer to represent him without payment, and he won refugee status. The Refugee Legal Centre, inadequately funded by the Home Office, and Asylum Aid, a charity funded by donations, provide free representation at appeals for limited numbers of people. Partly because they can choose the cases they take on, both exceeded the average 10 per cent success rate at appeals: the Refugee Legal Centre wins around 25 per cent of appeals; Asylum Aid won 100 per cent of its appeals in 1998/99 and around 88 per cent of them in 1997/98. A further element of uncertainty is of course the severity or otherwise of the adjudicators themselves; this is common to all judicial proceedings, but aggravated by the low level of training and skills of many of the adjudicators.

Immigration officials appear to see their role, both in their initial decisions and in their adversarial role at appeal hearings, as one of undermining the cases and credibility of asylum seekers and catching them out in 'inconsistencies'. Their attempts to undermine credibility are sometimes ludicrous. When the Ogoni refugee's lawyer produced evidence of torture at his appeal, the Home Office representative asked whether he had worked with agricultural machinery, and when he said he had, attempted to argue that his wounds could have been received in that way; even the adjudicator clearly found this ridiculous. In 1995 Asylum Aid published a document entitled *Adding Insult to Injury: Experiences of Zairean Refugees in the UK*, which states that:

Many of the reasons given by the Home Office for refusing asylum to Zaireans defy belief. For instance, it is regularly suggested by the Home Office that signs of torture displayed by Zaireans could have been caused accidentally. This implies, strangely, that dozens of Zaireans are opportunistically using accident scars as an excuse to claim asylum. The Home Office appears to think that it is a coincidence that so many people's scars resemble those left by handcuffs, whips or electrodes. Zaireans who have escaped from imprisonment are told they are lying about it because they could not possibly have escaped by bribery (in one of the notoriously most corrupt countries in the world!). In other cases they are informed that their escape, however fortuitous, means they cannot any longer be of interest to the authorities. One Zairean was told his claim to have been involved in student politics was not accepted because he had not explained how he found time for his political activities at the same time as his studies and in any case he had apparently failed to mention how he paid for his studies.

A refugee said at his initial examination that on one occasion he wore a T-shirt; at his appeal hearing he described it differently; this was held to undermine his credibility. Another refugee initially said that the cell he had been locked up in had no window; at his appeal he said that it had only a grid above the door; he was said to have lied. Asylum Aid carries a regular feature in its *Newsletter* on the 'unfair, unsubstantiated and sometimes plain bizarre reasons given by the Home Office for refusing asylum claims'. It has also produced two further documents, *'No Reason At All': Home Office Decisions on Asylum Claims*, published in 1995, and *Still No Reason At All: Home Office Decisions on Asylum Claims*, published in 1999. They contain a mass of evidence on the failings of Home Office decision-making. *'No Reason At All'* gives this example, among many others:

B.Z. ... escaped from prison and took a canoe across the River Zaire to Brazzaville, in Congo. The Home Office replied:

'The Secretary of State ... considered your account of crossing the River Zaire at night to be totally implausible. The Secretary of State is aware of the size, strength and considerable dangers posed by the river such as shifting sandbanks and crocodiles.'

Challenged to provide evidence of the extent of the crocodile population in this part of the River Zaire, the Home Office was unable to do so. It withdrew the statement, but instead produced a completely different set of reasons for refusing B.Z.'s asylum claim. In reality, canoes are a frequent means of transport across the River Zaire, as the Home Office could easily have established.

Zaireans refused refugee status, at a time when Amnesty International was reporting the 'worst human rights crisis', were over 90 per cent of applicants. *Adding Insult to Injury* quotes the following statements in refusal letters, the third and fourth of which contradict the first two:

We do not automatically assume that members of legal opposition parties are free from persecution in Zaire.

There is no general assumption that simply because political parties have been legalised human rights abuses and persecution cannot occur.

The UDPS has been a legitimate political party since 1990. ... The Secretary of State is of the view that UDPS members now have no reason to fear return to Zaire.

The Secretary of State is aware that a new government was formed in Zaire in July 1994 and that the main opposition parties hold various Vice Presidencies, Ministries and Vice-Ministries. He was of the view therefore that there was no reason why you should fear harassment or persecution because of your membership of [an opposition party] were you now to return.

'No Reason At All' gives examples of misapplication of the UN Convention and the UNHCR *Handbook*. A Kenyan was told that, although he had been arrested and beaten up for his membership of the Islamic Party of Kenya, that did not entitle him to refugee status because the party was illegal:

The Secretary of State is therefore of the opinion that anyone taking part in such activities would automatically put themselves at risk of arrest or prosecution by the police.

But the convention was intended to provide protection for people persecuted for their political beliefs. An Indian who said he had been tortured by Indian security forces was told:

the Indian government does not condone such actions. As the authorities have given assurances that all accusations of wrong doing would be investigated and action taken against those responsible, the Secretary of State does not regard such persons as agents of persecution.

But, says Asylum Aid, quite apart from the value or otherwise of assurances from the Indian government (which, as Amnesty International has reported, has notably failed to prosecute its agents who have engaged in torture and other abuses against Sikhs in Punjab), a torturer is *ipso facto* an 'agent of persecution', as per paragraph 65 of the UNHCR *Handbook*. A Burmese refugee, who had said that he took part in pro-democracy demonstrations at the Burmese embassy in London, was first accused of not having said so earlier when he in fact had, and then accused of having demonstrated simply in order to enhance his claim for asylum.

Four years later, as reported in *Still No Reason At All*, a refugee was told in his refusal letter:

You state that the men drove you to a place one and a half hours away and told you to run before they opened fire on you. The Secretary of State ... considers that if the men had intended to kill you they would have done so straight away rather than give you a chance to escape.

A Nigerian asylum seeker was told that, because he got the date of Ken Saro-Wiwa's sentencing wrong by one day, the secretary of state 'is of the opinion that these discrepancies must cast doubt on the credibility of your claim to be a MOSOP leader'. A Chinese refugee was told that 'the Chinese authorities are taking positive steps towards eradicating [human rights abuses]'. And so it goes on. *Still No Reason At All* comments:

The stories of asylum-seekers – the stories Asylum Aid hears daily – bear no relation to the self-serving mendacity they are accused of in Home Office refusal letters. The insult is all the greater when the recipients see that the reasons for refusal scarcely address the substance of their claim, and often draw on some irrelevant detail to refute the entire case. Their disillusionment is complete when they realise that the reasons they receive are standard cut-and-paste paragraphs and not an assessment of the merits of their individual claim.

Problems also arise frequently from poor reporting and interpretation. Initial interviews usually take place without legal representation and are conducted by an immigration official with minimal skills and knowledge of the situation in the countries the refugees have fled from; interpreters frequently make mistakes, and refugees later find it hard to convince officials that the mistakes were the interpreter's rather than their own. Interpreters sometimes make the elementary mistake of translating 'we' as 'they', thus giving the impression that the refugee was an observer rather than a participant in political actions. In 1994 a refugee with a virtually incontrovertible case travelled 70 miles to an appeal hearing in Birmingham, with several supporters including two people in their eighties; the interpreter was so unable to understand him that the hearing had to be cancelled; when his supporters complained of the waste of time and money, they were told that his 'patois' was difficult to understand; the refugee in question spoke standard French, easily understandable by those who had accompanied him to court.

Initial interviews usually take place soon after refugees arrive, at a port or airport. They may be traumatised and exhausted, and leave out some important information, but be accused of lying when attempting to remedy the omission later. This is a problem which particularly affects women who have been raped by soldiers or police but may be initially unable to explain it clearly to a strange and unsympathetic male official, or may be mistranslated. A leaflet produced by Black Women's Rape Action Project (BWRAP) and Women Against Rape (WAR) reports that:

A student activist in Côte d'Ivoire, Ms T, was raped by soldiers when the military raided her university campus. ... She applied for asylum but her claim was rejected. ... Legal representatives submitted inaccurate and badly translated statements on Ms T's behalf, e.g. Ms T saying she was raped was translated as 'the soldiers misbehaved'. ... BWRAP's report was submitted to a special adjudicator who accepted that Ms T had been raped because of her political activities. ... Ms T was awarded refugee status.

Women persecuted as women, principally through rape, have had difficulties in having their claims accepted, although some recent court victories have begun to change the situation. Another leaflet produced by BWRAP and WAR based at Crossroads Women's Centre gives the following example:

Ms P from Lithuania was raped by pimps attempting to force her into prostitution. After she reported the attack to the police, the rapists came to her home with a copy of her statement, saying it was pointless for her to expect help from the police. ... Ms P fled to Britain. The Home Office rejected her claim, ignoring evidence of police collusion with the rapists ... At her appeal, leading QC Ian Macdonald argued that young women in Lithuania constitute a 'social group', vulnerable to rape and other violence to force them into the sex industry. This was not simply criminal activity but persecution and torture involving police collaboration. Ms P was granted full refugee status.

Some recent decisions by the regular courts have overturned Home Office decisions. For example in 1999 three Court of Appeal judges, under the master of the rolls, Lord Woolf, ruled that the secretary of state had acted illegally in proposing to return three asylum seekers from Somalia, Algeria and Sri Lanka to France and Germany on 'safe third country' grounds, since France and Germany do not regard persecution by non-state agents as qualifying for refugee status and the three asylum seekers were therefore not safe. Also in 1999 the House of Lords found that two women, named Shah and Islam, who feared being stoned to death for adultery in Pakistan, under state-approved policy, should be treated as members of a 'social group' subject to persecution under the terms of the 1951 UN convention. Since these cases the Home Secretary Jack Straw has said he wants to 'curb' judges who take 'an over-liberal approach' to asylum seekers, and to use the 1999

European summit at Tampere in Finland to establish common criteria for the determination of asylum claims, aiming for a European directive which would overrule any decision by British judges. The *Guardian* reported on 12 October 1999:

'For good or ill, our courts interpret our obligations under the 1951 convention to a much more liberal degree than almost any other European country,' claims Mr Straw.

'One example is the case in which it has been held that women who are in fear of domestic violence in Pakistan may come under the terms of the convention. Now, I am concerned about women in fear of domestic violence in Pakistan, but there is no way it can be realistically argued that was in contemplation when the convention was put in place.'

But the violence with which Shah and Islam were threatened was not 'domestic' violence. Hugo Young wrote an article in the *Guardian* of 26 June 1999 pointing out that Straw is not a liberal. Straw claimed to be in tune with working-class voters from Blackburn, and told Hugo Young that 'liberal' was 'not an adjective I use a great deal about myself. I don't think I ever have done, actually ... that's not been part of my lexicon.' But, Young said, one way in which he did not resemble his Tory predecessor Michael Howard was that he believed in the independence of the judges: 'As a matter of principle, he says, he would never dream of telling judges what sentences to pass.'

Asylum Aid, the JCWI, the Refugee Council, lawyers and others have established a mass of evidence and critical comments on the absurdities and cruelties of the system of determining asylum claims in Britain, and the waste of time and money involved in not making proper decisions with good legal representation at an early stage in the process. Labour, and Straw in particular, have chosen to ignore all this. The problem is that there is little point in demanding improvements in legal processes when the real purpose of Home Office officials is to find whatever pretext they can, however nonsensical and inhumane, to refuse asylum.

THE CRIMINALISATION OF REFUGEES

Refugees are being criminalised by deliberate government policy. The words 'asylum seeker' and 'illegal immigrant' are constantly bracketed together. Technically, about half of all asylum seekers are 'illegal' (see below). Worse, the government forces refugees into reliance on criminal networks through visa restrictions, carriers' liability, airport liaison officers and the 'safe third country' rules. Government publications and official meetings throughout Europe lump together as 'problems' immigration and international crime, the trafficking of people and the trafficking of drugs. The association of 'immigrant' and 'refugee' with 'drug smugglers' and 'terrorists' was made as long ago as the mid-1980s in Europe by the Trevi Group and the Ad Hoc

Group on Immigration. The link was continued recently at the European summit in October 1999 at Tampere in Finland, which discussed common policing plans to deal with asylum, illegal immigration and cross-European crime.

The criminalisation of refugees and migrants has the effect, deliberately or otherwise, of creating a group of people who are subject to extreme forms of exploitation as 'illegal' workers. It also feeds racist prejudice. The government uses language about refugees which differs little from that of the gutter press. Its attacks on abusive, fraudulent, bogus asylum seekers have given the media a field day. It is then a small step, encouraged at times by the selective release of crime statistics and the results of government investigations into international crime rings, to accuse asylum seekers of cheating on social security, scavenging tube tickets and other rackets. No wonder a local freesheet such as the *Oxford Journal* carries a banner headline saying 'ILLEGAL ALIENS ON THE INCREASE' and proceeds to allege that:

Oxfordshire is being plagued by an influx of illegal immigrants who are making their way into the country by hitch-hiking on lorries. ... The pair, who claimed to be brother and sister, were fleeing the Serbian trouble-zone of Kosovo and are believed to have sneaked on to the lorry in France or Belgium.

The reality is different. Recently Asylum Welcome, a charity in Oxford, was looking for emergency accommodation for an Iraqi Kurd. He was a nurse and an activist for women's rights and socialism who had been threatened by the Kurdish Democracy Party, who he says are supported and armed by the US and Turkish governments. He had had to flee across Europe, partly on foot and partly in lorries, with the hope of finding refuge in Sweden where he had contacts. He was put onto a lorry by the 'mafia' and spent 24 hours without food or water, and in extreme cold, in the casing of the spare tyre under the lorry. In the middle of the night the lorry stopped and the driver said 'Out', the only word he spoke to him. He was left on a motorway, and realised he must be in Britain rather than in Sweden 'because the cars were driving on the left'. He went towards lights in a service station and asked to be directed to the nearest police station. The police came for him and he was given food and spent the rest of the night in relative comfort in a police cell. In the morning the police told him to go to the Immigration and Nationality Directorate in Croydon. But he had no money to get there, so eventually he was directed to Asylum Welcome, who made an appointment for him to see someone from Oxfordshire's social services department and found him a lawyer to help him claim asylum. He will not receive benefits, because he is categorised as an 'in-country claimant' and an 'illegal immigrant', and he is not allowed to work for six months. Such people risk being treated as though they were criminals. Governments spend large amounts of money in the attempt to catch them. As the barrister Frances Webber related in a 1995 speech later published under the title *Crimes of Arrival*, sniffer dogs discovered

51 illegal immigrants in the back of a lorry in July 1995; they had come from India, Pakistan, China and Turkey, and:

As well as the sniffer dogs, the Home Office has teams of immigration officers equipped with night vision equipment trawling the lay-bys and petrol stations near Dover and other ports seeking evidence of people being transferred from containers to cars.

Germany uses helicopters, patrol boats and three kinds of heat-seeking equipment to detect illegal immigrants along its border with Poland, operated by military personnel in police uniforms. ...

Vast amounts of money and time are devoted to improving the technology of control. Millions are spent on detection of forged passports and travel documents. A sub-group of the Ad Hoc Group on Immigration ... holds bi-monthly seminars on detecting forged travel documents. Western Europe's junior partners, particularly Hungary, the Czech Republic and Poland, which have been recruited as buffer states and act increasingly as the frontline of immigration control, are being supplied urgently with equipment such as automated travel document scanners, UV-IR lamps, security laminate verifiers and video-spectral comparators. And biometric controls are being developed, which could do away with the need for passports. Digital fingerprinting and electronic scanning of the iris of the eye are being explored, and there are already pilot hand-scanners in use at JFK and Frankfurt airports. ...

Those whom Europe's interior and justice ministers have called on to develop European immigration and asylum policy behind closed doors are policemen, security officials, immigration officers and civil servants. It is no wonder that what they produce smacks of a European police state, in which refugees are described as 'disorderly movements' and measures designed to combat them.

All asylum seekers and illegal entrants to Britain are fingerprinted, in part so that their fingerprints can be held on the Schengen information system (SIS), a central European electronic database to deter 'asylum shopping'.

The attempt to stop refugees begins well before they arrive at European borders. The only way of becoming a refugee outside the country of asylum is through the UNHCR resettlement programme, but its provisions are restrictive, and only 27,000 refugees were resettled by the UNHCR in 1997; 61 of these were resettled in Britain, where they had close family ties. In 1999 Britain eventually accepted a few hundred Kosovans under this programme; by April 1999 it had accepted 330 Kosovans out of a UNHCR-programme total of 22,253, of whom 9,974 were in Germany and 2,000 in France. Most refugees therefore have three main possibilities: to apply for a visitor's, student's or business visa at a British embassy or high commission, to buy a (very expensive) forged visa, or to stow away or be smuggled (the latter, again, at great expense). Approaching a British diplomatic post can itself be extremely dangerous, because of security guards outside and local employees inside. To get a visitor's or other visa requires proof of the possession of money and contacts; any mention of asylum will lead to immediate refusal, although there are a few cases of embassy officials befriending a refugee. Immigration officials appear to recognise that refugees are unlikely to be able to travel on their own documents. A Nigerian detainee in Campsfield immigration detention centre told the author that he had had to spend at least half an hour arguing with immigration officials at Heathrow airport who (wrongly) claimed his passport was his own passport, and so he could not be a genuine refugee. Asylum Aid's document *'No Reason At All'* quotes a letter of refusal from the Home Office, sent to a Ugandan woman who had been persecuted by soldiers who claimed she was associated with a rebel group, as follows:

> The Secretary of State also notes that in spite of your claim that you were being harassed by the Ugandan authorities and you left that country in fear of persecution you were able to leave Uganda through normal channels using a passport issued in your own name. ... The Secretary of State ... considers that ... the use of your passport further undermines your claim to have fled Uganda in the circumstances you allege.

Damned if you do and damned if you don't.

Obtaining false documents is expensive and risky. It will be made more expensive still if visitors have to put up a £5,000 bond (see p. 84). The next obstacle to overcome is carriers' liability. Britain continues to be the country which applies this form of control with most severity, although it is now a requirement of the Schengen Convention. In the British case carriers are expected to be able to detect all forgeries that are 'reasonably apparent'. They are assisted by Home Office officials called airport liaison officers (ALOs). Refugees who are caught out in this process are likely to end up in the hands of local security forces. The third possibility is to travel clandestinely. Refugees have travelled across borders on foot, on horseback, in cars, in the backs of lorries and underneath them, in the undercarriage of aeroplanes; and they have swum, travelled in small boats, and stowed away in ships. On part of the border between Mexico and the United States, and on the border between Morocco and the Spanish enclave of Ceuta, migrants negotiate razor-wire fences in incredible feats of skill and endurance. Many have died or suffered greatly in the process.

Once refugees arrive in Britain they can avoid being labelled as illegal immigrants only if they identify themselves, hand over any false documents or explain why they have no documents, and claim asylum at the port or airport of entry, *before* they go through immigration. In recent years approximately half of them have done so. Those who do not, and are therefore 'illegal', have actually been more rather than less successful in obtaining refugee status; in 1992–94, for example, almost twice as many of those who applied for asylum after entry were granted it as of those who applied for asylum before entry. Since the 1996 act 'in-country' applicants have not been entitled to welfare benefits. But 'port applicants' are almost as likely to be detained; in the late 1990s between a third and half of detained asylum seekers at any one time were *not*, even technically, 'illegal immigrants'. In addition if refugees do apply for asylum before entry, and have travelled overland or changed planes, they risk falling foul of the 'safe third country' rule, becoming 'refugees in orbit' and being returned to a country they have travelled through, which may or may not be 'safe' in reality. Germany and France changed their constitutions to enable them to return asylum seekers to neighbouring states. The only way to be sure of avoiding this is to claim 'in-country', when the authorities must finally consider a claim. Frances Webber, in *Crimes of Arrival*, cites, as examples of what can happen to those who claim asylum at port of entry,

the 17-year-old Somali boy who had witnessed his mother being killed and had fled via Italy to join his only surviving relative in the UK, who was returned to Italy. Or the Somali man with shrapnel lodged in his head, given painkillers and put back on the plane to Italy ... the examples are legion.

Detention centres and prisons in Britain contain people who are bemused and distressed because they have been picked up and detained when they were on their way to another country. Worse, in early 1999 there were, in addition to the 800 or so people detained under immigration rules, 450 people imprisoned in ordinary prisons, including Wormwood Scrubs and Holloway, with criminal convictions for travelling on forged papers; most of them were picked up at Heathrow on their way to claim asylum in the United States or Canada, a claim that their criminal records would now cause to be ruled out, and had been advised by duty solicitors to plead guilty to shorten their sentences. In July 1999 two judges in the High Court, in response to cases brought by an Algerian, an Iraqi Kurd and an Albanian, ruled that the government was in breach of its obligations under article 31 of the Geneva Convention which states that asylum seekers should not be penalised for entering a country illegally; Lord Justice Simon Brown said that:

It must be hoped that these challenges will mark a turning point in the crown's approach to the prosecution of refugees for travelling on false passports. Article 31 must henceforth be honoured.

The judge added that the combination of visa requirements and carrier's liability 'has made it well nigh impossible for refugees to travel to countries of refuge without false passports'. Criminal prosecution of refugees holding false documents has now been put on hold. But those still in prison were told they could not simply be released but would have to reopen their cases through the courts. One of the 'reasons' the Home Office gives for detaining refugees continues to be their use of false documents.

Most asylum seekers have little idea what they ought to do on arrival in Britain. An African who later got refugee status went through immigration control on arrival, spent the night sleeping rough in Trafalgar Square, and eventually managed to get to Croydon and apply for asylum there. Refugees may not wish to approach uniformed officials until they have taken advice from friends. Usually their only source of advice before arrival is the agents who have brought them to Britain, whose interests may not be the same as those of the refugees. Some are told by these agents that they will get some money back if they go through immigration and hand over their false documents to them once they are outside. Some destroy their documents, not wishing to have a false identity. A UNHCR note submitted to the British government in May 1998 (quoted by John Morrison in *The Cost of Survival*) said it was reasonable for them to do so:

There are also circumstances in which an asylum seeker may be driven, for perfectly valid reasons, to destroying, damaging or disposing of his [or her] travel documents which do not belong to the asylum seeker. The primary reason for such action is the asylum seeker's fear of being returned to his [or her] country of origin or a third country which, rightly or wrongly, he [or she] considers unsafe. ... It is common for asylum seekers to be instructed on what to do with their passports by agents (eg. destroy them on arrival or return them to the agent). Persons who fear persecution if returned to their own country, or an unsafe third country, are not normally inclined to ignore the instructions of an 'agent' to whom they have entrusted their journey to perceived safety.

Yet if refugees get it wrong, they may be accused of not providing a 'reasonable explanation' for their lack of documents, or of failure to disclose immediately that their documents are false, and of therefore 'lacking credibility' (a favourite accusation). They can also then have their rights of appeal drastically curtailed. Some who hide in lorries cannot tell when they arrive at frontiers and ports, have no means of getting out until they are released or found by drivers and may have no idea of their destination. Some may cross the Channel by choice, for example because of the brutality of French police, warehouse accommodation in Calais, the new French laws which make it illegal for support groups to help them materially, and the probably vain hope that the grass is greener elsewhere. But others have little choice once they have handed over their money to agents. In *The Cost of Survival* John Morrison notes that, of the 27 individuals whose cases he studied, under a third had chosen to come to Britain, mainly because of family, friends and community; in the rest of the cases either 'the facilitation of the agent play[ed] an important if not decisive role in determining the outcome', or the refugees had 'no idea at all where the final destination would be, other than it might be somewhere in Europe', or 'there is no real choice at any stage of the journey', or any choice occurred only after they have already fled their country. Morrison says that these findings were confirmed by the more general experience of community organisations in London.

Internal controls to detect illegal entrants are becoming more pervasive. In France the police routinely check Algerians and other black people, under wide powers given to them by the 1993 Pasqua laws; subsequently laws were introduced requiring anybody who had a foreigner living in their house to report their arrival and departure to the police, although they were withdrawn after mass demonstrations including celebrities who pledged to break the law. In the Netherlands identity and residence checks have been introduced at work and elsewhere. In Switzerland the authorities register both foreigners and those who invite them. In Britain police raids on workplaces and street searches resulted in a doubling of the number of illegal immigrants caught between 1993 and 1994. Under Labour's new act powers are to be extended to immigration officers to check, presumably in the street as well as elsewhere, the immigration status of people who are already within Britain, rather than merely at frontiers. The withdrawal of benefits and the consequent destitution of many asylum seekers itself has the potential to criminalise them, to turn them and their children into social outcasts and to drive them into begging or worse. When refugees are detained, this means in the eyes of many that they are criminals; hence the banners, made by protesters inside and outside Campsfield immigration detention centre for example, proclaiming 'REFUGEES ARE NOT CRIMINALS'.

Deportations are on the increase, and sometimes involve considerable violence against asylum seekers. In May 1999 Aamir Mohammed Ageeb, a Sudanese asylum seeker, died when border police at Frankfurt airport put shackles on his hands and feet and forced a motor-bike helmet onto his head. Frances Webber in *Crimes of Arrival* says:

Deportations of rejected asylum seekers have involved the use of sedative injections, straitjackets, stretchers, face masks, handcuffs, leg irons, surgical tape. Face masks were introduced in the Netherlands after surgical tape wound round the head and face of a Romanian deportee resulted in his suffering brain damage. ... After the death of Kola Bankole in Germany, while being sedated for deportation, the Nigerian embassy accused the German authorities of responsibility for 25 such deaths.

Several dozen Zairean deportees were said to have been handcuffed and bound with tape throughout their journey, on two specially chartered planes, from France. The appeal of special chartered flights for deportation is obvious; passengers travelling to a third world destination for profit or pleasure don't want to see distraught deportees, sometimes shouting, lashing out and having to be restrained, or already under restraint, drugged or bound and gagged. They might be moved to intervene, as passengers have on occasion, refusing to travel unless deportees were taken off the plane. ... The entry into force of the Schengen agreement resulted in the first joint mass deportation, in which the French, Dutch and German authorities chartered a plane to deport 44 Zaireans, in the spirit of solidarity and burden-sharing.

After Bankole's death the German Medical Council issued a statement warning doctors that those who sanction forced deportations are in breach of medical ethical codes; its president stated that 'all measures using direct force are a danger to life and, as such, constitute bodily harm', and warned the government not to resort to sedation. The World Doctors' Association passed a resolution which states that 'If somebody resists, one is not allowed to make him fit for travel with drugs.' Some protesters resort to the tactic of persuading pilots and passengers to refuse to fly with deportees. French protesters have engaged with the Air France trade unions, and Belgians have demonstrated in airports to persuade passengers to refuse to sit down until deportees have been removed from planes.

The more measures governments introduce to detect and punish asylum seekers and other migrants, the more elaborate, ingenious and expensive the countermeasures by refugees have to become. Their only alternative to this is to stay where they are and face possible imprisonment, torture and death. And the more the dangers and the controls, the greater the potential for exploitation. There are of course examples of friends and family members organising escapes. Some of the agents who organise the procurement of false passports and other aspects of escape may act more like travel agents than criminals, even possibly with humanitarian purpose. Jeremy Harding in his *London Review of Books* article 'The Uninvited' (now a book) describes with admiration the exploits of the *scafisti* or boatmen who evade coastguards to land refugees and migrants safely in Italy. But refugees are often forced to put their lives in the hands of unscrupulous people, most of whom act for profit. One estimate of the total annual income derived by those who profit from organising escape and migration, quoted by John Morrison in *The Cost of Survival*, is that it is between US$5 and US$7 billion a year. The British authorities triggered this industry in the 1950s, when their attempts to persuade the Indian government not to issue passports to intending migrants resulted in the creation of forged passports, which were sold in Indian villages. Governments are themselves responsible for the growth of the international criminal networks which they condemn. These in turn exploit people desperate to flee, and sometimes cause extreme hardship for them.

One of the consequences is a growth in media stories which, while exposing scandals, also have the effect of further feeding prejudice against migrants and asylum seekers. The *Daily Mail* of 24 November 1998 carried an article on a 'Briton, "the Godfather of human smuggling"', alleging that he had smuggled 12,000 Indians into the United States and 'netted £133 million in just three years'. Their journeys 'often took months or even years'; 'Once inside America they were kept in houses until relatives paid the £17,500 smuggling fee. Those who failed to pay were expected to work off their debt. The [US Immigration and Nationality Service] said it had a list of 1,000 US employers who used the illegal immigrants as a form of cheap labour.' The *Guardian* of 12 October 1999 reported that four members of a Chinese gang were convicted of taking part in an extortion racket in which immigrants were kept prisoner and beaten in order to extract money from their relatives in Chinese villages, although they had already paid up to £18,750 to be brought to Britain. The *Guardian* of 18 May 1999 carried a full-page article entitled 'Highway robbery', which described the 'sinister effect' of lorry drivers' financial problems: 'they are causing a boom in the secret trade in contraband and refugees from mainland Europe'. Some lorry drivers, the article said, stick to 'beer and baccy'; but others are tempted by the larger sums available for smuggling drugs and people. A random 3 per cent of incoming lorries are diverted to 'the pride and joy of Eurotunnel security, Britain's biggest X-ray machine'. If the drivers get caught, even if they did not know they had human beings in the back of their lorry, they are liable to end up in prison, sometimes taking the rap themselves rather than accusing others because of their fear of the gangs. The *Guardian* of 7 September 1999 reported that 'security experts' from the government's National Criminal Intelligence Service (NCIS) warned that 'The Albanian mafia is targeting Britain in an effort to expand its European-wide illegal immigration, drug trafficking and arms dealing operations', and that 'many Albanians seeking asylum in Britain were criminals posing as refugees'. The Albanian mafia, the article added, 'is thought to control many of the people-smuggling routes from east to west and has muscled in on the heroin trafficking trade run by Turkish mafias'. However the article added that John Abbott, the NCIS director-general, said that 'the trafficking of illegal immigrants into Britain was currently run by 50 gangs', nearly all of which were British led.

Not surprisingly, all this has led to great hardship, and even deaths, for refugees and migrants themselves, whether or not criminal networks are involved. UNITED, a refugee support organisation based in Amsterdam, has documented over 1,000 deaths related to governments' enforcement policies between 1995 and 1998. Stowaways risk being killed and thrown overboard if they are discovered, partly to avoid carriers' liability fines. Or they may be locked into containers in holds, in appalling temperatures and without food and water, and unable to make themselves heard. They may be sprayed with pesticides or crushed by moving cargoes. Sometimes they die before they are discovered. Many drown in overloaded small boats; at least 1,000 people are said to have drowned since 1988 crossing from North Africa to Spain, and a further 547 crossing the Adriatic to reach Italy. Others drown swimming the river Oder between Poland and Germany. In North America, the *Financial Times* of 23 February 2000 reported, US border patrols 'yearly find about 300 corpses at desert and river crossings'; some drown in the Rio Grande, others die of heat exhaustion and in road accidents with exhausted drivers. Two Indian brothers travelled to Britain in the undercarriage of a plane; one of them miraculously survived. In August 1999 two stowaways, aged 15 and 16, from Guinea were found dead in the landing gear of a plane when they arrived in Brussels, having landed in Mali on the way; a note was found with one of them which said:

Excellencies, gentlemen – members and those responsible in Europe, it is to your solidarity and generosity that we appeal for your help in Africa. If you see that we have sacrificed ourselves and lost our lives, it is because we suffer too much in Africa and need your help to struggle against poverty and war. ... Please excuse us very much for daring to write this letter.

In December 1996 a ship carrying hundreds of refugees, organised by traffickers, was rammed in the Adriatic, and 280 people drowned. In 1995, 18 Tamil asylum seekers, having paid £500 each in Romania to a smuggler who promised to get them into Germany, were locked into a lorry trailer whose driver ran away near the Austrian border, and they suffocated. Of five Romanians who travelled to Britain in the back of a lorry, four died from the inhalation of toxic fumes; the sole survivor, having been locked up for a while in Britain, was returned to France and then deported. In Sweden another sealed container was found to contain 64 Iraqis, 24 of them children, who had paid $2,000 each; there was hardly any oxygen and the temperature was 70°C. Others have travelled in refrigerated lorries. Most of those who travel in lorry containers suffer from hunger, thirst, extremes of temperature and disorientation. John Morrison quotes a Chechen woman:

I travelled for a very long time. Alone, in complete darkness, knowing neither the time nor whether it was night or day. It was very hard for me. My wound hurt, I could only sit, lie and pray. It was also very cold. But I bore it and waited. Eventually, after a long time, the door opened ...

Women are particularly vulnerable, and there are many reports of rape and other abuses during clandestine escapes.

There is a good deal of speculation about how many 'illegal immigrants' there actually are. In the United States the estimate is that there are around 6 million. In Britain nobody seems to know. In the policy document written in opposition, *Fairer, Faster and Firmer: Labour's Approach to Asylum and Immigration*, Jack Straw and Doug Henderson wrote:

it is time to put a stop to inflammatory speculation with accurate research. It is astonishing that after 17 years in government the Home Office has not sponsored any proper research into the scale of illegal immigration. Labour will commission the necessary research.

But it has not done so. It has, instead, made its own contributions to 'inflammatory speculation'.

One problem is that it is unclear what is meant by 'illegal immigrant'. In many people's minds, an illegal immigrant must be someone who has entered Britain when they have no right to do so, for example in order to work illegally. But about half of asylum seekers are labelled illegal immigrants, even though they have a legal right under international conventions to claim asylum in Britain. In addition, and inconsistently, ministers have a tendency to equate numbers of illegal immigrants with numbers of people refused asylum, although the majority of those refused asylum in recent years have been port applicants and therefore not illegal. Moreover declines in the percentages of people granted asylum do not mean in reality that the number of illegal immigrants, or economic migrants, has increased; it means merely that the criteria for acceptance of refugees have become more restrictive. Speculation, as the *Guardian* of 12 May 1998 reports, nevertheless continues.

Tory MPs point out that 250,000 people have applied for political asylum in Britain over the last ten years and the official figures show that 10,700 have been granted asylum and 13,000 deported. 'Where are the other 226,300 people?' they ask. This ignores the 70,000 people whose cases are still stuck in the backlog and that some

5,000 a year are granted exceptional leave to remain. But undoubtedly some thousands have overstayed and simply disappeared.

People who enter clandestinely are all automatically 'illegal', and are generally assumed to be so by public opinion and the media. But an unknown but certainly large proportion of these people are refugees, many of them Kurds, Tamils, Kosovans and Algerians. So when immigration officials report, for example, that the number of people who have been caught entering clandestinely through Dover has gone up from 850 in the whole of 1997 to 650 in the first four months of 1998, this does not mean that there has been a big increase in people trying to enter Britain illegally to work. It may mean that there has been an increase in refugees. Or it may simply mean that the authorities are spending more money on new devices for detection. According to the *Guardian* of 12 May 1998, the Immigration Service said the number of 'illegal entrants' found trying to enter Britain clandestinely was stable until early 1998, when they suddenly increased sharply; but officials themselves said this had more to do with sniffer dogs and better detection techniques than with a new influx: 'They say that they now pick up 50 per cent of clandestine entries where before they were only catching 20 per cent.' The Home Office minister Mike O'Brien told the House of Commons on 30 March 1998 that in 1997 '14,150 people were traced and served with illegal entry papers, but many of them may have entered in previous years.' Again, many of them may have been refugees; and others will not have been caught.

What is clear is that the government's intensification of repressive measures has not been followed by significant declines in the numbers of refugees coming to Britain. Moreover the long-drawn-out process of refusing asylum is not, generally speaking, followed by removal. All it achieves is suffering.

DESTITUTION

Probably most people who flee to escape persecution take a drop in their standard of living. Even when they are allowed to work, they usually cannot obtain employment which fits their skills and qualifications. Doctors and professors end up as sandwich makers and security guards. University students cannot continue or start their studies until they get refugee status, which may take years. For those who cannot get jobs at all, living on welfare benefits, supposing they are available, is hard, especially without relatives or friends.

Nevertheless the contradictory myth is perpetrated that refugees come to sponge off the state and take the locals' jobs. Therefore, the argument goes, they must be deprived of even these possibilities. The German and Dutch governments do not allow asylum seekers to work, either during their applications or after refusals. In Britain they are not allowed to work for the first six months after they have arrived. After that they can, in theory and if someone tells them about it, apply to the Home Office for permission to work. If their application for asylum has not yet been decided, the Home Office will normally, but not always, give permission and issue them with a document, a standard acknowledgement letter (SAL) which may enable them to get a National Insurance number and employers to employ them without falling foul of the employers' liability provision in the 1996 Act. On the other hand, because of delays and inefficiency, some asylum seekers have to wait more than six months before receiving an initial interview with the Home Office and being issued with SAL. Others are in detention and remain there until after their applications are turned down. And if, when their six months is up, refusal is imminent, the Home Office may not issue an SAL. The asylum seeker will then never be able to get a National Insurance number. After a refusal, the SAL and permission to work are withdrawn, or not granted, and it becomes unlawful for an employer to employ the asylum seeker (even though he or she may be legally in the country, waiting for an appeal). If an asylum seeker already has a National Insurance number, he or she may be able to continue to work, though without permission, since employers who can prove they have seen such a document are immune from prosecution. But if asylum seekers do work without permission they may increase their vulnerability to deportation and exploitation by employers.

In Germany, the Netherlands, Sweden, Belgium, Switzerland and Denmark, asylum seekers are compulsorily housed in reception centres, where they are vulnerable to racist attacks, the most notorious of which have been the firebombing of refugee hostels by the extreme right in Germany. Britain is moving in this direction, with the opening of Oakington (see p. 122). The provision of welfare benefits to asylum seekers is being eroded. In Germany all state benefits are paid in kind, with a small cash allowance. In the Netherlands asylum seekers who have their claims turned down are to be deprived of benefits altogether, presumably in the hope of more or less literally starving them out. In Britain asylum seekers were until 1996 entitled to 90 per cent of normal benefits. In 1996 the Conservative government introduced new regulations, entitled Social Security (Persons from Abroad) Miscellaneous Amendment Regulations 1996, to deny benefits to asylum seekers who did not claim asylum before entry and to all asylum seekers once they had had a first refusal from the Home Office. A young Zairean woman went to court to challenge the new regulations, and won. One of the two appeal judges, Lord Justice Simon Brown, said the following:

Parliament cannot have intended a significant number of genuine asylum-seekers to be impaled on the horns of so intolerable a dilemma: the need either to abandon their claims to refugee status, or to maintain them as best they can but in a state of utter destitution. Primary legislation alone could, in my judgement, achieve that sorry state of affairs. ... [this] uncompromising draconian policy contemplates a life so destitute that to my mind no civilised nation can tolerate it.

The Tory social security secretary, Peter Lilley, proceeded to demonstrate that that was exactly parliament's intention. He asked parliament to reverse the Court of Appeal's ruling by passing new primary legislation. In spite of strong opposition in the House of Lords, the 1996 Asylum and Immigration Act was passed, incorporating the new rules on benefits for asylum seekers. Lawyers then went to court against Kensington and Chelsea Council, and won the judgment that somebody without any money could be held to be vulnerable under homelessness legislation, and should therefore be housed. In a third case, in the High Court on 8 October 1996, four asylum seekers won the judgment that they were eligible for support under the 1948 National Assistance Act, which obliges local authorities to provide shelter and food for anybody who is destitute for whatever reason, and that this had not been changed by the 1996 Act, which did not mention it. Mr Justice Collins commented that he found it:

impossible to believe that Parliament had intended that an asylum seeker, who was lawfully here and who could not lawfully be removed from the country, should be left destitute, starving and at risk of grave illness and even death because he could find no one to provide him with the bare necessities of life.

He added that if parliament attempted to pass a law restating its intentions, it would be in breach of the European Convention on Human Rights and the Geneva Convention on Refugees. His judgment was upheld in an appeal on 17 February 1997 by the master of the rolls, Lord Woolf, and two other judges, who wrote that 'The plight of asylum-seekers who are in the position of the respondents obviously can and should provoke deep sympathy. Their plight is indeed horrendous.' *The Times* reported that:

The four asylum seekers who brought the case are a Romanian who arrived aboard a lorry last July, has slept rough under Waterloo Bridge and has nowhere to live, no money and speaks no English; an Algerian who arrived last July and has slept rough in Hyde Park, London; a Chinese citizen who arrived last May; and an Iraqi Kurd who arrived secretly last August.

After this, and until the introduction of Labour's plans for a Home Office-run voucher and accommodation scheme, asylum seekers were more or less supplied 'with the bare necessities of life'. In addition, the 1989 Children's Act was used to help families with children. The changes meant that asylum seekers were supported not from the central government-funded social security budget, thus making a 'saving' of approximately £200 million a year, but from the already much depleted social services budgets of a fairly small number of local authorities, most of them in deprived inner London. The much-publicised 'burden' on local authorities is of the government's making. Although the Conservative government decided to reimburse local authorities at the rate of £165 a week for each asylum seeker, this was said not to cover their actual costs, which were £200 a week, which was also a good deal more than the cost of providing and administering normal welfare benefits from central funds. In Oxford refugees were in a slightly better situation than they were elsewhere. Oxfordshire social services initially paid asylum seekers £65 a week; when the government instructed the council not to pay cash, it paid landlords for asylum seekers' rooms and their bills, and supplied them with £30 a week in £5 food vouchers. However these vouchers had to be spent in Co-op branches; they were not available for tobacco or alcohol and change could not be given. The Co-op shops are often several miles from where the asylum seekers live. There was no money for bus fares or the telephone. Asylum Welcome, the charity set up to help asylum seekers in Campsfield immigration detention centre and after they are released, was faced with dramatic increases in the numbers of visits to its office by asylum seekers with desperate needs for housing and cash. Elsewhere, especially in some London boroughs, the situation was worse. Kensington and Chelsea Council initially put asylum seekers in a hotel near Heathrow and gave them £2 a day; fares to the centre of London were £3.90. Brent was also giving people £2 a day. When money payments were stopped, Camden put people in bed and breakfast and fed them with meals-on-wheels. In Southwark social workers spent their time shopping for refugees. The Refugee Council carried out a survey and concluded, according to its *Update* of February 1997, that 'The physical and mental health of some of the participants deteriorated dramatically during the tracking period and two individuals made suicide attempts.' Another Refugee Council survey concluded that over 70 per cent of the 200 people interviewed did not have enough to eat, and nearly 75 per cent were completely penniless, with no money for bus fares or other necessities. The stories began to multiply of the suffering caused to refugees who often had to walk many miles across London, with small children and sometimes injuries, to the designated shop for spending their vouchers; who were subjected to racist abuse when their attempt to spend the exact amount of their vouchers held up supermarket till queues; whose children were taunted at school as 'voucher kids'; who ran out of milk for their children in mid-week, having spent their single £25 voucher, and could not go to the local shop to get some. Local authorities and others trying to help asylum seekers were, according to Nick Hardwick, chief executive of the Refugee Council, 'at their wits' end'. The *Guardian* of 14 June 1997 reported that councils were housing asylum seekers in substandard hotels and hostels and that 'Welfare workers fear that social and racial tensions will rise as single men without money or work cluster round hostels for months.' Councils such as Westminster were sending refugees out of London. Comic Relief, without publicising its efforts for fear of a backlash from Middle England, spent an increasing proportion of the funds it raised to support destitute refugees *within* Britain. In January 1997 the Red Cross started to distribute food parcels to asylum seekers in Britain, saying that without them asylum seekers would starve. *Big Issue*, the magazine for homeless people, ran a 'Stop the Vouchers' campaign. The Churches Commission for Racial Justice urged local churches to provide 'basic subsistence', including shelter, clothing, food and money for destitute refugees.

If charities and refugee communities provided support, or if refugees seemed not to be destitute, some local authorities provided even less. The June 1999 issue of the Refugee Council's magazine *iNexile* relates that:

One London council, for example, refused to give vouchers to a Congolese man because he was wearing a gold watch and chain. They told him to pawn the items and live off the proceeds. Only thereafter would he be considered destitute. When he dutifully visited the pawnbrokers, he discovered that the watch and chain weren't, in fact, gold. But he was still asked to pawn them, before he could present himself back to social services to ask for help.

In another case, a Sierra Leonean man, who was already on vouchers, went to pick up his weekly £25 voucher from social services. He was told that, because he was wearing new-looking trainers, he was obviously not destitute and therefore would no longer qualify for vouchers. Even though he explained that the trainers were a gift from a friend, he was still refused. He was told that, in order to qualify as destitute, he would have to give the council his friend's address so that they could confirm that the trainers had, indeed, been a gift.

The Labour government's 1998 white paper said this system was 'messy' and 'expensive', costing £400 million a year and placing an intolerable burden on local authorities (but not, apparently, on refugees). Its 1999 act takes nearly all asylum seekers outside the minimum standards of social support normally provided to people in Britain. Instead they receive accommodation and food vouchers, administered by the Home Office through locally constituted 'consortia'. Many of them are not be allowed to work (see p. 106), which rather destroys the point of the argument, in paragraph 8.23 of Labour's white paper, that 'social services departments should not carry the burden of looking after healthy and able bodied asylum seekers'. The policy began to be implemented under interim provisions in December 1999. It was intended to be fully operative in April 2000, but the local consortia failed to come up with sufficient offers of accommodation. The implementation of the scheme was therefore postponed, with local social services, mainly in London and Kent, left to administer vouchers and find accommodation for 'in-country' applicants, a task for which they were unqualified.

Initially the Home Office claimed it would require perhaps 100, and no more than 200, new staff to perform its new tasks. In a written parliamentary answer on 5 November 1999 it admitted that it would need over 500 staff, at an administrative cost of £11.5 million per year. The marginal cost of administering normal benefits for the same number of people would be minimal. Figures published on the Internet by the Home Office research department are that the unit cost per month of supporting an asylum seeker on benefits was £405 in 1998/99, rising to £425 in 1999/00. The unit cost of local authority support in those years was £650. The cost under the 'new support arrangements – white paper proposals' was expected also to be £650 in 2000/01, and to rise to £666 in 2001/02. All these extra costs, and more, are accounted for by the extra costs of administration; asylum seekers themselves actually receive less. Since the number of unresolved asylum cases is now over 100,000, and depending how many of them are allowed to work, the government thus appears to be willing to spend up to £270 million of public money to make life harder for refugees, in the hope of deterring future applications. The white paper, in paragraph 8.20, put it like this:

Cash based support is administratively convenient, and usually though not inevitably less expensive in terms of unit cost. Provision in kind is more cumbersome to administer, but experience has shown that this is less attractive and provides less of a financial inducement for those who would be drawn by a cash scheme. The number of asylum applications fell by 30 per cent following the withdrawal of some social security benefits in 1996.

Asylum seekers are to subsist on vouchers and small amounts of cash worth 70 per cent of income support. Although the home secretary Jack Straw claimed that the support on offer amounted to 90 per cent of normal benefits rather than 70 per cent when utility bills were taken into account, most interpretations are that even on this basis it would amount to at most 76 per cent. Asylum seekers are to be denied the protection of the National Assistance, Housing and Children's Acts. For the first time families are to be included as well as single people, and local authorities are prohibited from helping them. Outcry about the needs of children in particular in committee in the House of Commons resulted in a residual role for the Children's Act, and an increase in the amount of cash from £1 for adults and 50p a day for children to £10 a week for each adult or child. But this concession was deducted from the value of the vouchers. The vouchers, as before, are usable only in designated shops and issued in fixed amounts, from which no change is to be given. *iNexile*'s article (see above, p. 109) concludes as follows:

Vouchers will be stigmatising, humiliating and degrading for those asylum seekers who flee to the UK after April 2,000. 'If the vouchers are to work', Bob Ilunga [of the Zairean Congolese Community Association] told iNexile, 'then they need to be flexible, in smaller denominations and exchangeable at other shops. Then people could exist in dignity and the scheme would work'.

The reality, of course, is that we already have a system like that in place. It's called cash.

The 1999 act states that support will be 'discretionary', in the sense that it will be based on an assessment of whether the person is destitute or not. Asylum seekers will be expected to go to their communities and families first before seeking support from the Home Office. At a conference organised by Joint Council for the Welfare of Immigrants, the National Assembly Against Racism and the Jewish Council for Racial Equality in October 1999, the

Labour MP Diane Abbott related that she had asked the home secretary whether refugees would have to take their rings off before they could get support; Straw had said 'Yes'.

The Labour government, citing the experience of other European countries, moreover intends to give all asylum seekers only one, 'no choice', offer of accommodation. The scheme disperses asylum seekers away from London and other ports and airports, specifically banning any consideration of asylum seekers' personal preference to be near relatives and friends. If they refuse this enforced dispersal, they will lose their right even to vouchers. The policy of dispersal had been tried in the 1980s in the case of Vietnamese 'boat people'. A Home Office study, entitled *Vietnamese Refugees* and published in 1995, concluded that within two years more than half had moved to London, because of the isolation, unemployment and racism they experienced in the areas they were assigned to. The government has stated that it intends to move people to 'cluster areas' of refugee or immigrant settlement. But the reality is likely to be that they are dispersed to available housing on sink estates and hostels in areas of high unemployment, perhaps in towns where there are no existing immigrant communities. If so, they are being set up as targets for racist attack. The new dispersed will probably return to London boroughs and perhaps elsewhere, where at least there are support networks, lawyers, communities, friends, and the possibility of being absorbed into places where there is a relatively high level of tolerance and diversity. Hackney, for example, will not have fewer refugees. What it will have is more destitute people, more outcasts, more people who will be forced to resort to begging, prostitution and crime. They will be the objects, perhaps, of Jack Straw's hostility to squeegy merchants, targets for zero tolerance. In March 2000, in a forestaste of what may be to come, a few Roma women begging 'aggressively' with their children gave rise to a prolonged barrage of xenophobic front-page headlines and statements by ministers against asylum seekers in general.

In a further twist of the screw, the Home Office announced in a draft manual published on 17 February 1999 that asylum seekers would not receive even this support if they decided to go for judicial review of Immigration Appeals Tribunal decisions, stating that:

Support will not be provided where Judicial Review is pursued. Apellants should look to their own community or the voluntary sector for any support. The Immigration and Nationality Directorate is considering the case for providing grant aid for such functions.

The announcement followed a successful appeal against deportation by Mohammed Arif, a teacher. He had fled Kashmir in 1992 after being tortured in gaol, and had been sentenced in his absence to seven years' hard labour, on charges of incitement to murder at a political demonstration against the then ruling Muslim Convention party. In Britain the Immigration Appeals Tribunal had ruled in 1996 that as Arif's party, the PPP, had since returned to power, he would be able to appeal against his sentence on return to Kashmir. The three Appeal Court judges, presided over by Lord Justice Simon Brown, ruled that it was not enough for the Home Office to assume he would be safe when he returned but that it would have to prove this was so. According to his lawyer, this judgment might affect 50,000 other refugees threatened with deportation to countries where the Home Office was claiming the situation had improved. The Home Office's reaction was to threaten to starve out anyone who might attempt to pursue a similar course in the exercise of their legal rights.

DETENTION

Governments' other main form of deterrence is to lock up refugees. The UNHCR, in particular, has been highly critical of the practice of detaining asylum seekers, which it says in its *Guidelines on Detention of Asylum Seekers*, published in Geneva in January 1996, is 'highly undesirable'. Guideline 2 states:

The right to liberty is a fundamental right, recognised in all the major human rights instruments, both at global and regional levels. The right to seek asylum is, equally, recognised as a basic human right. The act of seeking asylum can therefore not be considered an offence or a crime. Consideration should be given to the fact that asylum seekers may already have suffered some form of persecution or other hardship in their country of origin and should be protected against any form of harsh treatment.
    As a general rule, asylum seekers should not be detained.

The *Guidelines* refer to article 31 of the 1951 UN Convention on Refugees 'which exempts refugees from penalties for illegal presence or entry when "coming directly" from a territory where their life or freedom was threatened' and says that 'coming directly' should not be restrictively interpreted, for example if an asylum seeker transited briefly through another country. The *Guidelines* also state that:

Detention of asylum seekers which is applied ... as part of a policy to deter future asylum seekers is contrary to the principles of international protection. ...
    Escape from detention should not lead to automatic discontinuance of the asylum procedure, nor to return to the country of origin, having regard to the principle of non-refoulement.

An article in *The Economist* of 14 February 1998 quoted Peter van der Vaart, deputy representative of the UNHCR in London, as saying that 'Britain's detention of supplicants breaches the European Convention on Human Rights. "What we object to" he says, "is that detention is being used to deter asylum seekers."' The UNHCR *Guidelines* further state that, if asylum seekers are, in exceptional circumstances and for a 'minimal period', detained, they should have the right to be given reasons for their detention, should be able to challenge the decision before an impartial authority, and should be provided with legal assistance to do so. People under the age of 18 should not be detained, and asylum seekers should not be held with convicted criminals.

The British government, with Finland and Denmark, was the earliest in Europe to engage in the practice of detaining asylum seekers. But others have followed. There are now well over 100 detention centres in Europe. Detention of asylum seekers is practised in the Netherlands, Germany, Belgium, Greece, Norway, Switzerland, France, Italy, Austria, Spain, Portugal, Poland, Romania, Lithuania, Latvia, the Slovak Republic and Hungary, and also in the United States and Australia. In March 1997 FASTI (the Fédération des Associations de Solidorite avec les Travailleurs Immigrés) organised a conference in Lille, entitled '*Europe Barbelée*' (whose proceedings were edited by Jean-Pierre Perrin-Martin). Delegates described the detention situation in their countries. In France, in the 1970s, administrative detention of people who the authorities wished to deport took place in secret at Arenc in Marseille, without judicial process, and caused scandal when it was discovered. Since then, unlike in Britain, detention has been subject to judicial process. It has a time limit of a maximum of 20 days and has to be endorsed by a judge within 48 hours of the arrest. Detention is prior to deportation and if deportation cannot be effected within the 20-day period, the person has to be released. However the judges, who initially had sometimes freed people and in 1992 condemned the minister of the interior for assault, were progressively, and especially under the Pasqua laws, transformed into appendages of the administrative process. A further scandal occurred when a report by the European Committee for the Prevention of Torture revealed in 1990 that foreigners were being kept in a detention centre in a basement under the Palais de Justice in central Paris, in inhuman and degrading conditions. At FASTI's Lille conference Sabine Mariette, a judge, said the report revealed that 'foreigners were dumped in rooms without sanitary arrangements worthy of the name, sharing mess tins to eat', and subjected to violence by the Paris police, while the judges pronouncing on their detention in the courts above them refused to take the trouble to go downstairs to observe their situation. However, when in 1995 a man barely able to walk after this treatment was brought before a judge, this particular judge decided to see for himself; when the police refused entry to the lawyers representing the man, the judge ordered the release of all 22 occupants of the detention centre. Now, according to Sabine Mariette, 'They are trying to scrap the role of the judge.' Twenty-six new detention centres were opened in France after the mid-1980s. In addition, a small number of foreigners who have resisted deportation, around 100, are locked up in detention centres for periods of up to three months, again after judicial process. At the FASTI conference Madgiguène Cissé, spokesperson of the Saint Bernard *sans-papiers* in Paris (see p. 142), said:

When people are picked up for questioning, you don't know where you'll find them. ... We came across a secret detention centre, one, that is, which isn't on any of the lists kept by police prefectures. It is a detention centre at Genevilliers, in the Hauts-de-Seine *département* north of Paris. We held a demonstration in front of it. In this detention centre, you're kept in a room 10 metres square with 17 mattresses on the ground. *Sans-papiers* were crammed in there, from ten to 17 at a time, prior to their deportation. There was no possibility of telephoning out. ... What is special about this detention centre is that it is located in the depot of a dog brigade, a place where they train police dogs. When we visited this detention centre we had the shivers, because we could hear the dogs barking. The detainees were put in a room and, right outside, the dogs being trained barked all day and night ... it's something that sticks in your mind, you can never forget it. You can't forget how, in order to carry out a policy of closing borders, men, women and children are treated like animals.

In Germany, according to a report to the FASTI conference by Helmut Dietrich of the Forschungsgesellschaft Flucht und Migration (FFM), detention is more recent. In 1988 there were 'only' 59 refugees detained prior to their expulsion. After the fall of the Berlin wall, in 1992, the first detention centre was opened; more followed; the largest, at Büren, has 600 places; another, at Berlin-Grünau, has 330. Most failed asylum seekers and other 'illegals' are detained 'prior to expulsion'. By 1997 some 25,000 persons were detained per year, for a maximum of 48 hours, in inspection centres at the German-Polish frontier and then expelled, with no opportunity to contact lawyers or put their case. Some 4,000–5,000 people a year are detained at German airports with no clear time limit, and sometimes for several months. Some 18,000–20,000 people are detained prior to expulsion, about 2,000 of them at any one time, mostly in some 100 prisons and detention centres, some run by the police or by private companies. Detention may last up to six months and for a maximum of 18 months; most people who are expelled are detained first, but over 10 per cent of them have to be freed because the authorities fail to expel them. There is a token judicial process, with judges signing requests for detention by the police and immigration services without examining cases. Helmut Dietrich told the FASTI conference that:

People collaborating with the administrative services for foreigners visit detainees regularly, in order to get them to crack. Detainees must reveal their identity and sign a passport request for the embassy of the country to which they are going to be expelled. If the detainee refuses, pressure is applied. As punishment, he is confined to a punishment cell, bound, and bullied particularly. This is why, unlike those detained provisionally, and those who have been convicted, detention prior to expulsion is distinguished by still more arbitrary restrictions and racist brutality. Reports of extraordinary institutionalised brutality regularly come to light. Some detainees – this has happened for years at Kruppstrasse in Berlin – were undressed and stuffed in rags or refuse-bags, or – as in the Büren detention centre – put in punishment cells and given the 'Schaukelfesslung' treatment (in which hands and feet are tied behind the detainee, who is thus forced into a rocker shape), a practice recognised as torture and internationally proscribed. In these cases, judicial investigations were set up in Berlin and Büren. In revenge, the policeman who made these abuses public became the subject of threats and complaints. At Büren, the 'Schaukelfesslung' treatment has not even been outlawed or excluded from being used in the future.

... people have committed suicide while detained prior to expulsion.

There have also been several rebellions, some of them 'veritable insurrections lasting for weeks', in which especially Kurds and Algerians were involved, and there have been hunger strikes at airport detention zones.

The FASTI conference was also told, by a participant from Zurich, that in Switzerland 5,000 people were detained in 1995 for varying lengths of time in prisons prior to deportation. In 1997 a special centre for deportation prior to removal was opened. People in this centre were 'subjected to big pressures': 'They are beaten to make them confess what country they come from and what their true name is. We know of cases where people have been shoved onto aeroplanes, bound with wire and drugged.' Sweden has kept asylum seekers in detention on ships, as Britain did Tamils in an earlier period, and confines some refugees on tents. By 1997 it had four detention centres, in which people may be held for eight or nine months. In the Netherlands, according to Rens den Hollander of the Autonoom Centrum in Amsterdam, more than 1,000 detention cells have been created in special prisons for refugees and 'irregular' foreigners. Two new 'mega' prisons were being built, and there were plans for an expansion of capacity to 2,000 places. Normal prison and police stations were also used; the latter have no facilities to receive visitors. And there are reception centres at the airport and at land frontiers, where decisions are made in 24 hours and may be followed by transfer to detention. In addition, although moves to surround reception centres, or open camps, with high fences were thwarted by protesters, every effort is made to deter asylum seekers from going out; if they do, they are electronically monitored. There is no time limit to detention. This, and the lack of any organised activities or adequate medical attention, leads to disorientation and depression among detainees. 'Once', said Rens den Hollander, 'I brought a dead leaf to a detainee to give him the sense of seasons' passing that he had lost. Not allowed! Regulations!' Standard punishment for any form of protest is two weeks in an isolation cell. Many are released, with no change in their circumstances and sometimes after many months in detention. Rens den Hollander commented:

These detention centres are part of a real exclusion machine. For detention is an instrument of deterrence much more than it is an efficient means of control. In the Netherlands, 50 per cent of detainees are not removed from the country but are simply thrown onto the street, where they find themselves once more in a condition of illegality, after spending months and months in prison. The period of detention is unlimited. It is a kind of administrative detention. This detention of refugees and 'irregulars' is supposed to send a signal to potential immigrants – 'Don't come here' – and to the governments of their countries of origin, to apply diplomatic pressure on them to take back their nationals.

In Britain detention is still for longer periods and with less judicial control than in other European countries. In an *Observer* league table of human rights abusers published on 24 October 1999, Britain scored worse than any other EU country, and worse than a long list of Third World countries. This was presumably because the criteria for rankings included arbitrary arrest and detention without trial. Amnesty International has argued, for example in *Prisoners Without a Voice*, that Britain is violating article 5 of the European Convention on Human Rights, article 9 of the International Covenant on Civil and Political Rights, the UN Body of Principles for the Protection of All Persons under Any Form of Detention or Imprisonment, and recommendations of the intergovernmental Executive Committee of the UN High Commissioner for Refugees (UNHCR). Britain violates virtually all of the UNHCR's guidelines (see above). In particular, numerous unaccompanied minors have been detained, including in Campsfield for example, 13-year-old girls, who have false passports for women in their thirties, whose denials are systematically disbelieved and whose birth certificates, if they can be found and sent to them, are said to be 'forgeries'.

Under the 1971 Immigration Act British immigration officials have a virtually unrestricted power to detain, after cursory examination, any person seeking to enter or remain in the United Kingdom who is subject to immigration control. There is no judicial oversight to their decisions. When the act was passed it was intended that these powers would be used to detain for brief periods, pending imminent removal, people refused entry to Britain as visitors, students or workers, and people caught as 'overstayers'. It was not intended that it would routinely be used to detain asylum seekers, as it was from the mid-1980s onwards. The overwhelming majority of asylum seekers are detained, moreover, not at the end of the process, after their claims have been rejected and pending their removal, but at the beginning. In 1998–99, according to the Home Office's *Statistical Bulletin*, 'around 40 per cent of those detained had applied for asylum at ports of entry', and were therefore not even in a technical sense, contrary to common belief, 'illegal immigrants'. Government claims that nearly all detained asylum seekers are bogus and have had their claims rejected are presumably based on the fact that, having initially been detained at the time they made their claim, they may still be in detention months later when the Home Office rejects it and after they have lost their appeals. Amnesty International carried out a survey of a representative sample of 150 asylum seekers in detention in June 1996; it published the results in a report written by Richard Dunstan, entitled *Cell Culture*. Eighty-two per cent of these asylum seekers had been continuously detained since the time of application for asylum. Eighty-seven per cent had been detained before the Home Office had made a decision on their case. Less than 7 per cent had been detained solely to achieve their removal, and even they had already spent long periods in detention. The Labour government's 1998 white paper stated baldly, in paragraph 12.1, that 'Effective enforcement of immigration control requires some immigration offenders to be detained', blithely disregarding the fact that most of those locked up have not 'offended' at all, under any definition, that many of them subsequently attain the holy grail of refugee status, and that most of them are eventually released, for reasons which are no more clear than why they were detained in the first place.

There is no time limit on detention. The 1999 act did not introduce one, the government's white paper merely claiming, in paragraph 12.11, that:

Often detainees are held for longer periods only because they decide to use every conceivable avenue of multiple appeals to resist refusal or removal. A balance has to be struck in those circumstances between immediately releasing the person and running the risk of encouraging abusive claims and manipulation.

Amnesty International's sample had been held for an average of five months, which was slightly more than the average length of detention for all detainees at that time; one person had been held for eight months without receiving an initial decision from the Home Office. Some people are detained for a few days, others for a year or more; one exceptional case was three years. The absence of any release date for detainees, unlike for ordinary prisoners, is one of the hardest and most demoralising aspects of detention, especially for new arrivals in detention centres and prisons when they discover that others have been incarcerated for months and even years. Detainees, including some who are initially resilient and even cheerful, gradually decline. Between 1987 and 2000 at least nine asylum seekers committed suicide or for other causes died in various forms of detention. A report by C.K. Pourgourides and other medical practitioners, entitled *A Second Exile*, gives a full account of the effects of detention on the mental and physical health of detainees, including many examples and quotations from detainees themselves. It says, 'the responses to detention, namely hopelessness, helplessness, powerlessness, despair, despondency, demotivation, distress, anxiety and so on are predictable and *understandable*. They are *normal* responses to an abnormal situation.' And it concludes:

Detention, based on the evidence presented, ... *recreates* the oppression from which people have fled. It places detainees in predicaments parallel to those they may have faced under torture or previous detention. It maintains the mechanisms of persecution which precipitated their flight. Detention is therefore clearly abusive and inhumane. This report has presented compelling evidence against detention, which is a noxious practice which should be opposed on medical and humanitarian grounds.

A Nigerian detainee sent the *Campsfield Monitor* the following poem from Bullingdon prison, where he was imprisoned following a protest at Campsfield detention centre, which said something similar:

> Arrived;
> Immigration;
> Interrogation;

Detention; detained; imprisoned.
Group 4: abuse, threat, discrimination.
Case: adjudicator, hearing, appeal dismissed.
Meanwhile: abuse, repeated; threats.
Fed up: protest, demonstrate.
Arrested; interrogated; charged.
Court; magistrates; Solicitors.
Remanded; suppressed; but supported.
Court; adjourned, Crown, Barristers; Court, case ...
And still ...
They continue to remind me of
Horrors faced back home.

The Labour government, while admitting that the purpose of much of its 'toughness' is deterrence, continues to maintain, as the Tories did, that detention is used only 'as a last resort', in cases where it is absolutely necessary. Britain locks up over 9,000 asylum seekers each year. At any one time there are now around 800 asylum seekers detained. In addition others, often the fathers of small children who, sadly, travel to visit them in detention, are locked up for violations of immigration rules, such as 'overstaying', or working without permission. The Home Office claims that less than 1 per cent of asylum seekers are detained. This figure is obtained by taking the numbers detained as a percentage of the total backlog of people with unresolved claims. The percentage of new applicants detained is much higher; immigration officials detain around 14 per cent of all those who arrive and claim asylum. Ministers have a stock response to questions about detention, which is pasted into all their replies to letters. The following quotation happens to be from a letter from the Conservative Home Office minister Charles Wardle to the Tory MP John Patten, dated 15 April 1994, in response to representations from one of his constituents; subsequent letters from Labour ministers have used exactly the same phraseology, presumably plucked from Home Office computers:

It is Immigration Service policy to use detention only as a last resort. Temporary admission is granted wherever possible and detention is authorised only when there is no other alternative and where there are good grounds for believing that the person will not comply with the terms of temporary admission. In deciding whether to detain account is taken of all relevant circumstances, including the means by which the person arrived in this country and any past immigration history, and the person's ties with the United Kingdom, such as close relatives here.

In practice, only a very small proportion of asylum seekers are detained. Detained cases receive a very high priority and the need for continued detention is reviewed regularly. It is not in our interest to detain a person for longer than is necessary and if there is any indication that asylum is likely to be granted then the person is released immediately.

However it is impossible to discern why some people are detained and others, whose cases and histories are similar, are not. It is therefore impossible to escape the conclusion that detention is merely intended to act as a deterrent, and performs no function whatsoever in controlling refugees once they have arrived in Britain. Apart from an increased vulnerability to detention of certain nationalities, the process is arbitrary. The best advice to any intending asylum seeker would be to make sure he or she was at the back of the queue at the immigration counters. There is much evidence that immigration officials simply fill up the available spaces in prisons and detention centres, and give the more fortunate latecomers 'temporary admission'. On the other hand some detainees are released, in equally arbitrary fashion, before they have had any response from the Home Office, as well as when they are granted refugee status. Release may be in response to appeals from friends and visitors, or it may be for no apparent reason at all, thus making it even harder to understand why detention was resorted to in the first place. No reasons have to be given, either for detention or for release. An immigration official, asked why he refused to give temporary admission to a Zairean student, said 'We believe he is likely to abscond.' Asked what evidence he had for this belief, since the asylum seeker had been detained when he applied for asylum at Heathrow airport, he said merely 'We are not a court of law.' The Zairean was eventually released on bail, with sureties of several thousand pounds. A few months later his appeal was heard and he was given refugee status. After similar interventions another Zairean, who had also been detained at Heathrow, was given temporary admission, which meant he had no need to find sureties and apply for bail. But his appeal against Home Office refusal has never been heard. Amnesty International in *Prisoners Without a Voice* reports that the government, repeatedly pressed for figures on asylum seekers 'absconding', finally vouchsafed that in the period 1992–94, of 37,120 people who were refused asylum, 220, or 0.59%, had absconded.

The other 'reason' sometimes given for detention, that the person had false documents, is incompatible at least with the spirit of article 31 of the UN Convention on Refugees (see p. 75). As Amnesty International comments in *Cell Culture*, 'international standards do not permit asylum-seekers to be detained simply because they have used false travel documents'. The arbitrariness of immigration officials' decisions to detain has been confirmed by many, including the government's own Chief Inspector of Prisons, Sir David Ramsbotham, whose report on Campsfield detention centre in 1998 said the following:

It is abundantly clear from our inspections of Campsfield House, Tinsley House, and the detention wing at HMP Rochester, as well as what we have seen at Haslar and other prisons in which immigration detainees are held, that in the view of the Immigration Service and contractor's staff there is little or no consistency, or logic, in current arrangements for deciding upon detention, nor in how detention is managed. The Immigration Service needs to re-examine the criteria and process of detention to ensure that they are readily understood by all involved and that detention is used for the shortest possible time.

In particular, Ramsbotham recommended, as have many other authorities, that detainees should be given written reasons for their detention and that there should be 'judicial oversight' of decisions to detain. However the Labour government's white paper claimed that 'There is no reason to believe that the administrative process has led to people being improperly detained.' Its 1999 Act, in spite of expectations to the contrary, introduced no provision of a judicial element in decisions to detain. There is not even any proposal to provide detailed and specific written reasons for a decision to detain; merely a 'checklist', to be ticked by officials.

The only recourse that detainees have is to apply for bail. Until Labour instituted automatic bail hearings (see p. 121), whether detainees did so depended, however, on whether they had determined lawyers, which probably depended on whether they had visitors. Above all, success depended, and continues to depend, on whether they happened to be visited by people who were willing to stand bail for them, or to find others who were. Commonly two sureties of £2,000 each are required. Although detainees have sometimes been released on much lower sureties, adjudicators have been known to demand larger amounts in court in front of detainees, thus putting enormous pressure on supporters to up the amount they are offering. Few asylum detainees have local contacts who can help them. Local support groups arrange visits, but who gets these visits depends on luck, for example on whether another detainee gives a name to a visitor. Until recently there was no presumption of liberty, as there is in criminal cases. Detainees and their sureties have to convince an adjudicator that they will not abscond, that they have an address to go to, and that someone will make sure they report at police stations and turn up in court. An Algerian, one of the sample of asylum seekers cited in Amnesty's *Cell Culture*, was refused bail four times, told by one adjudicator that he had 'no incentive to comply with any conditions' and by another that 'I do not believe I have to give reasons. I think there is a chance the appellant will not attend court'; a month later he was suddenly released on temporary admission, after over a year in detention, and granted asylum. Bail is granted or denied on the whim of adjudicators. The *Campsfield Monitor*, produced by the Campaign to Close Campsfield, relates the following in its July 1997 issue:

... I went to stand bail for a detained asylum seeker. A touching family scene; a father, mother and rather bright four-year-old in a public place, an immigration court ... the infant runs first to one parent, then to the other. ... This family group remains together for five hours, moving from room to room. ... Then they separate. The father is led off by a private Group 4 guard. ... Back to prison; there is to be no bail. The adjudicator refuses to say why.

The mother contains her grief just as far as the stairs ... then she throws her shawl over her head, collapses on the floor, and howls. ...

The Labour government's 1999 act provides for two automatic bail hearings. There is no provision for further bail hearings after the first two. Bail hearings may be heard in detention centres or prisons, even by TV link. There is no guarantee of legal representation, although the act does introduce legal aid for those fortunate enough to have found legal representatives. The requirement for large sureties is unchanged. The bill did not provide for a presumption of liberty. An acceptance of this right was one of the few concessions won in committee and incorporated in the act, but it was so hedged around with conditions as to be almost meaningless. Some legal observers believe that the changes will make the situation worse rather than better, providing a rubber stamp for the arbitrary decisions of immigration officials.

The more than 800 refugees who are currently detained are held in a variety of detention centres, in small holding centres at Heathrow, Gatwick and other ports, in police stations and in many ordinary prisons. Up to half are in the latter. The use of Pentonville prison was abandoned in the mid-1990s after its governor and Board of Visitors objected to holding innocent asylum seekers, and after several hunger strikes by Algerians and the death in 1993 of a Zairean, Omasese Lumumba, as a result, the inquest jury ruled, of the 'use of improper methods and excessive force in the process of control and restraint' by prison officers. Asylum seekers began to be detained in the mid-1980s. Initially the only detention centre available was Harmondsworth, a decrepit collection of buildings near Heathrow airport, with a capacity for 95 people; it had been used for immigration detainees since 1970 and was run by private security companies, first Securicor and then Group 4; it is now finally to be abandoned and replaced in 2002 by a new detention centre nearby at Hatton Cross, to be run by Burns Ltd, another private security company. In 1987, when the Home Office ran out of detention spaces, 100 refugees, mostly Sri Lankan Tamils, were detained in a converted ferry in Harwich harbour; the ship broke its moorings in a storm and ran aground, and the experiment was abandoned. In 1989 the Home Office opened a new detention centre, run by the prison service, in an old naval barracks at Haslar, near Portsmouth, with a capacity for 150 people; detainees are kept in two large and noisy dormitories, but have access to educational facilities and a sports ground. In November 1993 the government opened another detention centre, Campsfield immigration detention centre, which has a capacity of 200 and is run by Group 4. In July 1994 and May 1995 D and E wings of Rochester prison were redesignated as detention wings, with a capacity of 198. Campsfield and Rochester enabled more asylum seekers to be detained, rather than any reduction in the numbers held in ordinary prisons. While the latter rose higher than ever, to around 300, the total numbers detained increased from about 250 in early 1993 to over 600 in 1995 and about 750 in 1996. In May 1996 a new purpose-built detention centre was opened at Tinsley House (sic) near Gatwick airport, privately built by a subsidiary of the British Airports

Authority, and privately run by a US company, the Wackenhut Corporation, with a capacity to detain 150 men and women. The numbers detained increased to more than 800.

The Rochester detention wings are run by the prison service with a regime identical to that of a prison, with the sole exception that asylum seekers are not locked up on the same wing as criminals. As in prisons, no phone calls can be received, even from lawyers. Normally detainees are locked into their cells from 8 p.m. to 8 a.m. and the doors clang shut again at 11.30 and 4.30; sometimes they are locked in for 22 hours a day. In January 2000 HM Inspectorate of Prisons published a report on Rochester by its chief inspector Sir David Ramsbotham, who wrote in the preface that 'I know that this dreadful report will not make comfortable reading ... but it is my job to report what we find and not what people would like us to find.' He wrote of the 'disgrace' of 'filthy dirty accommodation' and said 'Most of all, I must express my concern at the poor treatment and conditions of the ... asylum seekers, immigration detainees and other foreign nationals who form almost half the prison population.' The cells on D wing looked 'rather like a cluttered toilet'. Two unoccupied cells were covered in congealed blood and the blood stains of an asylum seeker who 'had deliberately cut himself'. There was no attempt to explain procedures in languages the detainees could understand, and some were in segregation for failing to comply with them. And so on. Campsfield detainees are threatened with transfer to Rochester as a means of discipline. One of them reported that, at Rochester, he had a belt stolen by a guard. When he complained, he was accused of having threatened to beat the guard with it and was put into isolation for five days. Another reported that he was beaten 'for a whole day'. One detainee tried to retain his sanity by spending his days copying out articles from *Le Monde*.

The Labour government intends to expand the numbers detained. Its white paper was unspecific about this, saying merely that the use of dedicated detention centres is 'preferable' to the use of prisons, without any commitment to comply with UNHCR guidelines by ending detention in prisons. The government plans to open a detention centre at Aldington, near Folkestone, and another one by creating a detention wing to hold 110 refugees in Lindholm prison near Doncaster. In March 2000 it opened a 'reception facility' in a former military barracks at Oakington near Cambridge, with a capacity for 400 people, run by Group 4. Oakington is to be used to process on site the applications of asylum seekers, including families with small children, mainly people who arrived at Dover without papers or clandestinely in the back of lorries, whose claims are being 'fast tracked', and to deport them directly from there if they are rejected. The camp is virtually a prison, with its occupants allowed to leave only for specific purposes and with an escort. The families are to be separated, with men kept apart from women and children. A week after it was opened, six detainees climbed the fence and escaped. In June 2000 a new detention centre was opened at Thurleigh, north of Peterborough. In April 2000 William Hague, leader of the Conservative opposition, proposed that all new asylum seekers should be detained in 'secure reception centres'. The Home Office response, according to the *Guardian* of April 19 2000, was that this would cost 'an extra £850 million' a year. Nevertheless in June the government announced its intention to increase the number of detention spaces available from 900 to 4,000 so as to be able to detain all those whose applications for asylum had been turned down.

The detention centres are run by private security firms. Before the election, according to quotes from the 26 June 1998 issue of *Private Eye*, Jack Straw told the 1996 Prison Officers' Association conference that:

I find it morally unacceptable for the private sector to undertake the incarceration of those whom the state has decided need to be imprisoned ... almost all people believe that this is one area where a free market does not exist.

Once in government, he told the 1998 Prison Officers' Association conference that:

As a responsible government we have committed ourselves to providing best value and to achieve high performance, efficiency and effectiveness. Current cost comparison research indicates that privately managed prisons are between eight and 15 percent less costly than their counterparts in the public sector. The difference is accounted for almost entirely by lower staff ratios, lower staff costs, including pension arrangements and salaries; and greater availability of staff with fewer holidays.

Official figures reported in Amnesty International's *Cell Culture* were that in 1995 the average cost of holding a person in an immigration detention centre was 'about £560 per week', compared to about £450 in prisons. In 1997, after a mass protest destroyed some of the buildings, the cost per person per week of detention at Campsfield rose to over £700. But the detention centres continue to be run by Group 4 and Wackenhut. Group 4 lost the contract for Harmondsworth detention centre in 1999 to another private company, Burns Ltd, which according to the Home Office press release (which nevertheless felt obliged to praise Group 4 for its excellent work) put in a lower bid. Ominously, under Labour's new Act, the staff of private contractors are to be given more powers.

CAMPSFIELD IMMIGRATION DETENTION CENTRE

Campsfield 'House', as governments like to call it, has been open since 1993, and is still the largest of the detention centres. The great majority of its detainees are asylum seekers. Until 1997, around 50 of them were women. It has the aspect of a concentration camp. Its 20-foot high metal fences have mesh whose holes are slightly too small for fingers. There are 42 video cameras on the fence and inside. Periodically, as a result of protests inside and outside and attempted escapes, the fortifications are added to. Additional fences have been built parallel to the existing external fences. Razor wire has been put along the top of the entire length of the external fence.

Campsfield is run by the private security company Group 4 Securitas Ltd. Its guards are currently paid £4.50 an hour, work 12-hour day or night shifts, and receive virtually no training except, for some of them, in the use of control and restraint techniques and suicide awareness. The report on Campsfield by Sir David Ramsbotham, HM Chief Inspector of Prisons, carried out on 13–15 October 1997, quoted detainees as saying that 'staff were rude, racist, used inappropriate language, and teased and intimidated them'. The *Campsfield Monitor* has published numerous accounts of the racist behaviour of Group 4 guards and reports by detainees that guards call them 'fucking niggers', 'lazy pussies' and 'black monkeys', and tell them to 'go back to your own country if you do not like it here'. A man in his forties told the *Campsfield Monitor* that he was dragged out of the shower naked in front of women and men. Another detainee said Group 4 guards kicked him in the stomach 'to see if it really hurts'; he subsequently had a major operation.

Inside the high fences, detainees are not confined to their rooms, most of which are shared. There is a loudspeaker system which appears to be unceasing, with calls to the telephone, interviews and other announcements. There are two classes a week in basic English and one volunteer-run art class but no other educational facilities. There is a sports hall but outdoor access is confined to small paved areas; detainees have never had access to the centre's football field, on the grounds, variously, that it is 'waterlogged' or, as HM prison inspectors were told, that 'building work ... was taking place'. There are telephones, but no means of obtaining cash or phone cards to use them, for example through paid work, except from friends and visitors. Asylum Welcome, a charity set up in Oxford, arranges visits for as many detainees as possible, but is hampered by Group 4's refusal to provide lists of names and therefore relies on information supplied by other detainees. Visitors, especially former detainees, are sometimes unaccountably excluded by Group 4. Medical facilities are inadequate. Group 4 put a contract for medical services out to tender; none of the local GP practices was willing to bid for it because they considered that an adequate service could not be provided with the money on offer. Eventually Group 4 engaged part-time a retired GP who also worked at Bullingdon prison. Detainees, sometimes sick and traumatised and suffering the aftermath of torture, have difficulty in gaining access to the doctor or nurses, and when they do they are likely to have their problems ignored and merely to be prescribed paracetamol. Referral to hospital or to specialists is sometimes so delayed that illnesses which could have been treated at early stages become severe. The detainee who was kicked in the stomach, after complaining of severe pain for a week, eventually collapsed unconscious and had to be removed to hospital, where he had a major operation which could have been averted. A young Moroccan spent a year in Campsfield and lost most of his teeth. Some detainees, including several who were considered to be at risk of suicide, have been moved to the hospital wings of prisons on the grounds that Campsfield facilities are inadequate.

There have been two reports on Campsfield by HM Inspectorate of Prisons, the first by Judge Stephen Tumim, published in 1995, the second by Sir David Ramsbotham, published in 1998. Both contained strong criticisms. Tumim noted a 'prevailing sadness' and a 'settled misery' among detainees. Ramsbotham was particularly critical of the lack of rules governing the running of the centre, which he said constituted a danger for both detainees and staff. He noted that 'When detainees begin to behave in a disruptive way the only control option appears to be a removal to prison detention, which is a grossly inappropriate and unsatisfactory sanction.' The threat and actuality of removal to other prisons is one of the aspects of Campsfield that detainees find hardest to bear. The threat when Campsfield was first opened was Haslar; it is now Rochester. Not only are both places probably worse than Campsfield, although some detainees report that prison guards are less racist than Group 4, but removal often means the loss or partial loss of visitors, friends and other support networks. Detainees have also been transferred to Winson Green, Bullingdon, Wormwood Scrubs, Holloway and Blakenhurst prisons.

By 1997 at least 35 detainees had been removed to other prisons. During 1997, according to the Ramsbotham report, 24 detainees were removed 'at the request of Group 4 staff'. The process, like detention itself, is arbitrary and unaccountable. Decisions to remove are formally made by immigration officers, but they are generally at the request of, or after consultation with, Group 4. There are no legal processes, no time limits, no formal charges and sometimes no stated reasons, written or other. In reality removals seldom follow anything which might truly be described as 'disruptive behaviour'. Ramsbotham himself reported that the Group 4 centre manager had told him that 'the transfer of detainees to prison was dependent on available spaces; they could be moved arbitrarily regardless of good or bad behaviour'. Visitors speculate that 'arbitrary and unexplained transfers' might have as their purpose to separate detainees from visitors and friends and so make deportation easier. Dr Evan Harris, the Liberal Democrat MP in whose constituency Campsfield is, and who has been active in the defence of refugees and highly critical of detention at Campsfield, reported at a public meeting organised by the Campaign to Close Campsfield that the head of Home Office enforcement had told him that, since the 'detainee population' was 800–900 and the places in detention centres were only 500–600, when places became available in prisons it was necessary to take them up. In addition, Evan Harris said, people who are 'fingered' for transfer by profit-making private security companies are liable to include people who incur extra costs, for example because they are ill and require escorts to hospital. Who gets transferred also has much to do with the likes and dislikes of Group 4 guards. As the October 1996 issue no. 8 of the *Campsfield Monitor* reported,

One detainee, fleeing from a dictatorship in Africa, described the situation as 'almost like Africa': 'it's a dictatorship, if you don't do what they say, it will cost you'. Some detainees have a good relationship with the guards; others are disliked by them and often reported to immigration officials. A visitor reports that detainees are subjected to 'constant petty harassment'; 'their nerves are taut', but if they respond to provocation, transfer to Rochester is threatened.

A detainee wrote to the *Campsfield Monitor* to say that two other detainees were removed to prison 'because they were giving out information for help'. Removals from Campsfield commonly follow complaints. Most detainees therefore do not complain. The man who was dragged naked from the shower was removed to Rochester after he had complained of his shameful treatment. Removals have followed complaints about scalding water in the showers, under-cooked chicken, Group 4's behaviour. Four people were transferred from Campsfield to Winson Green prison in Birmingham, after a fire was started in a toilet. None of them had done it. One of them, an Algerian who now has refugee status, states that he was accused of setting the fire; his lawyer subsequently obtained a letter from the Home Office saying he was not suspected of participating in the arson incident. He nevertheless spent nearly two months in Winson Green, locked up with murderers. What he had done was to complain about Group 4 showing a pornographic video in the room next door to where they were trying to say their prayers; the supervisor ignored his complaint and he then, refusing to be intimidated, asked a visitor to transmit the complaint direct to the chief immigration officer at Campsfield. Another detainee was transferred to Winson Green after he was accused of using obscene language to a female Group 4 guard, who appeared to have misinterpreted the laughter of a group of Algerians as directed at her (another Group 4 guard later accused a detainee of using an identical phrase). The Algerian spoke no English; his friends described him as '*un pur*' and said they could not understand why he was picked on. They were told by an immigration official that there was no problem; obviously these things had not been said. A few weeks later ten Group 4 guards came into his room while he was asleep and told him to come with them; when he tried to refuse, they tricked him, telling him he was not being taken to prison. But he too spent months in Winson Green.

Detainees, most of the time, bear all this with extraordinary fortitude. Almost without exception, they are unfailingly polite to those who come to visit them. Their harsh treatment at the hands of Group 4 and the authorities does not prevent them from showing great appreciation for the efforts of those who do seek to help. Nevertheless detention is felt as bitter injustice. This sense of injustice, the uncertainty about when or whether they will be released and whether or not they will finally be deported to further persecution, has led in some cases to severe depression, and in many cases to increasing listlessness, inability to concentrate 'on anything', and despair. It has also led to a series of protests, hunger strikes and attempts to escape. Before the razor wire was added to the fences, there were over a dozen escape attempts, some of them successful. Although the razor wire appeared to make escape impossible, two Indian refugees threatened with deportation, astonishingly, attempted it; one severely gashed his legs and was caught and moved to the hospital at Tinsley detention centre; the other fell on his head and remained, at first in a coma, in Oxford hospitals for many weeks, and was then moved, still in a very fragile state, to Rochester prison.

Early in 1994, after some asylum seekers detained at Pentonville prison had won their release with a hunger strike, ten Algerians, including one woman, went on hunger strike at Campsfield. The woman was removed to Holloway prison and then released; the others were removed to a private hospital prison near York and, after local protests, they too were released. This was followed by a mass hunger strike, in which 180 of the 200 detainees in Campsfield took part. At the beginning of the strike several of them broke out into a courtyard and climbed onto a roof, where they could communicate with demonstrators outside. Others in other detention centres and prisons followed their example and went on hunger strike. After several weeks 15 of the Campsfield hunger strikers, described as 'ringleaders', were removed to Winson Green, Bullingdon and Blakenhurst prisons. Some of them were put in isolation cells, said, with grotesque inaccuracy, to be 'bad boys'. Two were put in bare strip cells as suicide risks, deprived of all their personal belongings including books and toothbrushes, given only an indestructible tunic and left shivering on the bare floor, a method of physical prevention of suicide which has since been ruled inhumane and inadmissable. They all ended up in hospital wings of the prisons but, convinced in part by their visitors that the authorities would allow them to do permanent damage to their organs but not to die, they eventually abandoned their hunger strike without being released. Since then there have been a number of other hunger strikes, at Campsfield, Rochester, Winson Green and Haslar, some of them coordinated across centres, although none on so large a scale.

In Campsfield, but not in other detention centres, there have in addition been protests which have taken the form of demonstrations and, on two occasions, large-scale physical destruction. On 5 June 1994, a mass protest followed the summary removal for deportation of Ali Tamarat, an Algerian. His fellow Algerians reacted angrily and climbed onto a roof to make their protest. They were joined by other detainees who came out into the courtyard. During a long night they caused material damage which the government claimed amounted to about £100,000. Group 4 left out a ladder which was used by six detainees to escape; a seventh was badly injured when an immigration officer pulled the ladder from underneath him; later detainees recaptured the ladder and another five people escaped. Group 4 fled and barricaded themselves in their offices. Riot police were called; detainees who were in the courtyard said some of them were beaten and that a Nigerian woman suffered a fractured kneecap; another woman was taken to Holloway prison with a broken leg; screams were heard by protesters outside after the riot police went in; several ambulances were called but observers, who counted their occupants as they left, failed to discover what had happened to them. One of the Algerians on the roof was seen jumping, head first, off it. The Home Office admitted only five serious injuries. Twenty-two detainees were taken to Oxford police station and then dispersed to various prisons. One of the few recommendations of the Tumim inspection report that has been implemented is that some of the Group 4 guards who run Campsfield have since been equipped with riot gear and trained to use it.

In May 1997, when the Algerian falsely accused of sexual harassment (see above) was removed to Winson Green prison, his friends, after spending the morning 'talking and talking', decided to climb onto a roof to protest and demand his return. They were joined by four others, demanding their own freedom. They stayed on the roof all night and most of the next day, with a little food and some blankets passed to them by detainees below. About 100 other detainees, refusing to be locked into their rooms, broke out into a courtyard and were eventually locked into another wing. Extra Group 4 guards were bussed into Campsfield in riot gear. An offer to mediate by Evan Harris MP was turned down. Eventually the rooftop protesters were forced down by the cold and the rain. They were eventually transferred to Winson Green, Rochester and Tinsley.

On August 20 1997 there was another mass protest, triggered by the early morning removal of two West African detainees. One of them was ill, resisted and woke everybody with his cries of pain. The detainees who saw his removal thought he was being strangled, and demanded to know why the two were being removed. Eventually nearly all of the detainees were outside in the courtyard protesting and displaying placards saying they were not criminals. Group 4 donned their riot gear, numerous police and extra guards were brought in, and, so the government claimed, £100,000 of material damage was caused by detainees. The next day Mike O'Brien, Home Office immigration minister, issued an inflammatory press statement headed 'BURNING BOOKS – IN A MOMENT OF MADNESS', ignoring the fact that library facilities were burned by one individual who was never identified by the authorities. 'The detainees', he said, 'destroyed their own facilities. ... The disturbance was firmly quelled and the police are now investigating whether to bring criminal charges against certain individuals.'

The government was clearly anxious for exemplary punishment, hoping this would deter future protests. Thirteen people were arrested. In the event, none of them was charged with starting a fire, although they were associated in the minds of many people with images of burnt buildings and smashed facilities. The charges were for violent disorder; they were later upped to riot, which carries a maximum sentence of ten years. Two lawyers told a meeting in Oxford, called to organise a Campsfield Nine Defence Campaign, that an officer at Banbury police station where police were taking statements said to them 'the charges were going nowhere' until they received a phone call from Jack Straw. Charges against three Caribbeans and one Lebanese boy were later dropped without explanation. The remaining nine were all West

African male asylum seekers, picked by Group 4. Yet 100 or so people of many nationalities and both sexes had protested. The process was a lottery, in which nine young West Africans were being scapegoated. Mike O'Brien nevertheless told demonstrators outside Campsfield that he confidently expected that the Nine 'would all go down'. Both before and after the trial, O'Brien repeatedly praised Group 4. Shortly before the trial the government announced it had renewed Group 4's contract, and O'Brien went to Campsfield to deliver an Investors in People training award to Group 4. During the trial defence lawyers told members of the defence campaign that they had clear indications from the prosecution that they were looking for a way of dropping the case but were under pressure to continue.

The case took ten months to come to trial. During this period, in Reading and Feltham Young Offenders Institutions and in Bullingdon prison, four of them made suicide attempts. Over half took anti-depressants. Four of them had been severely tortured by the Nigerian military regime from which they fled to find refuge in Britain; three were teenagers. Two now have refugee status, two have exceptional leave to remain. Members of the defence campaign visited the Nine in Bullingdon and Reading prisons and called for the charges to be dropped. They had little faith in the British justice system. The case might have hinged on the possible prejudices of the jury, who could have chosen to believe either the West African defendants or their white Group 4 accusers. Potential defence witnesses were nearly all fellow detainees, too scared to give evidence, unlikely to be believed if they did, and liable to deportation; the Home Office did in fact deport several potential witnesses. Most of the defendants were stuck with the solicitors who had represented them, or failed to do so, in their immigration cases. Supporters convinced some of them it was worth changing lawyers, and struggled with the administrative obstacles imposed by the prisons in obtaining letters and signatures from them, only to find that Judge King in pre-trial hearings refused the transfer of legal aid. He made an exception in one case. One of the Nigerians in Bullingdon prison, who was first on the indictment, decided to complain to the Law Society about his lawyer. He was allowed to transfer to Birnbergs and Nigel Leskin, who obtained refugee status for him at his second try, and he was then released on bail. Leskin worked on the case full time thereafter. Together they spent many hours in Banbury police station looking at film from the 42 surveillance cameras in Campsfield, returning with yet more evidence that Group 4 was telling lies, which Leskin and his counsel Henry Blaxland then used to devastating effect in court. Without them, the outcome could well have been different.

The trial at Oxford Crown Court started on 1 June 1998 and collapsed 17 days later. Nicholas Jarman, QC for the prosecution, said the case 'was based mainly on eye witness statements' by Group 4 guards. 'No prosecution properly conducted', he said, 'could or should invite a jury to convict on that evidence.' The prosecution's abandonment of the case came shortly after one of the Nine left the dock in acute desperation (the last Group 4 witness had, yet again, claimed to have 'recognised' him, this time carrying a 'heavy weight bar', although he had mentioned him in none of his three police statements), and a 17-year-old defendant had collapsed in uncontrollable sobs. The judge then directed the jury to give a verdict of Not Guilty, which it did with apparent relish. The jury consisted of eight white men and four women. None of them looked as though they might remotely belong to what Mike O'Brien on Radio 4 castigated as 'the extremist liberal chattering classes' who oppose Campsfield. Group 4's behaviour during the trial caused the jury to laugh in disbelief. After the trial collapsed, some of them spoke to protesters outside the court. One said quietly: 'Who should have been on trial was Group 4, not them.'

The court heard Chief Immigration Officer John Graham and 16 Group 4 witnesses, including Centre Manager John Jasper. These, the prosecution told the court, were all except two of the eye witnesses to be called. The prosecution had little video evidence it could use. Defence lawyers, in turn, had no need to produce any wider political defence. One by one, the witnesses were demolished. Over and over again, they admitted they might have been wrong or that they had told lies (an 'undeliberate lie', said one of them). Repeatedly they claimed to have 'recognised' defendants whom they had previously mentioned in none of their statements. Asked how they recognised them, they said it was through meal duties, or playing sports. 'Playing sports?' asked one defence lawyer. 'Yes.' 'Playing football?' 'Yes.' 'But my client never plays football, or any sport.' John Graham, the senior immigration official at Campsfield, claimed in his statement to the police to have 'recognised' at an incident the previous evening two of the defendants and one of the two detainees who were removed, and to have known them 'from my work at the centre'. In court he said, instead, that he had asked Group 4 for the names of 'the three most vociferous'. He said he 'could not understand his mistake', and also that he thought he had ordered the removal of one of the defendants. Tim Allen, former supervisor, who claimed to have been hit with a dumb-bell by one of the defendants, was shown a video by defence lawyer David Bright. He acknowledged that the defendant would have had to be on the film if he had indeed hit him, picked out a detainee on the film and then had to admit it was not the defendant, yet continued to maintain that he knew the defendant had hit him.

Witnesses repeatedly contradicted themselves. John Jasper, Group 4 manager, who said he was previously a chief superintendent in the West Midlands police force, was asked about notices recommending respect for detainees and avoidance of racial abuse. He said they were displayed in corridors but was unable to say where, and finally admitted that he did not know of any that were visible to detainees. Jane Essery told the prosecution she felt 'fearful' and 'panicky'. Henry Blaxland produced the transcript of a statement she had made to Group 4 management in which she said: 'I felt very calm, actually.' Her response was that she had 'never heard that tape; I never heard it would be used in evidence.'

Group 4 guard Caryn Mitchell-Hill said she had been alone in a corridor when a defendant took her by the shoulders and said 'Where are you going white bitch?'; 'I put my knee up, aiming for the groin area. In all honesty, I don't know whether I made contact.' Shown a video of herself at the same time in a different area with two other guards, she refused to identify herself though she identified the other two, surmised that she might have been another guard, finally admitted it must have been her but then suggested it must have been another day; 'at no point did I end up in the dining room area', she insisted. Various stories were told by different guards about Chris Barry, a 20-stone guard who collapsed in a corridor. He was said to have had a plastic bottle full of a chemical substance thrown at him, or been hit on the head by it, or not to have been hit at all, or to have fallen as he was being dragged through a door by a colleague. Barry himself said his shirt was soaked by a chemical and torn, that he was repeatedly hit and punched, and that he was 'concussed'. Videos showed him a few minutes later walking along in a clean and dry shirt, and then on a roof. Tim Allen, filmed on the roof with him, nevertheless continued to deny strenuously that Chris Barry had been on the roof.

Group 4 admitted to doing some damage themselves. Two of them, Mo Stone (stand-in supervisor) and Paul Bean (now a prison officer) admitted they had hit detainees with their batons on the head (although they had aimed for their arms as they were trained to do). Stone said he had not sought to discover who he had hit or whether the person was seriously hurt, had not made a report, and that: 'I don't regret doing it, but I regret that it happened.' Bean said he had drawn his baton because he had been hit by a dumb-bell and was 'scared'. In his police statement he had said that he drew his baton before he was struck. John Allen, supervisor, was questioned about the 'control and restraint' techniques used in the removal. Asked whether the detainee was held by the neck, he said 'No.' The defence then produced a video of the removal which showed the detainee being held by the neck. John Allen said: 'Like everybody who passes their driving test, they don't do it perfectly every time. ... It was not text book.'

Group 4 did some material damage too. Mo Stone was asked by David Bright whether he personally had smashed a telephone in the Ladies' Day Room. 'I did not.' Asked whether if witnesses gave evidence that he had done so, he would call them liars, he said: 'I will openly admit that I did take one of the phones apart. I was worried that detainees would communicate with the outside world. ... Some of them might have got back into the building, they could be used as a means of communication.' He did not tell the police he had done this. Told he had not dismantled the phone, but smashed it, using his baton, he said he used the baton 'to pull the cable out of its socket'. Four of them were 'trying to do it'. Later Terry Morley admitted he had 'smashed the handset off the telephone' because detainees were using it. Asked why there was no reference to this incident in his police statement, he shrugged. Asked why he thought photographs were taken of the damage, he said it was 'as evidence of what damage was done'. 'By whom? Detainees?' 'Yes.' 'Did it enter your mind to tell the police about the smashed telephone in case there was any doubt who did it?' 'No.' David Bright showed a copy of a letter written to campaigners on behalf of the Home Secretary, which said, explaining the decision to prosecute detainees: 'All the pay phones and other telephones were ripped from the walls.' He suggested that Group 4 might have done other damage as well.

The spectacle of Group 4 in court had a notable effect not only on the prosecution, but also on the judge. Judge Morton Jack initially made disparaging remarks about the detainees. In refusing to accept that one of the defendants, who had been held in Reading Young Offenders Institution, was 17, he said the defendant had 'told lies'. When detainees' lawyers asked for all of them to have hearing aids, he said he detected 'an element of fashion catching on'. His early decisions went against the defence. He refused to order the withdrawal from the jury's bundles of photographs of the fire damage to Campsfield, although lawyers argued that, as none of their clients was accused of this damage, to show it was prejudicial. He refused to accept Henry Blaxland's argument that, if the removal of one of the detainees could be shown to have been carried out unlawfully, this would be relevant to the defence. He said he would be strict on extraneous matter but allowed John Graham to make derogatory remarks about detainees who 'tore up their documents' and 'make applications in two or three names', yet refused to allow the barrister Frances Webber to refute what she called his 'inflammatory and inaccurate statements'. He ruled that a minor must come to court from mental hospital, heavily drugged and with an escort of two nurses, refusing to accept legal arguments by Frances Webber that this was inhumane and within his power to prevent, and only agreeing to discharge the jury in his case four days later, after the hospital refused to send him to court and he had given the prosecution the opportunity to seek a second medical opinion. Yet, as the case went on, the judge's attitude changed. By the end, clearly irritated by Group 4, he was intervening to help lawyers to clarify the contradictions in their evidence.

After the Nine's acquittal, five of them were transferred to Rochester prison, which they found hard to bear. After much pressure from their supporters and from the media, and two more suicide attempts, all of them were eventually released from Rochester on temporary admission. But most are left in limbo, their claims undecided, and still under threat of deportation. The brutal response from the Home Secretary, in a letter to campaigners over the signature of Graeme J. Kyle, was that the trial 'simply interrupted the arrangements for the removal of those who have no claim to remain in the United Kingdom. Now that the trial has been completed, the removal of those who have no further basis to remain will continue.' After the ignominy of Group 4 in court, and after the suffering inflicted by Group 4 and the British state on innocent people, ministers apparently intended to carry on business as usual, with no apology or compensation for the Nine, and no action against Group 4. Group 4 still has its contract to run Campsfield. Its staff have not been disciplined, sacked or even moved elsewhere. The Campsfield Nine Defence Campaign called for all the Nine to be freed and granted refugee status or exceptional leave to remain, for the resignation of Mike O'Brien, for an apology and compensation from Jack Straw, for criminal charges against Group 4 and the scrapping of its contract. So far Mike O'Brien has been moved to another job. Lawyers have embarked on claims for damages for malicious prosecution from Group 4 and the Home Office. In notable victories, they have won their case in the High Court that John Quaquah, one of the Nine, should not be deported by the Home Office while he is suing the Home Office and Group 4, because the case was of sufficient public importance and the Home Office had not taken adequate account of Mr Quaquah's human rights. In another High Court judgment Mr Justice Turner said that 'if the conduct of the Group 4 officers both during the incident of unrest itself as well as their conduct in giving unreliable/false evidence was established, then it satisfied the description of having been "wicked"'.

The authorities' heavy-handed action did not have its intended result. Shortly after the trial ended, the detainees at Campsfield protested again. Announcing their action, hunger strikers at Campsfield put out the following statement:

We've come to UK seeking shelter from injustice, hoping to get back our right to live full lives, just like you do. The right that has been taken away from us, back in our home countries. Maybe some of us have overstayed, or entered Britain illegally. But we didn't do this for ill purposes. We are not criminals, we are the victims. English people have acquired incredible fortune due to their pious nature. Why not share some of it with us. Give us a chance to prove ourselves. We don't need much.

Some of us have families here. They need our support and love. Why lock us up like animals, separate from our wives and children. We did not commit any crimes.

The hunger strikers' spokesperson, a Nigerian opponent of the military regime and a pastor, was removed to Rochester. Three months later he got refugee status.

4   RESISTANCE

RESISTANCE IN BRITAIN

The protests and hunger strikes by detainees themselves at Campsfield and other refugee prisons have done more than anything else to draw attention to the plight of refugees and other migrants. They have received a good deal of media coverage, some of it sympathetic, and attracted support from campaigners and other members of the public. Those who are locked up inside prisons and detention centres are driven to desperation, and, although they demonstrate great courage, perhaps feel they have little to lose by protesting. On the other hand refugees who are outside, on temporary admission and waiting for the results of their claims, and even those who have been granted refugee status, are hesitant about engaging in protest and demonstrations and any form of public activity which might land them back in detention or, they fear, damage their cases and make deportation more likely. An Algerian released after his hunger strike at Campsfield in early 1994 was detained again after he was interviewed on television at a demonstration outside Campsfield; the same fate befell a Ghanaian who spoke on television. The document granting refugee status states that the refugee may be deported 'if during your stay in the United Kingdom you take part in activities involving for example the support or encouragement of violence or the conspiracy to cause violence, whether in the United Kingdom or abroad, so as to endanger national security or public order'. In addition refugees may be reluctant to draw the attention of the authorities in their own countries to themselves in case they are later deported.

There are some exceptions to this reticence, among both individuals and groups. The Algerian who was falsely accused of setting fire to a toilet and removed to Winson Green (see p. 126) has been determined to publicise his treatment and not to let Group 4 get away with it. Some of the Campsfield Nine have been willing to speak publicly at meetings and to come to demonstrations. The Onibiyo family conducted a sustained public campaign to save Abdul and his son Ade from deportation; although Abdul was deported to Nigeria and imprisoned and tortured, he eventually escaped and won refugee status after more campaigning, and in spite of the Onibiyo family's frequently stated belief that Straw and O'Brien reneged on pre-election promises they had made. Abdul then continued to speak at public meetings. Others have campaigned publicly against their own deportation, often with success. Ivoiriens, as a national group, have demonstrated outside courts, at Campsfield and even outside their own embassy; some of them have been active in organising opposition groups with, unusually, a socialist orientation. Algerian and Zairean community groups have organised protests and spoken at meetings. Many in the Kurdish community, some of them PKK members, have been active protesters and demonstrators. But it is inherently hard for refugees, given the extreme precariousness of their situation, their vulnerability and the dangers they have faced and still face in their own countries, to organise active campaigns against their mistreatment by the British authorities.

It is a different matter for black communities who are already settled in Britain, many of whose members were born in Britain and who had from the start, unlike in other European countries, full political and voting rights if they had migrated from Commonwealth countries. Over the years there has been growing black self-organisation to assert black people's rights and against racism, police harassment, other forms of institutional discrimination and the far right. There have been a succession of organisations formed among black and Asian immigrants, sometimes jointly with white anti-racists, including the West Indian Standing Conference, the Campaign Against Racial Discrimination (CARD), the Joint Council for the Welfare of Immigrants (JCWI). The Institute of Race Relations, initially a white-led and staffed research organisation, later became radicalised and is now black-led; it produces the journal *Race and Class*. The Indian Workers' Associations (IWAs), first set up in the 1950s, with connections with the Communist Party of India, developed sometimes acrimonious relationships with the trade unions and the Labour Party. In the late 1960s Black Panthers were active in Brixton in South London. More recently Southall Black Sisters, the Southall Monitoring Group and the Newham Monitoring Project in London, in defending the rights of black people, have of necessity been engaged with asylum seekers, for example in protesting against the murder of Ibrahima Sey, a Ghanaian asylum seeker killed by police. Some black-led organisations, in particular in the late 1990s the National Assembly Against Racism (NAAR), have explicitly extended their campaigning to refugees and other persecuted so-called 'illegal' migrants. They have pointed out that the increasing abuses of human rights and racist attitudes to which refugees and new migrants are subjected affect also the settled black communities. Since it has become a criminal offence for employers to employ people who do not have the correct immigration status, employers have become even more wary of employing anybody whom they suspect of being a foreigner, and especially black people. The greater emphasis on internal rather than border checks by immigration officials and police, and the greater powers of arrest, entry to private premises and the use of force given to immigration officials, is likely to subject black people, including long-term residents, to yet more harassment, demands to produce documents to prove their immigration status, and possibly detention, and will probably lead to greater solidarity between new and long-established migrants. On the other hand some members of established immigrant communities have been unwilling to support refugees and so-called 'bogus asylum seekers and illegal immigrants', affected perhaps by the prejudice fostered by the authorities and the media, and believing that people who are locked up must have committed some crime. In particular some who migrated from eastern Europe, Germany and elsewhere before and soon after the Second World War differentiate themselves from the people who are now doing so, claiming that, unlike themselves or their parents, the latter are not refugees but 'economic' migrants in search of a better life.

Since the 1950s, there has also been a succession of organisations, some of them official, supporting the rights of immigrants and campaigning against racist discrimination in immigration controls and racism in general. The local branches of the Race Relations Board and then the Commission for Racial Equality, the Community Relations Councils (CRCs) and now the Race Equality Councils, have acted to defend individuals faced with immigration problems, as well as against racism in general. The UNHCR and Amnesty International, with varying degrees of commitment and radicalism, have attacked the policies of governments towards refugees and asylum seekers. The Refugee Council, which is funded by the Home Office, has been critical of government policies. In the voluntary sector, Asylum Aid, a charity based in London, has both campaigned and provided legal services for refugees. The Medical Foundation for the Care of Victims of Torture has done much to support refugees, especially by providing medical evidence of torture for use in asylum appeals, and it also campaigns on behalf of refugees. The Immigration Law Practitioners' Association (ILPA) coordinates information and criticises British asylum policies. These organisations, with the Churches Commission for Racial Justice (CCRJ), have set up an Asylum Rights Campaign. An organisation, Bail for Immigration Detainees (BID), has been set up to find sureties. Asylum Welcome, a charity in Oxford, has organised visitors to Campsfield and supported increasing numbers of refugees outside Campsfield with their legal, housing and other social needs. There is a network of visitors' organisations, the Association of Visitors to Immigration Detainees (AVID), which has included visitors to detainees in Harmondsworth and Tinsley detention centres and Winchester and Haslar prisons. These organisations tend to argue for improvements in the system, for more fairness, for less racism in the application of immigration controls, rather than for their abolition.

The left in Britain has generally had a position of opposition to all immigration controls and the repeal of the various asylum and immigration acts. There have been many anti-racist campaigns and committees in different cities, with the involvement of trade unionists, students and others. For a while in the 1970s the Anti-Nazi League was a prominent national movement against racism and fascism which attracted much publicity. The Campaign Against Racism and Fascism (CARF), set up in 1977, has a bimonthly magazine and publishes a mass of information on state abuses of human rights, on racist attacks by the white population and the police, and so on. *Statewatch* magazine monitors the state and civil liberties, including the treatment of migrants and refugees, in Britain and Europe; it has unearthed a large amount of information on Fortress Europe and forced the European institutions to reveal information on their secretive activities in joint policing of crime and immigration. Inquest provides support to the families of black people who have died in custody. A local group, Dover Residents Against Racism, has been set up to campaign for the rights of asylum seekers in Dover and to defend them against attack. Counter-demonstrations against the National Front have been held in Dover, and have generally been successful in preventing the National Front from marching and rallying, in spite of massive police protection; they have been supported by the Anti-Nazi League and by anarchist and green groups, as well as the left in general, and have been welcomed by the local people they encounter opposed to 'those people', the fascists. The National Coalition of Anti-Deportation Campaigns (NCADC) provides support and helps with publicity and organisation for campaigns against the deportation of individuals and families and also against detention and for more general campaigns for the rights of refugees and migrants. It publishes a newsletter, distributes information and organises numerous meetings, and has paid campaigning officers in Birmingham, London and Manchester. Its strong support for very large numbers of anti-deportation campaigns has helped to create a climate of resistance against the inhumanities of the immigration and asylum system and to politicise this struggle. When some in the Asylum Rights Campaign preferred to lobby behind the scenes against Labour's Asylum and Immigration Bill in 1997–98, the NCADC and NAAR set up the Campaign for Asylum and Immigration Rights (CAIR).

The Campaign to Close Campsfield was set up in response to the opening of Campsfield immigration detention centre in November 1993, mainly on the initiative of Bill MacKeith, president of the Oxford and District Trades Union Council. The campaign was set up with three main objectives: the closing of Campsfield, the ending of all immigration detention, and the repeal of 'racist immigration laws'. The last of these was a compromise. The campaign is broad-based and some of its supporters argue that some form of immigration controls are necessary; others believe that to abolish the racist ones would be to abolish them all. The campaign has held monthly meetings and has demonstrated at midday on the last Saturday of each month outside Campsfield ever since it started over six years ago. On a national demonstration on 4 June 1994, the day before the first major protest inside Campsfield, there were some 500 people. The campaign has received letters from detainees expressing their appreciation of the demonstrations. Possibly their main usefulness has been in showing detainees that there are people out there who care about them. Group 4 has made intermittent and strenuous efforts to block communication between demonstrators and detainees. In the early days the prisoners could see the demonstrations from windows at the front of the building. When one-way glass was installed and then detainees were barred from these windows, the demonstrators went round to the back of the site. When they discovered they could see over the fence and shout to detainees in a courtyard by climbing trees, Group 4 cut down the trees. They have since extended metal sheeting to the full height of the fence, saying detainees 'needed protection from the wind'. Recently they have taken to preventing detainees from going out into the yard during demonstrations. Partly because of the razor wire on the top of the fence, the protesters have not yet devised a method of seeing over it. Demonstrators have come with drums and musical instruments. They have had support from green activists. During the year or so after Campsfield opened, and before the razor wire, some of the latter climbed fences and draped banners on them; demonstrators climbed into the centre; a woman climbed inside and got onto a roof before she was violently dragged down by Group 4 guards, who had to call an ambulance. In the summer of 1995 there was a protest camp in a Ministry of Defence-owned piece of land adjacent to the prison which lasted for several weeks before the campers were evicted; campers have returned for brief periods over the years. Six supporters walked to London and delivered a 5,000-signature petition, in a box bound with barbed wire and red roses, to Downing Street. In 1997, after the Nine had been arrested and charged with riot, protesters paid what was meant to be a surprise visit to Jack Straw one weekend when he was staying at his period cottage in the Cotswold village of Minster Lovell. The plan was to put up a tall fence in front of his house. When the protesters arrived at the top of the rise above the village they saw police with a dozen vans and on horses, who allowed them to reach the main street some yards from Straw's house before pushing them back. Later two protesters camped outside Campsfield and announced to the media that they were digging a tunnel under the fence.

Supporters of the Campaign to Close Campsfield have also put resolutions to Labour Party branches and constituencies, to Labour's 1995 annual conference and to local councils and trade unions, with some successes. In 1994 Oxfordshire County Council passed a resolution critical of the practice of detention at Campsfield. Closure of Campsfield and all detention centres is the policy of both Labour constituency parties in Oxford. Oxford City Council failed to pass a resolution put forward by the Labour group calling for Campsfield to be closed only when a minority of right-wing Labour councillors allied with opposition councillors to vote against it. Closure of Campsfield and all detention centres is the national policy of the Manufacturing Science Finance Union (MSF), the National Union of Journalists (NUJ), the National Association of Teachers in Further and Higher Education (NATFHE) and the Transport and General Workers Union (TGWU), and of the trades council movement of England and Wales. A letter circulated in

1994 by Sir William Hayter, former head of New College at Oxford University, stating that 'Asylum seekers, who are innocent of any crime, should not be detained', expressing concern at 'a dangerous undermining of democratic principles and the rule of law' which 'could open the way to further abuses', and calling for the early release of the detainees, was sent to the then prime minister, John Major. It was signed by over 100 senior members of Oxford university, including ten present or former heads of colleges and 20 professors. Charles Wardle, Home Office minister in charge of immigration at the time, dismissed the protesters as 'a motley collection of the far left and liberals'. In 1998 a further letter, supported by Professor Michael Dummett and Dr Alan Ryan, current warden of New College, containing similarly strong criticisms of Campsfield, appealed to the prime minister, Tony Blair, 'to bring this cruel system to an end without delay' and supported the Campsfield Nine; it was signed by 112 senior members of Oxford university, including four current and three former heads of colleges and 27 professors.

There is also a Campaign to Close Harmondsworth which organises regular demonstrations. The Kent Campaign for Asylum Seekers and others have demonstrated outside Rochester prison during hunger strikes by detainees there. For a while there was a campaign against immigration detentions at Haslar near Portsmouth. A campaign has been set up in Cambridge, Cambridgeshire Against Refugee Detentions (CARD), to stop the opening and then call for the closure of the new 'reception facility' at Oakington. There are anti-detention campaigns elsewhere in Europe. In Italy demonstrations against the Trieste detention centre resulted in its closure. Also in Italy, during a demonstration by the Anti-racist Coordination of Milan at the via Corelli detention centre in October 1998, protesters climbed onto the roof of the detention centre. In spring 2000 there were large demonstrations in Italian cities following the death of four detainees in a fire at a detention centre in Sicily. The government announced the closure of the via Corelli centre, although it is to be replaced. In Denmark protesters symbolically cut the fence of a detention centre. In Belgium the Vottem detention centre at Liège has been a frequent target of resistance actions. Freedom camps have been set up along the eastern borders of Germany. Elsewhere protesters have actively assisted escapes.

In Britain most of the local campaigns against detention were initiated by trades councils, and trade unions have often been active in opposing racism. Nevertheless the history of trade union attitudes to immigration, immigration controls and refugees has been mixed and at times dishonourable (see Chapter 2). At the end of the nineteenth century the Trades Union Congress (TUC) was among the influences which led to immigration controls. Both the TUC and individual trade unions were opposed to immigration, on the grounds that Jews competed for jobs, worked long hours and were perceived to be the main causes of sweating. The TUC passed resolutions calling for restrictions on immigration in 1888, 1889, 1890,

1892, 1893, 1894 and 1895, although none thereafter. In the early twentieth century Chinese seamen were the object of much hostility from trade unions because of strike-breaking by a group of them; this hostility continued until many were deported in 1920. In the First World War, anti-German strikes were organised and, for example, led to the dismissal of 27 Germans from the Manningham Mills in 1915. The attitude of trade unions to European voluntary workers (EVWs) after the Second World War was restrictive and even hostile. Collective agreements were concluded in nearly 40 industries which laid down not only that EVWs should have the same wages and conditions as British workers and should join unions, but that they should not be employed where British labour was obtainable, that they should be dismissed first if there were redundancies, and that there should be maximum quotas of usually 10–15 per cent of the workforce. EVWs were completely excluded from some industries, for example the Welsh mines. This attitude continued with the later Commonwealth immigrants, who were at times excluded not only by the prejudice of employers but by workers and trade unionists who shared this prejudice. Black workers were excluded from several well organised industries, including the print industry, the docks and parts of the car industry, and from individual factories, and there are notorious examples of white workers betraying black workers who took strike action, sometimes as a result of employers giving their white workers special privileges. Employers' refusal to promote black workers was often claimed to be because white workers would not take orders from them. In 1968 Pakistani workers were refused membership of the skilled union in a Burnley mill, thus barring them from promotion.

On the other hand, left trade unionists have sometimes successfully struggled against such prejudice and exclusion. For example it was largely thanks to the left leadership of trade unions in Cowley, Oxford that black people finally managed to get into the Morris car assembly plant. Alan Thornett in his book *From Militancy to Marxism*, in a section headed 'Breaking the Morris colour bar', describes how the senior stewards Frank Horsman and especially Bob Fryer:

raised the issue with management continuously in the late 1950s and into the 1960s, but with no real success. The company recruitment officer appeared to be personally hostile to recruiting black people. As the shop stewards movement grew stronger, management eventually caved in and in 1967 agreed to open all jobs to black workers.

There was initial hostility from many of the white workers and stoppages on some of the tracks with groups of white workers using all the worst racist arguments to refuse to work with blacks. Fryer made no concessions to this pressure and every revolt was faced down.

This breakthrough, with black people on the production lines, was quite early in motor industry terms. ... Large numbers of black workers came into the plant ... [and] were loyal supporters of the trade union movement ...

Exclusion from the Cowley body plant lasted, however, much longer, and its labour force long remained overwhelmingly white.

In the 1950s and 1960s the TUC gave qualified support to the right of Commonwealth immigrants to come and work in Britain, while arguing that colonial exploitation was to blame for them coming, and should be eliminated to make migration unnecessary. The TUC opposed the Commonwealth Immigrants Bill in 1961, but after 1965 it tended to follow the Labour Party's about-turn on controls. It was also opposed to discrimination against Commonwealth workers, but its opposition was verbal rather than real. In the 1950s and 1960s it did little or nothing to stop discrimination, pursuing what Castles and Kosack in *Immigrant Workers and Class Structure in Western Europe* call a *laissez-faire* policy, and considering that any special services for immigrants were unnecessary and undesirable. When the possibility of extending the provisions of the 1965 Race Relations Act into employment discrimination was under discussion, the TUC formed an unholy alliance with the Confederation of British Industry (CBI) to oppose any such interference in industrial relations, and worked out joint voluntary schemes in a bid to stop legislation. Some local unions did, however, embark on special drives to recruit black workers, and for example printed leaflets in immigrants' languages. Nottingham Trades Council founded a local committee for liaison with immigrants as early as 1954 and published a booklet welcoming them to the town and urging them to join trade unions, which they did. Viraj Mendes, a NALGO member, and Abdul Onibiyo, a UNISON member, are among the best known of many trade union members whose campaigns against deportation in later years have been backed, sometimes strongly and effectively, by their trade union.

Left trade unionists have long held the position that racism and discrimination against black workers are a weapon used by employers to divide and weaken the labour movement, and should be resisted on those grounds. They have, moreover, argued against immigration controls, both on principle and because they may create an 'illegal' workforce which is vulnerable to exploitation and which employers hope to use not only as cheap labour but as a means of undermining organised labour, through strike-breaking for example. In practice there have been few examples of foreign workers allowing themselves to be used in this way, and in Britain they have been among the most militant sections of the workforce. A higher proportion of black people than of white are now members of trade unions. This has contributed to a sometimes grudging respect for them among white workers in general, and at times to active solidarity, such as the support by the labour movement for the Asian women who carried on a long and militant strike at Grunwicks and, by Liverpool dockers in particular, for the Asian women who struck with determination against contracting out and wage cuts in cleaning services at Hillingdon Hospital.

In Britain green activists have been overwhelmingly supportive of campaigns for the rights of refugees and migrants. There is no equivalent of the fascist infiltration of green movements including the Sierra Club in the United States, which use the argument that if people migrate to the United

States they will consume more (see China Brotsky, 'A defeat for the greening of hate'). While green activists are opposed to free trade and the free movement of capital, in Britain at least both they and Green Party spokespeople have supported the right of *people* to migrate freely. For the many who have anarchist sympathies, while they may advocate relative self-sufficiency in small communities, controls on free movement are anathema. The official policy of the Green Party in Oxford is to close detention centres and its councillors have supported the Campaign to Close Campsfield. Green activists have been frequent participants in demonstrations and protest camps at Campsfield. In November 1999 a new group called CAGE, set up to oppose prison building and privately-run prisons and supported by a variety of green, anarchist and non-violent direct action groups, mobilised for its first action for the end-of-the-month demonstration at Campsfield. Group 4 had spot-welded the bolts on the fence and locked the detainees inside in fear of what might happen. The police, there in large numbers and with horses, dragged the protesters from the fence. CAGE will doubtless return.

THE *SANS-PAPIERS* MOVEMENT

On 18 March 1996 in Paris 324 Africans, including 80 women and 100 children, occupied the church of Saint Ambroise. They thus began what has become known as the *sans-papiers* movement, which has grown into a movement for the legalisation of all so-called 'illegal immigrants' and even for free movement and the opening of frontiers. It is not a campaign to stop the deportation of particular individuals, but rather is for the 'regularisation' of *all* immigrants who do not have the correct immigration documents. The *sans-papiers*, or 'undocumented people', live in France but do not have papers, either because they came illegally, or because their residence permits have run out and not been renewed, or because they have had their asylum claims rejected.

The movement is led by the *sans-papiers* themselves. They have insisted on their autonomy and have accepted support from white-led organisations on the basis that it *is* support, rather than direction. One of their leading delegates, Madgiguène Cissé, a Senegalese woman, explains in a booklet published in English translation by Crossroads, *The Sans-Papiers: A Woman Draws the First Lessons*, that the struggle 'taught us first of all to be autonomous':

There were organizations which came to support us and which were used to helping immigrants in struggle. They were also used to acting as the relay between immigrants in struggle and the authorities, and therefore more or less to manage the struggle. They would tell us, 'Right, we the organizations have made an appointment to explain this or that'; and we had to say, 'But we can explain it very well ourselves.' ... If we had not taken our autonomy, we would not be here today, because there really have been many organizations telling us we could never win, that we could not win over public opinion because people were not ready to hear what we had to say.

The *sans-papiers* early on decided to refer to themselves as 'undocumented' rather than 'clandestine', their previous designation. Thus the essence of the movement is that people who were previously virtually in hiding, working illegally and in fear of deportation and for that reason vulnerable to exploitation, decided to come out into the open, declare themselves to the authorities and demand their regularisation. In the process they took, and take, great risks. As their manifesto, published by the newspaper *Libération* on 25 February 1997 (and translated for the Crossroads booklet), states:

We the Sans-Papiers of France, in signing this appeal, have decided to come out of the shadows. From now on, in spite of the dangers, it is not only our faces but also our names which will be known. We declare:

Like all others without papers, we are people like everyone else. Most of us have been living among you for years. We came to France with the intention of working here and because we had been told that France was the 'homeland of the Rights of Man': we could no longer bear the poverty and the oppression which was rife in our countries, we wanted our children to have full stomachs, and we dreamed of freedom.

Most of us entered France legally. We have been arbitrarily thrown into illegality both by the hardening of successive laws which enabled the authorities to stop renewing our permit to stay, and by restrictions introduced on the right to asylum which is now given only sparingly. We pay our taxes, our rent, our bills and our social security contributions – when we are allowed regular employment! When we are not unemployed or in casual employment, we work hard in the rag trade, the leather trade, the construction industry, catering, cleaning ... We face working conditions employers impose on us which you can refuse more easily than we can, because being without papers makes us without rights. We know this suits plenty of people. We produce wealth, and we enrich France with our diversity. ...

We demand papers so that we are no longer victims of arbitrary treatment by the authorities, employers and landlords. We demand papers so that we are no longer vulnerable to informants and blackmailers. We demand papers so that we no longer suffer the humiliation of controls based on our skin, detentions, deportations, the break-up of our families, the constant fear. The prime minister of France had promised that families would not be separated: we demand that this promise finally be kept and that the principles of humanity often proclaimed by the government be implemented. We demand that the European and international conventions, to which the French Republic has subscribed, are respected.

We rely on the support of a great many French people, whose own liberties may be under threat if our rights continue to be ignored. Since the examples of Italy, Spain, Portugal and on several occasions France itself, demonstrate that overall regularisation is entirely possible, we demand our regularisation. We are not in hiding. We have come out into the daylight.

Some of the *sans-papiers* who occupied Saint Ambroise church on 18 March 1996 were asylum seekers and some were people who had been made 'illegal' by the new laws; all were threatened with deportation. They were evicted on 22 March, and moved from place to place, with the women, who came to be known as *sans-papières*, playing a big role in keeping the movement going. In May some went on hunger strike. Hunger strikes started in several other places including Lille and Versailles, and in some cases led to regularisation. More than 25 *sans-papiers* collectives were set up around France. There were two big demonstrations in Paris in their support. In June the government gave the right to stay to 22 of the original Saint Ambroise occupiers. The *sans-papiers* then occupied the Saint Bernard church, also in Paris. Ten men went on hunger strike in the church, and they set up the Sans-Papiers National Coordinating Committee (*Coordination Nationale des Sans-Papiers*). On 23 August 1996 1,500 police violently broke into the church with clubs, axes and tear gas and evicted the *sans-papiers* and their children and supporters, separating black from white and women from men, detaining many of the blacks; the same evening 20,000 people went on the streets to support them. Most of the Saint Bernard protesters were released; by January 1997, 103 of the original 324 had received temporary papers, 19 had been deported, two were in jail. They joined a big march in Paris; there were demonstrations in Marseille, Bordeaux and Toulouse, and again in Paris. The Saint Bernard Collective moved into disused trade union premises at Faubourg-Poissonnière. Hunger strikes, demonstrations, petitions and occupations by *sans-papiers* in Paris and other parts of France continued at a high rate. In March 1998 *sans-papiers* occupied the Notre Dame de la Gare and Saint Jean de Montmartre churches, which led to mass arrests and deportations. After a low period, the movement revived with a march from Toulouse to Paris, an occupation of the embassy of the Holy See, many other actions and an increase in membership and groups.

The *sans-papiers'* protests followed the increasing harshness of immigration controls and restrictiveness of asylum procedures, and in particular the progressive illegalisation of people who had often lived, worked and paid taxes for long periods in France. French frontiers were closed against immigration in 1974. In 1980 deportations of people already in France, and detention to make this possible, began. The Socialist government of 1981 reversed some of these processes; protective measures were introduced which prevented the expulsion of foreigners who had strong links in France, including minors, foreigners who had been in France for ten years or more, the victims of accidents at work, the spouses of French people, and the parents of children born in France; in addition in 1982, 150,000 immigrants were 'regularised' by the Socialist government. In 1984 ten-year residence permits were introduced for people with links in France and who had lived there for over three years. In 1986 laws introduced by Charles Pasqua, the notoriously right-wing Gaullist interior minister, reversed some of these protective measures and made entry to France harder. In 1989 a Socialist government repealed the Pasqua laws, reintroducing the principle that people born in France, and the parents of children born in France, could not be deported. The right, and Pasqua, returned in 1993, and introduced a series of new repressive laws. In 1997, shortly before the Socialist landslide victory and, some argued, contributing to it, the Debré laws were introduced. These laws cancelled the automatic right to renewal of ten-year residence permits, making it subject to 'public order' and other conditions, and substituted temporary one-year permits for some categories of residents, thus immediately making the situation of thousands of people precarious and potentially illegal. They increased surveillance measures, including finger-printing, to check immigration status at work and elsewhere. They also attempted to introduce a measure obliging people offering hospitality to foreigners not only to obtain permission from the town hall, but to report when they left; this measure attracted huge protests and was withdrawn, after massive demonstrations which were joined by hundreds of celebrities who announced their intention of breaking the law.

In June 1997 the left regained control of parliament. There were high hopes that they would proceed to a general regularisation of the *sans-papiers*. Immediately after the elections, while Socialist Party supporters were celebrating inside, demonstrators were outside announcing their determination to hold them to their promises on refugees and migrants. Lionel Jospin, the new prime minister, met Ababacar Diop, one of the leaders of the *sans-papiers*, and announced that the regularisation of *sans-papiers* would be speeded up, but would be conditional on certain criteria such as ties with France. Officials made clear that regularisation would not be generalised as in 1982. Chévènement, the new minister of the interior, issued a decree inviting applications for regularisation. Some 150,000 applied, but only about 75,000 were granted papers, for one year only. Another 63,000, most of whom had lived in France for many years, were refused and made subject to deportation. The Chévènement decree came to seem more like a trap than an offer, since the 63,000 had revealed their names and addresses and were faced with a choice of deportation or going back into hiding, afraid each time they went out that that might be the last they saw of their families. In addition, an unknown number did not come forward, mistrusting the Socialists' promises. The Socialist government did not repeal the Pasqua laws. It allowed one hunger strike to continue for 78 days. The *sans-papiers* continued to demand the regularisation of all the undocumented, both those who declared themselves and those who did not.

On 27 March 1999 the Sans-Papiers National Coordinating Committee organised a big demonstration in Paris, together with many anti-racist organisations and trade unions and political parties, including the CGT, the CFDT-FGTE, the French Communist Party, the Greens, the Ligue Communiste Révolutionnaire and Lutte Ouvrière, and with participation from most European countries, including a delegation from the Campaign to Close Campsfield. A delegation of 3,500 Italians in special trains, accompanied by some Albanian refugees, was stopped at the French frontier, which was closed to all travellers by 1,500 special riot police and members of the French Foreign Legion. The European demonstration's demands were for the regularisation without conditions of all the *sans-papiers* in Europe; for freedom of movement and settlement; for the ending of deportations and the return of the deported; for the closing of all immigration detention centres; for the abolition of 'double punishment'; for the repeal of all discriminatory and xenophobic laws. The demonstration was marked by numerous slogans, banners and leaflets in favour of free movement, the opening of frontiers and the end of nation states. The Sans-Papiers National Coordinating Committee stated that 'we want the human right to move around to be recognised for all'. A slogan from the organisation Partisan said 'Capital is without frontiers; no frontiers for workers!' A leaflet from the Ile-de-France regional collective of *sans-papiers* and other organisations demanded a 100-year regularisation of all *sans-papiers* without quotas or restrictions and freedom of movement and settlement, saying that:

To accept the Europe as conceived by States and governments, both of the right and of the left, means to accept the vision of a world where inequality and misery reign while a minority which monopolises all wealth protects itself by every means possible. ... To tolerate this situation means to tolerate apartheid on a world scale ... as for poverty, exploitation and repression, they know no frontiers.

We join the activists of the European campaign against detention camps so that freedom of movement and settlement, as well as the reappropriation and sharing of wealth, can become reality and not mere statements of principle.

The Collectif Anti-Expulsions de Lille produced a leaflet which said:

We oppose deportations because freedom of movement is a principle on which there can be no compromise; because it does not seem acceptable to us that a mere piece of paper can determine the fate of individuals. We struggle for freedom of movement in its most concrete meaning, such as the ability to travel and to settle, wherever we wish to, without hindrance; because this struggle concerns also the refusal of social control which afflicts us all, whether or not we have papers.

The Fédération des Associations de Solidarité avec les Travailleurs Immigrés (FASTI), which campaigns against detention, receives state funding to visit detention centres and was one of the main organisers of the European demonstration, produced a leaflet headed 'Ouverture des frontières, libre installation' (Opening of frontiers, freedom to settle) which concluded:

- The establishment of individuals in regions which are not their native regions is a source of enrichment both for the receiving countries and for the countries of departure. ...
- Freedom of movement and settlement is an inalienable right, in the same sense as the right to work, the right to health. It does not depend on economic considerations, since the mobility of persons must not be imposed, but chosen.
- The concept of the universality of human rights implies for their application the abolition of frontiers. It would be wrong to defend 'human rights' and yet limit them to a few countries or to certain regions of the world. This is as true for rights which are said to be basic (work, health, education, housing) as for the right to travel and to settle.

- The arguments which separate rights of survival from rights of movement are indefensible. The history of peoples, in France and elsewhere, is rich in migrations. The reasons for these movements may be wars, famines, persecutions, unemployment. Nothing can stop peoples and individuals seeking places to settle in order to survive. Today, the right to the free movement of peoples is profoundly linked to the right to survival.

The Commission Immigration du Réseau No Pasaran wrote that the closing of frontiers and the hardening of conditions for migrants under Schengen:

has done nothing other than feed xenophobic and racist fantasies, while plunging thousands of people into clandestinity, a real enslavable workforce delivered to the mercy of employers. These policies of closing frontiers have never been able to prevent the rise of unemployment and go hand in hand with the policy of labour deregulation: insecurity, exclusion, poverty.

To complement the closing of frontiers, some people argue for a policy of immigration quotas. But such a policy would not stop individuals from travelling if they need to or want to. There will always be people who will die trying to cross the frontiers of Fortress Europe, as is happening at Gibraltar. Worse, a policy of quotas would mean that states determined the number of immigrants authorised to enter Europe in relation to their own economic needs. If this is not a new form of apartheid, of exploitation and domination of the countries of the South ... let someone tell us what it is. ...

We are pleased that all the organisations which have taken part in the European demonstration of 27 March and are here in this meeting [a rally the day following the demonstration] have expressed their support for freedom of movement and settlement. A great step has been taken. Now is the time to make this freedom real.

The leaflet also called for the liberation of all detainees and for a demonstration at the Vincennes detention centre, demanding the freedom of all the *sans-papiers* detained there, to be supported by 'all the signatories of the call for 27 March', including Madame Voynet of the Greens and Monsieur Gayssot of the Communist Party.

The *sans-papiers* movement is gaining ground in other countries in Europe, including Belgium and Italy. The Belgian organisation Frontières Ouvertes (Open Frontiers) distributed a leaflet at the European march which demanded the regularisation of all *sans-papiers*, the closing of detention centres and the ending of deportations, and the right of all people living in Belgium to full social, medical and employment rights, and said in part:

For ten years Frontières Ouvertes has been denouncing the implementation of more and more anti-democratic measures against refugees and *sans-papiers*. This fascisisation of the state is the consequence of the closing of frontiers which we are struggling against. This closing can only be effected by reinforcing the police, debasing rights and militarising certain frontier zones. It has the effect of meeting the demands of fascist parties and encouraging racism.

Migration has taken place since the dawn of humanity. From its origins, capitalism itself has in addition forced workers to move around the world. As long as this unjust system of wealth distribution subsists, forced movements of populations will take place. No closing of frontiers, however radical, will prevent migrations, it only has the effect of forcing those who wish to migrate to carry out their journey in danger of their lives and to join the ranks of clandestine immigration.

At the rally after the march a delegate from Frontières Ouvertes remarked that after the death of Semira Adamu (a Nigerian refugee who was killed by Belgian police who covered her face with a pillow when she resisted being deported), 'clandestine' people decided they no longer wanted to stay in the shadows, since they might be killed in any case. They too have set up a *sans-papiers* movement, beginning with the occupation of a church. A torchlit demonstration supporting Semira Adamu in July 1998 was followed by the escape of 31 *sans-papiers* from a detention camp at Zaventem airport. The protests forced the government to sack the interior minister and to introduce what a government spokesperson called 'radical' new asylum policies, to improve conditions in detention centres, simplify asylum procedures and regularise the position of 'illegal' immigrants already in Belgium.

In Germany a group called Kein Mensch Ist Illegal (No One Is Illegal) has existed since 1998. It took part in a caravan for the rights of refugees (Die Karavane) which passed through many German cities and set up an extensive network of groups. They organised a European conference of *sans-papiers* and related groups at Jena in April 2000.

The movement of the *sans-papiers* themselves has galvanised resistance in Europe against the injustice imposed by the attempt to enforce immigration controls, and has led to growing demands for the regularisation of all the undocumented and for freedom to migrate and to settle. But the movement has, as yet, made little impact in Britain.

5 RE-OPEN THE BORDERS

IMMIGRATION CONTROLS AND HUMAN RIGHTS

The strongest case against immigration controls is that they impose increasingly harsh suffering on migrants, including refugees. In the process they undermine a long list of human rights: the right not to be subjected to inhuman and degrading treatment, the right not to be tortured, the right not to be arbitrarily arrested and imprisoned, the right to a fair trial by a properly constituted court, the right to family life, the right to work, among others. Immigration controls as they are currently practised violate the provisions of several international treaties to which the British government is a signatory (see, for example, p. 116). They also tear families apart and prevent parents and children visiting each other, they force both migrants and refugees into the hands of often unscrupulous agents, they subject them to long periods of arbitrary detention and expose them to destitution, isolation and racial harassment. Refugees and asylum seekers in particular are punished not for anything which they themselves have done, but in a vain attempt to deter others. Proposals to reform and humanise the asylum system, even supposing they were realistic, would still leave refugees at the mercy of necessarily uncertain decisions on the genuineness of their claims. The only way to ensure that refugees are really protected would be if there were no immigration controls. The current posture of governments appears to be, on the contrary, to try to cut the numbers of applications for asylum, let alone acceptances, through the ever harsher application of extremely repressive immigration controls. Such cruelty is incompatible with the hard-fought-for gains of liberal democratic societies.

To stop immigration altogether, and to reduce the numbers applying for asylum, as governments apparently wish to, would imply still more drastic measures, still less compatible with the aims of liberal democracy. Even then they might not succeed. Such measures would affect the population as a whole, reduce its democratic rights, and risk turning Europe into a police state. Already immigration officials and private security guards at refugee prisons have large and unaccountable powers. The immigration detention centres are reminiscent of concentration camps. As the Oxford dons said (see p. 139), the current treatment of refugees amounts to 'a dangerous undermining of democratic principles and the rule of law' which 'could open the way to further abuses'. There is a danger of creeping fascisisation of society. The morality of frontiers, where human rights are at their lowest, is threatening to invade the interiors of countries. The extension of internal controls will mean an increase in random checks, which so far are mainly checks on people who look foreign, especially blacks, but which affect black citizens, and potentially other citizens, as well. This has been going on for some time in some European countries, especially, as a result of the much hated Pasqua laws, in France, where police raids in public places and demands for North Africans in particular to show their papers are commonplace. Although Britain does not yet have compulsory identity cards, they may be on their way. Meanwhile, black British people find it prudent to carry around proof of their right to be in Britain. A large amount of their time has to be spent in making sure their documents are in order. People have been caught, imprisoned and deported, sometimes after years of living in Britain with their families, as a result of failure to comply with some petty immigration procedure. The deprivation of welfare benefits for some sections of the population is, similarly, a slippery slope. After refugees, convicted criminals who fail to comply with community orders seem to be next in line. Since the British have a habit of adopting North American practices after a time lag, single mothers may soon be subjected to a maximum two-year limit on benefits. Immigration controls create illegal workers, who are vulnerable to savage exploitation. If the treatment of migrants and refugees is not opposed, it could become the norm and spread to other sectors of society. At the FASTI 'Europe Behind Barbed Wire' conference in March 1997, Roland Dyaye, a member of the Sans-Papiers National Coordinating Committee, said of their movement:

Basically, this is a struggle against illegal working. Illegal working in a capitalist system in crisis becomes an instrument, a tool of all the neo-liberal forces to make the world of work more precarious. Yesterday removals to countries of the Third World were denounced. There is a new kind of removal, that is, the continual spread of this form of labour, which costs practically nothing. This is a powerful and fundamental perspective in terms of the capitalist response to the current crisis. In simple terms, it is to subject an ever growing proportion of workers to Third World conditions, in the context of what used to be called 'the consumer society'. Today, these people are the *sans-papiers*. After that, it will spread to include people on income support, homeless people, and so on. Each section of workers will fall under the steam-roller.

It is in such a context in the West that fascist forces develop. 'Europe Behind Barbed Wire' is also a Europe where fascism has been reborn and is growing. In the past, in the context of an international crisis, of fascism come to power in a strong country like Germany, labour camps were transformed into death camps. If this goes on, what will be the future of these detention centres, of these transit zones?

They are dumping people there like cattle, in order to deport them. Beware! It's deportation today, but what will it be tomorrow? In this great regression of civilisation that threatens European countries, notably France, with those who lead the fascist menace sniffing the air, well, the *sans-papiers* movement is in many respects comparable to the Dreyfus affair. It's now or never, for the democratic forces in the country, to embrace this amazing movement of the most marginalised section of the working class and of society, the *sans-papiers,* who have no rights. Let there be some new Jaurès, some new Zolas, and let there be some trades union and political organisations in the working class that rise up to form a barrier to this fearsome danger of regression in society and civilisation.

At the same conference Helmut Dietrich from Berlin said that immigration policies create a 'new social layer of "illegals"' who are 'super exploited' and 'may end up in prison in the next raid. ... Existential fear, systematic harassment, intimidation and violent expulsion have become the daily lot of this underclass.' This treatment, Dietrich said, is being extended to others besides refugees and migrants, including small-time drug dealers, whose movements within German cities are being restricted.

One human right which, because it has not been recognised as a right, is not violated by current attempts to enforce immigration controls is the right to cross frontiers (from the outside in). The right to leave countries was proclaimed by the 1948 Universal Declaration of Human Rights, whose authors presumably had the Soviet Union and eastern Europe in mind; but nothing was said of the right to enter another country. As *Moscow News* ironically put it in 1993, 'Russia and the West have swapped roles. An iron curtain has been lowered against the majority of those who wish to enter Europe.' The Berlin Wall is being replaced by high fences, razor wire and increasingly sophisticated electronic devices, on the borders between Mexico and the United States, between the inner and outer countries of Europe, and around the Spanish enclaves in north Africa; people are killed and wounded by entry guards rather than by exit guards. The Universal Declaration also proclaimed people's rights to move around freely inside their own country. In the current state of opinion it would be considered unthinkable for people from Manchester not to be allowed to travel to Oxford unless they were very rich or skilled, or unless the authorities of Oxford decided that they had been so severely persecuted by the authorities in Manchester that their lives and liberty were in danger there. It is true that the rich inhabitants of north Oxford built a wall across a street to keep out the inhabitants of Cutteslowe council estate. But this was considered shocking, and did not last. Restrictions on immigration from the Commonwealth were also considered unthinkable by most people in the 1950s, and restrictions against aliens were unthinkable in the late nineteenth century. It is time for the idea of international migration to be rescued, and enshrined in international declarations as a normal and natural human right.

It is time also to question the assumption that governments and their citizens have the right to exercise control in their own interest over particular bits of land, any more than they have the right to appropriate the air and the sea. Most of the arguments for and against immigration controls are expressed in terms of the interests of nations and their current inhabitants, rather than of the peoples of the world as a whole. It is taken for granted that the former should take precedence. The governments and peoples of the rich countries see nothing immoral about arguing (whether or not this is in fact the case) that immigration controls are necessary to preserve their special privileges. Instead, it is somehow considered immoral for people to cross national frontiers to seek work or even refuge. And governments are prepared to go to extraordinary lengths to stop them doing so. It is from the denial of people's rights to travel to and settle in the place of their choice that some of the worst abuses of human rights in Western liberal democracies have sprung.

IMMIGRATION CONTROLS DO NOT WORK

If freedom to migrate meant that movements of people were so large that they led to catastrophic disruption, chaos and decline in living standards in the rich countries, then, however admirable the ideal, it would be understandable that it should be opposed. But the abolition of immigration controls, although it would doubtless lead to some increase in migration, would not have an overwhelming effect on numbers. This is, first, because immigration controls do not work. In spite of the ever-increasing paraphernalia of repressive measures, during the 1990s the numbers of asylum seekers have remained roughly constant. European governments and their officials are beginning to recognise that immigration controls will never be made to work. They are engaged in a last-ditch defence of what remains of national sovereignty, in a period of growing power of international private capital. The attempt to maintain freedom of movement for capital and prevent the movement of labour will not indefinitely resist the pressures of so-called 'globalisation'. The water metaphors commonly applied to immigrants can be applied to controls: controls are like a dam; when one hole is blocked, another one appears somewhere else. Migrants and those who facilitate their migration resort to staggering feats of ingenuity, courage and endurance to assert their right to move and to flee. The question is how much suffering will be imposed on innocent people, and how much racism will be stoked up, in a vain attempt to deny the right to freedom of movement before governments finally abandon the effort.

Second, officials despair at their inability to deport people. Having put refugees and migrants through months and sometimes years of suffering and uncertainty, possibly in detention centres and prisons, governments then cannot deport the great majority of those to whom they refuse the right to stay. This is because the governments of their countries of origin will not provide them with papers or agree to readmit them, because they have developed family links in Europe, because they cannot be found, or even because protesters succeed in stopping their air flights. There are not enough detention centres to lock up all those whose cases are turned down, and most countries apart from Britain have time limits on detention and must often release people before they can deport them. Even in Britain, lawyers have successfully used habeas corpus to get people released if they do not have documents enabling them to be deported. Governments may therefore end up releasing them onto the streets, sometimes with no access to any form of public support and no permission to work, thus turning them into, at best, illegal workers. At a meeting in Oxford a group of European officials discussed seriously how much denial of health facilities would be compatible with international human rights obligations. In the Netherlands, according to a Dutch official, 'they are just dumped on the streets', in an attempt literally to starve them out, or perhaps deliberately to create an illegal and exploitable workforce. The policies which are well established in the United States, and now appear to be be increasingly contemplated in Europe, are to use the migrants' (illegal and therefore cheap) labour, but deprive them of social and political rights.

Third, the numbers of people who would migrate if they were free to do so are often exaggerated. Some have argued that population increases and environmental catastrophes are such that, unless something is done, there will be massive population movements from poor countries to rich countries. Others appear to believe that if people were allowed to move freely, 400 million Indians would emigrate en masse to the rich countries in search of jobs. Orthodox free market theory suggests that, if there was free movement of labour, there would be large-scale movements of workers until eventually wages were equalised throughout the world. Neither of these things is likely to happen. While some enterprising people move because there are jobs and the possibility of higher pay in the rich countries, this does not mean that the entire population of the Third World would do so, or even a significant proportion of it. Britain, with great reluctance, offered 20,000 visas to Hong Kong citizens; 10,000 of them were taken up. In situations where there are no immigration controls, such as from the Commonwealth to Britain in the 1950s, from Puerto Rico and Cuba to the United States and from French Overseas Departments to France, migration has been large but represents only a small proportion of the population of both receiving and most sending countries. Between 1950 and 1980, for example, 0.6 per cent of the population of the Caribbean emigrated per year, taking advantage of the absence of restrictions in former colonial powers and the United States. Bob Sutcliffe in *Nacido en otra parte* has ventured an estimate that, on the assumption that these Caribbean rates of emigration were repeated worldwide, there would be an extra 24 million migrants per year, leading to a growth of 2.4 per cent per year in the population of the industrialised countries. Provided such an increase was fairly evenly distributed, which would imply international agreement to abolish controls, and in particular agreement among European countries, such an increase could well come to be seen as a useful means of counteracting declines in the birth rate and ageing populations. But it seems unlikely in any case that people would migrate from other areas at such high rates. Much of the Caribbean emigration took place in years when unemployment was high in the Caribbean and much lower in the countries of destination than it is now. Migration from the small islands of the Caribbean, where opportunities are relatively few, was facilitated by the existence of communities in the recipient countries and common languages and education systems. In many areas which do not have these characteristics there has been virtually no emigration. During the postwar period of free entry for Commonwealth citizens, which was also a period of job abundance in Britain, migration was only from a small number of areas. It also rose and fell in relation to the numbers of job vacancies, in response to information from already established communities.

On the whole most people do not want to uproot themselves, abandon their families, and suffer the hardships and risks of migration to a strange and possibly hostile place in order to do the dirty work of the natives. And, surprising though it may seem to racists quaking at the prospect of invading hordes, they like their own countries and cultures. In *Journey Without a Destination* Rohini Hensman quotes the Tamil refugees she interviewed giving depressing descriptions of their experiences of deprivation and racism in Britain, and expressing their wish to go back to Sri Lanka as soon as it was safe to do so. Even those who had found conditions in Britain more bearable still wanted to return to their families, the climate, the social warmth and neighbourliness, and perhaps their jobs, land and properties in Sri Lanka. 'The overwhelming majority' of her interviewees, she says, 'expressed a desire to go back if peace was restored.' Many others did not leave at all, saying they would prefer to die in their own country rather than flee to a strange and hostile land.

If migration for unskilled work was no longer illegalised, it is true that the costs of migration would go down because it would no longer be necessary to pay agents and buy false papers. But the costs would still be high. Most people cannot afford the fares, the loss of earnings when moving, and the expense of settling in a new country. Others might prefer to migrate for short periods, while they are young and strong, and to return when they have saved enough or learnt enough without losing the possibility of migrating again and without being forced to settle and to move their families. The migrants' lack of rights, and the existence of immigration controls, makes such flexibility more or less impossible. In Britain (see Chapter 2) most immigration occurred after and just before controls were introduced, because migrant workers were forced to settle and bring in their families. The *Financial Times* of 23 February 2000, describing Mexican seasonal migrants and 'the aspirations, humanity, sacrifices and courage of those daring to run the wire', says that 'More seasoned travellers now tend to stay longer, in part because tighter border controls increase the likelihood of being caught.' Abdul Onibiyo's troubles (see p. 134) started when he spent too long in Nigeria and so lost his right to stay with his family in Britain. And as Rohini

Hensman wrote to the author, agreeing that 'immigration controls may lead to more migrant workers settling down and bringing dependants over': 'I think the same is true of refugees, who by definition are unwilling migrants. ... I feel that many Tamil refugees, for example, would go back now that the situation has improved, *provided* they had the option of coming out if it deteriorates again, since things are still quite unpredictable. Lacking that option they will stay where they are rather than risk being cast adrift again.'

The predominant fear of the authorities at the moment seems to be not that there will be mass migration from the Third World, given the costs and distances involved, but that there will be an unstoppable movement of east Europeans across land frontiers in Europe. If this is a problem, it is one that west Europeans have partly imposed on themselves by demanding cuts in public expenditure to service foreign debt and the privatisation and closure of state enterprises in east European economies, which have reintroduced unemployment and extreme destitution in areas where they did not exist. Nevertheless, except in the case of mass refugee movements such as have occurred after the break-up of Yugoslavia, the migrants are still likely to be young and ambitious people, mostly young men, whose labour is in any case needed. In a few years' time European countries may again be competing for such people. Under extreme forms of repression and impoverishment, whole Roma families have fled across Europe. But they too are a small proportion of the total Roma population, and are only a few hundreds of people, who badly need protection and sympathy. It could be argued that many millions more people should migrate to seek refuge or a chance of economic betterment in the rich countries of the West. But it will not happen.

IMMIGRATION AND JOBS, WAGES AND CONDITIONS

It is in any case doubtful whether the prevention or reduction of immigration would serve the interests of the rich countries. Those who believe in the necessity of immigration controls often argue that, without them, the jobs and living standards of existing residents would be threatened. The governments of rich countries claim that their concern is about 'economic refugees', those who migrate to work or, allegedly, to live off the welfare state. Since governments turn down most asylum applications, they claim in effect that most people who migrate to Europe do so for economic rather than political reasons. The great majority of those who migrate to Europe, including refugees, would of course like to work. The governments' favoured category of people, the 'genuine refugees', might perhaps be supposed to be more willing to live on welfare benefits, because of their desperation, than those who are in governments' terms 'bogus'. But those who migrate to Europe for economic reasons, which means these days either those who have desired skills, or clandestine migrants, or perhaps some who claim falsely to be asylum seekers, do not do so in order to live off welfare benefits. People who are very poor usually cannot migrate to other countries and continents. Those who migrate tend to do so from slightly better-off areas and sectors of the population. Mostly they migrate because they want to work, save and probably remit their savings to their families in their countries of origin. The same was true in the past, before immigration controls, and will be so when controls have been abandoned.

Economic migration, to the extent that it exists, occurs in response to labour demand in richer countries. Saskia Sassen in *The Mobility of Labour and Capital* argues that there is currently a large increase in low-paid, often service-sector jobs, especially in the big cities of the United States and other industrialised countries, in declining industries, in new 'high tech' industries, and to service these industries and the expanding professional elite. This, she says, combined with increased so-called 'globalisation' and links created by the activities of multinational companies, is what is causing migration. Over the years capitalism has frequently been confronted by the problem of labour shortages, and has resorted to force to secure labour. More recently European countries, as well as the countries better known as countries of immigration including the United States, have satisfied their unmet labour needs through immigration. When their economies were expanding they obtained labour first from the poorer parts of Europe and then from the Third World. Now that European countries are in a period of low growth, and unemployment is high, immigration would have declined anyway. But these countries still need foreign labour to do jobs which the natives have ceased to be willing to do; it would have catastrophic effects on their economies if recent immigrants were to leave in any numbers. It is common for there to be vacancies in unskilled and casual employment in hotels, restaurants, supermarkets and hospitals even in places where unemployment is high.

In addition, it seems likely that the need for immigrant workers, of all types, will increase in the future because of static and even declining populations in Europe, and the ageing of these populations. Although an Organisation for Economic Co-operation and Development (OECD) report published in 1991 rejected the possibility of remedying the problem by allowing immigration, on the grounds it was 'politically unthinkable in the Europe of today', it is possible that official opinion will change. The United Nations Population Division published a report in March 2000 entitled *Replacement Migration: Is It a Solution to Declining and Ageing Populations?* The report said that the populations of Europe and Japan were expected to decline as a result of declining birth rates in the next 50 years. The population of Italy, for example, is projected to decline from 57 million now to 41 million in 2050. The declines in working-age populations and in the ratio of people of working age to people over 65 will be even greater. For Europe, whereas there are now five people of working age for each person over 65, by 2050 the projected ratio is only two to one. The UN report says that to maintain their working-age populations at their 1995 levels Italy would need about 350,000 migrants per year and Germany would need about 500,000. To maintain the ratio of young to old people at four to one, Italy would need 2.2 million immigrants and Germany would need 3.4 million per year over the period 1995–2050, a possibility dismissed by the report as unrealistic. Some European officials are now talking of the need to allow limited economic migration; this may be not merely because they hope to relieve the pressure on asylum procedures, but also because of potentially recurring labour shortages.

Illegal immigrants are particularly suitable for doing the jobs for which native workers are unavailable because they are exceptionally cheap, both for employers and for the state, partly because they do not have the alternative of welfare benefits and also because of their vulnerability to deportation and their lack of legal rights. As Saskia Sassen puts it: 'Border enforcement is a mechanism facilitating the extraction of cheap labour by assigning criminal status to a segment of the working class – illegal immigrants.' In the United States the practice of employing foreigners illegally as cheap exploitable labour is practically institutionalised, as a recognised part of the labour force, much valued by employers. The slogan is 'Immigration Yes, Welfare No.' Estimates of the number of 'undocumented aliens' in the United States range from 3 to 12 million. According to an article in the *Financial Times* of 23 February 2000 entitled 'Illicit angels of America's economic miracle', undocumented Mexicans provide 18 per cent of the Los Angeles area's construction labour force, 70 per cent of workers at peak fruit harvesting time in Washington state, 15 per cent of the total US farm workforce. The *Financial Times* commented that a local Kentucky newspaper said Kentuckians 'could not expect immigrants to undertake unseen and unheard the jobs now shunned by Americans. They also had cause to feel humbled by the realisation of the hardships and perils the newcomers were prepared to confront.'

Employers in Europe have been hesitant to argue publicly for more immigration, but they are not averse to employing illegal labour when they can. In the clothing industry in London attempts to unionise or to win better conditions can be thwarted by the owners calling the police. Rwandan women work in London for £1.50 an hour. *The Observer* of 14 March 1999 reported that Filipinos and Mauritians were working on oil rigs in 'slave' conditions for 81p an hour, 'sold' by agencies in their countries. Chinese businesses employ Chinese 'illegals', sometimes recruited by Triads and Snakeheads, seven days a week, give them no money and little food and force them to sleep on the floor. Some British farmers employ illegal immigrants for a pittance. A large-scale farmer in Oxfordshire rang up a supporter of the Campaign to Close Campsfield to enquire about the possibility of Campsfield detainees being temporarily released to pick his vegetables; when offered former detainees who were refugees with the legal right to work, and who asserted their rights, he found no use for them. But, although it could be argued that immigration controls are good for employers in the sense that they create an especially cheap labour force, even immigrants with legal status can be useful to employers because of their willingness to work for low wages and long hours and in poor conditions, and because of pressures on the labour market. Immigration, legal or illegal, is clearly good for employers. The *Wall Street Journal* favours not only increased immigration but, consistent with its free market ideology, free movement. In January 2000 Alan Greenspan, head of the US Federal Reserve, said that 'Not only in high-tech and in the farm area but throughout the country aggregate demand is putting pressure on an ever-decreasing supply of unemployed labour.' He suggested that if growth was to continue without inflation, immigration policies would have to be relaxed.

A different question is whether immigration is good for the native workforce. Greenspan's remarks tend to reinforce the widely held belief that competition from immigrants forces down wages and deprives the locals of jobs. But the likelihood is that immigration has little effect on wage levels and conditions, and that its effect on employment levels is if anything positive. A great deal has been written on this question. One neo-liberal US economist, George B. Borjas, wrote in a 1993 OECD publication that:

The methodological arsenal of modern econometrics cannot find a single shred of evidence that immigrants have a major adverse impact on the earnings and job oppor-tunities of natives of the United States.

It is nevertheless often argued that general wage levels might have risen faster in the absence of immigrants. Another orthodox economist, Charles P. Kindleberger, argued in *Europe's Postwar Growth: The Role of Labor Supply*, that the availability of labour was the major factor which determined whether European economies grew fast or not. Countries such as France and Germany which had high levels of net immigration grew faster than Britain where there was net emigration. Kindleberger argues that this was because immigration kept down inflationary pressures on wage levels. On the other hand wage levels in France and Germany are now much higher than those in Britain.

The thesis that immigrants cause unemployment seems to have little or no basis in reality. As is well known, unemployment was higher in the 1930s, when there was hardly any immigration, than it is now. Unemploy-ment in Europe was lowest in the period of major immigrations after the Second World War. It is clearly caused by capitalist recessions rather than by immigration. Even the effects of sudden large-scale immigration on unem-ployment seem to be short-lived. Nigel Harris, in a paper presented in Paris in September 1999, says that when Algeria became independent in 1962 about 900,000 *pieds-noirs* (white settlers) moved to France; unemployment around Marseille peaked at 20 per cent a few months later, but was down to 6 per cent one year later and 4 per cent the next year. The return of Portuguese colonists from Africa had no more effect. OECD figures show a correlation between immigration and employment levels in the mid-1990s which is the opposite of what some people assume: the countries with lowest levels of immigration, including Spain, have the highest levels of unemployment, while the opposite is true of Switzerland. It can be argued, in fact, that an influx of refugees and migrants may cause boom conditions, as the Cuban exiles have in Miami and the *pieds-noirs* possibly have in the south of France.

A principal argument for the thesis that immigrants do *not* cause unemployment is that they tend to take jobs which are shunned by the natives, and therefore provide an essential means of enabling economies to function and expand. Some have argued that if immigrant workers had not been available there would have been more modernisation, and that employers would have been forced to improve conditions and so make the jobs attractive enough for local workers to take them. But it is perhaps more likely that the jobs would have disappeared altogether, or been moved abroad. If this is so immigrants have enabled industries and services to survive and thus created more jobs for the population as a whole, both in these industries and from the demand they create, as well as contributing to the general expansion of the economy. Nigel Harris in his Paris paper comments:

Many of the sectors involved are relatively marginal so the lack of a labour supply would lead to closure rather than raising wages to meet local native expectations and/or increasing the capital intensity of production. Imports would then presumably replace local production, and key services would not be provided. Almost certainly this would reduce native employment – for those natives employed in the sectors concerned, for those employed in providing goods and services to the former labour force, and for those dependent upon the complementary inputs of those industries. The benefits of forcing closures here are difficult to see.

The economic studies are, as usual, not necessarily conclusive, and are often contradictory and confusing. But supposing there was, after all, any negative effect on wages and conditions arising from the availability of the cheap labour of immigrants, the biggest effect would arise from their illegality. This is what makes it hardest for migrants to struggle for better conditions and wages, and most useful to employers in supplying, they hope, a malleable and docile workforce. Once immigrants have a secure legal and residence status, as Commonwealth migrants have since they first came to Britain in the 1950s, and as all workers would once immigration controls were abolished, all the evidence is that they are as willing to join trade unions and organise as the native workforce, or more so. Supposing it were true that immigrant workers and their legally inferior position weakened the bargaining strength of the working class as a whole, then the obvious response is to make more effort to incorporate them as fully as possible into union structures and to fight for their full access to all the rights enjoyed by local workers. However what has the most potential to weaken and divide the working class is not the existence of immigrants, either legal or illegal, but the racism of white workers. The hostility of some of the latter towards immigrants may cause them to blame immigrants rather than their employers and capitalism as a whole for high unemployment and worsening conditions in a period of recession. It may even cause them to identify with their employers, as they obtain relatively higher status and promotion from the worst jobs which come to be filled by immigrants, and may thus weaken their will to engage in collective struggles for the interests of the working class as a whole. Some have argued that this is a reason why governments have deliberately created, through immigration controls, an illegal workforce. Marx, writing in 1870, commented as follows on the hostility of English workers towards Irish immigrants:

Every industrial and commercial centre in England now possesses a working class divided into two hostile camps, English proletarians and Irish proletarians. The ordinary English worker hates the Irish worker as a competitor who lowers his standard of life. In relation to the Irish worker he feels himself a member of the ruling nation and so turns himself into a tool of the aristocrats and capitalists of his country against Ireland, thus strengthening their domination over himself. He cherishes religious, social and national prejudices against the Irish worker. His attitude towards him is much the same as that of the 'poor whites' to the 'niggers' in the former slave states of the USA. The Irishman pays him back with interest in his own money. He sees in the English worker at once the accomplice and the stupid tool of the English rule in Ireland.

This antagonism is artificially kept alive and intensified by the press, the pulpit, the comic papers, in short, by all the means at the disposal of the ruling classes. This antagonism is the secret of the impotence of the English working class, despite its organization. It is the secret by which the capitalist class maintains its power. And that class is fully aware of it. (Marx 1970)

The opportunity to work in industrialised countries is clearly seen as a benefit by immigrants themselves, harsh though the exploitation they are subjected to sometimes is. Even if their ability to migrate caused some redistribution of wealth in their favour, this should be welcomed rather than condemned. Alan Thornett, former TGWU deputy convenor at the British Leyland car plant in Oxford and a Trotskyist, said at a meeting in Oxford that he would favour the abolition of immigration controls even supposing its effect on wages and conditions in Britain was negative: 'British workers have no God-given right to special privileges.' Nevertheless, the likelihood is that migrants increase, rather than diminish, the economic well-being of the native inhabitants of the countries they migrate to. It has generally been the case that the incomes and jobs of the mass of the people depend on an expanding labour supply. In a rare example of the consistent application of the neo-classical competitive paradigm, B. Hamilton and J. Whalley in 1984 in the *Journal of Development Economics* estimate that, because migration of labour is potentially a means of increasing the productivity of labour, an international free market in labour and the abolition of all immigration controls would cause a doubling in world incomes.

IMMIGRATION AND PUBLIC EXPENDITURE

A common argument put forward by the proponents of immigration controls is that free movement would be impossible to accept because of the existence of the welfare state and the burden immigrants would put on it. In 1963 Frank McLeavy, Labour MP for Bradford East, said in the House of Commons:

We cannot afford to be the welfare state for the whole of the Commonwealth. We have a responsibility to our people from a trade union point of view ...

Such attitudes are frequently expressed, and not just by trade unionists. Apparently the benefits of the welfare state should be reserved for the native inhabitants of the rich countries. They are not for sharing. The effects of immigration on public finances are much debated. But, as Bob Sutcliffe argues in *Nacido en otra parte*:

This is really an extraordinary debate. First, both sides share the assumption that immigration is desirable only if it has a positive fiscal balance. That is, immigrants are welcome only if they improve the economic situation of the current inhabitants. If not, they must be excluded. A debate based on similar assumptions in relation to national groups would be almost universally considered barbaric. If, for example, and as is likely, in general people over the age of 70 receive more from public expenditure than they contribute to it, an argument corresponding to the one on immigration would have to be that such persons are undesirable and should be expelled from the country. Doubtless the same would apply to the unemployed, the severely incapacitated, perhaps to religious people and artists. The only reason why the argument is not rejected is that it concerns foreigners. To take this argument seriously is to contribute to the dehumanisation of the migrant.

Nevertheless those who wish to protect the privileges of the inhabitants of the rich countries need not worry too much. Most research concludes that the effect of immigration on public finances is slight. Seventeen studies on the matter were examined by the OECD in a 1997 report on *Trends in International Migration*; 4 said the effect of immigration on public finances was zero or positive, 6 that it was zero or negative, and 7 could not decide; none of them was said to be conclusive. Immigrants when they first arrive probably contribute more to the welfare state than they take from it. They are generally young men, and sometimes women, of working age, self-selected as fit and enterprising. Provided they are allowed to work they do so; they pay taxes and do not require welfare benefits. The rich countries get the labour they need for the functioning and expansion of their economies without having to pay what Marxists call the reproduction costs of labour: the support and education of children and care and medical attention for people who are ill. Usually they fail to make any attempt to provide immigrants with adequate housing. Refugees, it is true, sometimes come with medical problems, including the aftermath of torture, but they too are mostly young and would work if they were allowed to. The very rich come for medical attention and education, and pay for it. Only the fit, and often skilled, come to work.

Immigration controls put an end to the possibility of coming to work or find refuge for short periods and leaving again, or replacing one wage earner by another younger member of the family. They are thus partly responsible for the fact that young workers, especially from the Asian subcontinent, began to consider the alternative of permanent settlement and to bring in their families. Their families included initially non-working wives and young and old dependants. As a result their need for public services began to increase. But they only differ from native workers in the sense that they are, or were, foreigners. They continue to be part of the workforce. Like other workers, they need housing for themselves and their families, medical care and education. They impose no more of a burden than any other part of the workforce, and for the first generation at least, probably less. The condition of course is that they are allowed to work. When the British government talks of the 'burden' imposed by asylum seekers on local authorities, this is a 'burden' it has itself created, first by not allowing them to work, and second by depriving them of normal and administratively cheaper welfare benefits, which are centrally funded, thus transferring the cost of supporting them onto locally administered and much-cut social services.

On the other hand immigration controls are expensive, and becoming more so. The apparatus of controls is mushrooming and becoming ever more sophisticated and oppressive. According to estimates published by the OECD and the 'Intergovernmental Interior Ministers', quoted by Nigel Harris in *The New Untouchables*, European governments spent between US$4 billion and US$8 billion per year in the early 1990s on refugee control and assessment alone, equivalent to roughly one-seventh of their total foreign aid budgets. The figure will by now have increased by a large amount. An estimate made a few years later by Bob Sutcliffe in *Nacido en otra parte*, referring to all types of immigration, is that 'more is probably spent on the administration of current restrictions against citizens of the Third World than is transferred in aid or investments'. In the EU innumerable committees and working groups, usually operating in secret and with the participation mainly of security forces, discuss an ever-expanding arsenal of control techniques, including massive computer systems, the introduction of constantly updated surveillance and detection equipment, and even physical barriers. On top of this there is expenditure on the immigration bureaucracy, including staff and premises. In Britain, according to a House of Commons answer to Eric Forth MP on 7 February 2000, the cost of Immigration and Nationality Directorate operations was £268.6 million in 1999/2000. There is expenditure by the police on arrests and removals, at a cost which the Home Office refused to divulge when asked in parliament by Evan Harris MP on 6 April 2000. There is the cost of detention centres and prison places. In a House of Commons written answer of 23 March 2000, the immigration minister Barbara Roche said that the 'total average monthly cost of holding a detainee' is 'slightly over £5,000'. This means that the cost of detaining 800 people in British detention centres, prisons and police stations, and escorting them between them, is around £48 million a year, about twelve times what it would cost to pay them income support and housing benefit, let alone allow them to work. Detention centres also have to be built or refurbished; the initial cost of opening Campsfield detention centre, for example, was £20 million. There is the cost of paying welfare benefits for asylum seekers who are not allowed to work, and the even greater cost of the current British proposals for voucher and dispersal schemes. The latter have required the Home Office to take on 500 new staff and cost about 50 per cent more than welfare benefits for the same number of people would cost; in a parliamentary answer to the Liberal Democrat MP Simon Hughes on 6 April 2000, Barbara Roche said these 'support costs' were £475 million in 1998/99 and £597 million in 1999/2000. According to figures supplied by the Home Office press office, the total cost of supporting asylum seekers and other immigrants and of the operations of the Immigration and Nationality Directorate to determine whether or not they have a right to stay, to detain them, to deport them, to detect them, etc., at Croydon, at the ports and in the London head office, was £800 million in 1999/2000. On top of this there is the cost of public funding for legal aid and the Refugee Legal Centre. The Immigration Service Union has said, possibly with some exaggeration, that it costs £2 billion a year to support and process asylum seekers.

The money would be better spent on making migrants and refugees welcome, and on improving housing and other public provision for the population as a whole, including recent immigrants, and thus reducing the scope for racist scapegoating.

IMMIGRATION CONTROLS AND RACISM

There remains the question of racism. If it is true that objections to immigration on economic and welfare grounds have little basis in reality, it follows that immigration controls exist mainly because of racism in the countries which apply them. This conclusion is reinforced by the fact that, in Britain as in many countries, controls have discriminated between black and white immigrants (see Chapter 2) so as to stop the former and encourage the latter. To some extent this racism has a material base. It may suit employers and the state, who hope to make immigrants into scapegoats and so divert attention from the deficiencies of capitalism. It divides the workforce and provides employers with exploitable labour, both within the industrialised countries and in the world as a whole. But objections to immigration are also based on irrational notions that cultural mixing is undesirable and objectionable, and that cultural homogeneity is the goal. This is what drives the far right, and what in turn has probably been the major force in the introduction of immigration controls.

In a peculiar twist of logic, governments now say that their reason for introducing ever harsher immigration controls are that they want to promote 'good race relations' and assuage the fears of the racists. But immigration controls do not stop racism. On the contrary governments, in introducing controls, give official endorsement to the notion that immigrants are a problem. The racists are never satisfied. One concession to their prejudices gives rise to demands for more. It is hard for governments, as they do, to call for integration and condemn racism when at the same time, at least implicitly, they fail to refute the prejudice that immigrants are responsible for poverty, poor housing, crime, disease and unemployment, and therefore must be kept out.

Politicians also claim that, in introducing or reinforcing controls, they are responding to popular pressures. There is a danger, they and others claim, that the public might react violently to any increase in immigration. But the process operates in both directions; people, and the media, react to what the politicians tell them. Mostly they have no idea what the numbers of recent immigrants are, and both politicians and media feed exaggerated stories to them (see Chapter 2). When Margaret Thatcher said in a radio interview in 1978 that she sympathised with people's fears that they would be 'rather swamped' by immigrants, the proportion of people saying in public opinion polls that immigration was an urgent issue rose from 9 per cent before her interview to 21 per cent after it. Jack Straw claims to be against racism. But he also claims he has only ever met one genuine asylum seeker and, at a time when Roma refugees were being harassed by racists in Dover, accused British 'travellers' of defecating in doorways. It has to be asked why he was not prosecuted for incitement to racial hatred. The language used by the current Labour government is inflammatory and abusive, unlike the asylum seekers the government so describes. The government, with its big majority in parliament, had an opportunity to set the record straight and tell the truth about refugees, asylum seekers and migration. When it briefly did, in the case of the Kosovan refugees, it uncovered a well of good feeling and sympathy towards their plight. The liberal immigration and asylum policies of Canada, for example, have apparently not led to any racist backlash. The British Labour government could have faced up to Middle England. Instead, it chose to pander to people's basest instincts and to curry favour with the gutter press, whose language mirrored the government's. Presumably following the guidance of focus groups, the government appears to believe that the path to re-election lies in proving that it is capable of acting towards asylum seekers with even greater cruelty than the Tories.

By forcing asylum seekers and immigrants into illegality, governments moreover not only impose hardship on the migrants themselves, but further feed prejudice. They increase, rather than diminish, the extent of international criminal activities which are sometimes said to be the reason why border controls are necessary. Immigration controls, as Prohibition in the United States once did, have pushed people into the hands of criminal gangs and the mafia, who trade in human beings, drugs and stolen goods. Refugees and migrants are therefore associated in people's minds with crime, and the process provides rich hunting-grounds for the prejudices of the media. Even the broadsheets carry sensational stories of the doings of the human 'traffickers' and the terrible effects they have on the people who put themselves in their hands, including forcing them into prostitution.

Governments also seem determined to transform refugees into objects of contempt and targets for racist attack by making them destitute. The government says it wishes to combat social exclusion, and threatens zero tolerance. It is nevertheless creating another category of people who will be driven into begging and providing services on the streets, when they find it difficult to survive on vouchers worth 70 per cent of the minimum amount considered necessary for the rest of the population. In addition, the plans to disperse asylum seekers into sink estates and impoverished regions, blighted by the lack of jobs and facilities, will subject them to racist harassment and abuse. The situation of refugees forced by the Tories' denial of access to the benefits system to stay in south Kent, an area impoverished by mine closures and the decline of English seaside resorts, provides an indication of things to come. Refugees will be blamed for the condition of the housing in which they are placed and will be isolated from their own communities, and they will return, to London and other places, to survive by whatever means possible. Again, when governments lock refugees up in detention centres and prisons many people make the logical, but false, assumption that they must have committed some crime. Such treatment of refugees makes it harder to counter the unfounded assertions that immigrants are especially prone to criminal activities, as well as to disease, squalor and all the attributes which the racists regularly ascribe to new immigrants of whatever origins, and which have been refuted in numerous official reports and by reality (see first section of Chapter 2).

Immigration controls are inherently racist. Even supposing a system of controls was adopted which did not discriminate between foreigners on the basis of their colour, they would still discriminate against foreigners in general, and in favour of the native inhabitants of the country operating controls. Yet racism remains hard to understand. Why the English, or the British, should consider themselves superior to foreigners, and how the English, or British, should be defined, is a mystery. Notions of national culture and national homogeneity have little basis in reality. Britain, like most other countries, is the product of of immigration. The two things that immigrants have in common is that they have nearly always been the object of prejudice and hostility when they first arrived in Britain, and that they have subsequently in different ways made large and valued contributions to the wealth and culture of the country. In practice the racist opponents of immigration are generally white, even though the nations they are defending contain a great diversity of peoples, and their prejudices for the last 40 years or so have been directed mainly at black people. When supporters of the far right are interviewed on television, it becomes even harder to understand how such specimens can consider themselves to be of superior stock.

MIGRATION AND THE THIRD WORLD

A big question is whether or not migration is in the interest of the peoples of the Third World. If it is beneficial, or at least not harmful, for the countries that the migrants go to, it could be that it was damaging for the countries they leave. This argument is sometimes used, either cynically or sincerely, by the proponents of immigration controls. Usually it is a self-serving argument; it is hardly likely that those who resort to it genuinely believe that the justification for immigration controls, and all the suffering they impose on individuals, is that they help the Third World. Quite apart from the question of the enforced flight of some people for whom the alternative would be death, imprisonment and torture, and the economic benefits to some of the individuals who migrate, it is likely that migration leads to some redistribution, however imperfect, of the world's wealth in favour of the Third World.

One of the largest international flows of resources in the world today is 'remittances', or money saved by migrant workers and sent back to their families. The amounts are difficult to estimate. The World Bank publishes figures on remittances transmitted through official channels. These are widely considered to be serious underestimates since remittances are often made through unofficial channels, or made in kind, carried by migrants when they return home, and not recorded in the statistics. In addition, the fact that exchange rates are often undervalued in Third World countries magnifies the purchasing power of the foreign exchange remitted. Nevertheless even the official figures for remittances are higher than the figures for foreign aid. The World Bank figure for remittances in 1998 was $52.8 billion. Its figure for foreign aid was $50 billion, of which only $23 billion was actually grants to developing countries. The figures are roughly equivalent to 1 per cent of the national income and 5 per cent of the exports of all middle- and low-income countries.

Remittances are of course not evenly distributed. They are concentrated precisely in the areas of high emigration, and therefore not necessarily in the poorest countries and regions. But they have many advantages over other forms of international financial transfers. They are not the result of any 'charity' from the rich countries, but are the product of the hard work of the migrants themselves, who have come to recuperate some small part of the wealth that has been stolen from them over centuries of imperialism. They are without doubt preferable to aid from the World Bank, the International Monetary Fund (IMF) and other official sources. Unlike bank loans and most official aid, they do not have to be repaid. Although remittances are not a secure form of income, nor are aid and foreign bank loans. And remittances come without conditions. They are not tied to purchases of doubtfully useful goods and services from the countries from which they come. Whereas foreign aid and the conditions attached to it have on balance impoverished rather than helped the peoples of the Third World, remittances go direct to the families of the people who have emigrated, to use as they think fit.

With their usual self-serving hypocrisy, the authorities and some orthodox economists of the rich countries argue that remittances are misused. Much the same argument is, wrongly, used to justify tying aid to projects chosen by 'donors' and the conditions attached to it. The recipients of remittances are accused of using them for consumption rather than investment. But the argument makes little sense. The native inhabitants of the industrialised countries are not expected to invest their wages, and their failure to do so is not used as a justification for not paying them. The reality is that remittances are used for a variety of purposes, ranging from the satisfaction of elementary needs to the acquisition of consumer durables and sometimes for investment, in particular to buy land. Remittances may at times cause some economic problems, but it is unlikely that they do so more than other sources of foreign exchange, including exports. And alternative sources of foreign exchange, superior or otherwise, may in any case not be available. The criticisms of the economic effects of remittances are in reality yet another example of the way in which the general prejudice against immigration is reflected in a critical assessment of its effects. In the current unequal state of the world, emigration and the resulting remittances are probably one of the best mechanisms currently available for redistributing the world's income in favour of poorer countries.

Others display concern that migration causes a loss to the Third World of skilled and enterprising people, even a new form of pillage of the Third World, using the brains and skills of its peoples for the benefit of the rich countries. Calculations of 'losses' are made on the basis of totting up the costs of educating the migrants in their countries of origin. This concern is hardly compatible with the fact that existing immigration controls impose few restrictions on the movement of people with skills that are needed or desired in the industrialised countries, such as scientific, business, medical, computing, artistic, cultural and sporting skills. It is estimated, for example, that in the period up to 1987 sub-Saharan Africa lost 30 per cent of its highly qualified people through legal emigration. It is the unskilled whose movements are restricted or prevented altogether. To be consistent, this concern ought to imply that restrictions on the movement of unskilled people should be removed, while skilled people should be forced to stay where they are (which of course would contravene the provisions on free movement in the Universal Declaration of Human Rights). It is true that many immigrants who work, sometimes illegally, in unskilled jobs in the industrialised countries are people who are enterprising and sometimes also highly educated and skilled in a formal sense. This is particularly the case with asylum seekers and refugees. In their case it might even be argued that they should stay at home and carry on their struggle against repressive and corrupt regimes. But it is not up to the governments of rich countries to make the decision that they should not migrate. People have many reasons for doing so and, in addition, their migration may make a contribution to the development and well-being of their own countries, for example if they remit their savings, or if they return home with additional skills and experience, or if they help to increase opportunities for those who remain, or perhaps if they help to organise political opposition to their governments while they are in exile. Immigration controls make it less likely that the skills and experience of those who emigrate can be used to benefit their countries of origin, since they tend to force people to stay in the countries they have migrated to rather than risk leaving them and not being able to return if necessary. The alternatives to migration may be death, torture and long imprisonment, as well as frustration, blocked opportunities, unemployment and greater poverty. The arguments put the supposed, but largely unproven, interests of Third World nations above those of the individuals who live in them. Above all, it is clear that the authorities' reasons for denying freedom of movement have nothing to do in reality with any concern about the well-being of the inhabitants of the Third World. It will not do to argue, as some do, for immigration controls on the grounds of opposition to the so-called 'brain drain'.

Opponents of immigration sometimes place their hopes for stopping or reducing it on the promotion of development in the Third World. There are at least two problems with this argument. One is that its adoption can be politically and morally dubious, since it implies acceptance of the notion that migration and an increased diversity of peoples are evils rather than a sign of human progress. Le Pen, leader of the fascist National Front in France, is in favour of development aid. Recently attempts have been made to make EU aid to associated countries conditional on their governments controlling emigration: 'co-development' was adopted as EU policy at the Tampere summit in October 1999. Trade access to the EU has been made conditional on governments agreeing to take back 'illegal' immigrants. The French Socialist government has been negotiating bilateral co-development deals with African governments. The February/March 1999 issue of *La Voix des sans-papiers* carries an article headed 'Co-development, aid for repatriation: Who are they trying to fool? Are immigrants just a currency?', in which Prime Minister Jospin is quoted as constantly repeating on his tour of Africa that 'co-development is one of the means which the government will use to control migratory flows'. The article comments that while Jospin was assuring the Malien government that he would no longer use charter planes to deport its citizens,

he was asking the African governments to help him to control immigration. To put it more clearly, aid money was to be conditional on the willingness of the countries of origin to exercise tight control over emigration to France.

African governments were in a sense being called upon to sell their nationals: to stop those who wished to leave without the unattainable visa, and to accept the enforced return of irregular migrants.

Subsequently the report of Sami Naïr, adviser to Chévènement, on the theme of 'the policy of co-development linked to migratory flows' was revealed to the press. It proposed 'the creation of social conditions to help potential migrants stay at home'. But who can believe that emigration will be reduced by micro-projects? Especially when we know the devastating effects of IMF structural adjustment programmes. Sub-Saharan Africa is crushed by foreign debt. ...

In addition, immigrants are human beings, not a currency! And they contribute much more effectively to the development of their countries of origin than official aid which is largely absorbed by corruption. Many villages have been equipped with electricity, or supplied with wells or maternity hospitals – thanks to the funds sent directly by the immigrants working here.

But is it really a question of co-development? Is it not really more a question of using fine words to ease the conscience of those who are preparing expulsions? ... The government is only talking about 'co-development' to get itself out of a problem which it has itself created by refusing to regularise. We prefer to remain mobilised for the regularisation of all *sans-papiers!*

The second problem with such arguments is that development, or faster growth, may increase rather than diminish the likelihood that people will migrate. One of the largest recent migratory flows was from the so-called 'Asian tigers', including South Korea, Taiwan and Hong Kong, mainly to the United States, during the period of high growth and increased employment and incomes in Asia before the 1997 crisis. Various official US studies have concluded that migration is likely to increase with development, at least in the short term, as people become more educated, and as the role of women changes, for example. Globalisation and investment by multinational companies create links with the metropolitan countries and knowledge of the opportunities there. Development may break down traditional ways of making a living, causing movements of people from rural areas into towns. Higher incomes create the opportunity to move. Many writers have argued that migration is caused by 'pull' factors rather than 'push' factors, in other words by the opportunities available in the immigration countries rather than by the situation in emigration countries. Although there is no precise correlation, there is on the whole less emigration from very impoverished countries than there is from countries where there are more opportunities and wealth. The biggest exception is forced migration from countries where there are wars and political conflicts, which include for example some of the poorest countries in sub-Saharan Africa; and other factors, such as pre-existing community and family links, explain some migration. But in general official and academic studies seem to concur that the promotion of development is likely, at least in the short term, to increase rather than diminish migration. Obviously this is not a reason for opposing development.

Nevertheless it could be that it is skewed and unequal development that causes people to migrate, and above all the repression and impoverishment associated with such development. While people should be free to migrate if they wish to or need to, many people are forced to migrate against their will.

Saskia Sassen in *The Mobility of Labor and Capital* argues that the growth of export-orientated industries sometimes leaves people, especially young women, stranded when they are thrown out of factories once the intensity of work has worn them out; they then cannot return to their villages and have little alternative but to migrate to low-wage jobs in US cities. IMF and World Bank structural adjustment programmes have, sometimes quite deliberately, created unemployment especially among urban workers in public services, and required wage cuts. Their demands for cuts in public services and wages have been in the cause of extracting repayment of foreign debt. This creation of poverty must have increased the relative attractiveness of migration, and the need for it. It has also sometimes led to political upheavals and more repression, from which people have been forced to flee. In the clear-cut case of Yugoslavia, the policies of the IMF created poverty and unemployment which was then exploited by nationalists and led to war, ethnic cleansing and mass flight. The *sans-papiers* have increasingly argued that, while they do not relish their exploitation in wretched jobs which the native inhabitants of Europe reject, they have been forced into this situation by imperialism. At the FASTI conference in Lille (see pp. 113), a *sans-papiers* asylum seeker, who was able to remain in France because her son is French, and who goes around with her son's identity card in case she gets stopped, said in a speech to the conference:

The Europeans come to Africa. They take all its riches. ... We only own 13 per cent of our natural resources. It is France that is there, everywhere. ... It would be better to go home, if we could work there in true cooperation. We'd be better off in the sun, under the coconut palms.

At the same conference Madgiguène Cissé, a leading spokesperson of the Saint Bernard *sans-papiers*, after speaking about the horrors of detention camps, said it was not enough to demand their closure; it was necessary to examine the root causes of migration from the South to the North. Describing the effects of structural adjustment programmes, the disproportion between the sums spent on debt repayment and the sums required for education and health programmes, and the support by France for repressive regimes in Africa, she concluded:

I shall end by saying that today demanding the closure of detention centres, or an amnesty for *sans-papiers* who want their situation to be regularised, should mean starting by demanding the inauguration of new relationships between the North and the South, and the cancellation of Third World debt.

In other words an end to exploitation of the Third World and development which in reality improved conditions there, and so made migration a matter of choice rather than of desperation, would be welcome. Madgiguène Cissé also made the point that the imperialists supply arms to the oppressors:

They tell you about the debt we must pay back, they tell you about public assistance for development, but what they don't talk about is that a large proportion of this public assistance serves to arm the dictators. They say, 'We gave you *x* billion in aid', without mentioning that those billions were used to arm dictators such as Mobutu or Habyarimana. ...

We in the French-speaking countries, we can't even confront our regimes, or rather our dictators; we can't even get face to face with regimes that perpetuate oppression, because the French army is there too. ... Whenever there are public disturbances, when the people are in the street, the French army is there to restore order. There are some very recent examples of this: Zaire, and Bangui where the French army took the liberty of conducting reprisals.

Zaireans opposing Mobutu's corrupt and right-wing regime have been one of the largest groups of refugees in Europe. In Angola the imperialist powers, through their surrogates in South Africa, fomented and financed fighting against the left-wing liberation movement that ousted the Portuguese colonialists, and thus created one of the most persistent flows of refugees from Africa to Europe. All over the world refugees flee wars, repression and torture which are made possible with weapons and equipment manufactured and exported by the West. These are often financed by official loans. The opponents of immigration sometimes talk about the infringements of human rights in Third World countries creating refugees, and demand measures to address the problem. But it should be remembered that these opponents' own governments themselves bear much responsibility for these infringements, by supporting right-wing repressive regimes and selling arms to them.

It would clearly be wrong and opportunistic to use the prevention of migration as an argument for debt cancellation and the ending of the arms trade, since that would imply endorsement of prejudices against migration. Nevertheless debt cancellation and the end of the arms trade are goals which are both desirable in themselves, and likely to go some way towards easing the conditions that force people to flee. Campaigners for the cancellation of debt, such as Jubilee 2000, and against the arms trade, such as the Campaign Against the Arms Trade (CAAT), are natural allies of those who campaign in support of migrants and refugees. Probably most people who migrate now do not do so out of choice. A more just world order, politically and economically, would be one in which no one is forced to migrate by wars, repression or impoverishment. The ideal is that people should be able to migrate of their own free will. The compulsion to move should be reduced to a minimum. But freedom to move should be total.

FREE MOVEMENT

There is now a flagrant contradiction between the current, regressive, promotion of the ideology of the free market as far as goods and capital are concerned, and its denial where people are concerned. But too much should not be made of the analogy. Migrants are human beings, and they should be treated differently from mere material goods and flows of capital. The current situation should, in fact, be reversed. It is quite possible, and right, to oppose free trade and uncontrolled movements of capital, and the domination of the World Trade Organisation by the interests of big capital, and yet to be in favour of the free movement of people. In an ideal world investment would be planned and democratically controlled so that its benefits were widely spread, to reduce inequality, share necessary jobs and improve working conditions and social conditions worldwide, and to protect the environment and other essential interests which are now threatened by profit-seeking private capital. Within Britain some argue that workers who have been made redundant in the North of the country, rather than being forced to migrate south where there are jobs but no housing, should have access to jobs in the North. But people should have the right, internationally as they do within Britain and the EU, to chose freely either to stay where they are or to migrate. Free movement of people will enable workers and the mass of people to share ideas and organise internationally. It too will require international agreement, so that some governments do not maintain restrictions while others abolish them. To deny people the right to migrate is harsh and oppressive, and is leading to unbearable extremes of cruelty.

Cultural diversity exists within nations. In the world as a whole it has existed for thousands of years. It is to be celebrated. It has the potential to enhance human progress. The opening of borders could make the world a more harmonious and peaceful and less racist place, and make possible cooperation and democracy and greater mutual understanding worldwide. Immigration controls should be consigned to the dustbin of history, recognised for what they are: a cruel but relatively short-lived twentieth-century aberration.

APPENDIX: MANIFESTO OF THE NO ONE IS ILLEGAL GROUP, SEPTEMBER 2003

NO ONE IS ILLEGAL! FOR A WORLD WITHOUT BORDERS! NO IMMIGRATION CONTROLS!

Defend the outlaw!

Immigration controls should be abolished. People should not be deemed 'illegal' because they have fallen foul of an increasingly brutal and repressive system of controls. Why is immigration law different from all other law? Under all other laws it is the act that is illegal, but under immigration law it is the person who is illegal. Those subject to immigration control are dehumanized, are reduced to non-persons, are nobodies. They are the modern outlaw. Like their medieval counterpart they exist outside of the law and outside of the law's protection. Opposition to immigration controls requires defending all immigration outlaws.

Beware the fascist! Understand the enemy!

Immigration controls are not fascism. Detention centres are not extermination camps. However immigration laws are different from other laws in one other significant way. They are the result, at least in part, of organized fascist activity. This country's first controls were contained in the 1905 Aliens Act and were directed at Jewish refugees fleeing anti-semitism in Eastern Europe and Russia. A major, perhaps the major, reason for the implementation of this legislation was the agitation of the British Brothers League. This was a proto-fascistic organization which was formed in 1901 specifically around the demand for controls, which organized major demonstrations in London's East End and which can legitimately be viewed as the main force behind the legislation. The first controls directed against black people – the 1962 Commonwealth Immigrants Act – quickly followed events in Notting Hill and Nottingham in 1958. These were the so-called 'race riots' – so-called to give a spurious impression of both spontaneity and non-political street fighting. The reality was that these physical and political attacks on black people were engineered by explicitly fascist organizations such as Oswald Mosley's Union

Movement and Colin Jordan's White Defence League. And these organizations had a specific demand – immigration controls. Fascist front organizations such as the British Immigration Control Association subsequently continued the agitation until legislation was enacted. Oswald Mosley himself was quoted in the left-wing *Reynolds News* as claiming the Bill leading to the 1962 Act was the 'first success' for fascist activity in this country.

Immigration laws are inherently racist, since their purpose is to exclude outsiders. And they feed and legitimize racism. Far from being a natural feature of the political landscape, they are a relatively recent and disastrous distortion of it, explicable only by racism. This, together with the fascist origins of such laws, renders problematic the notion of 'reform', as opposed to abolition, of immigration controls.

Immigration controls are more than they seem. Immigration controls deny people's right to freedom of movement and the right to decide for themselves where they wish to live and to work. They also deny people access to rights such as the right to work and the right to social and legal protections enjoyed by some of the current inhabitants of the place to which they migrate. In the process they cause intolerable suffering to many people. The sole purpose of this suffering is to deter others who might come to this country to claim asylum, to work or to join family here. People are thus punished not for anything they have themselves done, but for what others might do in the future.

Controls are not simply about exclusion and deportation. They are a total system. A system of extremes of pain and misery. They are international in the sense that virtually all countries, particularly all industrial countries, use controls. They are also international in the way the old British Empire was international. British Embassies, British High Commissions, British Consulates encircle the globe denying visas or entry clearance to the unchosen. A vast edifice of repression is built to prevent the movement of people. Those who attempt to flee wars and repression, or to improve their situation through migration, are forced to resort to buying false papers from agents or, worse, to travel clandestinely, again usually with the help of often unscrupulous agents. In the process many of them suffer great hardship, and thousands die. The answer is not to abolish agents, unscrupulous or otherwise. It is to abolish the controls on which the agents, the pain and the misery breed.

Controls are also internal to the modern state and in particular to the modern British state. They require the expansion of repressive and violent activities such as surveillance, security, prisons and policing, changes which threaten to permeate society as a whole. The deaths of Joy Gardner and others at the hands of immigration officers are a portent for the future. Immigration officers have become part of what Karl Marx's colleague Frederick Engels described as 'the armed bodies of men' who constitute the state. Under immigration laws around 2,000 immigrants and asylum seekers who have not been charged with any crime, including children, babies and pregnant women, are locked up without trial, without time limit, and with minimal access to bail. Asylum seekers who are not detained are no longer allowed to work. Since 1996 employers have become an extension of the immigration service, responsible for the immigration status of their workers and liable to criminal sanction for employing undocumented workers. Over the last two decades entitlement to most welfare state benefits and provision has to some extent or another become linked to immigration status. Those without the required status go without. They are excluded from virtually all non-contributory benefits, child benefit, social housing and homelessness accommodation, in-patient hospital treatment, significant areas of community care legislation relating to the destitute, the sick, the elderly and the otherwise vulnerable, protection under child care legislation, state education provision in prisons and detention centres and in the proposed new accommodation centres. So much for the idea that those coming from overseas obtain priority treatment! Instead since 1999 asylum seekers from overseas have been deliberately transformed into an underclass subject to a regime that is the direct copy of the nineteenth century poor law. Like the poor law there is maintenance below subsistence level (70 per cent of income support). Like the poor law there is forced dispersal into accommodation over which those dispersed have no choice. Under legislation introduced in 2002 many asylum seekers are no longer to have even this miserable entitlement, neither supported by the state nor allowed to work.

Immigration controls are not only about refugees. This is just the latest government myth. Migrants and immigrants – those coming to work and those wanting to join family here – along with visitors and students are all equally subject to controls along with refugees. Except unlike refugees they are not even entitled to the fake safety net of the poor law. History is important. It is the immigrant communities, especially of the Indian sub-continent and the Caribbean, who from the 1970s launched a direct attack on immigration control by organizing around campaigns against deportations and for family reunion. It is these campaigns which laid the foundations for the present movement in defence of refugees.

Can there be non-racist or fair controls?

Immigration controls are racist. The first post-war controls, contained in the 1962 Commonwealth Immigrants Act, were directed at black people. However all those subject to immigration control are not black. Within the last decade there has emerged or re-emerged a racism against those from Eastern Europe often combined with an anti-Islamic racism which ensures controls are directed against all those from Bosnians to Serbs to the Roma to the nationalities of the new Russian empire. There is nothing new about this. The first immigration controls, contained in the 1905 Aliens Act, were imposed against refugees – Jewish refugees fleeing persecution in Eastern Europe and Tsarist Russia. Controls were again imposed on Jews attempting to escape Nazism. In short the first half of the twentieth century was about controls against Jews, the second half about controls against black people and the last decade has been about controls against anyone fleeing war, poverty or mayhem or anyone wanting to join family here. Today there exists, however fragmented, a movement against immigration control – a movement which challenges deportations, which opposes detention centres, which offers solidarity to refugees. The great strength of this movement is that it has united and formed a coalition between liberals and socialists, between reformists who don't challenge controls on principle and socialists who are opposed to all controls – and who argue no one is illegal.

The greatest weakness of this movement is that on the level of ideas liberalism dominates. Many of those critical of controls believe that such controls can somehow be sanitized, be rendered fair, be made non-racist. Even socialists are sometimes reluctant to raise the demand for the abolition of all immigration controls or to take this demand to its logical conclusions, in case this alienates potential allies against the abuses that follow from them. The result is that the argument against controls is simply not presented. Many people, perhaps most fair-minded people, if they are presented with the case, do agree that in principle immigration controls are wrong, but may also believe that to argue for their abolition is unrealistic. But ideas matter and so too does the struggle for ideas. Wrong ideas can at best lead to confusion and dead-ends and at worst collusion with the present system. It is our position – a position which denies anyone is illegal, a position that is for a world without borders – that immigration restrictions can never be rendered fair or non-racist. This is for the following reasons. First, controls are inherently racist in that they are based on the crudest of all nationalisms – namely the assertion that the British have a franchise on Britain. Second, they are only explicable by racism. Their imposition is a result of and is a victory for racist, proto-fascist and actual fascist organizations. It is impossible to see how legislation brought into being by such means, legislation accompanied by the most vile racist imagery and assumptions, can ever be reconfigured and rendered 'fair'. Third, the demand for 'fair' controls simply ignores the link between immigration controls and welfare entitlements. This link is itself intrinsically unfair – and racist. Finally, controls can never be 'fair' to those who remain subject to them.

The demand for no controls – based on the assertion that no one is illegal – is frequently derided as utopian and is compared adversely to the 'realism' of arguing for fair controls. However this stands political reality on its head. The struggle against the totality of controls is certainly uphill – it may well require a revolution. However the achievement of fair immigration restrictions – that is the transformation of immigration controls into their opposite – would require a miracle.

More problems with arguments for reforms

The proclamation, our proclamation, that No One Is Illegal means what it says – it does not mean some people are not illegal or only some people are legal. The demand for no controls means no collusion with either the arguments for controls or with controls themselves. However controls have become so politically legitimized over the relatively short period of their existence that it has become all too easy to accept their existence whilst simultaneously opposing them. Here are some examples of what we are arguing against – deliberately difficult and we hope provocative examples:

First, we are absolutely and unconditionally in favour of campaigns against deportation. However we are critical of the emphasis given to so-called 'compassionate' grounds – in particular the re-occurring themes of sickness, age, vulnerability of children, violence towards women and destruction of family relationships. Of course we accept that these issues have to be presented, and presented forcibly, to the Home Office in private as part of any legal argument. The present balance of power – with the Home Office having most of the power – requires this presentation.

However this does not require campaigns against deportation to construct themselves politically and publicly around such compassionate grounds. What this does is make a distinction between the 'worthy' and the 'unworthy' – between those with compassionate grounds and those without. It legitimizes the racist-inspired obligation that people feel to justify their presence here. In doing this it transforms what is normally undesirable – for instance ill health – into something highly desirable in order to try to remain here. Under the guise of gaining support on humanitarian grounds it actually dehumanizes individuals, and denies them their dignity, by reducing them to the sum total of their disabilities and vulnerabilities. It creates a competition between those subject to immigration controls as to who has the more 'compassionate' grounds.

Ultimately it makes it virtually impossible for young, fit, childless, single people without an asylum claim to fight to stay. This is why we support the slogan 'Solidarity not Pity'. We support unconditionally the right of all people to stay here if they wish to, and irrespective of their personal circumstances.

Second, we are absolutely in favour of exposing the lies and hypocrisies of those advocating immigration controls – such as the lie that people coming here are a 'burden' on welfare or are 'flooding' the country. It is important to reject the notion that if immigration controls were abolished this country would be invaded by the populations of entire continents; the reality is that the vast majority of people prefer to stay where they are if this is at all possible. However we are opposed to building a case against immigration controls on the grounds that immigration is in the economic self-interest of the current inhabitants of this country, both because such an argument is wrong in principle and because the situation can change.

For example although it was true until recently that more people left this country than came here, this is no longer the case. And while migrants, immigrants and refugees are currently net contributors to the welfare system, supposing it could be shown that new arrivals are somehow accessing a 'disproportionate' percentage of welfare, would that mean we now have to support controls? Statistics are useful to refute distortions and lies, but cannot be the bedrock of our opposition to controls. Statistics can be a hostage to political fortune. Principles cannot. This is why we support the principle of No One Is Illegal.

Third, we recognize the many contributions made to British society by migrants, immigrants and refugees stretching back centuries. Britain has been constructed out of waves of migration – the very idea of there being an 'indigenous' population is both politically racist and historically nonsensical. However we are opposed to all arguments that seek to justify the presence of anyone on the grounds of the economic or cultural or any other contributions they may make. It is not up to the British state to decide where people should or should not live, or anyone else but migrants and refugees themselves. We support the unfettered right of entry of the feckless, the unemployable and the uncultured. We assert No One Is Illegal.

Gains for some mean exclusion of others. No 'equal opportunities' immigration controls! An obvious, if often overlooked feature of immigration control and the struggle against it, is that defining who may be excluded from it by necessity entails defining who is included in it. No One Is Illegal means that reform of immigration control, in whatever way such reform is presented, is at best problematic, at worst unacceptable because it would leave some people subject to control. It would still leave immigration outlaws. The degree to which any demand falling short of total abolition of controls is acceptable can only be measured by the degree in which it takes up the fight for all outlaws. All specific demands against controls need to be put in the context of and worked out through a position of opposition to all controls. Again we present some deliberately controversial examples:

First, we are critical of the demand for a government 'amnesty' against immigration outlaws. The level of our criticism will depend on the level at which the amnesty is pitched. Who is to be included in this demand? More importantly who is to be excluded? What gives anyone opposed to controls the right to define who is to be excluded? No One Is Illegal means what it says – anyone in the entire world who wishes to come or remain should have the right to do so. On a pragmatic basis amnesties have to be criticised as they will be used by the Home Office to entrap those not included in the amnesty. This is precisely what happened when in 1974 a Labour government declared a tightly defined amnesty – deporting many of those who applied under the mistaken belief they fell within the definition.

Second, we are critical of demands which, however well meant, leave even more vulnerable and exposed to immigration controls those not contained within the demand. An example is the demand that women coming here for marriage who are subsequently subject to domestic violence should not be subject to the requirement that they remain living with their partner for twelve months in order to acquire full immigration status. After years of campaigning this demand has now been met in part. As such it is clearly a tremendous gain for those women who otherwise would have the impossible choice of remaining in a violent relationship or being deported.

However where does this leave all those women not subject to violence who wish for whatever reason to leave the relationship? For them not being battered by their partner has now become a positive disadvantage for immigration purposes. This is yet another example of how something morally outrageous – abuse of women – has become something highly desirable in immigration law. It is simply not a tenable position to argue. The only tenable position is to fight for the right of all, men or women, to remain irrespective of their personal situation.

Third, immigration controls are not just racist. In their nationalism they encompass virtually all reactionary ideology. So unsurprisingly they are homophobic. Until recently there has been no provision for a gay partner to come or remain. However we are critical of the campaign for 'equality' with heterosexual relationships for gay relationships within immigration control. There cannot be equal opportunities immigration controls – unless one is in favour of the equality of the damned. For the last forty years immigration control has systematically attacked, undermined and wrecked tens of thousands of mainly black extended families from the Indian subcontinent, the Caribbean and Africa. Demanding equality with heterosexual couples simply ignores the inherent racism of controls and therefore the relationship between racism, sexism and homophobia. An additional problem is that the demand for the rights of gay couples elevates romance into a political goal – what about the single gay person, the celibate, the lonely, those of no sexual orientation or the promiscuous of any sexual orientation? Including gay couples within immigration law and its spurious 'rights' means that all these other people are by definition excluded. Their status as outlaws is intensified. The way forward is to fight for the rights of all gay women and men along with everyone else to be able to come and remain irrespective of personal circumstances or relationships. The only equal opportunities immigration controls are no immigration controls.

Fourth, demanding to be 'included' within controls – in the sense of demanding specific provision for gay couples – seems itself quite strange in that everyone else is fighting to be excluded from the tentacles of controls. However this contradiction only exists because, given the existence of controls, then absolutely everyone is already 'included' in them to a greater or a lesser extent – in that everyone remains liable to investigation as to whether or not they are subject to them. In this sense women experiencing domestic violence still very much remain subject to controls – as they are obliged to undergo the humiliation of reliving the violence by having to prove its existence. The only political answer to these issues is to fight for no controls.

Fifth, each piece of immigration legislation going back to 1905 (and dramatically intensified in the last decade) can be seen as another brick in the wall – the wall preventing entry of the undesirable, the unchosen. It is therefore not sufficient to demand the repeal of the latest piece of legislation, to remove the latest brick – the whole wall has to go. Otherwise all those excluded by previous legislation remain outlaws and, what is worse, forgotten outlaws. Simply demanding the repeal of the most recent, and only the most recent, laws only serves to legitimize those preceding them. An example is the agitation against that part of the Nationality, Immigration and Asylum Act 2002 (the latest legislation) which denies support to asylum seekers who make 'late' asylum applications – thus rendering these refugees destitute. However in 1999 there was a campaign against the then latest legislation – the Immigration and Asylum Act. This was the legislation which created the poor law of forced dispersal and below-subsistence support. But now the agitation is to include late asylum applicants within the poor law! Again this is not a tenable political position.

At the same time there is being forgotten all those undocumented nonasylum seekers, migrants and immigrants, who have effectively been without any support due to provisions in various pieces of legislation prior to 1999. These statutes were themselves once new, were once campaigned against and are now forgotten – along with those subject to them. No One Is Illegal means fighting to destroy immigration controls in their entirety and at the same time fighting to break the link between welfare entitlement and immigration status.

Socialism

Many if not all of the arguments used to justify immigration controls are simply ludicrous and are more the result of racist-inspired moral panic than of any connection with reality. Such is the notion that the entire world population would come to this country if there were no controls: even if such an absurd notion were true, it should prompt concern for their reasons for coming rather than fear. Nonetheless these objections to open borders need to be answered and they require a socialist and anti-imperialist analysis. The objections about 'overcrowding' can only be answered by discussing socialist use of resources – use based on needs not profits. The objection, the surreal objection, that migrants, immigrants and refugees obtain luxury housing and endless welfare compared to British workers needs to be answered both by pointing out the truth (namely that just the opposite is the case) but also by a recognition that benefits and welfare are woefully inadequate for everyone – both for the documented and the undocumented and that both have a shared interest in fighting for better welfare. The objection that those fleeing the devastation of the Third World have no right to come here can be met by pointing out the imperial responsibility for this devastation, both in the past and currently. As the Asian Youth Movement used to say 'We are here because you were there'. The objection that a state has the right to control its own borders can only ultimately be answered by questioning the nature of the nation state and borders. We agree and sing along with John Lennon:

'Imagine there's no countries'

The way forward – break the links, pull the plug!

- To build the widest possible alliance in all struggles against immigration controls amongst those of differing political views. But to do this without collusion with controls and without compromising with the principle of no controls. To do this on the basis of challenging and winning over those involved to a position of opposition to all controls. No One Is Illegal – No Exceptions, No Concessions, No Conciliation.
- To raise the demand for no immigration controls within all actions and campaigns in support of migrants and refugees. A no-controls position should not be a necessary precondition of support for any particular campaign, but we should argue constantly within all campaigns for such a position. We should argue for campaign slogans to reflect a position of opposition to controls, not refugees are our friends or refugees are welcome here but slogans which recognize that we are in favour of freedom for all as a right, not a charity: No One Is Illegal – Free Movement; No Immigration Controls.
- To support and build every single campaign against deportation. To do this on the basis of solidarity not compassion. No One Is Illegal – No Need for Justification of Presence!
- To support and build every campaign against detention/removal centres, since these are one of the clearest and most outrageously brutal and unjust consequences of immigration controls. No refugees or migrants should be detained simply because they want to be in this country. All detention/removal centres, and also all accommodation, induction and any other repressive 'centres' designed to enforce the unenforceable, should be closed. No One Is Illegal – No Detentions!
- To fight against all forms of collusion with immigration control and with the Home Office. In particular this means local authorities and voluntary sector organizations refusing to implement the new poor law. Local authorities should refuse to act as sub-contracted agents providing accommodation (often otherwise unlettable) for the forced dispersal scheme. Voluntary sector agencies should likewise refuse

Home Office monies to enforce the poor law either through the provision of accommodation or advice. No One Is Illegal – Break the Links Between Welfare Entitlement and Immigration Status!

- For workers within the welfare system to refuse to comply with the denial of benefits or provisions based on immigration status. Most workers within the welfare state, at either local or national level, entered their jobs in the belief they would be providing some form of socially useful service. Instead they now find they are denying services and have become part of the apparatus of immigration control. No One Is Illegal – No Compliance, Be In and Against the State!

- Of course non-compliance by individual workers would leave them absolutely vulnerable to victimization and dismissal. Non-compliance requires major trade union support. It is manifestly important to try and win trade unions to a position of no immigration controls. To do this it is equally important to form rank and file groupings within unions of welfare workers who are being obliged to enforce internal immigration controls. No One Is Illegal – Workers' Control Not Immigration Controls!

- For a massive trade union campaign of recruitment of undocumented workers – of immigration outlaws. Such a recruitment campaign would help break the division between the documented and the undocumented. It would enable a campaign to develop against sweated labour and for the protection of migrant rights – rights to a fair wage, right to proper work conditions and, most of all, the right to work itself – as now it is unlawful to work without the correct immigration documentation. It would also provide another base for the undocumented to resist deportation and to fight for the regularization of their status. No One Is Illegal – Everyone has the right to work, the right to be in a union, and the right to have proper working conditions!

We are not alone!

No One Is Illegal is a phrase first used by Elie Weisel, a Jewish survivor from Nazi Germany, a refugee and a Nobel Prize winner. He was speaking in 1985 in Tucson, Arizona at a national sanctuary conference in the USA in defence of the rights of refugees to live in the USA . The sanctuary movement undertaken by religious communities in the USA (and to a far lesser extent in the UK) in support of those threatened by immigration controls is one of many pieces of resistance to controls. Over the last few years No One Is Illegal groups have been formed throughout Europe and North America – for instance in Germany (Kein Mensch Ist Illegal), Spain (Ninguna Persona Es Ilegal), Sweden (Ingen Manniska Ar Illegal), Poland (Zaden Czlowiek Nie Jest Nielegalny) and Holland (Geen Mens Is Illegaal).

In August 1999 anarchists organized a demonstration in Lvov against the deportation of Ukranian workers under the banner of No One Is Illegal.

In France the *sans-papiers* campaign under the slogan 'personne n'est illégal/e'. There have been No One Is Illegal/No Border camps at the joint borders of Germany, Czech Republic and Poland, and No Border camps at Frankfurt, southern Spain and Salzburg. In June 2002 there was a demonstration against war, globalization and in defence of refugees under the same slogan in Ottawa, Canada. In England groups are emerging calling themselves No Borders. The demand for no controls, rather than being seen as extreme, operates as a rallying call to the undocumented and their supporters. Our aim in producing this, our initial manifesto, is to encourage the formation of No One Is Illegal/No Border groups throughout this country – groups specifically and unreservedly committed to the destruction of all immigration controls.

> Steve Cohen (Manchester), Harriet Grimsditch (Bolton),
> Teresa Hayter (Oxford), Bob Hughes (Bristol),
> Dave Landau (London)

Contacting us

Please contact us if you wish to add your or your organization's name as a supporter of this manifesto – or if you would like a speaker at one of your meetings. If you would like to help us financially in the production of campaign material please make cheques out, in sterling, to 'The No One Is Illegal Group'.

Postal address:
No One Is Illegal,
Bolton Socialist Club,
16 Wood Street,
Bolton, BL1 1DY
Email: info@noii.org.uk
Phone: 01865 726804
Website: http://www.noii.org.uk

6 September 2003

BIBLIOGRAPHY

Academic Group on [Im]migration – Tampere (AGIT) (1999), 'Efficient, effective and encompassing approaches to a European immigration and asylum policy', final draft, 9 June, University of Oxford, mimeo.

Amnesty International (1995), *Prisoners Without a Voice: Asylum-Seekers Detained in the United Kingdom*, London: Amnesty International.

Amnesty International (1996), *Cell Culture: The Detention and Imprisonment of Asylum-seekers in the United Kingdom*, London: Amnesty International.

Amnesty International (2003), UK/EU/UNHCR: 'Unlawful and Unworkable – Extraterritorial Processing of Asylum Claims', mimeo, London: International Secretariat, 1 Easton Street, London WC1X 0DW.

Asylum Aid (1995), *Adding Insult to Injury: Experiences of Zairean Refugees in the UK*, London: Asylum Aid.

Asylum Aid (1995), *'No Reason At All': Home Office Decisions on Asylum Claims*, London: Asylum Aid.

Asylum Aid (1999), *Still No Reason At All: Home Office Decisions on Asylum Claims*, London: Asylum Aid.

Bail for Immigration Detainees (2002), *A Crying Shame: Pregnant Asylum Seekers and Their Babies in Detention*, London: The Maternity Alliance, Bail for Immigration Detainees, London Detainee Support Group.

Barbed Wire Britain: Network to End Refugee and Migrant Detention (2002), *Voices from Detention: Testimonies from Immigration Detainees in Their Own Words*, Barbed Wire Britain.

Borjas, G. J. (1991), 'The impact of immigrants on the employment opportunities of natives', mimeo, Paris: OECD.

Brotsky, C. (1998), 'A defeat for the greening of hate' in *Political Environments: A Publication of the Committee on Women, Population and the Environment*, issue no. 6, Fall 1998, Amherst, Mass.: Population and Development Program, Hampshire College.

Campaign to Close Campsfield (1994), 'Secret State', *Index on Censorship*, no. 6, November/December 1994.

Castles, S. and G. Kosack (1973), *Immigrant Workers and Class Structure in Western Europe*, Oxford: Oxford University Press.

Castles, S. and M. J. Miller (1993), *The Age of Migration: International Population Movements in the Modern World*, London: Macmillan.

Chossudovsky, M. (1996), 'Dismantling former Yugoslavia, recolonising Bosnia', published on the Internet, *chosso@travel-net.com*

Cissé, M. (1997), *The Sans-Papiers: The New Movement of Asylum Seekers and Immigrants without Papers in France: A Woman Draws the First Lesson*, London: Crossroads.

Cohen, R. (1988), *The New Helots: Migrants in the International Division of Labour*, Aldershot: Gower Publishing.

Cohen, R. (1994), *Frontiers of Identity: The British and the Others*, London and New York: Longman.

Cohen, S. (1988), *From the Jews to the Tamils: Britain's Mistreatment of Refugees*, Manchester: South Manchester Law Centre.

Cohen, S. (2003), *No-one Is Illegal: Asylum and Immigration Control Past and Present*, Stoke-on-Trent, UK and Sterling, USA: Trentham Books.

Cohen, S. (undated), *Imagine There's No Countries: 1992 and International Immigration Controls against Migrants, Immigrants and Refugees*, Manchester: Greater Manchester Immigration Aid Unit.

Cohen, S. (undated), *Still Resisting After All These Years: A Century of International Struggles against Immigration Controls 1895–1995*, Manchester: Greater Manchester Immigration Aid Unit.

Cohen, S. (undated), *Workers' Control Not Immigration Controls: Why Trade Unionists Should Oppose Immigration Restrictions*, Manchester: Greater Manchester Immigration Aid Unit.

Cohen, S., B. Humphries and E. Mynott (2002), *From Immigration Controls to Welfare Controls*, London and New York: Routledge.

Deakin, N. (1970), *Colour, Citizenship and British Society: An Abridged and Updated Version of the Famous Report*, London: Panther.

Dummett, A. (1973), *A Portrait of English Racism*, Harmondsworth: Penguin.

Dummett, A. and A. Nicol (1990), *Subjects, Citizens, Aliens and Others*, London: Weidenfeld and Nicolson.

Dummett, M. (2001), *On Immigration and Refugees*, London and New York: Routledge.

Edgar, D. (1977), *Racism, Fascism and the Politics of the National Front*, London: Institute of Race Relations.

European Council on Refugees and Exiles (ECRE) (1995), *Safe Third Country: Myths and Realities*, London: ECRE.

European Council on Refugees and Exiles (1998), *Detention of Asylum Seekers in Europe: Analysis and Perspectives*, The Hague: Kluwer Law International.

Fekete, L. (1994), *Inside Racist Europe*, London: Institute of Race Relations.

Foot, P. (1965), *Immigration and Race in British Politics*, Harmondsworth: Penguin.

Ghaleigh, N. S. (1999), *Immigration Detention and Human Rights: Deserving the Name of Democracy*, London: Asylum Rights Campaign.

Glover, S. et al. (2001), *Migration: An Economic and Social Analysis*, London: Home Office Research, Development and Statistics Directorate.

Gott, C. and K. Johnston (2002), *The Migrant Population in the UK: Fiscal Effects*, London: Home Office Research, Development and Statistics Directorate.

Greater Manchester Immigration Aid Unit (1991), *For a World Without Frontiers: A Collection of Writings from the First Two Years (1990–91) of the Greater Manchester Immigration Aid Unit's Newsletter – No One Is Illegal*, Manchester: Greater Manchester Immigration Aid Unit.

Greater Manchester Immigration Aid Unit (1991), 'The Immigration Service Union: A scab union', in *For a World without Frontiers*.

Hamilton, B. and J. Whalley (1984) 'Efficiency and distributional implications of global restrictions on labor mobility: calculations and policy implications', *Journal of Development Economics*, no. 14.

Harding, J. (2000) 'The uninvited' in *London Review of Books*, vol. 22, no. 3, 3 February.

Harding, J. (2000), *The Uninvited: Refugees at the Rich Man's Gate*, London: Profile Books.

Harris, N. (1995), *The New Untouchables: Immigration and the New World Worker*, Harmondsworth: Penguin.

Harris, N. (1999), 'Should Europe end immigration controls?' Paper given at 9th General Conference of the European Association of Development Research and Training Institutes (EADI), Paris, 22–25 September.

Harris, N. (2002), *Thinking the Unthinkable: The Immigration Myth Exposed*, London: I. B. Taurus.

Hatton, T. J. and J. G. Williamson (1998), *The Age of Mass Migration: Causes and Economic Impact*, New York and Oxford: Oxford University Press.

Hayter, T. (1971), *Aid as Imperialism*, Harmondsworth: Penguin.

Hayter, T. (1981), *The Creation of World Poverty*, London: Pluto Press.

Hayter, T. (1997), *Urban Politics: Accommodation or Resistance?*, Nottingham: Spokesman.

Hayter, T. (1998), 'Laughed out of court' in *Red Pepper*, no. 52, September.

Hayter, T. (1999), 'Free movement: A case against immigration controls', *Political Environments*, no. 7, Amherst, Mass.: Hampshire College Population and Development Program.

Hayter, T. and D. Harvey, eds (1993), *The Factory and the City: The Story of Cowley Automobile Workers in Oxford*, London: Mansell.

Hensman, R. (undated), *Journey Without a Destination: Is There a Solution for Sri Lankan Refugees?* London: Refugee Council.

HM Inspectorate of Prisons (1995), *Report by HM Chief Inspector of Prisons Judge Stephen Tumim of an Unannounced Short Inspection: Immigration Detention Centre Campsfield House*, London: Home Office.

HM Inspectorate of Prisons (1998), *Report by HM Chief Inspector of Prisons (Sir David Ramsbotham) of a Full Inspection 4–7 August 1997: Tinsley House Immigration Detention Centre Gatwick Airport*, London: Home Office.

HM Inspectorate of Prisons (1998), *Report by HM Chief Inspector of Prisons (Sir David Ramsbotham) of an Unannounced Short Inspection 13–15 October 1997: Campsfield House Detention Centre*, London: Home Office.

HM Inspectorate of Prisons (2000), *HM Prison Rochester: Report by HM Chief Inspector of Prisons (Sir David Ramsbotham) of an Unannounced Short Inspection 31 August–3 September 1999*, London: Home Office.

Home Office (1993), *Asylum and Immigration Appeals Act*, London: The Stationery Office.

Home Office (1996), *Asylum and Immigration Act*, London: The Stationery Office.

Home Office (1997), *Statistical Bulletin 1997*, London: Home Office.

Home Office (1998), *Fairer, Faster and Firmer: A Modern Approach to Immigration and Asylum*, London: Home Office CM 4018.

Home Office (1998), *Statistical Bulletin 1998*, London: Home Office.

Home Office (1999), *Immigration and Asylum Act*, London: The Stationery Office.

Home Office (2002), *Nationality, Immigration and Asylum Act*, London: The Stationery Office.

Home Office (2002), *Secure Borders, Safe Haven: Integration with Diversity (White Paper)*, London: The Stationery Office.

Home Office, J. Dudley, G. Turner and S. Woollacott (2003), *Control of Immigration: Statistics United Kingdom*, London: Home Office, Research Development and Statistics Directorate.

House of Commons (1972), *Police–Immigrant Relations*, report by the Select Committee on Race Relations and Immigration, Session 1971–2, London: HMSO.

House of Commons, Home Affairs Committee (2003), *Asylum Removals*, London: The Stationery Office.

Hunte, J. A. (1966), *Nigger Hunting in England?*, London: West Indian Standing Conference, London branch.

Institute of Race Relations (1969–), *Race Today*, quarterly/bimonthly journal, London: Institute of Race Relations.

Institute of Race Relations (1986), *The Fight Against Racism*, London: Institute of Race Relations.

Institute of Race Relations (1987), *Policing Against Black People*, London: Institute of Race Relations.

Institute of Race Relations (1991), *Deadly Silence: Black Deaths in Custody*, London: Institute of Race Relations.

Institute of Race Relations (1991), *Europe: Variations on a Theme of Racism*, London: Institute of Race Relations.

Joly, D. with C. Nettleton and H. Poulton (1992), *Refugees: Asylum in Europe?* London: Minority Rights Group.

Kindleberger, C. P. (1967), *Europe's Postwar Growth: The Role of Labor Supply*, Cambridge, Mass.: Harvard University Press and Oxford: Oxford University Press.

Lambeth Council, The Voice and South London Press (1988), *Forty Winters On: Memories of Britain's Post War Caribbean Immigrants*, London: Lambeth Council.

Layton-Henry, Z. (1992), *The Politics of Immigration*, Oxford: Blackwell.

Malden, H. E., ed. (1905), *The Victoria History of the County of Surrey*, London: Constable.

Marx, K. (1870), 'Letter to Bloch', in McLellan, D. ed. (1971) *Karl Marx: Selected Writings*, Oxford: Oxford University Press.

May, E. T. (1997), *A Treatise on the Law, Privileges, Proceedings and Usage of Parliament*, 22nd edn, London: Butterworths.

Merriman, N., ed. (1993), *The Peopling of London: Fifteen Thousand Years of Settlement from Overseas*, London: Museum of London.

Monahan, J., C. Howard and K. Fletcher (2003), *Asylum Voices: Experiences of People Seeking Asylum in the United Kingdom*, London: Churches Together in Britain and Ireland.

Morrison, J. (1998), *The Cost of Survival: The Trafficking of Refugees to Britain*, London: Refugee Council.

Organisation pour la coopération et le Développement Economique (OCDE) (1991), *Migration: les aspects démographiques*, Paris: OCDE.

Organisation for Economic Co-operation and Development (OECD)/SOPEMI (1999), *Trends in International Migration*, Paris: OECD.

Panayi, P. (1994), *Immigration, Ethnicity and Racism in Britain, 1815–1945*, Manchester: Manchester University Press.

Pentonville Board of Visitors (1993), *Annual Report 1993*.

Perrin-Martin, J.-P., ed. and Bill MacKeith, trans. (1998), *Europe Behind Barbed Wire: Immigration Detentions in Europe*, Oxford: Campaign to Close Campsfield.

Pourgourides, C. K., S. P. Sashidharan and P. J. Bracken (1996), *A Second Exile: The Mental Health Implications of Detention of Asylum Seekers in the United Kingdom*, Birmingham: Northern Birmingham Mental Health NHS Trust, University of Birmingham and Barrow Cadbury Trust.

Refugee Council (1995), *Beyond Belief: The Home Office and Nigeria*, London: Refugee Council.

Royal Commission on Population, Report of the (1949), Cmnd 7695, London: HMSO.

Sassen, S. (1988), *The Mobility of Labor and Capital: A Study in International Investment and Labor Flow*, Cambridge: Cambridge University Press.

Scarman, Lord (1981), *The Brixton Disorders, 10–12 April 1981*, Cmnd 8427, London: HMSO.

Shuster, L. (2003), *The Use and Abuse of Political Asylum in Britain and Germany*, London: Frank Cass.

Shuster, L. (2003), 'Common sense or racism? The treatment of asylum-seekers in Europe', *Patterns of Prejudice*, vol. 37, no. 3.

Singh, P. (1992), 'Punjab issue in British politics', *Economic and Political Weekly*, vol. XXVII, no. 13, 28 March.

Sivanandan, A. (1978), *From Immigration Control to Induced Repatriation*, London: Institute of Race Relations.

Sivanandan, A. (1983), *A Different Hunger: Writings on Black Resistance*, London: Pluto Press.

Sivanandan, A. (1986), *Asian and Afro-Caribbean Struggles in Britain*, London: Institute of Race Relations.

Skran, C. (1995), *Refugees in Inter-war Europe: The Emergence of a Regime*, Oxford: Clarendon Press.

Socialist Workers Party (1978) *The Case Against Immigration Controls*, London: Socialist Worker Distributors.

Spencer, I. R. G. (1997), *British Immigration Policy since 1939: The Making of Multi-racial Britain*, London: Routledge.

Stalker, P. (2001), *The No-Nonsense Guide to International Migration*, Oxford: New Internationalist and London: Verso.

Straw, J., MP and D. Henderson, MP (undated), 'Fairer, faster and firmer: Labour's approach to asylum and immigration', mimeo.

Stroud, H. (1999), *The Ghost Locust*, Hong Kong: Asia 2000 Ltd.

Sutcliffe, B. (1994), 'Immigration: rights and illogic', *Index on Censorship*, no. 3, 1994.

Sutcliffe, B. (1998), *Nacido en otra parte: Un ensayo sobre la migración internacional, el desarollo y la equidad*, Bilbao: Hegoa.

Thornett, A. (undated), 'The case against EMU' in *Even More Unemployment: A Socialist Outlook Pamphlet*, London: Socialist Outlook.

Trades Union Congress, European Union and International Relations Department (2003), *Overworked, Underpaid and Over Here: Migrant Workers in Britain*, London: Trades Union Congress.

United Nations High Commissioner for Refugees (UNHCR) (1992), *Handbook on Procedures and Criteria for Determining Refugee Status*, Geneva: UNHCR.

United Nations High Commissioner for Refugees (UNHCR) (1996), *Guidelines on Detention of Asylum Seekers*, Geneva: UNHCR.

United Nations Population Division (2000), *Replacement Migration: Is It a Solution to Declining and Ageing Populations?*, New York: United Nations.

Webber, F. (undated), *Crimes of Arrival: Immigrants and Asylum-Seekers in the New Europe*, London: Statewatch.

World Bank (1999), *Global Development Finance, 1999*, Washington DC: World Bank.

ORGANISATIONS AND CAMPAIGNS

Amnesty International
99–119 Rosebery Avenue, London EC1R 4RE
Tel. 020 7814 6200

Association of Visitors to Immigration Detainees (AVID)
c/o Sally Tarshish, Bartlemas House, Oxford OX4 2AJ
Tel. 01865 727795

Asylum Aid
28 Commercial Street, London E1 6LS
Tel. 020 7377 5123

Asylum Welcome
276a Cowley Road, Oxford OX4 1UR
Tel. 01865 722082

Bail for Immigration Detainees (BID)
28 Commercial Street, London E1 6LS
Tel. 020 7247 3590

Bail for Immigration Detainees (Oxford)
c/o Viva Network, 53 Westway, Oxford OX2 0JE
Tel. 0845 330 4536

Barbed Wire Britain: Network to End Refugee and Migrant Detention,
www.barbedwirebritain.org.uk

Campaign Against Arbitrary Detentions at Yarl's Wood (SADY)
PO Box 304, Bedford MK42 9WX
Tel. 07786 517379

Campaign Against the Arms Trade (CAAT)
11 Goodwin Street, London N4 3HQ
Tel. 020 7281 0297

Campaign Against Criminalising Communities (CAMPACC)
www.cacc.org.uk, tel. 020 7586 5892, e-mail knklondon@gn.apc.org

Campaign Against Racism and Fascism (CARF)
BM Box 8784, London WC1N 3XX
Tel. 020 7837 1450

Campaign to Close Campsfield
17c West End, Witney OX28 1NQ
Tel. 01865 558145/726804 or 01993 703994
www.closecampsfield.org.uk

Campaign to Defend Asylum Seekers (CDAS)
BCM Box 4289, London WC1X 3XX
Tel. 07941 566183

Centre for Research on Ethnic Relations (CRER)
University of Warwick, Coventry CV4 7AL
Tel. 01203 522641

Churches Commission for Racial Justice
Inter-Church House, 35–41 Lower Marsh Street
London SE1 7RL
Tel. 020 7620 4444

Close Harmondsworth Campaign
10 Endsleigh Road, Southall UB2 5QL
Tel. 020 8571 5019

Commission for Racial Equality (CRE)
10–12 Arlington Street, London SW1E 5EH
Tel. 020 7828 7022

Crossroads Women's Centre
PO Box 287, London NW6 5QU
Tel. 020 7482 2496

Detention Advice Service (DAS)
308 Seven Sisters Road, London N4 2AG
Tel. 020 8802 3422

Dover Residents Against Racism
105 Priory Hill, Dover CT17 0AD
Tel. 07803 680053

European Council on Refugees and Exiles (ECRE)
Clifton Centre, 110 Clifton Street, London EC2A 4HT
Tel. 020 7729 5152

Greater Manchester Immigration Aid Unit
400 Cheetham Hill Road, Manchester M8 7EL
Tel. 0161 740 7722

Immigration Advisory Service
71 Grove Road, Middlesex TW3 3PR
Tel. 020 8814 1115

Immigration Law Practioners' Association (ILPA)
Lindsey House, 40–42 Charterhouse Street, London EC1M 6JN
Tel. 020 7251 8383

Inquest
Alexandra National House, 330 Seven Sisters Road, London N4 2PJ
Tel. 020 8802 7430

Institute of Race Relations/Race and Class
www.irr.org.uk
2 Leeke Street, London WC1X 9HS
Tel. 020 7837 0041

Joint Council for the Welfare of Immigrants (JCWI)
115 Old Street, London EC1V 9JR
Tel. 020 7251 8708

Kent Campaign for Asylum Seekers
126 St Mary's Road, Faversham, Kent ME13 8EE
Tel. 01795 537334/537741

Kent Refugee Action Network
PO Box 294, Dover CT17 9GY
Tel. 01304 201131

Liberty
21 Tabard Street, London SE1 4LA
Tel. 020 7403 3888

Medical Foundation for the Care of the Victims of Torture
96–98 Grafton Road, London NW5 3FJ
Tel. 020 7813 7777

Migrant Media
90 De Beauvoir Road, London N1
Tel. 020 7254 9701

National Assembly Against Racism (NAAR)
28 Commercial Street, London E1 6LS
Tel. 020 7247 9907

National Civil Rights Movement
14 Featherstone Road, Middlesex UB2 5AA
Tel. 020 8843 2333

National Coalition of Anti-Deportation Campaigns (NCADC)
c/o John O
110 Hamstead Road, Birmingham B20 2QS
Tel. 0121 554 6947
c/o Alison Bennett
Room 228, Tudorleaf Business Centre, 2–8 Fontayne Road, London N15 4QL

c/o Tony Openshaw
c/o GMIAU, 1 Delaunays Road, Manchester M8 4QS
Tel. 0161 740 7113
c/o Kath Sainsbury
66 Dovecot Street, Stockton-on-Tees, TS18 1LL
Tel. 01642 679298

Newham Monitoring Project
PO Box 273, London E7
Tel. 020 8552 6284

No One Is Illegal
Bolton Socialist Club, 16 Wood Street, Bolton BL1 1DY.
E-mail: info@noii.org.uk, website: www.noii.org.uk, tel. 01865 726804

Refugee Council
3 Bondway, London SW8 1SJ
Tel. 020 7820 3000

Refugee Legal Centre,
Sussex House, 39/45 Bermonsey Street, London SE1 3XF
Tel. 020 7827 9090

Sans-Papiers National Coordinating Committee (Coordination Nationale des Sans-Papiers)
22 rue Pajol, 75018 Paris
Tel./fax 0033 146 07 1619

Searchlight Magazine
37b New Cavendish Street, London WC1M 8JR
Tel. 020 7284 4040

Southall Black Sisters
52 Norwood Road, Middlesex UB2 2DW
Tel. 020 8571 9595

Southall Monitoring Group
14 Featherstone Road, Middlesex UB2 5AA
Tel. 020 8843 2333

Statewatch
PO Box 1516, London N16 0EU
Tel. 020 8802 1882

United Nations High Commissioner for Refugees (UNHCR)
Millbank Tower, London SW1
Tel. 020 7828 9191

West Midlands Anti-Deportation Campaign, c/o Asian Resource Centre,
101 Villa Road, Handsworth
Birmingham B19 1NH

INDEX

60 WAYS
to Lower Your
BLOOD
SUGAR

DENNIS POLLOCK

HARVEST HOUSE PUBLISHERS
EUGENE, OREGON

Cover by Koechel Peterson & Associates, Inc., Minneapolis, Minnesota

60 WAYS TO LOWER YOUR BLOOD SUGAR
Copyright © 2013 by Dennis Pollock
Published by Harvest House Publishers
Eugene, Oregon 97402
www.harvesthousepublishers.com

Library of Congress Cataloging-in-Publication Data
Pollock, Dennis, 1953-
    60 ways to lower your blood sugar / Dennis Pollock.
        pages cm
    ISBN 978-0-7369-5258-3 (pbk.)
    ISBN 978-0-7369-5259-0 (eBook)
    1. Diabetes—Popular works. 2. Diabetes—Treatment—Popular works. 3. Reducing diets—Popular works. 4. Low-carbohydrate diet—Popular works. I. Title. II. Title: Sixty ways to lower your blood sugar.
    RC660.4.P655 2013
    616.4'62—dc23
                                                                    2013000620

To my sweet lady and my best friend,
my wife, Benedicta,
who is truly a gift from God to me.

Contents

Foreword

The relationship of obesity to blood-sugar problems and type 2 diabetes has been known for years. In this country today, the weight problem is epidemic. Just look around the next time you go to a restaurant, supermarket, or anyplace there are lots of people and see how many of them are overweight.

Dieting to lose weight is important, of course, but just what foods are better for your health to accomplish this task? The author has spent much effort selecting not only foods but a lifestyle to deal primarily with his blood-sugar problem—and with great success. The changes he suggests are not necessarily easy, but the end result is what is important. Eating a healthy diet will prevent many medical problems and decrease or eliminate the need for expensive medications. As I would tell my patients, all the food God made is good. But, what people do to it may not be—and this is manifested by what you see today in this country.

How earnestly do you want to be healthy? How motivated are you? How committed are you? Moderation in all you eat, as well as motivation to select healthy foods, are essential; both are wisely stressed by the author. As you read this book, may you be inspired to deal with your own issues for the sake of your better health.

Paul Saneman, MD, ABOG

The Simple and Basic Keys

Diabetes is on the rise in America. This is not a new phenomenon. It has been steadily increasing for years and shows no signs of letting up. It is projected that within another 50 years one in three Americans will be diabetic.

There is a note of hope in this, however. The fact that the rate of diabetes can increase reveals that there are factors we can control—things we can do to decrease our chances of becoming diabetic, or if already diabetic, to begin to reverse the process. If diabetes were totally unrelated to lifestyle factors, it would neither increase nor decrease from one age to another, or from one culture to another. This is clearly not the case.

As is true in so many areas of life, our primary problem is not ignorance of what we should do; it is a lack of motivation to do what we know we need to do. In my previous book, *Overcoming Runaway Blood Sugar*, I shared my own experience with blood sugar that rose precipitously high and dropped dangerously low. By the time I was in my forties my blood sugar was totally out of control. My pancreas was working just fine, but it was being overworked by a body that was no longer processing carbs and sugar efficiently. A high-carb meal could raise my blood sugar to twice the normal level or higher, and then within a couple of hours, after my abused pancreas had gamely dumped prodigious amounts of insulin into my bloodstream, it might fall to half of normal. I would be trembling violently and feeling like I was about to pass out, which I did in public once, to my shock and embarrassment.

At first I had no clue as to what was going on in my body, but had some suspicions that it had to do with blood sugar. After obtaining a blood-glucose monitor, I started checking my blood sugar several times a day. I soon realized that what I put in my mouth an hour or two previously had everything to do with the kind of numbers I was seeing on the monitor.

Lots of pasta, a big dessert, and a soda to wash it all down led to disastrous numbers. But a large chef salad with eggs, ham, and garden vegetables, with water to drink, produced beautiful numbers.

Not content to merely observe, I started reading different books and articles related to blood sugar. Trying to stay mainstream, I discovered that the most reputable and conservative authors came to the same conclusions. The three basic means of controlling blood sugar are *reducing carbohydrates, regular exercise,* and *shedding excess weight.* Now I had hope! As fearful as those trembling episodes had been, my attitude was, *Give me something concrete to do about this, and I'll do it!* I plunged into making the necessary changes and was thrilled to see my numbers go down and stay down. They have now been that way for years.

Most diabetics know the steps they must take to bring their blood sugar to a normal state and prevent long-term damage to their body. But making the necessary changes seems just too tall a mountain to climb. Besides, at the present they may feel just fine. They still have pep, they feel great—in fact, after eating a high-carb meal they feel especially good! They do not realize that they are well along on the journey to sores that refuse to heal, heart disease, kidney failure, leg amputations, and premature death. The irony is that the changes they are avoiding, while not unsubstantial, are not nearly as difficult or painful as they think.

This book does not take the place of a good doctor! **If you are diabetic you absolutely need to be seeing a doctor.** If you suspect you are diabetic you need to go to a doctor and get yourself checked. The ideas in this book are made to complement the advice and care of your physician.

In this little book I intend to put some very simple basic keys in your hand that will help you, step by step, make the necessary changes with the least amount of pain. I have never particularly liked pain. In fact any time I can avoid it, I surely will. The idea of being some kind of a grim diabetes martyr, never enjoying a meal, forcing myself to do physical workouts I hate, never indulging my sweet tooth (actually teeth), and walking away from every meal constantly hungry is something I have no interest in. The good news is—*it's not necessary.*

This is not a complex book. If you are looking for theories and large words and scientific terms, you won't find too much here. But if you are struggling and failing to keep your blood sugar under control, you will find some simple steps you can take to turn the thermostat down that controls the raging fire of your runaway blood sugar.

Nor is there anything wacky here. As I mentioned, the changes suggested have been known and recommended by the professionals for decades. But what is different about this book is that it puts in your hands a game plan you can easily understand and implement, along with some inspirational thoughts to stay the course. It is written by a regular guy for regular people who want to live out their lives in health.

As you read through the chapters, you will find some thoughts and concepts repeated. This is deliberate. We humans need to hear things more than once to really get them. Nor are the chapters necessarily sequential. They are ideas, tips, things to do, things to stop doing, and even some recipes.

These "ways" are not the end-all of behavior modifications for diabetics, but they make up a powerful set of adjustments and insights that can make a significant improvement in your prospects for a healthy life and a place at the weddings of your grandchildren.

Go ahead—dare to make some changes. You'll find that you can feel better now—and better yet in the future!

1
. . . .
Monitor Thyself

Most of the concepts we will be looking at could be read and embraced in no specific order. However, this particular thought really does need to be first. If you have blood-sugar issues, or merely suspect that you have them, you need to get a blood-sugar monitor. If the idea of frequently having your blood drawn turns you off—well, better to draw a little speck of blood a couple of times a day rather than to have your blood filled with sugar, destroying your organs, sapping your strength, and bringing you to an early grave.

I will never forget the first time I checked my blood sugar. I was at my office, and our assistant brought me an extra monitor from home (her husband was diabetic). I had shared with her and some of the others at the office some of my "shaky" experiences, and she wisely perceived that this was a problem with blood sugar. I suspected as much, but didn't want to face the truth.

I was terrified. I had read enough to know that 80 to 120 mg/dl was the ideal, and I was fearful about what mine would be. What if I was a raging diabetic with a level of 500? In fact I was so nervous I couldn't seem to get a full drop of blood on the stick, and we had to try several times and several pricks. I watched the monitor with a racing heart as I waited for the verdict that might determine the rest of my life. Finally it came, and it was decent—in the 120s as I remember.

Feeling emboldened, I checked myself a couple of hours later, and my level had dropped to around 60 (too low). I was too ignorant at this point to know why it would drop so much, but at least I was off and running. I would be taking hundreds of blood-sugar readings in the next year. Eventually I began to use these readings to make decisions about what

---

Mg/dl stands for **"milligrams per deciliter,"** the standard of measurement for blood glucose.

. . . .

kinds of foods were best for me to eat. Lo and behold, I found out that the higher the carbohydrate content of the foods I ate, the greater the rise in my blood sugar (no surprise, right?). Like most people I assumed that foods known for being sugary were the main things I should avoid. But my glucometer taught me an interesting lesson: carbs (carbohydrates) will affect our blood sugar, regardless of their source.

For example, if you place a bagel next to a candy bar and ask people which is more likely to affect blood sugar, most people would say the candy bar. Yet the candy bar may have 28 grams of carbs and the bagel may have 50. And if you say no to the candy bar but yes to the bagel, feeling very proud of yourself, and then go and check your blood sugar when it is at its peak, you will be shocked that your body wasn't particularly impressed with your choice. Your blood sugar most likely soared higher after the bagel than it would have had you eaten the candy bar.

If you read any competent articles or books they will unanimously tell you to check your blood sugar frequently if you have diabetes. It is also a good idea to check yourself if you are hypoglycemic (have low blood sugar frequently) or if you bounce up and down (as I used to). But why is this necessary? There are two primary, very powerful reasons to do this, and they have to do with assessment and accountability.

First, people always do better where there is accountability. When there is tangible evidence of how well or poorly we have been doing there will be far more motivation to improve than when we are left in the dark to guess our performance. Early on in my blood-checking I ate a meal of a hamburger with a large bun and a bunch of Fritos. I waited about an hour and a half, took my blood sugar, and felt sick to see the meter read well above the normal range. From that point on I had a fresh view of burgers with large buns and Fritos.

If you are to succeed in your struggle against high blood sugar, you need motivation, motivation, and more motivation! Anything that will increase your motivation you must embrace; anything that decreases it must be avoided. And there is hardly a better motivator than one of these little blood-glucose monitors. They will not lie to you and will tell you the truth, the whole truth, and nothing but the truth.

There are a gazillion books on the market about diabetes and blood sugar, and myriads of theories. Some folks will tell you to swear off all animal products and become a vegetarian. Others will tell you to pile on the meat, cover it with cheese, and then pile on more meat. Some will tell you that diabetes has no cure and others will swear that they alone possess the knowledge that will totally cure you. Who do you trust?

My suggestion, first of all, is to go mainstream. Don't take too much stock in the writings of someone who writes about diabetes and then mentions that he has also found a cure for cancer, has discovered the secret to living to be 200, and uncovered 100 different conspiracies by our government. And—oh yeah—he was once abducted by aliens, who taught him the secrets he now shares with you.

Second, believe your blood-glucose monitor. Some folks will tell you that fruit is so healthy for us and contains so many important vitamins that you can eat as much of it as you like. "Go ahead—indulge in that pineapple, eat that huge orange, and gulp down that big glass of apple juice. It's good for you!" Well, if you want to do that, be sure to have your blood-glucose meter nearby. About an hour later check and see what your fruit orgy has done to your blood sugar. You'll think twice about overdosing on fruit again. (I am not saying to avoid fruit. But you cannot give it a free pass and eat as much as you want without considering the carbs you are ingesting. More in a later chapter.)

There are two types of readings that are important. First you will want to check your fasting blood sugar. This is done when you first rise in the morning, before you eat anything. Readings in the 80s are ideal, in the 90s, decent, and over 100 is problematic. The ADA (American Diabetes Association) considers you diabetic if you consistently are over 126. Your fasting blood-sugar level is like a report card. If you are diabetic or prediabetic and have not been eating right for some time, your fasting blood sugar will usually rise and tattle on you. If you have been behaving yourself and doing what you should be doing it will tend to go down toward an acceptable level and stay that way.

A second highly significant reading is the one that tells us the effect of our last meal. This is especially critical in the early stages of discovering the dietary changes and adjustments that must be made. Not all people have their blood-sugar peak at the same time. For most people it will be about an hour to an hour and a half after they take the last bite of their previous meal. Take enough readings to find out the typical amount of time after a meal for your blood sugar to reach its peak. If your pancreas is still working well, the time will be shorter and the peak won't last too long, but if it is on the way out the peak may stretch out for a couple of hours.

Your tests will soon reveal your peak time, and this should be when you test yourself to discover how a particular meal has affected you. Ideally your blood-sugar level should not peak any higher than 140 to 145 mg/dl. Start with some of your favorite meals and see how they affect your blood sugar. It will be enlightening, and give you the courage to make the changes and adjustments that need to be made to keep your blood sugar under control.

Mirrors are something we take for granted, but where would we be without them? Almost all of us make use of mirrors every day. Is our hair looking all right? Does this shirt really work for us? Do we have anything in our nose that doesn't belong there? Of course mirrors can be a bit cruel. When we gain weight they expose it mercilessly. But they tell us the truth and they motivate us. If our hair is mussed, we will take the extra time to deal with it. If there is dirt on our face, we will wash ourselves.

So it is with your friendly little blood-glucose monitor. Those bold black numbers will either compliment you and encourage you to keep on with what you're doing, or they will shout at you to stop, turn around, and go the other way. Your meter is your friend. Treat it well, think fond thoughts of it, and listen when it speaks.

Carb-Cutting

There is no getting around it. If you want permanent control over blood sugar, you are going to have to cut some things out of your diet. You are going to have to control your carbohydrate intake. No, you will not need to do away with all carbs. That would be unwise, unhealthy, and just plain stupid. Our bodies need some carbohydrates daily for optimum health. But we don't need nearly so many as most Americans continually eat!

In earlier days, processed food was unheard of. Today's desserts did not exist. A dessert in those days was to eat an apple or some grapes or a watermelon. There was no soda, no doughnuts, no sugary cereals in dazzling colors, and nobody had ever heard of pizza. People worked hard, most stayed slim, and they ate whole grains, meat (when they could get it), vegetables, and enjoyed a little fruit in season. Diabetes was rare.

That was then; this is now. We have discovered thousands of ways to fill ourselves with sugar, stuff our stomachs with pasta, and glut ourselves on white rice and white bread. To make matters worse we wash all these things down with supersized sodas loaded with, you guessed it, more sugar. What's wrong with this picture?

As I began to research the causes of runaway blood sugar I began to discover some of the basics of good health and learned why the standard American diet is so pathetic, and why it leads folks like me straight to the land of diabetes once our youthful metabolism begins to give way to its slower, middle-aged replacement.

It is not that our bodies need no sugar; they most definitely do. They simply don't need nearly as much as we are shoveling into them. Many nutritionists believe a glass or two of red wine each day may be healthy for you. But drinking a dozen glasses of wine at each meal will destroy you. So it is with carbohydrates. A thin slice of whole-grain bread with an otherwise low-carb meal is no problem. A small portion of brown rice, along with some grilled chicken and a salad is reasonable. But a breakfast of a large bowl of sugary cereal, a couple of slices of bread, and a big glass of orange juice is dietary suicide. You are throwing so many carbs at your abused and overworked pancreas it has no idea where to even start. All it can do is dump out as much insulin as it can possibly manage.

If your pancreas hasn't yet been severely damaged by your abuse, it will provide enough insulin to eventually get the job done, but most likely you will experience a blood-sugar spike initially and then a miserable sinking feeling in a couple of hours when all that insulin forces your blood sugar toward dangerously low levels. If your pancreas is no longer capable of providing sufficient insulin, your blood sugar will stay elevated for many hours, damaging organs and nerves. When this goes on for years it will eventually take an enormous toll on your health and your life.

If you are starting to show rising blood sugar you need to start making some changes, and the first change on the list needs to be a significant reduction of high-carb foods. It is not spinach or cucumbers or tuna that are making your blood sugar soar; it is Sugar Smacks and doughnuts, and chocolate cake and lasagna and Dr. Pepper, and cinnamon rolls and… well, you get the idea!

There are many offenders in the high-carb category, but here are some of the worst:

Potatoes are one of the highest-carb foods on your table. What's more, the many carbs they possess break down with blazing speed into sugars once inside your body. Other than the fact that you get some extra nutrients, there is not much difference between eating a potato and eating a very large candy bar. A large baked potato or a large helping of mashed potatoes will contain about 60 grams of carbs. A normal Snickers bar has around 34 grams of carbs. Many well-meaning diabetics wouldn't dare touch the Snickers bar, and yet feel no concern over flooding their bloodstream with massive amounts of sugar from potatoes every evening. Whether you get hit by a bullet from a cheap, scratched pistol or an expensive, shiny new one, a bullet is still a bullet, and you're in trouble either way.

Bread seems like such a natural food that it is hard to imagine anyone having anything bad to say about it.

Bread in its whole-grain form isn't a bad food, but there is no getting around it—for people with blood-sugar problems it is problematic. Even whole-wheat bread can spell trouble for diabetics and people who are insulin-resistant. Its carbs may break down into sugar a little slower than the white bread, and it is definitely more nutritious, but those carbs can still rise up and bite you.

Rice is awesome, as far as taste is concerned. To drench it with some kind of sauce and have some pieces of meat throughout the mix is a taste sensation. But like bread, rice is a high-carb food. You cannot eat it as often as you like or as much as you like. And don't be fooled into thinking this only applies to white rice. A cup of white rice contains 49.6 grams of carbs (a candy bar and a half). Depending on the brand, brown rice is not far behind, and certain brands actually contain slightly more carbs. Granted, the brown rice has more fiber, but those carbs are still going to be a problem for people who struggle with blood sugar.

Desserts and sugary foods and drinks. If something tastes sweet, there is a good reason for that. Unless it has been artificially sweetened it is going to be loaded with sugar. And when that sugar hits your bloodstream, your blood-sugar level is going to soar.

I grew up (in the 1960s) hearing a never-ending commercial that told me, "Wonder Bread **builds strong bodies 12 ways.**" (Back in the 1930s they used the same slogan, but it promised a mere 8 ways.)

If you ever plan to get your blood sugar under control you are going to have to cut back on these kinds of foods. It would be marvelous if you could corral your blood sugar without changing your diet. If we could just keep on eating those same good old foods that we grew up on—breads and pasta and rolls and biscuits; heaping helpings of rice and beautiful, plump baked potatoes. Finishing each meal with a big bowl of ice cream drenched in chocolate syrup. We dare to dream, *Perhaps there is some new plan or medicine that will make that possible.* Forget it—it's not going to happen.

When you sit down at a table you need to immediately begin to assess the foods laid out before you. *There's a bowl of green beans—no problem there. I can have a big helping of those. Look at those beautiful avocados—I'm going to really enjoy one of those. Uh-oh, there's a problem! Look at that bowl of rice. I'm going to have to make sure my portion is about the size I would give my six-year-old daughter.*

To be effective at lowering your blood sugar you must become sensitive to and aware of the blood-sugar-raising potential of the foods you consume. You need to be able to look at a food and instantly be able to categorize it as safe, unsafe, or so-so. The unsafe foods may be perfectly wonderful foods for people without blood-sugar problems. But not for you. You can still eat them occasionally, but not in the quantity that you did before. You now march to the beat of a different drummer.

3
. . . .
Nuts to You!

One common problem for people who switch to a low-carb diet is that they often figure out what *not* to eat far more quickly than what they *can* eat. Stay away from that cake! Don't go near those doughnuts! Watch out for that nice baked potato! The "thou shalt not's" loom large, but the "thou shalt's" are sometimes hard to determine. Allow me to give you a major "thou shalt." Thou shalt eat nuts, all kinds of nuts, and frequently!

So what's so great about nuts? For starters, they are high in protein and relatively low in carbs. (One little problem is that the nut many people find the tastiest of all, the cashew, has twice the carbs that most nuts have, and is probably the one you should go easy on.) But as a whole, nuts are nutritious and pack a lot of power in their nutty little shape. Years ago they were thought to be problematic since they contain a lot of fat, but they have made a tremendous comeback as researchers are finding that they actually promote a healthy heart. Consider the following:

> Researchers from Harvard Medical School and the Harvard School of Public Health have examined the effect of eating nuts on cardiovascular health, reports the *Harvard Men's Health Watch*. "Their work shows that nuts really are healthy, especially for men at risk for heart disease," says Dr. Harvey B. Simon, editor.

Studies show that healthy men, and those who have already suffered a heart attack, can reduce cardiovascular risk by eating nuts regularly. Doctors theorize that:

- nuts may help lower cholesterol, partly by replacing less healthy foods in the diet

- nuts contain mono- and polyunsaturated fats known to benefit the heart
- the omega-3 fats found in walnuts may protect against irregular heart rhythms
- nuts are rich in arginine, a substance that may improve blood vessel function
- other nutrients in nuts (such as fiber and vitamin E) may also help lower cardiovascular risk.[1]

For those with blood-sugar problems, nuts are truly a godsend. Nuts of all kinds—almonds, Brazil nuts, pistachios, walnuts, and even the lowly peanut (which is actually related more to beans than to tree nuts)—are gifts from heaven. Giving up those salty, bad-for-you snack foods doesn't mean you have to go hungry. Nuts are your replacement for those blood-sugar-spikers like potato chips, nachos, french fries, Cheetos, Doritos, and the like. Not only are nuts much lower in carbs than nearly all our favorite American snacks, but they rank low on the glycemic index, which means that they break down very, very slowly in your body. And this means that the few carbohydrates that they do contain will be broken down into sugars slowly, gradually, and gently. Be sure to get unsalted nuts where possible, however.

Nuts are pretty high in calories so if weight is an issue for you, it would be best to eat them in moderation. In my case, when I first went low-carb I lost so much weight that if it weren't for nuts, I would have been in real trouble. As I learned more about what I could eat, that became less of an issue, but nuts have been a regular part of my diet for years now.

For those whose blood-sugar levels can go in either extreme, nuts are a terrific food for keeping things humming along smoothly. When you eat a meal, the high-carb, high-glycemic-index foods are going to break down first and rudely shove their sugars into your bloodstream. If those were the only foods you ate, your body would be forced to produce prodigious amounts of insulin in a hurry to deal with all those carbs. And after two or three hours, when the insulin had done its job and dealt with all that sugar, there would likely be a lot of leftover insulin looking for sugar to neutralize, but finding none. And when this happens, your blood-sugar levels can drop precipitously. This is when you find yourself shaking and feeling like you are about to faint. This occurs most often when your body is becoming insulin-resistant (becoming highly inefficient at cooperating with the insulin produced by your pancreas), and yet your pancreas is still capable of producing insulin in large amounts. This can also happen when you take pills to stimulate insulin production.

The Mayo Clinic folks say this about nuts: "**Eating nuts reduces your risk of developing blood clots** that can cause a fatal heart attack. Nuts also improve the health of the lining of your arteries." [2]

When you include nuts in your meal, the nuts "hang around" much longer than the baked potato or chips ever could, and the slow release of their carbs gives the leftover insulin something to munch on, so it doesn't take its revenge by driving your sugar levels too low. Thus no shaky or fainting episodes. Nuts also have the advantage of being extremely portable. Sure, you can take a bag of chips with you, but it's harder to carry around. You can keep a small bag of nuts with you in your purse or pocket and have an easy snack that will barely budge your blood sugar. Sometimes I take them with me to McDonald's to enjoy with a hamburger and a diet Coke. They are about a zillion times better for you than the french fries.

In short, enjoy nuts often. They are the new chips for you. They taste just as good (I think better), evidence suggests they are good for your heart, and without a doubt they are far better in helping you to manage your blood sugar.

4

Pizza Made Possible

Making dietary changes is not that hard. Losing weight is not particularly difficult. Lots of people do it every year. But making *permanent* dietary changes, especially when it involves giving up foods you have cherished and delighted in all of your life, is extremely difficult. Most people who lose weight by a change in diet will sooner or later, and probably sooner, return to their old ways, habits, and foods and gain back every pound they have lost—with interest!

In order for a new, improved diet and lifestyle to be permanent there have to be two factors present: 1) there must be some real motivation to make those changes, and 2) the new lifestyle has to be as realistic and easy as possible while still bringing the desired results. This is why drastic, draconian, unrealistic cutbacks on everything that has ever given us comfort and pleasure are simply not going to work. Most folks can make those sacrifices for a few weeks; almost nobody can make them for a year, let alone a lifetime.

As we seek to turn from the lifestyle that led us into the land of runaway blood sugar, there will have to be some serious changes made—no doubt about it. But we want to make it as much like your old lifestyle as possible. Although you need to turn from the standard American diet, you don't need to stop being American. Superman used to make it his motto to fight for truth, justice, and the American way. And the American way is to go out to restaurants frequently: Italian restaurants, Chinese restaurants, steak restaurants, Mexican restaurants, and yes, pizza restaurants.

Is it possible to go out for pizza and stay low-carb? It is indeed. Let's consider the makeup of a pizza. While most health purists consider pizza a monstrous concoction, in truth many of the ingredients are either harmless or actually good for you. Pizza sauce is mostly tomatoes—a little higher in carbs than we would prefer, but not too bad. And of course pizzas have to have cheese—a fairly low-carb food. No problem with any meats they might have on top—meats have so few carbs they're not worth mentioning. Mushrooms—no problem there. Jalapeno pepper slices—no carbs to speak of (if you can take the hot sensation).

This brings us to the real problem—the bread, the foundation upon which the pizza stands. If only we could put all those ingredients on a huge lettuce leaf! (Actually, we could, but nobody would want it.) It is this bread that will go into your stomach, be quickly converted to sugar, surge through your blood, and raise your blood-sugar level through the roof.

So when our friends invite us out, how do we avoid looking silly as we munch on our lowly salad, drink a glass of water, and look longingly at everybody else's heaping plates of pepperoni pizza? There are three basic guidelines for eating pizza and keeping your blood sugar under control.

First, *make sure to eat a large salad.* In some pizza restaurants they have a salad bar where you take as much as you want. Take a lot! Be sure to eat the salad first, with a low-carb dressing like ranch or Italian. By starting here you will dull your appetite and won't be tempted to overeat on the pizza. This is especially important in buffet-style pizza restaurants, where you can keep coming back for more pizza—and more and more and more.

Second, *order thin-crust pizza.* Remember, the cheese, the sauce, the pepperoni or sausage, and the mushrooms are not the problem. If you can just reduce the amount of bread you are eating, you can win. If you can cut the bread in half, you will only be dealing with half the carbs and will have done your overworked pancreas a great favor. So by all means choose the thin crust. You have just cut the carbs your body must process in half (more if you compare it with the thick-crust pizza).

Finally, *deal with the edge of the pizza*, which is always the thickest part. Thick dough: more carbs; thin dough: fewer carbs. So do yourself a favor and break off that fat edge and save even more.

By taking these steps you will have turned a blood-sugar disaster into a meal that is manageable. (You still cannot eat as much as you want. Limit yourself to three or four pieces.)

Be sure to check your blood sugar about an hour after you have taken your last bite. If it has risen to no higher than 140 to 145 you have done it! You have eaten out at a pizza restaurant, enjoyed pizza, laughed and joked with your friends or family, and still kept your blood sugar in check. If your monitor reads 150 or above, take one less piece the next time. Keep reducing the number of pieces until your post-meal reading falls within the desired range (This number varies depending on who you read, but about 140 to 150 mg/dl is about as high as you should ever want to see on your blood-glucose monitor for your post-meal reading.)

You can't exactly do it the way you used to, but you can still eat pizza at a pizza restaurant. You can play your part in truth, justice, and the American way—well, at least the American way!

I don't really know why this is, but it just seems flat wrong to eat pizza without drinking a soda. If you can get by on water or unsweetened tea, then by all means do that. But if (like me) you feel you just have to have soda to wash down that wonderful pizza, **make it a diet soda**. A regular soda is absolutely loaded with sugar and will ruin your good intentions no matter how much you watch your pizza. Sodas are right up there with candy bars, baked potatoes, and cotton candy. They are monsters that will kick your blood sugar into orbit. There can be no compromising here—if you must drink a soda, **make it a diet soda**. But don't drink these too often.

5

....

Bun Surgery

Americans love buns. We put hamburgers on buns, chicken patties on buns, fish on buns, hot dogs on buns…if it's a meat we find a way to put it on a bun, wrap it up, and sell it as fast food. We even put vegetable burgers on buns. When you assess foods placed between two buns, the reality is this: buns are a problem for people with blood sugar; what's inside is not (unless it has a bread coating).

Not only are buns a major source of carbs but they are almost always made from white flour, which is the least healthy type of flour. Buns have little fiber and high carbs. They lounge in your colon too long, block things up, and cause general mischief. Consider the common McDonald's cheeseburger. It is made up of the following ingredients: the bun, the beef burger, cheese, some bits of onion, and ketchup. There are a total of 33 grams of carbs in this burger. The carb grams break down as follows: 28 come from the bun, 1 from the cheese, 1 from the onions, and 2 from the ketchup. Those 33 grams are too much and are actually about the same you would get from a candy bar.

But you can do a quick carb-reduction surgery and make the situation much more to your needs. I have done it over and over again. Open the wrapping, pull off the top bun, use the top bun to wipe off most of the ketchup (you can leave a little on for taste), place the top bun in the wrapper, squish it thoroughly for satisfaction, and eat the burger minus the top bun. We might assume we have just cut our bun carbs in half. But in most cases we will have done a little better than that. Usually the top bun is plumper and heftier than the bottom bun, so by taking off the top bun you have probably cut the carbs by about 60 percent.

A Big Mac contains a total of 45 grams of carbs, 39 of which come from the bun. The Big Mac bun actually contains a middle bun layer as well as a top and bottom. By removing the top and middle layer, you have gone from a 45-gram carb meal to something like an 11-gram carb meal—and have done a significant favor for your pancreas and the rest of your body. Obviously you could save more carbs by getting rid of the bottom bun as well, but now you've got a really messy meal you won't be able to hold in your hands and eat without looking like a complete idiot, or else you'll have to eat it with a knife and fork. Besides it no longer feels like a hamburger.

One of the goals of our lifestyle change is to make changes we can live with. Most people are going to feel cheated by giving up the bun altogether, but you should be able to live with losing only the top half of the bun. At fancy restaurants that serve monster hamburgers smothered with cheese, onions, and mushrooms, I do sometimes remove both top and bottom bun. Since the hamburger is so filling, I don't feel cheated. I add a garden salad and I'm a happy guy.

I have done this so often it is second nature to me. Sure, there probably have been a few folks here and there who have observed my unusual practice and wondered what kind of odd character I was. But that is a small price to pay to keep the roaring lion of diabetes away from my door. And the practice of removing the top half of the bun works with more than hamburgers. Do it with subway sandwiches, hot dogs, Philly steak sandwiches, and any other foods that come between a top and bottom bun.

Some of the burgers you get from restaurants have **buns that significantly outsize the beef within** (remember the "Where's the beef?" campaign?). Whoppers from Burger King are especially notorious for this. Here is a great opportunity to save a few more carbs. Move the burger over to far edge of the bun and see how much the bread overlaps the meat on the one side. Tear off the overlapping bread until the bottom bun matches the patty.

Another thing you can do if you're especially hungry is to order two burgers, remove the insides from one and put them on the other bun, and then remove the top bun from that assembly. This works great with roast-beef sandwiches. Now you have twice the beef but all on only one half of a bun. You have done yourself a great favor!

I know I am suggesting you do some things very few people do, and maybe some folks will comment or look twice at your little surgeries. But high blood sugar is an incredibly destructive force in your body, and you have to get a little radical. You can't put out a forest fire with teaspoons of water, and you can't bring your blood sugar under control with tiny little minor modifications. This practice, by itself, is not going to make all the difference, but when you add this practice to the other suggestions in this book, it will make a huge difference. The life and limbs you save may be your own.

Confessions of a Cereal Lover

When I was a child I was an extremely finicky eater. I hated most vegetables. Just looking at beets made me sick. My salads consisted of lettuce
only, with French dressing. But I made up for my lack of variety by eating
huge doses of cold cereal. I loved almost all of them: Sugar Smacks, Sugar
Pops, Frosted Flakes, Shredded Wheat, Corn Flakes, Wheaties, Cocoa
Puffs...you name it; I would eat it. For some reason my mom decided Trix
was an unhealthy cereal (I think all the bright colors offended her) and
wouldn't buy it much, so whenever I could get it, this was a special treat.

In fact I owe a debt to cereal, for it was the means God used to get my
attention in a big way to my growing insulin resistance. In church one
Sunday I decided to slip out just before the end of the service to beat the
crowd. I didn't realize when I got up that my foot had fallen asleep, and
when I started to take a step the sleepy foot didn't do what it was supposed to do, and I ended up stepping on it the wrong way and sprained
my ankle. I hobbled out in pain but felt strangely weak. When I got to the
hallway outside the sanctuary I knew I was losing it. I put my back against
the wall and slid to the floor. The next thing I knew a lady was holding me
and told me I had passed out.

Medics were called, and they immediately did a blood-glucose test on
me. The meter didn't show a number. It simply read "Lo," which meant
my blood sugar was dangerously low. They wanted to take me to the hospital, but I refused and instead had my wife drive me home, after I had
eaten a few snacks to bring my blood sugar back up. I had no clue what was
happening but knew that somehow it had to do with blood sugar. I ana-
lyzed what I had eaten for breakfast that morning—a large bowl of Raisin
Bran, considered one of the healthier cereals. How could my blood sugar
have gone so low?

After I became more educated I figured out exactly what had happened.

Raisin Bran may appear to be a far more natural cereal than, say Cocoa Puffs or Trix, but in fact it has an enormous amount of carbs in it. The raisins themselves have quite a bit of natural sugar, the bran has a lot of carbs, and on top of that they sprinkle sugar liberally all over the raisins and inject more sugar into the bran flakes. The result is a tremendously high-carb food. You get about as much sugar and carbs in one large bowl of Raisin Bran as you would stuffing down three Hershey's chocolate candy bars.

And what's more, the Raisin Bran is very high on the glycemic index, meaning its carbs and sugars are going to hit your bloodstream fast—very fast! Your pancreas is going to exhaust itself trying to keep up with all those incoming carbs. And if you are suffering from insulin resistance, as I was, and yet have an active, functioning pancreas, you are going to overload your body with insulin. Had I checked my blood sugar an hour after I ate the cereal, it would have read way too high. But now that torrential flood of insulin was driving my blood sugar dangerously too low.

The simple truth is that **cereals are made from some type of grain**. There are no beef or chicken cereals, nor are there any cereals I know made from cucumbers or green peppers. And this makes them a problem.

The moral here: if you are going to control your blood sugar you are going to have to be very careful when it comes to cereal. And I am not just picking on Raisin Bran. Most cereals are just as bad; some are worse.

If you look at the nutrition information you can quickly see that they are quite high in carbs. But wait a minute! Look more closely. You will see that their nutrition information is usually based on a tiny serving that no one would ever eat: one-half cup or three-quarters of a cup.

Go get a half-cup measure, fill it with cereal, and put that in a cereal bowl. Would you ever eat that small amount? Of course not! To fill a moderately sized bowl you would need at least two cups of cereal; a large bowl would require three cups. This means you will need to triple (or more) the carbs listed on the label in order to find out the amount of carbs your breakfast will contain. And if you eat two bowls you should multiply that number by six. So why would the cereal manufacturers give their nutrition information based on such a minuscule portion? I can only conclude they don't dare give it to you in the portion size they know most people would eat. The calories and especially the carbs would overwhelm anyone who bothered to check it out.

Nearly all of the cereals commonly sold in the grocery stores should be off-limits for anyone wanting blood-sugar control. In fact the only one I found acceptable is Special K Protein Plus. And then that which I greatly feared came. One day I saw the Special K on the grocer's shelf with those horrible words "now tastes even better" proudly displayed on it. I knew instantly what that meant—more sugar! And sure enough, they had significantly increased the sugar and reduced the fiber, turning it into something off-limits. At this writing there is no cereal I find in ordinary grocery stores that meets my standards, save for those puffed wheat and rice bags you can buy for about a dollar. These manage to keep carbs low because they are more air than anything. However, they do give you that cereal taste, and with a packet of Stevia sprinkled on them they are pretty nice. You can add a little flaxseed meal to give them a little more substance.

There are decent low-carb cereals you can order over the Internet. Go to your favorite search engine and type in "low-carb cereal," and you will find them. The biggest drawback with them is that they cost double the price of ordinary cereals. And then there are shipping charges. But if you love cereal they will be worth it. You can get through a lovely cereal breakfast without overtaxing your pancreas or sending your blood-sugar levels into orbit.

As with all foods let your blood-glucose monitor be your guide. Check your blood-sugar level with your meter about an hour after you have taken your last bite of cereal. You may be surprised to find that even the "healthy" cereals will do a number on your blood sugar.

About the worst thing people can do for breakfast is to have a couple bowls of cereal, and then wash them down with sweet orange juice. That is a true blood-sugar nightmare. Don't get your day off to a terrible start by shocking your body with a truckload of carbs. If you like cereal (like I do), eat a low-carb cereal, eat one bowl only, have a few nuts with it, and don't eat it more than a couple of times a week. And watch out for the milk. Regular milk has too many carbs. See the next chapter for some ideas about milk alternatives.

Milk Musings

Milk is awesome! It tastes great as a stand-alone drink, it makes a wonderful ingredient in smoothies, and it is indispensable with cereal. And it certainly has fewer carbs than soda or fruit juice. But it still has too many carbs for those who want strict control over their carbohydrate intake. One cup of milk has around 11 grams of carbs. An average-sized glass of milk would probably have around 18 grams of carbs—far less than the 36 grams of the average soda, but still more than desirable.

Most alternatives are not any improvement and can actually be worse. You can find all sorts of milk-type products in your grocery store, such as rice milk, soy milk, and almond milk, to name a few. Typically they taste worse than regular milk, and more importantly they don't save you any carbs or calories. In fact they often make up for their lack of taste and body by simply adding sugar!

Soy milk is about the same as regular milk in its sweetened form. If you can find an unsweetened version of it, there are very few carbs, but it tastes nasty!

Some rice milk contains **22 grams of carbs per half-cup**. If you drank a normal-sized glass you would be getting 66 grams of carbs, the same amount as in three Dove dark chocolate candy bars!

Some health experts tout the benefits of skim milk. In their view, skim is better since it is fat-free. But fat is not nearly the monster the experts have assumed it is. Sugar is far more destructive than fat. When it comes to milk, our concern must be with the amount of sugar and carbs our body has to process, not the amount of fat. For the diabetic and those prone to blood-sugar problems, we will choose fat over sugar any day of the week. Skim milk will not save you any carbs.

All is not lost! There are two simple solutions, both of which not only enable you to still drink milk (or a version of it) but in fact may taste better than the milk you have been drinking. For many years I have been drinking milk sold by the Hood Company called Calorie Countdown, the one milk product commonly available in grocery stores that is both low-carb and great-tasting. They used to tout it as low-carb, but now they emphasize the low calories more. Whereas a glass of ordinary milk (skim, 2 percent, or whole) will have 12 grams of carbs, Hood milk has 3 grams. And the Hood milk has fewer calories: 70 compared to 150 for regular milk. On top of that it tastes richer than ordinary milk. It certainly beats the pants off that anemic, watered-down skim milk that folks force themselves to drink and pretend to like.

If you prefer, you can create your own low-carb milk. This is a simple feat. Buy a quart of heavy whipping cream and mix it with water, about 40 percent whipping cream to 60 percent water. Heavy whipping cream has very few carbs. In fact the carton may say that it has 0 grams per 1 tablespoon, but this simply means it has less than half a gram. When you mix it with about 60 percent water you have a low-carb milk that tastes awesome. If the 40-to-60 mix isn't to your taste, feel free to try a different ratio.

When you go out for a latte at your favorite coffeehouse, make sure you get them to do two things to insure your latte is kosher. First have them use artificial sweetener to sweeten it. (Another option is to have them not sweeten it at all—then you add your own packet of stevia to it. Or if you don't need the sweetening you can do away with it altogether.) Second, have them make your latte with heavy whipping cream (or whipping cream and water if you prefer). Starbucks will do this for you but they'll charge a little extra. It's worth it; pay the sixty cents. Now you've got a latte you can enjoy without feeling guilty.

Granted, milk is not nearly the danger to our blood-sugar levels that ice cream, cinnamon rolls, doughnuts, and chocolate cake are. But in your efforts to bring your blood sugar under control and extend your life and health, you must give attention to the lesser dangers as well as the greater. And in the case of milk, the solution is not at all radical.

8

. . . .

Take a Hike! (or at Least a Walk)

One simple assessment tool for deciding what activities are worthwhile is this: Is it natural? Men and women for thousands of years were physically active. They walked, climbed, bent over, carried heavy loads, jumped over puddles, swam across streams, dug holes, built houses, repaired roofs, carried children, and worked in their gardens.

Today our two favorite exercises are watching television while sitting on the couch and surfing the Internet while sitting on a computer chair. We can even sync our large-screen TVs to our computers so that we can surf the Net from our couches while snacking on chips and taking swigs of soda. And we mustn't forget playing video games, which started as a kid thing but now has become a significant part of the lives of most 20- to 30-year-old men. Not very natural, and definitely not very good for diabetics.

Some of this is unavoidable of course. I use a computer constantly throughout the day, and I do enjoy watching a movie on TV in the evenings. I am not advocating a return to the 1800s, or encouraging everyone to go join the Amish in Pennsylvania. But we must find a way to incorporate physical activity into our life.

People who say they don't have time for something are almost always deceiving themselves. We have time for the things we consider the most valuable or the most fun. We always seem to make time to eat meals, watch television, buy Christmas presents, drool over Internet ads, and even read interesting spam in our in-box. We really do have time to exercise; we just have to be convinced that it really will do us good.

Does exercise promote better health and better blood-sugar management? Of course! This is one thing that people from every discipline agree on. They may argue fiercely over other points, but nobody denies that exercise helps against runaway blood sugar. If you don't believe this, go to your favorite search engine and type "benefits of exercise on blood-sugar levels" or "benefits of exercise for diabetics." You'll find enough material to keep you reading for the rest of your life. Exercise lowers insulin resistance—one study found that regular exercise reduces the demand for medication by 20 percent in diabetics.

I enjoy going to garage sales and love finding nearly new things for sale that cost me about a tenth of what I would pay in the stores. And **one of the most common large garage-sale items is the exercise machine**. Rowing machines, treadmills, climbing machines…you name it, you can find it. And often they look like they've hardly been used. Do you know why that is? Because they have hardly been used. They usually sit a year or two in the garage while the owners suffer from twinges of guilt, until finally they quit kidding themselves and sell them for a fraction of what they cost.

· ·

The question then becomes, "What kind of exercise should I do?" I won't presume to tell you, but I will give you a few guidelines. Most type 2 diabetics are approaching middle age if not already there by the time they figure out they have a problem. They are in no position to try to train like one of the Dallas Cowboys or Los Angeles Lakers. If you get too intense in your exercising you'll probably strain something and that will be the end of that. Second, you will never be able to keep it up. In three months your fitness program will be history. And third, it isn't necessary.

You don't have to be buff; you don't have to have a six-pack abdomen, and you don't need the stamina of a Kenyan long-distance runner. But you do have to graduate from couch-potato status. The two rules to follow are these:

1. You should choose an exercise that will get your heart rate up a bit for about 30 minutes and will not be so unpleasant that you can't keep it up long-term. We are talking lifestyle change here, not a crash program to get you in shape so you will look good in a bathing suit.

2. The exercise should not be so violent that it damages your joints or strains your muscles.

For most folks a brisk 30-minute walk four or five times a week is about right. Physicians recommend walking daily for half an hour. If you have a treadmill in your home or in a nearby fitness center, that will do the job. Treadmills have the advantage that, since they are indoors, you can still exercise during a snowstorm, or when the temperature drops below freezing, or when it is raining all those cats and dogs. If you have medical concerns or issues, ask your doctor before beginning an exercise program.

Whatever exercise you choose, determine to stick with it. In the fight against diabetes you need every possible advantage. Granted, diet is far more important than exercise, but this is not an either-or situation. Eat a proper diet, exercise, and stay at a decent weight. The good news is, with these weapons (along with medication or insulin shots if necessary) you can avoid being a victim. You can keep the lion at bay.

Watch Those Peaks

We have already discussed this a bit in chapter 1, but I want to go into a few more specifics and challenge you to have a deliberate plan to monitor the regular meals that you eat. Most of us fall into habits and routines with our meals. We have our spaghetti nights and almost always include a salad and some bread. On taco night we may serve beans to go with the tacos. When we have homemade hamburgers we usually have the same accompanying foods. For most folks this would be french fries, but hopefully you have removed those little monsters from your diet. Of course we sometimes have unusual meals or unusual combinations, but most of the time we dine on old favorites and combinations of foods we have eaten many times before.

There is nothing wrong with that. In fact regular times and meals are believed by some to be very healthy for us. Our bodies become adjusted to these rhythms. But now that you have blood-sugar issues it is not enough to keep the status quo. You absolutely must find out what your meals are doing to your blood-sugar levels. You need to start monitoring your post-meal blood-sugar peaks and discover just what works for you and what doesn't.

There are about as many different opinions on the preferred diets for diabetics as there are boxes of high-carb cereals on your grocer's shelves. Some would tell you to go strictly low-fat and avoid meat altogether (a perfectly ridiculous idea). Some would tell you that you can eat as many grain products as you please, as long as they are made from whole

> In her great book *Blood Sugar 101*,[3] Jenny Ruhl advises people to **"eat to your meter,"** meaning you should allow your blood-sugar meter to dictate what foods and meals are acceptable for you, and which ones to avoid.

grains (just as ridiculous). But you don't have to take my word for it. Let your blood-glucose monitor settle the matter.

Keep in mind that having your blood-sugar levels high for long periods of time throughout the day (or constantly) will ruin your health and bring you to a premature grave. Every hour that your blood sugar is significantly higher than normal you are being robbed. Your kidneys are being ravaged, your heart is weakening, and your eyes and feet are under attack. The big question then becomes, how high is too high?

Again there are differences of opinion on this. The American Diabetes Association tells diabetics to strive for a blood-sugar level of 180 two hours after eating.[4] The American Association of Clinical Endocrinologists says people with diabetes should keep their blood-sugar levels under 140 mg/dl as much as possible.[5] Research indicates that when blood-sugar levels stay at 140 to 150 for prolonged periods of time, beta cells (the cells in the pancreas that produce insulin) start to die, neuropathy can set in, eyes can be damaged, and the potential for heart disease rises dramatically.

You can do your own research, but a good rule of thumb is to make sure your blood sugar peaks no higher than 140 to 150. With this in mind you are now ready to start monitoring your meals. As we mentioned before, everyone will not peak at the same time, so you will need to test yourself at several different points after meals to find your normal peak. Also, a meal high in fiber will break down more slowly and your glucose level will peak later. A bowl of beans is probably going to lead to a blood-sugar peak later than a bowl of Corn Flakes. A good starting place is to test yourself one hour after you take the last bite of your meal.

As you do this and find your levels too high for certain meals, don't get discouraged. Identify the offender and adjust appropriately. A high reading doesn't condemn all the foods that make up the meal. It means you need to figure out the major culprit for the high reading, and next time eat much less of that or else substitute some other food for it.

One test is not sufficient to condemn or justify a particular meal or food. There are other factors involved besides food that can alter our blood-sugar levels, so you should take at least three tests before deciding a particular meal or food is to be justified or condemned. But there is no doubt that eating thick-crust pizza washed down with soda is going to raise your blood sugar a great deal higher than a chef salad with a glass of water.

Buy a box of 50 or 100 test strips and get going. Get a little fanatical about it for a while. Check your post-meal peaks after every typical breakfast, lunch, and dinner you eat. You'll be amazed at some of the things you discover. Some meals you thought were no problem may turn out to be not so great, and others you worried about may prove to be better than you thought.

Suppose you determine that your post-meal peaks will not rise any higher than 140 to 145. As you keep your blood sugar in check something interesting will happen. You will find that as you bring your post-meal blood sugar close to normal boundaries, your fasting blood sugar (the reading you get when you wake up in the morning, before eating) will go down as well. Often your blood-sugar levels will become so nearly normal that any doctor who tests you would swear you were not diabetic or even prediabetic. Of course you know that this could change in a hurry, were you to eat the way you used to. But you're not about to do that, are you?

This is the absolutely best way to keep a prediabetic from becoming a full-fledged diabetic. It is also the means by which a diabetic can avoid all the complications of diabetes and live a full, healthy, and long life. When your post-meal blood-sugar peaks are kept "in bounds" meal after meal and day after day, you are on the road to victory! Your fasting blood-sugar tests, your A1C tests, and your general health will all start to fall in line. By giving your overworked pancreas a rest, you will allow it to recover, and it may well serve you faithfully for the rest of your life. But even if it can only limp along,

The **A1C test** uses the condition of certain of your red blood cells to measure your average blood sugar over the previous three months. (More in chapter 48.)

contributing just a fraction of the insulin it did when you were young, as long as those post-meal blood-sugar levels stay in a decent range, all is well. If it also requires medication to help make this happen—do it! If it takes insulin shots—do it! (Under a doctor's care, of course.) But by all means keep that blood sugar down.

Sandwiches and Bread

Once you understand that blood-sugar control has to involve a reduced-carbohydrate diet, you might conclude that sandwiches must become a thing of the past. You would be wrong. Bread is not something you need to forsake, but you do have to be discriminating about the type of bread you eat, and the amount.

Before we get to what is allowable, first let me dispel a myth that has been perpetuated by well-meaning but deluded folks: just because a bread is whole wheat does not mean you can eat as much of it as you like. Whole-wheat bread is definitely more nutritious than white bread, but it is almost exactly like white bread in its propensity to break down into sugar and hit your bloodstream with blazing speed.

A blogger named Richard Smith decided to run a test on himself and compare the effects of whole-grain foods on his blood sugar to a 12-ounce Pepsi. The Pepsi, containing 42 grams of carbs, raised his blood sugar to 156 one hour after eating. But eating two slices of whole-wheat toast with milk raised his blood sugar to 173. Oatmeal and milk spiked his blood sugar to 163. Most doctors and medical "experts" would roundly condemn drinking the Pepsi (for diabetics) but would give the oatmeal and the whole-wheat toast a free pass. Smith concluded, "It is no surprise that meals with whole-grain starches have about the same effect on my blood sugar as drinking a 12-oz. Pepsi."

Laura Dolson, who writes extensively about blood-sugar and diet issues, comments, "Whole wheat and white bread have essentially the same impact on blood sugar, which is to say **you might as well be eating a big spoonful of sugar.**" [6]

· ·

In a word, bread can be a good food in moderation, but you have to be extremely careful. Let's get back to sandwiches. You do not have to give up sandwiches! You just have to be discriminating about the bread that you use and the ingredients you place between the bread. You can order low-carb bread and bread mixes from any number of Internet companies. Check the carbs, but almost all of these are low enough to allow you to use two slices in a sandwich without running up your blood sugar. But if you're like me, you prefer items that can be purchased at your local grocery stores. They're almost always cheaper, you don't have to pay for shipping, and they're more convenient. And if possible you would prefer foods already made and ready to consume rather than things you have to bake.

So what can you find by way of bread at your local grocer? Go on a discovery trip to the bread section. Check out the whole-wheat breads there, deducting the fiber grams from the total carb grams to get the net carb content (fiber doesn't digest so it will not normally raise your blood sugar). Most breads will be too high, but you can normally find one or two that end up in the eight or ten grams of net carbs per slice range. One of the best breads I have found is Nature's Own Double Fiber Wheat bread, which has 13 grams of carbs per slice. But you can subtract the 5 grams of fiber, leaving only 8 net grams per slice. This means you can have a sandwich with this bread and only be getting 16 grams of carbs from the bread itself. That's not too bad. As long as the stuff you place between the bread has few carbs your blood sugar should not rise very high.

Consider the lowly tuna sandwich for example. As long as you don't use sweetened pickle relish, this is normally a very low-carb sandwich filler. The tuna's carbs are not enough to mention. Traditional mayonnaise has hardly any carbs, and neither will the unsweetened pickle relish and bits of celery (and egg if you choose to include that). So when you eat a tuna-salad sandwich almost all your carbs are going to come from the bread. And for most type 2 diabetics and prediabetics, 16 grams of carbs is something you can handle in one meal. Your post-meal blood sugar should stay under the 140 mark. I usually have some low-carb yogurt with my sandwich and I'm good for hours.

Tuna is just one example. Sliced beef or chicken with cheese would be just as good, as would many other combinations. Another type of bread that should do the job for you is what is commonly called "sandwich rounds." These are round, fairly flat bread slices that look like a condensed bun. Sometimes another version of this is known by "bagel thins." These are very similar in carbs, with a top and bottom making up around 15 grams of net carbs.

It pays to read the nutrition information! Other breads on the shelf that look just as healthy and not much different in size may have as much as 25 to 29 grams of carbs per slice—50 to 58 grams for a sandwich. This is nearly double what the previous breads have, and it will "break the bank." (You and your pancreas can't afford it!)

One way to get truly low-carb bread is to make it yourself in a bread machine. The beauty of bread machines is that they do most of the work for you. You put the ingredients in them, turn them on, and go about your business. A few hours later you have a loaf of bread that is far lower in carbs than anything you can buy in the stores.

Bread is kind of deceptive. It doesn't taste all that sweet, certainly not like Twix bars and chocolate shakes and Lucky Charms cereal and rocky-road ice cream. And it looks so natural and so healthy! But the little grains that make up those slices of bread are just waiting to be mixed with the acids in your stomach, where they will almost instantly turn into sugar molecules and surge into your bloodstream. Bread is a high-carb food. Don't do away with it, but be careful, be discriminating, be moderate, and read those labels!

Low-Carb Bread for Bread Machines
This bread only has 2 or 3 grams of carbs per slice, so you can eat without guilt.

Ingredients:
1/2 cup water
1 egg
1 tablespoon butter or margarine
2 tablespoons Splenda sugar substitute
1/3 cup ground flaxseeds
1/4 cup soy flour
3/4 cup vital wheat gluten flour
1 teaspoon dried yeast

Directions:

Using a 1-pound capacity bread machine, combine ingredients according to order given in bread machine manual.

Select "light" browning setting.

Don't remove bread until it is cooled.

Cut into slices and store, covered, in the refrigerator.

Yields 10 to 11 slices.

Note: This makes for a pretty spongy bread that tastes good but is a little hard to cut. If you prefer a harder bread that is easier to slice, you can be a little generous with the soy flour and flaxseeds. This will increase the carbs a bit, but not much.

Beware of Snacks

America is a nation of snackers! We love our chips and popcorn, our Cheez-Its and our candy bars, our peanuts and our cheese sticks. It seems like such a long time from breakfast to lunch, and even longer from lunch to dinner. And who can resist a nice evening snack as you watch that long movie or surf the Internet? Munching on something and sipping a drink just seem so natural while watching television or a computer screen. And going out to the movies just wouldn't be the same without popcorn and a soda.

There are two major problems with snacks for those who struggle to keep their blood sugar in check.

1. Most of the snacks we love are high-carb and will wreak havoc on our blood sugar. The sweet things like cake, ice cream, pie, and so forth are loaded with sugar. Check your blood sugar an hour after you eat them and see what they can do to a perfectly normal state of things. But it is not just the sugary, sweet snacks that will do this. The chips, pretzels, and popcorn will do the same thing. Anyone who is going to get serious about corralling their blood sugar is going to have to look long and hard at the snacks they are eating and, to quote the song made famous by Bing Crosby, "eliminate the negative."

2. Your base blood-sugar level is the level your body reverts to once it has dealt with the current load of blood sugar. When you have gone several hours without eating your blood sugar will drop and then remain fairly constant. This is called your fasting blood sugar. Although doctors normally want to measure this after you have gone eight or more hours without eating (usually in the mornings after a night's sleep), most people will approach something close to that after going three or four hours of not eating, which is about the time that passes between breakfast and lunch, and between lunch and dinner. By the time you start your meal your blood sugar should have dropped down close to its base level, and your body is now ready for a moderate rise in blood sugar with the intake of your next meal.

But this never happens when you constantly snack in between meals. Many people will go only two to three hours before putting more food into their stomachs in the form of a snack. As a result their blood sugar never has a chance to get down to its base level.

For young people this is not much of a problem. Their bodies produce insulin in abundance and handle it efficiently. Often they will be back to their base level an hour and a half after eating. Not so with older, insulin-resistant folks like me (and probably you, since you are reading this book). When we snack between meals our blood sugar never has a chance to return to normal before being raised again by our snacking. The result of this is that our base level drifts upward. It typically goes from the 80s (healthy and normal) to the 90s (a bit high) to over 100 (too high) to the 126 mg/dl that is considered the mark of a diabetic.

The good news is that what comes up can also come down. By limiting your carbs, exercising, and avoiding so much snacking, you can give your overworked pancreas and blood-sugar mechanisms some rest, and they will express their gratitude by gradually lowering your blood-sugar levels overall, and your fasting blood sugar as well.

I used to feel my night was not complete until I had watched something on TV and had a snack with some coffee. After realizing that I was prediabetic I knew I could no longer eat the cinnamon rolls and coconut pie like I used to. It took me a while but gradually I built up a repertoire of "approved" snacks to go with my coffee. Life was sweet again! I tested them and could see that they weren't raising my blood sugar to dangerous levels. But they *were* raising my blood sugar, and as a result my fasting blood-sugar levels weren't nearly as good as they should be. As I cut down on the evening snacks (didn't quite cut them all out, but made them the exception rather than the rule) my fasting blood-sugar numbers began to look a lot better. And I'm quite sure my pancreas greatly appreciates the extra time to chill, knowing that most nights, once it has dealt with my supper carbs, it has nothing more to do until the next morning.

Does this mean you can never have a snack? No, there is no need for fanaticism here, but it would be wise to limit your snacks as much as is reasonable and possible. And definitely make them as low-carb as possible. A handful of almonds and a slice of cheese will barely bump your blood sugar up, if you have any pancreatic function at all. The same with a couple of boiled eggs.

Of course people taking insulin shots have special needs in regard to eating regularly and may not be able to go nearly so long without eating as others. But even for them low-carb snacks are clearly preferable to the high-carb ones.

12

. . . .

Fear Not…Meat!

For some time meat has had a bad reputation. Of course no health writers or "experts" were going to stop most of us from eating meat, but they have succeeded in making many folks feel guilty about it. The big issue? Meat is bad because it has fat in it, and surely we all know that fat is bad. Fat in foods makes fat men and women, and fat boys and girls. Fat is evil, fat is nasty, fat is disgusting. We must all drink low-fat milk and eat low-fat meals, and any meat we dare place on our plate must have the least amount of fat possible. A dried-out slice from the skinniest, scrawniest, toughest old turkey on the farm might be okay, if you have to eat meat at all!

Those who have led the way into low-fat nirvana have to have something to replace the fat with, and their answer has almost always been high-carb foods. Of course they don't describe them as pancreas-abusing, turn-into-sugar-in-your-bloodstream-in-a-heartbeat foods. They prefer to tell us that they are from "the bread group" or the "bread, cereal, rice, and pasta group." They insist that the majority of all the food that we eat must come from this group. This is the base of the famous food pyramid. So rolls, and cornflakes, and bagels, and doughnuts are healthy for you, but meat is a nasty food we should avoid as much as we possibly can.

Eating whole-grain bread in moderation is okay, but for people with diabetes or prediabetes, you cannot make "the bread group" the heart of your diet. It will flat kill you. Your blood sugar will be constantly elevated, your fasting blood sugar will rise higher and higher, your blood circulation will grow more and more sluggish, and your organs will start to fail. The low-fat diet sounded like a great idea when it was introduced, but time and research have shown it is in fact the worst possible diet for diabetics.

We have assumed that since meat contains cholesterol and grains do not, the less meat we eat the lower our cholesterol will become. But if we eat lots of meat, our cholesterol levels and heart problems will go off the chart. The only problem with this idea is that it just isn't borne out in the studies and research that have been done. Over and over again studies have shown that low-carb diets lower bad cholesterol, improve triglyceride levels, and reduce heart disease.

Of course we want to be moderate in eating meat, but we need to understand this basic fact: when you see a piece of meat on your plate you can forget about how many carbs it has or how much it will affect your blood-sugar levels. Meat has so few carbs they are not worth worrying about. You will get more carbs from a handful of Cheerios than a huge steak. Have you ever taken a look at the carb content of a can of tuna? Starkist tuna lists the carbs as 0 grams. The McDonald's Big & Tasty burger totals 37 grams of carbohydrates. But if you take away the bun you are down to 6 grams. And if you take away all the other ingredients until only the meat patty is left you are down to 1 gram.

What this means is that, since you are going to have to go light on the breads, and since you have to eat and cannot live on water, most diabetics and prediabetics are going to need to make peace with the idea of eating and enjoying meat.

The one meat you have to watch out for is meat with a bread coating on it, such as chicken-fried steak. The meat here isn't the problem, but that coating can rise up and bite you. Choose grilled meat over fried meat and stay away from chicken or fish with a bread coating.

When you find yourself out at a friend's house and they serve a dinner with some high-carb items along with some type of meat, the best way to eat their meal without offending them or raising your blood sugar through the roof is to major on the meat and vegetables and minor on the rolls, potatoes, and pasta. This way you can still get full, they can still have the satisfaction of seeing you enjoy their meal, and your blood sugar stays at a reasonable level.

Enjoy meat! Don't let the low-fat fanatics make you feel guilty. Don't go "hog-wild" (pardon the pun) but don't shun it either. You are going to have to eat something, and if you are struggling with blood-sugar issues, meat and vegetables are about a zillion times better for you than bread and pasta. A steak and salad dinner will barely move your blood sugar, assuming you still have some pancreatic function. But a meal loaded with rice and rolls and pasta will drive your pancreas crazy. But don't take my word for it. Your blood-sugar monitor will faithfully testify to this.

13

· · · · · · · · · · · · ·

Salads—the New Potatoes

What could be more American than potatoes? We love our potatoes. To quote the noble Sam Gamgee, Frodo's faithful companion in the Lord of the Rings trilogy, "You know—potatoes? Boil them; mash them; stick 'em in a stew!" Of course we do a lot more with potatoes than that. We fry them, we bake them, we create a strange dish we call potato salad with them— and how we love our french fries! For many people potatoes are a staple of nearly every dinner, in some form or fashion.

The problem is that, although potatoes are somewhat nutritious, they are about the worst possible food we could eat if we are having trouble with blood-sugar levels. Imagine eating at the house of a man who is known far and wide for his fanaticism about eating healthy food. Knowing his reputation, you are curious as to what he will be serving. As everyone sits down to the table you note carefully the items on his plate: a small piece of chicken, a beautiful spinach salad, a generous portion of cauliflower, a heaping helping of broccoli—and two Milky Way candy bars. You would probably be more than a little puzzled.

Yet many diabetics and prediabetics regularly eat baked potatoes, french fries, and potatoes in other forms without thinking twice about it. A large helping of potatoes in most forms will have as many carbohydrates as two candy bars, and the sugars those carbs turn into will hit your blood-stream just about as fast as those in the the candy bars!

Part of the answer is obvious: severely limit your potato intake. But that in itself is not enough. We have to eat, and nobody is going to stay on a dietary regimen that leaves them still hungry when they get up from the table. The potatoes must be replaced. The most obvious replacement is something we are all familiar with—the salad. Packed with far more vitamins than potatoes, and far more fiber as well, salads are a much better food for you, even if you don't have blood-sugar problems. But if you do, salads must become a regular item at the dinner table.

It is not that garden vegetables don't have any carbohydrates. They do, but they don't have nearly as many as potatoes do, and the carbs they do have are converted to sugar much more slowly and released into your bloodstream in a far more gentle and gradual way. Of course all vegetables are not created equal, carb-wise. Be careful with beets, carrots, yams, peas, parsnips, and of course corn. But greens, broccoli, zucchini, cauliflower, cucumber, lettuce, cabbage, and a number of others are quite low in carbs. You get pretty much a free pass with these.

Be careful with your salad dressing. What you gain by switching to the garden vegetables you can lose through an unwise choice in dressing. French dressing and Thousand Island dressing are notoriously sweet and have far too much sugar. Ranch and Italian dressings typically are pretty low in carbs. But sometimes a manufacturer can attempt to spice up their dressing by adding extra sugar. So to be sure, check the labels and go for the dressings that have the lowest carbs. Salad dressing carbs are usually listed per two tablespoons. Most people are going to use more than this on a good-sized salad, so keep this in mind.

Get creative with your salads. There are so many different kinds of vegetables you can use. Try different combinations, and remember that you can add various bits of meat in them without affecting the carb count (as long as it is not bread-coated meat). Sometimes add a couple of boiled eggs in your salad. They taste great and will make the salad more filling.

Salads may not be able to compete in taste with a baked potato drenched in butter with little bacon bits sprinkled on top. But they can do wonders in keeping your blood sugar under control. If you need a little extra motivation to "go salad," try the following experiment. Have a meal one night with a large baked potato. Check your blood sugar at its peak afterward (one to one and a half hours after you eat). The next evening have the exact same meal but switch out the potato with a garden salad. Check your blood sugar at its peak. You'll need no further convincing on the value of salads over potatoes.

The One-Portion Rule

One of the simplest things you can do to keep your blood sugar under control is to get to a reasonable weight and maintain it. There is a definite correlation between obesity and diabetes, between excess pounds and over-the-top blood-sugar levels. If you are 50 pounds overweight you have increased your chances of being diabetic exponentially. And if you drop those 50 pounds you most likely have also reduced your blood-sugar levels significantly.

One simple rule for keeping your weight in bounds is what I call the one-portion rule. When we place a portion of vegetables or beans or meat or rice on our plate we often have every intention of eating that and only that for our meal. But when we finish eating, that food tasted sooo good that we decide to have "seconds." Here is where the battle is lost.

This is pretty elementary but it needs to be said: when you eat 30 percent more food than originally planned, you are getting 30 percent more calories and 30 percent more carbs. When you double the portion you double the calories and carbs. If your small helping of brown rice contained 18 grams of carbs, and then you take another helping of equal size, guess how many carbs you have now ingested? That's right—you went from 18 grams to 36 grams. And the calories doubled as well.

Often it is those second helpings that drive our blood sugars sky-high and pack on the extra pounds. Had we stayed with our original good intentions we would have been fine. The answer is to make a firm commitment to stay with one helping. This may mean taking a little more than you otherwise would initially, knowing that there is no second chance. That's okay. It is far better to do that than to go for the seconds, because once our plate has been cleaned we can put more food on it and still not look like a glutton. So take a little more at first, and having finished what was on your plate, shut down shop! No more food until your next meal.

At first your stomach, spoiled little brat that it is, will scream and protest, and whine and snivel. But after a while it will get used to its new rules and behave itself. Just remember, you are the boss, your stomach is the servant.

When you monitor your post-meal blood-sugar peak and find that it is too high, it doesn't mean you have to do away with those particular foods and never have that meal again. It may be you just need to take less of the high-carb foods and more of the low-carb foods. And having eaten what you dished out for yourself, don't go back to the well again.

People with diabetes or prediabetes can't afford to be overweight. This has nothing to do with vanity or looks; it has everything to do with staying healthy, enjoying a better quality of life, and avoiding the terrible diabetic complications that will surely come your way if you live with raging blood sugar. Take reasonable portions for your breakfast, lunch, and dinner, and then shut your stomach down. Between this and eating a reduced carb diet, it will be extraordinarily difficult for you to stay overweight.

Our eyes generally have a pretty good idea of how much food we should take. But our eyes have an adversary—our stomachs. What seemed good and reasonable to our eyes seems pathetically small to our stomachs. And far too often our stomachs overrule our eyes. We yield. And we pack in the calories—and the carbs.

15

. . . .

Artificial Sweeteners—
the Supplement Everybody
Loves to Hate

When a person learns they are diabetic, one of the most painful prospects they face is the idea of cutting sugar out of their diet. Of course many folks simply refuse to do this and live with elevated blood sugar (and the consequences). Others learn of artificial sweeteners and begin to use them as a replacement.

The evidence is solid and beyond all contradiction. You must wean yourself off all forms of added sugar. Even in its natural forms, like honey and in fruit, you cannot bear too much of it. Of course your body needs some sugar, which it will ideally produce through complex carbohydrates, but simple sugar, added sugar, and the sugar you get through eating fudge, pies, and candy bars will eventually bite you. In general, sugar is not your friend.

Artificial sweeteners certainly have their critics. It is not within the scope of this book to deal with all the pros and cons here, but let me give you a few simple thoughts about the matter. We know that normal sodas are laced with sugar and will make your blood-sugar level soar. Diet sodas do not have sugar and generally have 0 carbohydrates. They will not normally raise blood sugar, with the exception of sodas containing caffeine, which may make your blood sugar rise slightly. So if you have to drink soda, choose diet soda over real soda. Likewise, if you have to eat sweetened foods, choose foods sweetened with artificial sweeteners over foods sweetened with sugar.

I know I am making the purists gasp, but I am not a purist. And notice I said, "If you have to…" Obviously, since artificial sweeteners are artificial it would be ideal to avoid them altogether. And if you can do that, more power to you. But many of us are not eager to give up on ever tasting sweet things again for the rest of our days. And it is my conviction that the "purists" are usually the ones that can never stick with a low-carb diet for a lifetime. At the time of this writing I have been doing it for ten years and don't feel the least deprived. I enjoy diet sodas once in a while, and I occasionally treat myself with a dessert sweetened with Splenda. This I can live with.

Diet sodas and artificial sweeteners have been around since the 1950s. The government has had a long time to try to prove that they cause cancer and result in all sorts of maladies. But they have never been able to do so. When a well-meaning friend tries to tell you that artificial sweeteners will kill you or drive you mad, the best they can usually come up with is some anecdotal evidence. They know someone who heard about someone who had a grandma who used to drink a lot of diet soda and one day fell over in a seizure. Her nose started twitching, her legs kicked the air uncontrollably, and soon afterward she died while screaming, "The diet soda did all this!"

That makes an interesting story, but it is meaningless. Diet sodas are drunk by the billions every year and still there is no hard evidence that the artificial sweeteners they use are harmful. The FDA says aspartame is "one of the most thoroughly tested and studied food additives the agency has ever approved." They have searched and searched for a reason to condemn it and haven't found one. But there *is* a preponderance of hard, solid, incontrovertible evidence that excess sugar is extremely harmful to the human body.

Of course as in nearly all things in life, moderation is vital. You shouldn't be drinking five or six diet sodas or eating large desserts sweetened with artificial sweeteners every day. But when you weigh the totally conclusive evidence against sugar against the slight (nearly nonexistent) evidence against artificial sweeteners, you have to conclude that if you must sweeten your tea or coffee, or have a soda, go with the artificial sweeteners.

One sweetener that is natural and still has almost no carbs or calories is *stevia*. This little gem is preferred by those who don't want to risk the artificial sweeteners. It has been used for centuries in South America. It is quite sweet and is great for sweetening tea or coffee. In powdered form it doesn't mix readily in cold drinks, however. The only drawback to stevia is the price—it is significantly higher than artificial sweeteners, especially when you buy it in packets at your local grocery store. However, you can get it online from various sources in bulk, and in this form the price is much more reasonable. I buy 1000 packets at a time, and they provide me many happy (and sweet) cups of tea.

For those of you who would like to enjoy something—anything—that tastes like a dessert and still won't send your blood sugar through the roof, allow me to give you one of my favorites. The following recipe is not merely some wimpy substitute for a real dessert. This tastes better than most desserts, sugared or otherwise. It is awesome! Yet it should not raise your blood sugar significantly.

Chocolate-Drizzled Orange Sour-Cream Cheesecake

Pie crust ingredients:
3/4 cup ground almonds (1-1/2 cups before grinding)
4 packets Splenda
3 tablespoons unsalted butter

Preheat oven to 350° F. Mix Splenda and ground almonds; set aside. Melt butter in microwave or on stovetop, then add to nut mixture and stir until evenly distributed. Spray 9-inch pie plate or small spring-form pan with cooking spray. Pat nut mixture into pie plate or pan, using a spoon or fingers to cover bottom and sides. Bake for 11 minutes, being careful not to overcook. Cool on a wire rack.

Filling ingredients:
2 8-oz packages cream cheese (not low-fat or fat-free)
1/2 cup sour cream
3/4 cup Splenda
1-1/2 teaspoons pure orange extract (or 1/2 teaspoon orange oil)
2 eggs

Preheat oven to 350° F.

Mix all the above ingredients in a blender until smooth. Add the cream cheese last, and add it in small pieces rather than all at once. Pour into cooled crust and bake at 350° F. for approximately 40 minutes. Allow to cool for one hour on wire rack.

Topping ingredients:
1/2 cup sour cream
4 packets Splenda
1 teaspoon pure orange extract (or 2 drops orange oil)
3 pieces of sugar-free chocolates (the small ones that come 6 or 8
    to a package)
1/8 cup sliced almonds

In a small bowl combine first three ingredients and whisk until well blended. Spread on top of chilled cheesecake. Melt chocolate pieces in microwave until they resemble a chocolate sauce, but try to avoid letting them bubble or boil. Cool for approximately 30 seconds. Drizzle top with chocolate. Immediately sprinkle with almonds.

Place in refrigerator and chill, covered, 6 to 8 hours or overnight. *Yields 8 to 10 servings; 5 to 7 grams of carbohydrates per serving (depending on piece size).*

The recipe for the crust is invaluable. It is truly one of those low-carb gems that tastes as good as or better than what you are replacing. And while I am on the subject, let me give you a quick way to enjoy pumpkin pie for Thanksgiving and Christmas without breaking the low-carb bank.

Easy Low-Carb Pumpkin Pie
Follow the directions on a can of Libby's pumpkin with these alterations:

1. Use the almond crust above in lieu of a normal pie crust.

2. Substitute Splenda for sugar.

3. Substitute heavy whipping cream for the evaporated milk the recipe calls for.

These three substitutions will save you a fortune in carbs and turn a sugar nightmare into a very nice and very manageable dessert. I've never had anyone who tried this who didn't like it, and some even say it's better than a regular pumpkin pie. I agree!

Using Low-Carb Muffins as Fillers

It is unnatural to sit down to a plentiful table with a healthy appetite, eat only a small portion of what is available, and then leave the table almost as hungry as when you sat down. Yet that can often be the case when you are determined to only eat those foods which will keep your blood sugar within healthy boundaries. "Those potatoes look great—but no, I dare not touch them. The corn on the cob would sure be nice, but I'd better avoid it. I'll take some of the main dish, but I won't have too much." You pick and choose, and you test your blood sugar when it peaks an hour after your meal, and it is fine, but the problem is, you're still really hungry. What do you do now?

As you test your blood-sugar peaks frequently you will find basically three types of foods: the good, the bad, and the so-so (you thought I was going to say ugly, didn't you?). You will learn that you can eat smaller portions of those so-so foods, but you absolutely can't pig out on them like you used to. You take one taco rather than three; you eat a small portion of lima beans rather than a big one. All of this is prudent, but too often it will leave you hungry at the end of your meal. Small portions just don't fill our stomachs like big ones.

The answer to this dilemma is to have a ready stock of foods and snacks that can fill us up without taxing our pancreas and raising our blood sugar to obscene levels. Allow me to introduce one very wonderful such filler, the low-carb muffin. At many a meal these babies have allowed me to leave the table feeling well satisfied, rather than deprived. Not only does this muffin serve as a filler, but it also satisfies a psychological need most of us have to eat bread products. Since our childhood we have eaten bread, rolls, buns, pancakes, doughnuts, cornbread, bagels, and all kinds of other bread products. To be told we can never taste any kind of baked flour food for the rest of our days is depressing. It's enough to bring our inner rebel to the fore, and soon we are stuffing ourselves with bread of every variety.

And some foods seem to simply call for bread of some kind. I love to eat eggs and sausage, but the meal seems sort of incomplete if there isn't a muffin to go with the eggs, or a piece of toast or a pancake. Low-carb muffins fill the bill. They taste great and you can even put several blueberries or pieces of strawberries in each one to make them especially delightful. Another nice thing about these muffins is that they are portable. Sometimes I have taken them into a restaurant in a jacket pocket, and when they serve the eggs, sausage, and toast, I snub their toast and go for my muffin instead.

In past years there were low-carb muffin mixes available in stores, but now you rarely see them. The good news is you can make your own without too much trouble. You may have to invest 15 minutes of your time to prepare them, but what a small price to pay for the benefits received! And how marvelous it will be on Saturday night to put an old Humphrey Bogart movie on, make yourself some coffee, and enjoy one of these bad boys with your coffee as you see Humphrey get the bad guys (or be the bad guy who gets got).

Dennis's Favorite Low-Carb Muffins

1. Preheat oven to 375 degrees.

2. Spray a muffin tray with cooking spray.

3. Mix 2 tablespoons of oat bran with one tablespoon of soy flour.

4. Sprinkle the oat bran / soy flour combination on the muffin tray.

5. In a large bowl mix the following:

   2 eggs

   1/2 cup of heavy whipped cream

   1/2 cup of Splenda

   Just under 1/2 cup of water

   1 cup of soy flour

1 teaspoon of baking powder

6. Mix the ingredients together with a spoon.

7. Place in 6 or 7 holes in the muffin pan.

8. Cook in oven for 20 minutes.

If you're like me, you may want to double this recipe and then freeze some of the muffins, which ensures you'll be enjoying great muffins for a while!

Managing Rice

To me rice is awesome. Chicken chow mein over a bed of rice, shrimp gumbo over rice, pepper steak over rice, teriyaki over rice…there are so many tasty combinations possible! The rice soaks up the juice of the stew or sauce and every bite is sweet and satisfying. When you are invited to friends' homes for dinner, there's a pretty fair chance rice will play a role in the meal they serve you.

What to do? First know that rice *is* a high-carb food. The minute you see rice in a bowl, sirens should sound in your head. It's not that you can never eat rice, but if you have blood-sugar issues, you can never shovel it in like you did in your youth—not if you value your health above your taste buds!

When you indulge in rice, always choose brown rice over white rice. Although the carb content isn't significantly different, the brown rice has about seven times more fiber than the white, plus it provides far more nutrients. This does not mean that brown rice gets a free pass. If you think whole grains don't affect blood sugar, think again! If you don't believe me, eat a big bowl of brown rice for breakfast, and then test your blood sugar an hour later. The next morning eat a big plate of eggs and sausage for breakfast and test yourself in an hour. You'll need no more convincing!

You can eat rice dishes, but you'll need to know how much your body can handle. To find this out, have a dinner with rice as the only major source of carbs (no biscuits, bread, desserts, or fruit). Make it something like pepper steak over rice, with green beans and a garden salad with a low-carb dressing, such as Italian. Measure the rice you take. You might start with a half-cup portion. Check your blood-sugar level about an hour after your last bite and see what the meal and the rice did to you. If you stay within your desired limit, you're good. If you were somewhat below the limit you might be able to eat a bit more rice the next time. If you were somewhat above the limit you will have to cut down a bit.

Judging ourselves by a monitor is far superior to an "I can eat this but I can't eat that" approach. To be told we can never have rice again would likely result in our having a few "pig-out" rice meals just to satisfy our inner rebel. But when we understand that the goal is to keep our blood sugar under a level that will ensure we do not suffer from diabetic complications, we find we can live with this a lot better. So have a bit of rice under that teriyaki or shrimp gumbo. But know that the days of heaping up huge mounds of rice and then smothering them with our favorite stew are gone. It wasn't particularly good for you even when your pancreas was working well, and it certainly isn't good for you now!

There are rice substitutes you can try. Keep in mind that rice really doesn't have that much taste. Most of us like it as a kind of gravy or sauce sponge that sits under the main dish. You can use spaghetti squash to this end. Or you can take a low-carb pancake made from soy flour and break it into small pieces and use it in place of rice. Sure, these don't taste exactly like rice, but they're not bad and they are far easier on your sugar-processing system. If they make the difference between 190 mg/dl and 135 mg/dl when your blood-sugar peaks, they are well worth it.

Once, when staying in a hotel in a small town in Uganda, my wife and I ordered chicken and rice (I never eat raw salads in Africa, so my choices are limited). They served us an enormous plate of rice and a single drumstick from what must have been the scrawniest chicken in all of Africa. This was the exact opposite of what I hoped for, since I was planning to **go heavy on the chicken and light on the rice**. I ended up relying on snacks brought over from America to satisfy my appetite that night.

Portion Size

Some things are so obvious you may think they're hardly worth saying. But trust me, they are. The first thing is that portion size is extremely important in your quest to keep your blood sugar under control. Let me give you an example.

On the Honey Bunches of Oats cereal box you will find that a three-quarter-cup serving contains 26 grams of total carbs. Deduct two grams of dietary fiber and that leaves you with a net 24 grams of carbs (without the milk). That doesn't sound too bad, does it? But have you ever measured out a 3/4 cup serving of cereal? I just did to remind myself of how small it is—and it is exceedingly tiny. No adult would eat that little amount; in fact, no child would either. Most of us would eat about three times that much, which brings the carb count up to 72 grams. Add 15 grams for the milk and you're up to 87 total grams. Throw in a slice of whole-wheat toast and you're over 100 grams—the equivalent of eating three good-sized candy bars! Your pancreas is going to go crazy trying to keep up with that sugar load.

Let me illustrate the concerns about portion size another way. (Now this gets really, really obvious, but you still need to hear it.) If a small portion of mac and cheese contains 30 grams of carbs, guess what you'll get when you double it and make it a medium portion? That's right—60 grams of carbs. And suppose you want a little more so you add yet another portion. Now what do you have? That's right—now you're up to 90 grams.

I realize I haven't dazzled you with my brilliance in arithmetic, but stay with me here. What this means is that the size of the portions you take when you eat a meal are going to make a huge difference in the number of carbs you ingest, and therefore in the blood-sugar level you read on the monitor when you test yourself. By controlling your portions you control your blood sugar.

Fortunately for us all, there are nutritious foods that do little to raise blood sugar, and some foods so low in carbs we can pretty much eat as much of them as we want. Spinach is a good example. Yes, spinach has some carbs, but so few carbs for so much nutrition! Green beans and cucumbers are in this category as well. In fact most of the garden vegetables that make up our salads are the same. Carrots and tomatoes are a bit higher and need to be limited somewhat, but there are so many vegetables that are nutrient-dense, carb-light, and just plain good for you. Meat, although not having so many nutrients, is loaded with protein and has almost no carbs.

Knowing this, what we need to do should be self-evident. We need to take big portions of the low-carb foods and small portions of the high-carb foods. And by all means, never take a second helping of a high-carb food. Take second helpings of the chicken or avocado or celery or low-carb muffin if you must, but leave the potatoes and rice and noodles and bread alone.

Theoretically you could eat anything you want and keep your blood sugar under control—doughnuts, chocolate cake, cotton candy, and so on. The problem is, with highly sugar-laden foods and starchy foods, you could only eat tiny little portions of them—nowhere near enough to satisfy yourself. On top of that, sugary and starchy foods are usually not particularly nutritious (except for fruit). In most cases you would not only be perpetually hungry, you would also be nutrient-starved.

It feels a little freakish to eat out with friends or eat at someone's house and have to flatly refuse a food that everyone else is eating. Sometimes it is probably good to do this, but often we can get by with simply having a small helping of the high-carb foods. Chances are, nobody will even notice that you went heavy on the vegetables and meat and light on the starches and sugars.

Keeping Breakfast Beautiful

I love breakfast! It is my favorite meal of the day. No matter how busy I'm going to be that day, I always take the time to enjoy it. I'll pick up the pace a little later, but at breakfast time I want to relax and savor my tea and food. But how are we to keep breakfast beautiful in the blood-sugar arena too?

When we first wake up in the morning our blood sugar is at its lowest level. For many of us it will never drop this low again until the next morning. The last thing we want to do is spoil this beautiful low blood sugar by

stuffing ourselves with cinnamon rolls, bagels, bananas, and then washing them down with sugary orange juice. If we can eat reasonably we'll be on a roll—we'll continue to have low blood sugar at least until lunchtime, provided we avoid a high-carb mid-morning snack.

Americans have for whatever reasons designated some foods as breakfast foods and others as definitely non-breakfast. No one is forcing us to do this, but most of us are such creatures of habit we have a hard time breaking out of the mold. In this step toward low blood sugar let us focus on the traditional breakfast foods, and note the good, the bad, and the terrible.

When you think about breakfast, you can hardly avoid thinking about eggs. This is good news for the diabetic! Eggs have virtually no carbs. You can eat one egg or ten eggs and the effect on your blood sugar won't be much different. For years health experts have solemnly warned us about the evil of eggs, with their high cholesterol content. Surely they will raise your cholesterol through the roof, lead to a massive heart attack, and you'll be dead before you're 50.

The only problem with this advice is that research keeps contradicting it and proving it to be flat wrong. Eating eggs, meats, and other foods high in cholesterol does not lead to high cholesterol of itself. The problem is eating these foods while stuffing ourselves with carbs and keeping the insulin level elevated in our bodies. This can indeed be a problem. But in the context of a low-carb diet, eggs are a great choice. A plate of several eggs and bacon is going to have almost no effect on your blood sugar, and on top of that will taste awesome. So enjoy your eggs fried, scrambled, over easy, over hard, or hardly over!

Another favorite breakfast food is cereal, which is not such good news. Many folks think they can overcome the problem with cereal by choosing the healthy cereals. "I'll skip the Trix and the Frosted Flakes, and choose the Wheaties or the Shredded Wheat." But hold on a minute. Have you checked the carb count on those cereals? You'll be surprised that they are just about as bad. And remember, to your body a carb is a carb. Whether it comes from a healthy-looking cereal like Wheaties or a blatantly sugarfied cereal like Lucky Charms, your body will hardly know the difference. There are low-carb cereals you can order online, but they are somewhat expensive by the time you pay for the product plus shipping. Best to order several boxes at once if you go this route.

Now let me recommend two of my favorite breakfasts that will treat your pancreas kindly and avoid the hazards of cereal. Eat and enjoy!

The "continental breakfast" is one of the worst breakfasts for someone watching their blood sugar. Sometimes in hotels I'll go down to look over the complimentary breakfast and be dismayed to see it is "continental." What this means is you can eat as many cinnamon rolls, bagels, or bowls of cereal as you like. They'll usually throw in some bananas as well. When I see these kinds of foods laid out, I say to myself, "Carbs, carbs, carbs." Then I go back to my room and munch on snacks I have brought with me, or else go to a real restaurant and order a decent breakfast.

Favorite #1: The first breakfast idea revolves around a bagel—yes, I said bagel. But not just any bagel. Normally the bagel is one of the worst offenders you can find in carb content. But amazingly there are some pretty great low-carb bagels around. They manage this by jacking the fiber content way up, which reduces the net carb content tremendously. Check your grocery-store shelves, and if you can't find them there, order several packages online and freeze what you don't plan to use for a while.

Fry one egg and one slice of ham. Melt a slice of cheese on one half of a low-carb bagel. Then place the fried egg on it and top the egg with the fried slice of ham. This simple concoction takes almost no time to make, tastes great, and is pretty filling. Notice I do not put the other half of the bagel on top. Most of the low-carb bagels have about 9 net grams of carbs per half. I don't find any need to double this number by eating the other half, although even 18 grams wouldn't be too bad, since the other ingredients' carbs are so negligible. Fix yourself some tea and enjoy a breakfast that will do very little to raise your blood sugar.

Favorite #2. When I first realized I would have to eat low-carb for the rest of my life, one of the most depressing things I had to face was that pancakes were going to have to go. Since my early adulthood it has almost been my "theology" to have pancakes every Saturday morning. But of course a stack of white-flour pancakes drenched in sugary syrup spells blood-sugar disaster. Guess what? The pancakes have resurfaced in my life in an altered form and they taste as good as ever.

The pancake recipe I share with you in this section is terrific. These pancakes make a great breakfast, and I have found that I can eat two or three of them with a touch of sugar-free syrup, a few blueberries mashed on top, and the whole thing covered with some whipped cream—and it barely budges my blood-sugar levels. If someone were to see me eating this delightful breakfast, they would surely think I couldn't be serious about watching my blood sugar. But they would be wrong. With these pancakes, you can still enjoy an amazing breakfast. Add a couple of sausages (virtually no carbs there) and you have a meal fit for a...happy diabetic!

The pancakes use a combination of soy flour and heavy whipped cream, both of which are great tools. Soy flour is God's gift to diabetics. Whereas white wheat flour contains about 95 grams of carbs in a cup, soy flour has about 30 grams. This can make a colossal difference when you are reading those black numbers on your blood-sugar meter. There are a few unfortunate individuals who find soy disagrees with them, but as long as you aren't one of them, you will find soy to be a great friend to you for the rest of your days.

Low-Carb Pancakes

Ingredients:

3 eggs

1/2 cup heavy whipping cream

1/2 cup water

3/4 cup soy flour

3 tablespoons sugar substitute (recommended: stevia or Splenda)

1 heaping tablespoon wheat (or oat) bran

1/3 teaspoon baking powder

In a blender mix all the ingredients. Then cook in a pan or on an electric griddle just as you would wheat pancakes. Feel free to butter them, put a dab of sugar-free syrup on them, mash a few blueberries and place on top, and then cover them with a light coating of whipped cream. These are so good you won't miss the old-style pancakes at all, and if you serve them to friends who don't know what they're getting, they'll never guess they are eating low-carb!

Another option for a low-carb breakfast is a couple of waffles. I like to have these with my hot cereal. In most cases, waffles and hot cereals are terrors for diabetics. But here are a couple of recipes that you should be able to eat and enjoy without seeing a significant rise in your blood sugar:

Simple Waffles

Blend (a personal mini-blender is perfect for this):

1 egg

1/3 cup soy flour

1/4 cup heavy whipping cream

1/4 cup water

1 packet of stevia (or Splenda)

1/2 teaspoon of baking powder

1 teaspoon oat bran

Makes 2 waffles.

My waffle maker takes about five minutes to cook these. These waffles aren't quite up to the kind you would get at Waffle House, but they are so much better for you, and with a little butter and some sugar-free syrup, they are really nice.

Low-Carb Hot Cereal
1 cup flaxseed meal (ground flaxseeds)
1 cup protein powder (I use Jillian Michael's Whey Protein—
    just don't use the sweetened kind—check the labels!)
1/2 cup oatmeal
1/4 cup oat bran

Combine the ingredients. You can store the remainder for later use, preferably in the refrigerator. To prepare one serving, pour one cup of water in a pot and bring it to a boil, then lower the heat slightly and start adding the mix gradually, stirring vigorously. When it gets to the proper consistency, put it in a bowl, pour a little heavy whipping cream over the top, sprinkle some sunflower seeds over it if you like, and top it with a packet of stevia.

This makes a really nice hot cereal that is ridiculously low in carbs and easy on your blood sugar.

The Virtues of Whipped Cream

In the world of foods, whipped cream is an anomaly. It looks and tastes like it ought to be saturated with sugar, but in fact it is not. It is such a simple way to turn bland, dull, unexciting foods into tantalizing taste sensations. If you check the labels you will find that many whipped creams that come in a can contain a puny 1 gram of carbohydrates per two tablespoons. This is incredibly great news for people with blood-sugar problems. The reason whipped cream can be so sweet and still have so little sugar and carbs is that it is extremely light and a little bit of sugar goes a long way. On top of that, the creamy texture fools us into thinking it is sweeter than it actually is.

Spritz some on top of your coffee to give it that coffeehouse taste. Have a few strawberries topped with whipped cream. Or if you really want a treat, take a low-carb muffin (see recipe in chapter 16), split it in half, cut and mash about five strawberries, place them on the two muffin halves, and then put some whipped cream over the top. If someone were to come in and find you eating this amazing and sweet concoction, they might say you're breaking your low-carb diet. But in truth, you haven't broken it at all. You are eating a snack that should not seriously raise your blood sugar (for most type 2 diabetics), and tastes amazing.

Almost any low-carb bread (low-carb bagels, low-carb pancakes, low-carb soy bread, and so on) can be used as a foundation for diabetic strawberry shortcake. Make sure to cut up and mash the strawberries thoroughly so the juice sinks deep into the bread. (What you *don't* want to do is use those "store-bought" shortcakes that come about six in a package. Each little cake contains 17 to 20 grams of carbs, far too many for such a small serving.) Or, instead of the low-carb muffin in its normal form, you can take your low-carb muffin mix and bake it in "mini-cake" pans, and the finished product will seem even more like the old strawberry shortcake.

When I first realized I was prediabetic and went low-carb, all I knew was what I couldn't eat. I didn't realize how many lovely foods, snacks, and desserts were still available to me. As a result I lost weight like crazy. As I explored and found all sorts of great things that were still lawful, the weight began to come back, and I had to be more careful. But that's a good thing. It's great to have options and choices! Who wants to stay slim just because you're forced to eat the same tired foods with little taste, foods that never fill you up? Far better to be slim because you are exercising self-control—and to know that you can occasionally reward yourself with snacks and sweet foods that are still low in carbs and won't drive your blood sugar through the roof.

Try whipped cream on sugar-free Jell-O, on berries of various kinds, on low-carb pancakes, and in your coffee. Be creative. Enjoy.

Fruit Juice—Don't Be Fooled!

Fruit juice sounds so totally healthy. Drinking a sweet drink made from apples or oranges surely must be about a thousand times better than drinking a Coke or a Pepsi. Many parents would rather cut off their arm than put a nasty old soda in their baby's sippy cup. Yet they go ahead and pour sickeningly sweet, sugar-laden apple or orange juice in their little ones' cups and flood their fresh little bodies with one of the most dangerous elements known to man—sugar. CBS *HealthWatch* reports,

> A growing body of science is linking sweet drinks, natural or otherwise, to a host of child health concerns, everything from bulging bellies to tooth decay. "All of these beverages are largely the same. They are 100 percent sugar," Dr. David Ludwig, an expert on pediatric obesity at Children's Hospital Boston, said recently. "Juice is only minimally better than soda."[7]

Well-known health advocate Dr. Joseph Mercola refers to fruit juice as "soda's evil twin."

When you pick up a bottle of juice at your local grocery store, you may notice several things on the label that are very deceptive. First, you may notice the sugar and carbs don't seem as high as what you read on your soda label. But not so fast! Check out the portion size and you will probably find it does not represent the entire bottle. Factor in the amount of sugar and carbs for the whole bottle and you'll see that the fruit juice has as much sugar as the soda has, ounce for ounce—and in some instances more.

Another deception (and this is not limited to just fruit juices) is the bold pronouncement "No sugar added." Yes, it does mean that there is no sugar added, but that doesn't tell the whole story. There is a pretty good reason why they added no sugar—the fruit juice was totally saturated with sugar already. And if it isn't sweet enough in its original state, they can simply extract a little water and it will become proportionately sweeter—and they still haven't added a grain of sugar! The key is not whether sugar has been added; it is how many grams of sugar you are bombarding your body with when you drink that glass of juice.

And then there are the "fruit drinks." These are doubly deceptive. They mix a tiny bit of fruit juice with a lot of water, throw in a little color, and then dump in loads of sugar. To make up for what they take away they add a vitamin or two and proudly call it "fruit drink."

Juice doesn't get a free pass just because it contains "natural" sugar. When it comes to sugar, your body will pay the same price whether you get it from orange juice or a Dr. Pepper. Admittedly fruit juice has more vitamins and nutrients than soda, but you can easily get your vitamins from vegetables, which will not overload you with nasty, pancreas-exhausting sugar.

The truth is this: if you are serious about watching your blood sugar you will have to say goodbye to fruit juice and fruit drinks. Far better to eat an orange than drink orange juice, or to eat an apple rather than drinking apple juice. At least with the whole fruits you get some serious fiber. But even with apples and oranges we need to be careful. I once saw my blood sugar jump to over 200 mg/dl primarily because I ate a large, sweet apple. When it comes to fruit juices, there is really not a lot of room to compromise. (I suppose you could mix 10 percent fruit juice with 90 percent water and get the sugar to a manageable level, but what kind of drink would that be?)

Far better to have a cup of hot green tea sweetened with a packet of stevia, or a tall glass of iced tea with a slice of lemon and a packet or two of Splenda. If you aren't opposed to artificial sweeteners, there are all sorts of diet drinks that contain zero or almost zero carbs. Make these the exception rather than the rule, but remember this: continually overdosing on sugar can be lethal. But, artificial sweeteners have been tested again and again for decades and still there is no hard evidence that they are harmful. And of course stevia is not artificial anyway.

So stay away from the fruit juice and "fruit drinks." Don't let their pretty, bright colors and their claims of vitamin C lead you down the garden path.

Eating at Other People's Houses

When I was a boy it used to make me nervous when we would eat at other people's houses. I was an extremely picky eater, and I was sure they would serve me broccoli or Brussels sprouts or some other horrible food that would make me gag. I could trust my mom to make me foods I liked; everyone else was trouble! When I became a teenager I became so embarrassed about telling people I didn't like this or that food that I started eating foods that were on my don't-eat list. And I found out they weren't so bad after all. In time I became fairly normal (at least in this respect) and ate pretty much what everybody else ate.

And then I developed blood-sugar problems. Once again I began to dislike the idea of eating at other people's homes. I knew what my system could handle and had begun to tailor my meals to my weakness. But at other people's houses I was likely to encounter things like lasagna, macaroni and cheese, baked potatoes, rice dishes, and chocolate cake with ice cream. Eventually I learned ways and means to cope in these situations and I wanted to pass along a few tips to you.

Invitations to eat at people's homes can be broken down into two categories: people you know well, such as relatives and close friends; and people you don't know so well. With family and close friends no real problem should present itself. If you are serious in your efforts to avoid diabetic complications, there is no way you will be able to keep it a secret, nor should you want to. People you spend time with and care about will soon discover that you are either a diabetic or a potential diabetic, and that you are absolutely serious about keeping your blood sugar low and living out your years in good health without all the miseries diabetes can bring. In 99 percent of the cases these people will applaud your efforts and admire your discipline. When they invite you to their house for a meal they will probably attempt to provide foods that will work for you. I have had some amazingly tasty low-carb meals served by people who don't normally eat that way themselves, but were eager to provide me a meal I could enjoy without guilt.

That brings us to the other category: people you don't know well, and who have no clue that you struggle with blood sugar. In this case there are two routes you can go, and I have done both, depending on the situation. Sometimes I tell them in advance that I am prediabetic and eat a low-carb diet. Almost nobody takes offense at this when you present it as a health issue—and especially if you mention the "D-word." This usually takes care of matters.

However there are times when, for one reason or another, I don't say anything and simply determine to make the best of the food they make available. In such cases the first step is to survey the table once the food has been laid out. What are your enemies? Do you have many friends there? Usually the table will contain several of both. Especially if you don't eat in such situations too often, you can decide to allow yourself a little more leeway than you normally would at home.

But don't just surrender! Much of your meal can be handled by portion control. For example, if you are served spaghetti and salad, go easy on the spaghetti and big on the salad. If you are served a rice-and-stew dish, take a small amount of rice and drench it with a great big portion of the stew. If you are served steak and a baked potato, take a large steak and only half a potato. When the bread is passed around, pass it on. No one is going to get too upset with you for not eating the bread. In this way you can still eat what has been prepared for you without doing nearly so much damage to your body as you would going whole hog (or "whole carb" in your case).

This brings us to the worst villain of all—the inevitable dessert. That sweet-tasting, mouthwatering concoction loaded with sugar stares at you, daring you to pass it up. My advice is, take the dare! Here is a great time to share that you are diabetic and cannot indulge in a dessert. Of course if you are the only guest and they have labored for over an hour on this sweet treat, they may be a little put out. In such cases it might be better to take the smallest amount you can get away with. But if you are there with your family or other families and everyone else partakes of the dessert, you can probably get by with turning it down altogether. Just let them know why.

If this seems way too much trouble and you are tempted to simply eat everything there—or worse, to eat as much of the out-of-bounds foods as possible since you are now presented with an excellent excuse, let me suggest something. Take your blood-sugar monitor with you in a purse or jacket pocket. An hour after you have stuffed yourself with sugar and starches, excuse yourself to go to the restroom and quickly take a reading of your blood sugar. The objective little monitor will faithfully rebuke you for making such a bad decision. That reading of 200 or 300 will (hopefully) make you sick at heart and encourage you to be a little more proactive in your food choices even when eating in other people's homes.

Read Those Labels!

The ability to read nutrition facts labels and quickly assess the value of a food is a vital survival skill for the diabetic. Without it, you'll be like a sheep among the wolves when you visit your local grocery store. As you wander the aisles considering what your next meals might be, you must be armed with the ability to discriminate the good from the evil, the healthy from the health-destroying foods that catch your eye.

And though after a while you will begin to possess a pretty good idea what you can eat and what you can't (I never stand next to the pretty boxes of Frosted Flakes debating with myself whether they're allowed), still there will always be new foods to check out. And sometimes you simply need reminding.

As you look at the nutrition facts on the label or package, you will not be nearly so concerned with what worries most people—fat and calories. Fat is not the enemy of the diabetic, and in truth is not really the enemy of anybody else, in normal amounts. Our society's fear of fat and passion for sugar and breads is what has made us the most diabetic generation in the history of the planet. As for calories, they may be some concern if you are considerably overweight, but in most cases those who are faithful to stick with a low-carb diet are going to get down to their proper weight without worrying much about calories. So as you peruse the nutrition facts label, the first few categories are not what we are interested in.

You should be, however, very much

Nutrition Facts

Serving Size 1 slice (34g)
Servings per Container 20

Amount Per Serving

Calories 80   Calories from Fat 10

	% Daily Value
Total Fat 1 g	2 %
Saturated Fat 0 g	0 %
Trans Fat 0 g	
Polyunsaturated Fat 0 g	
Monounsaturated Fat 0 g	
Cholesterol 0 mg	0 %
Sodium 150 mg	6 %
Total Carbohydrate 17 g	6 %
Dietary Fiber 2 g	8 %
Sugars 3 g	
Protein 2 g	

Nutrition info from a popular bread

interested in the first two lines under "Nutrition Facts": *serving size* and *servings per container*. Many food companies are downright deceitful. They list the facts based on a totally unrealistic serving size, a portion that no adult would ever be satisfied with. Cereal is one of the worst offenders. Not daring to list the actual amount of carbs most folks are going to be getting from a normal bowl of cereal, they often list their nutrition facts based on three-quarters of a cup or sometimes even half a cup. This is a ridiculously small amount that hardly covers the bottom of the bowl. Sometimes sweet drinks list their serving size as only about a third or a quarter of the drink. The carbs and sugar are still high, but they don't look too bad. But when you measure how much you actually drink, those carbs are going to be multiplying.

For some strange reason bread sometimes does it the other way. Its nutrition information is listed for two slices rather than one (I suppose since most people use two slices for a sandwich). In this case you will need to divide by two to get the information for a single slice.

The *servings per container* measurement is also useful as it gives you a good idea of just how much their serving size amounts to. If you are looking at a can of beans and it says that there are five servings per container, you can imagine that one fifth of a can of beans is going to amount to some slim pickings.

Nutrition Facts		
Serving Size ¾ cup (27g)		
Servings Per Container About 13		
	Sprinkles	with
Amount	Cookie	½ cup
Per Serving	Crisp	skim milk
Calories	100	140
Calories from Fat	10	10
	% Daily Value**	
Total Fat 1g*	**2%**	**2%**
Saturated Fat 0g	**0%**	**0%**
Trans Fat 0g		
Polyunsaturated Fat 0.5g		
Monounsaturated Fat 0g		
Cholesterol 0mg	**0%**	**1%**
Sodium 150mg	**6%**	**9%**
Potassium 40mg	**1%**	**7%**
Total Carbohydrate 23g	**8%**	**10%**
Dietary Fiber 1g	**5%**	**5%**
Sugars 10g		
Other Carbohydrate 12g		
Protein 1g		
Vitamin A	10%	15%
Vitamin C	10%	10%
Calcium	10%	25%
Iron	25%	25%
Vitamin D	10%	25%

Nutrition facts from a popular cereal

After checking out the serving size and servings per container, go straight to the carbohydrates category. You will find total carbohydrates, and under that you should see subcategories that list the sugars and fiber. Don't be too impressed if the sugar count is low (if the carb count is high). Your body really doesn't care whether the carbs are coming from sugar or from starches that will quickly turn into sugar. Both can be big trouble.

The fiber category *is* significant. Fiber is the one carbohydrate you don't have to fear. It will quietly pass through your body without raising your blood sugar. Indeed it will help flush out your colon and do you good. For this reason you can deduct the fiber grams from the total carbs to get the "net carbs" you should consider. The slice of bread (see the first sample label) has 17 total grams of carbs and lists 2 grams of fiber. You can subtract the 2 fiber grams from the 17 total grams and get 15 net grams of carbs for the slice of bread.

This is not too much of a discount, but there are some products, such as some low-carb bagels, that are loaded with fiber, and the subtraction makes a huge difference. I eat Nature's Grain Carb Check bagels, which contain 36 grams of carbs per bagel. But 18 of those 36 grams are fiber grams, which are going to have little effect on my blood sugar. To put it in shopper's terms, this is a phenomenal discount! On top of that I only eat a half bagel at a time, so I am now dealing with only 9 grams of carbs.

Speaking of beans, if you check out some of the popular pork-and-beans on the Internet, you will find they list around 24 grams of carbs per serving. But the serving size they list is half a cup. **Do you know how many beans are in half a cup of pork-and-beans?** I do. I counted those in one sauce-heavy brand and found 19 beans. Who in the world is going to be satisfied with 19 beans?

Some food products, such as the vegetables you see in the produce section, don't have nutrition facts listed on them. (It would be kind of tricky to put nutrition facts on grapes!) You can use the Internet for these and quickly find their carb content. You can also do this with foods you commonly buy at chain restaurants. Want to know how many carbs in a Big Mac? I just searched for it online and in a few seconds found it to be 47 grams—too many!

One thing I do as I check the carbs of various foods is make what I call the candy bar comparison. The average normal-sized candy bar will have between 32 and 40 grams of carbs. So when I find foods such as the Big Mac we just mentioned or evaluate a bowl of cereal, I just imagine what it would do to me to eat one or two candy bars for a meal. Lots of diabetics would never eat a candy bar, yet they think nothing of eating a large bowl of cereal, or some toast and pre-sweetened oatmeal, or a generous helping of lasagna that will have twice as many carbs as the candy bar.

Granted, it is a bit of a hassle to be a carb checker and nutrition facts analyzer. But what a small price to pay for your health. Go ahead! Read those labels.

Vegetables—Your Best Friends (Mostly)

In the battle against high blood sugar your greatest allies are the vegetables. Granted, you could live on meat and eggs and keep everything under control, but you would get precious few vitamins. If you are serious about maintaining reasonable blood-sugar levels and getting the necessary nutrition to maintain excellent health, you will need to become good friends with the vegetable family.

There are a few veggies that are high in carbs, but most are not. It is not that they have no carbs. All vegetables have carbs—they're not like that can of tuna that lists a big fat zero for the carbohydrate amount. But many vegetables have so few carbs and so many vitamins and nutrients they are nearly perfect as food for diabetics. In many cases you would have to eat so much of the veggie to accumulate a significant amount of carbs that you can forget the need to count their carbs. And the carbs they do have are locked into the fiber of the food, so that they hit your bloodstream slowly and gently.

Here is a list of most of the vegetables you will see in your local grocery store, with their net carb content (total carbs minus fiber carbs) *based on a cupful of each vegetable*. Keep in mind that carb counts are tricky things and there are gobs of carb charts available. The numbers can vary pretty widely based on whether the foods are boiled, cooked, or raw, and the portion size listed. And, people being people, some charts simply differ from others. So while I won't guarantee that others may not come up with somewhat different numbers, the categories are what you need to focus on.(The actual figures are from the website www.fatsecret.com.)

The Really Good	
(under 5 grams of carbs per cup—enjoy these freely)	
Asparagus	2.40 grams
Broccoli	3.64 grams
Brussels sprouts	4.58 grams
Cabbage	2.97 grams
Cauliflower	2.80 grams
Celery	1.40 grams
Cilantro	0.19 grams
Cucumber	3.28 grams
Eggplant	1.87 grams
Green peppers	4.41 grams
Mushrooms	1.60 grams
Radishes	2.04 grams
Romaine lettuce	0.54 grams
Spinach	0.39 grams
Tomatoes	4.86 grams
Zucchini	2.75 grams

The Iffy	
(5 to 9.9 grams per cup—be a little careful with these)	
Artichoke	6.55 grams
Beets	9.20 grams
Carrots	8.66 grams
Pumpkin	6.94 grams
Squash	8.26 grams
Sweet red peppers	5.98 grams
Turnips	6.06 grams

Veggies Not Worthy to Be Called Iffy *(10 to 20 grams per cup—eat sparingly, if at all)*	
Chili peppers	11.02 grams
Green peas	13.57 grams
Leeks	10.99 grams
Parsnips	17.43 grams

The Candy Bars of the Vegetable Family *(over 20 grams per cup—avoid these if you possibly can; they are not your friends!)*	
Potatoes	22.9 grams
Sweet potatoes	22.76 grams
Yams	35.62 grams
Yellow sweet corn	25.09 grams

As you can see, not all vegetables are created equal. Sadly, two of the tastiest and most popular vegetables (potatoes and corn) are the absolute worst ones you can eat, sugarwise. The key to successful blood-sugar control is being willing to load up on the low-carb foods and go easy on the high-carb ones. Many Americans fill up on potatoes, breads, chips, and pastas, drink sugar-saturated drinks, and enjoy prodigious desserts and candy way too often. Not good! Those of us who battle high blood sugar have to reverse this and make vegetables, meats, eggs, and cheese foundational in our diet, supplemented by low-carb, high-fiber breads and lesser portions of some of the other foods.

You really do have a say in what your blood-sugar monitor reads when you prick your finger and wait for the results. Choose wisely and make low-carb vegetables an important part of your diet.

Fruits—Be Discriminating

I saw an article on the Internet in which the author gave a blistering defense of fruit. When she gives lectures on nutrition and speaks of the benefits of fruit, she reports that she is often challenged by her students. They tell her that fruit is filled with carbs or loaded with sugar and shouldn't be considered a "healthy food."

In righteous indignation this woman declares how much better fruit is than most of the sweets Americans eat. She details how that fruit comes complete with fiber, antioxidants, minerals, and phytonutrients, and is bursting with vitamins. On top of that, much fruit is relatively low in calories, far lower than the "sweets" we normally eat. She compares an orange to a cola drink, and shows that the orange has less sugar, fewer carbs, fewer calories, and more vitamins, minerals, nutrients, and fiber.

I have no argument with her, as far as she goes. If someone were to set an orange and a Coke in front of me, put a gun to my head, and tell me I had to ingest one or the other, I'd go for the orange in a heartbeat. (No one has ever done that, and I have a suspicion that I will live out my years without that ever happening.)

However, for the diabetic and prediabetic the question is not whether oranges are healthier than soda, or apples better for us than Snickers bars. Our major concern is keeping our intake of carbs from driving our blood sugar sky-high and eventually leading us into the land of sores that won't heal, terrible circulation, amputations, and all the other diabetic complications that will destroy our health. With that in mind I make a simple observation: there is a reason why little Johnny refuses to eat his broccoli and his cauliflower but has no problem finishing his apple chunks and his pear slices. Ounce for ounce, fruit has considerably more sugar in it than most vegetables. And for people watching their sugar intake, that is not insignificant.

I am not suggesting that diabetics never eat fruit. Fruit is a great source of vitamins and can be a part of a healthy diet. But we must be discriminating, and we must not be naïve. You cannot eat as much fruit as you want, any time you want, and any type you want, if you want blood-sugar control. Your body doesn't give natural sugars a pass while reacting violently to the sugar in sodas and candy bars.

One simple rule for diabetics is to eat half—half an apple, half an orange, half a pear, and so on at a meal rather than a full one. Remember this simple thought: reduce the portion size—reduce the carbs your body has to deal with. Don't eat several fruits at one setting. Eating a large sweet apple, a big banana, and a bunch of grapes will quickly get you near 75 to 80 grams of sugar your pancreas has to try to deal with. If these are a part of a meal that includes significant other sources of carbs, you have put an enormous load on your body, and rising blood sugar will be inevitable.

Carb-wise, the worst fruits of all are the dried fruits. With these the water has been mostly evaporated but the sugar remains. And since they are smaller in size, you get the impression you can eat quite a lot of them without really eating too much. What you are ingesting primarily is sugar, sugar, sugar. One cup of dried figs is 130 grams of carbs! A cup of prunes, which are dried plums, contains around 106 grams, and a cup of raisins has 130 grams. You might as well eat three candy bars (blood-sugar-wise—yes, they do have more vitamins and so on.).

Some fruits are far more acceptable than others. A small tangerine is only about 7 or 8 grams of carbs, which is quite good for the vitamins you are getting. Melons and berries aren't too bad, as long as you don't consume them in large quantities.

The chart below, from diabetescare.com, gives a good comparative guide to the carbs in fruits. As with the vegetables chart, there are slight differences in the numbers in various charts you find. But it is a good resource for making comparisons.

And don't forget that ultimately it is the net carbs, not the total carbs, that count. The chart lists raspberries as having 14.4 grams of carbs per cup, but this amount includes 8.4 grams of fiber. Thus, you really are having to deal with only 6 grams of carbs for a cup of raspberries, which isn't bad at all. You can put some of these babies on a low-carb pancake with-out guilt, and it will be a great treat. You can see how a little knowledge can make a big difference. The mangos have 25 grams of net carbs per cup, whereas papayas (which I really enjoy) have only around 11 grams per cup. Switching from mangos to papayas cuts your carbs in half, and a little more.

Food Item	Portion	Carbs (grams)	Fiber (grams)	Net Carbs (grams)
Apple, medium	1 each	21.0	3.7	17.3
Applesauce	1 cup	27.6	2.8	24.8
Apricots, dried	1 cup	24.9	3.6	21.3
Apricots, fresh	1 each	3.9	0.8	3.1
Avocado, whole raw (all varieties)	1 med	15.0	10.0	5.0
Banana, small	1 each	23.7	2.4	21.3
Blackberries	1 cup	18.4	7.6	10.8
Blueberries	1 cup	20.4	4.0	16.4
Cantaloupe	1 cup	13.2	1.2	12.0
Cherries	1 cup	19.2	2.8	16.4
Cranberries, raw	1 cup	12.0	4.0	8.0
Currants, dried	1 cup	106.8	9.6	97.2
Dates, chopped	1 cup	130.8	13.2	117.6
Figs, dried	1 cup	130.0	23.2	106.8
Figs, fresh	1 each	9.6	1.7	7.9
Grapes	1 cup	28.4	1.6	26.8
Honeydew melon	1 cup	15.6	1.2	14.4
Kiwifruit	1 each	11.3	2.6	8.7
Mango	1 cup	28.0	2.8	25.2
Nectarine	1 each	16.0	2.2	13.8
Orange	1 each	16.3	3.4	12.9
Papaya	1 cup	13.6	2.4	11.2

Peach, medium	1 each	10.9	2.0	8.9
Pear, medium	1 each	25.1	4.0	21.1
Pineapple	1 cup	19.2	2.0	17.2
Plums	1 each	8.6	1.0	7.6
Prunes	1 cup	106.8	12.0	94.8
Raspberries	1 cup	14.4	8.4	6.0
Seedless raisins	1 cup	130.4	6.8	123.6
Strawberries	1 cup	10.8	3.6	7.2
Tangerine	1 each	7.8	1.6	6.2
Watermelon	1 cup	11.2	0.8	10.4

Ultimately the test for any and all fruits is what they do to your blood-sugar levels. If you enjoy a lunch that includes an apple or a pear, fine. Test yourself about an hour and 15 minutes afterward and see what happened. Remember, 120 mg/dl as a peak is normal, 140 is acceptable. But when that number goes north of 150 it's probably time to make some changes. Try half an apple or half a pear next time, and test again. Keep cutting back until the number becomes something you can live with (literally).

Fantastic Fiber

Nearly every nutrition expert agrees that fiber is very, very good for us. Fiber is classified as a carbohydrate, but it is the one carb from which you have nothing to fear. It will pass through your body without being digested, so it has almost no impact upon blood sugar. When you read the nutrition information on the label of the food, you will see that the fiber is placed within the carbohydrate category, but you can deduct the fiber amount from the total carbohydrate count to discover how many sugar-producing carbs you are going to have to deal with. We call this the *net carbs*.

Fiber is categorized by two different types: *soluble fiber* and *insoluble fiber*. Neither will impact your blood sugar and both are beneficial, but they have differing benefits. The insoluble fiber doesn't break down at all in your digestive system. It passes through pretty much "as is" and heads for the exit door with haste. So how can this be beneficial, if it isn't digested? There are several things it does do. First, the insoluble fiber keeps your bowel movements more regular and prevents constipation. We sometimes call it "roughage" and it not only passes through your bowels quickly, but tends to carry the other foods along with it on a faster journey. Since it helps your food not be clogged up in your intestines, it is thought to be a colon-cancer-preventative agent. Another benefit of this fiber is that it adds bulk, attracts water to the colon (making your stool softer), and gives you a feeling of fullness, preventing you from overeating.

The soluble fiber does break down, to a degree, and forms a gel-like mass that has been shown in many studies to reduce blood-sugar spikes. Yet like the insoluble fiber it does not affect blood-sugar levels. The *New England Journal of Medicine* reports the following:

> *Beneficial effects of high dietary fiber intake in patients with type 2 diabetes mellitus:* A high intake of dietary fiber,

particularly of the soluble type, above the level recommended by the ADA, improves glycemic control, decreases hyperinsulinemia, and lowers plasma lipid concentrations in patients with type 2 diabetes.[8]

Basically, this gel-like mass keeps other carbs from being too quickly absorbed and turning into sugar. The release of glucose in your body is of a kinder, gentler (and slower) nature than it would be otherwise.

It is not the purpose of this book to delve very deeply into theory; I am more concerned about getting you traveling in the right direction. Let us sum up what research has learned about fiber with these two simple but important facts: 1) Fiber is really good for you; and 2) the higher the ratio of fiber carbs to total carbs, the better a food is for the diabetic. For example, if a slice of bread has 22 grams of carbs with 1 gram of fiber, that is not impressive. But if, as in the case of some "double fiber" breads, a slice has 13 grams of carbs with 5 of those being fiber carbs, that is significant. You are dealing with only 8 sugar-producing grams of carbs for that slice, which isn't too bad.

The fiber percentage you need to consider is found by dividing the fiber grams by the total grams of carbs. Peanuts are listed as having 5 grams of carbs per ounce, and 2 of these carb grams are listed as dietary fiber. Divide 2 by 5 and you get .40, which means that 40 percent of the carbs in peanuts are fiber, which is quite good, far better than most foods.

Just because a food is high in fiber doesn't mean that it is low in net carbs. There are some high-fiber cereals that still blow the roof off in terms of net carbs. Don't be taken in simply by a high-fiber label on the food. The true test of the food is the net carbs. Many granola cereals look so crunchy, healthy, and fiber-full that they surely must be great for the diabetic. Not! In fact, most granola-type cereals have a naturally high carb count and then (to add insult to

A low-carb bagel sounds like an oxymoron but researchers have been able to create these wonders by ratcheting the fiber carbs to absurd levels. The low-carb bagels I eat contain 36 grams per bagel but exactly half of these (18) are fiber carbs which don't affect blood sugar.

injury) they add loads of sugar, so that they become some of the highest carb cereals on the shelf.

Foods highest in the ratio of fiber carbs to regular carbs. The mother of all foods when it comes to the ratio between fiber carbs and total carbs is the lowly flaxseed. When you buy flaxseed meal you find an amazing fact on the nutrition information: the number of total carbs and fiber carbs in a serving is exactly the same! In truth there is a slight difference, but so little that they don't bother to list it. (Something like 4.0 total carbs to 3.84 fiber carbs.) This is why flaxseed meal is found in so many low-carb recipes, as in flaxseed muffins (see chapter 28) and low-carb bread (chapter 10) With flaxseed you can pretty much eat as much as you can stand, without worrying about carbs or blood sugar.

Other great fiber-to-regular-carb-ratio foods include wheat bran, spinach, collard greens, broccoli, avocados, and blackberries. All these have more fiber carbs in them than digestible carbs. Asparagus, celery, eggplant, lettuce, mushrooms, radishes, and red raspberries have about an equal amount of fiber to digestible carbs, which is great. Almost all nuts are high in fiber and fairly low in carbs, and are great foods for diabetics.

Wheat flour fares pretty low in this category compared with soy flour. A serving of wheat flour contains 3 grams of fiber, as does the same amount of soy flour. But the soy flour contains only 8 grams of total carbs, whereas the wheat flour contains 21 grams. So the soy flour's ratio of fiber to total carbs is 37 percent, but the wheat flour's percentage is 14 percent.

To sum up, fiber is tremendously beneficial, and no diet should be without it. However, those concerned with blood sugar should not assume "high fiber" makes a food safe for them. Watch for the net carbs, and also be aware of the fiber-to-total-carbs ratio.

Managing the Cost of the
Low-Carb Lifestyle

As you move toward a low-carb lifestyle you will soon find that there is a cost involved. In my early days I used to eat a lot of low-carb candy bars, and I would be so envious when I looked at the regular candy bars sitting proudly on the racks as I waited in line to check out. Whereas I might be paying a dollar and a half for my low-carb bar, these sugar-filled delights were sitting there selling for a mere fifty cents. It just wasn't fair!

And it still isn't. Food retailers know they have the low-carbers over a barrel. Some years ago I used to buy a low-carb bagel that was absolutely delicious, but pricey. I think I was paying around five or six dollars for a bag of six. After a while the product disappeared from the grocery shelves. I called the company to order some and they told me an interesting story about that particular bagel. They said the FDA had decided that these bagels weren't as low-carb as they had been advertising, and forced them to change their nutrition information. They were still lower in net carbs than most bagels but were no longer low enough to be advertised as low-carb. The company took the "low-carb" boast off the label and started selling the same bagels for about a little over half of what they had been charging before. Since they were no longer low-carb they figured they could never get the former price. Such is the nature of the low-carb food business.

Another issue that raises the cost of low-carb foods is that these days you can't find many of them in regular grocery stores. You can find low-carb products through various specialty stores on the Internet. If you live in a big city there are probably a few low-carb stores scattered throughout the city, but you aren't likely to find many of these foods at Walmart or Kroger.

Going to a low-carb store is the essence of mixed emotions. At first your eyes light up as you see all kinds of low-carb foods, candies, syrups, desserts, mixes, muffins, and so forth. But then you start checking the prices. Suddenly your elation turns into dismay. The prices seem ridiculous, far higher than those for their starchy, sugar-filled counterparts at your local grocery store. If you are cheap and not all that wealthy, and a little bit stubborn (guilty on all counts!), you tend to rebel. You buy a token product or two and leave most of the pricey items for others.

There is hope! While you cannot do away with paying a little above and beyond the normal cost of eating, you can modify the cost quite a bit. First, you can make a number of foods yourself. At one point I got excited about low-carb bread. I had been eating bread with about 8 net grams of carbs per slice, but found there was one for sale that had only 1 net gram of carbs for each slice. Wow! The bread looked great in the picture, it had all kinds of fiber, and I decided to track down the one store I could find in the Dallas area that carried it.

But when I arrived at my destination my excitement turned to disappointment. The bread sold for about eight dollars a loaf. And the loaf was soooo scrawny! I was intending to buy two loaves, but changed my mind and picked up one instead. But I never got out of the store with it. As I carried it around, looking for other products, I became more and more upset with the idea of spending this much money for a puny little loaf. I knew I would never be able to make this my "go-to" bread, and sadly placed it back where I found it, next to its high-priced brothers.

The story sounds discouraging, but it has a happy ending. I went home and started checking out low-carb bread recipes. I found one that looked encouraging, bought a bread machine, and made myself a delicious loaf of low-carb bread. Not only was it much cheaper (I estimate the ingredients might have cost a little over $2) but it was a larger loaf. And with the bread machine there was very little work to it. I simply dumped the ingredients in, turned it on, and a few hours later had wonderful low-carb bread. And to make the whole process even more of a deal (now, don't tell anybody this!), I found the bread machine in great condition at a garage sale for $20.

Another cost-cutting step is to refuse to be bullied by complex recipes. You will find a number of recipes that call for all sorts of spices and other small items that can safely be forgotten about. Remember that recipes aren't the Bible—they are not divinely inspired. You can leave things out, and you can substitute a cheaper item for a pricey one.

Feel free to experiment. When my low-carb muffin recipe called for a third of a cup of club soda I tried it that way. But I never use club soda for anything else and it seemed a waste to buy a liter of it for the sake of the one-third cup. So the next time I tried good old tap water and couldn't see or taste any difference. Au revoir, club soda!

There are so many low-carb recipes for great foods, snacks, muffins, breads, and desserts on the Internet that you could spend a hundred lifetimes trying them all and still never be finished. With a little effort you can find all sorts of foods and recipes that won't raise your blood sugar much and will allow you to eat to your heart's content. And check out the low-carb Internet websites. Their shipping fees are painful, but by ordering a lot you bring the price per item down. Freeze what you won't eat for a while. Low-carb bagels are often hard to come by in stores, and by ordering six or more packages and then freezing all but one, you won't do too badly.

There is a price to be paid in time spent when you make foods from scratch. Being the cheapo that I am, I am nearly as tight with my time as I am with my money. But the way to keep this from being too much problem is to **make large recipes and freeze part of the food**.

Yes, low-carbing will probably cost you a bit more than what you would spend on the standard American diet. But in truth you are saving, not losing. The extra money you spend is one of the best investments you'll ever make, and could end up saving you a fortune in medical bills, lost time spent in hospital rooms, and years of your life cut off. Make the necessary sacrifices, and spend the money and time required to live a healthy lifestyle. You're worth it!

The Humble Yet Mighty Flaxseed

When our Creator designed the flax plant, He surely must have had diabetics in mind! The flaxseeds it produces are nutritious, tasty, bursting with fiber, and have almost no net carbs. Any diabetic who does not become close friends with flax is missing something good. Laura Dolson, writing for about.com, comments,

> The flaxseed carries one of the biggest nutrient payloads on the planet. And while it's not technically a grain, it has a similar vitamin and mineral profile to grains, while the amount of fiber, antioxidants, and Omega-3 fatty acids in flax leaves grains in the dust.[9]

The amazing thing about flaxseed is that when you compare the total carbs with the fiber carbs they are nearly one and the same. My box of milled flaxseeds lists 4 grams of total carbohydrates per 2 tablespoons, and then lists 4 grams of dietary fiber for this same amount. This means almost none of what you are eating is having any effect on your blood sugar. You will totally stuff yourself on flax long before you ever do any serious raising of your blood-sugar level.

Along with spinach, cucumbers, chicken, fish, and a number of other foods, here is a food you can enjoy and indulge in without any concern. If only there were a way to incorporate this stuff in our diets. The good news is—there is! The long-ignored flaxseed is starting to get the press it deserves, and we are beginning to see it pop up all over the place in various recipes for diabetics and low-carbers. Of course one of the simplest ways to use it is to add it to various foods you are already eating. It has a delicate, nutty taste that will most likely improve them in flavor, help fill you up, and provide you with nutrients without adding a smidge of blood-sugar-raising carbs. (Okay, maybe it will add a smidge, but not more than that. Definitely not three smidges!)

Milled flaxseed got a major boost in popularity when a fitness trainer showed a television doctor how you can make a muffin in a mug in your microwave, using flaxseed as its primary ingredient. This sounds unbelievable, and when I first heard about it I had my doubts. But when I tested it I found it not only produces a muffin, but the muffin tastes pretty good. Here is the recipe:

Flaxseed Muffin-in-a-Mug
Ingredients:
1/4 cup of ground (milled) flaxseed
1 teaspoon of baking powder
2 teaspoons of cinnamon
1 teaspoon of coconut oil
1 egg
1/2 packet of stevia (or any sugar substitute)

Instructions:
Thoroughly beat the egg in a mug first, then add the other ingredients and mix until well blended. Put the mug in your microwave and set it for about 90 seconds. Voilà! The muffin pops easily out of the mug and you can put butter on it or cream cheese and have a real treat. Granted, it doesn't brown this way as muffins do in the oven, but the taste is decent, especially with a little sugar-free jelly on it. And you almost feel guilty enjoying something this much, fixing it this easily, and knowing that it has almost no effect on your blood sugar.

There are an infinite number of variations and substitutes that you can incorporate. You can leave out the cinnamon if you don't care for it. You can use regular cooking oil instead of coconut oil. You can add all sorts of low-carb items, like a few berries, sliced almonds, or sunflower seeds. You can also microwave the mixture in a large bowl or a plate with upturned edges rather than in a mug, and it will turn out more in the shape of flat bread. You could even make a couple of these and use them as hamburger buns.

This is just one example of what you can do with flax. You can use milled flaxseed to make extremely low-carb pizza crust, you can use it in bread recipes (see chapter 10), you can make hot cereal with it, you can use it in making protein fiber shakes, and there is even a recipe for "miracle brownies" based on flaxseed. And if pure flaxseed is too much for you, in many recipes you can substitute a corresponding amount of soy flour for about half the flaxseed called for, which will produce a slightly milder taste.

Get on the Internet, go to your favorite search engine, type in "flax-seed recipes," and start trying things. And don't be afraid to experiment and make changes to suit your taste, as long as you are not substituting a high-carb product for a low-carb one. To keep your meals from being boring and increase your chances of staying low-carb for life, you need as large a repertoire of meals, snacks, and recipes as possible. Flaxseed can be one of your go-to ingredients that helps to enlarge that repertoire.

One word of caution: when you start eating quite a bit of flaxseed you will probably be ingesting more fiber than your body is used to. It may take some time for it to get used to it, and there may be some protest at the beginning. So you may want to go a little slow at first and gradually work your way to more fiber.

Bean Power

High in protein, high in fiber, rich in antioxidants, and loaded with minerals, the humble bean is a powerhouse food. Studies abound that show positive effects of beans for diabetics and prediabetics. Trading in pastas and regular bread for beans has been shown to lower overall blood sugar, as well as fasting blood sugar, and prevent the post-meal spikes in blood sugar that are so common for insulin-resistant diabetics.

The bean has been blessed with over-the-top levels of fiber—far more than most other foods. These fibers not only can be deducted from the total carbohydrate count, since they don't raise blood sugar, but they actually work to prevent other foods from spiking your blood sugar as they make their way through the intestines. From myhealingkitchen.com:

> Beans also are high in soluble fiber, which binds to carbo-hydrates and slows their digestion into the bloodstream, preventing wild swings in blood-sugar levels. They also contain generous amounts of resistant starch, which means that beans are less digestible than other carbs in the small intestine, so they move into the large intestine faster. Once there, they behave like a dietary fiber, limiting the sharp rise of glucose levels and insulin that can follow a meal, even one that is filled with refined carbohydrates.

One could write a large book about beans, but for our purposes we focus on the knowledge that you really need to get them in your diet.

First, though, we do need a few words of wisdom about beans. Beans do have significant carbohydrates, and even with their high fiber content, there are still a number of carbs that can raise your blood-sugar level.

Second, canned beans are always going to be worse, in every way, than a bag of dried beans you cook yourself. They will have more salt, often added sugar, and they will affect your blood sugar more. Give up the canned beans and invest a little time working with the dried ones.

Because beans do have a significant amount of carbs (even deducting their fiber) you want to be moderate. A large bowl of beans in a soup with little else but beans is probably not the way you want to go. It is far better to put a more moderate amount of beans over a very low-carb bread. With the low-carb bread as a base you don't need as many beans to fill you up.

Beans are slow to digest, so your blood-sugar levels will take longer to reach their peak after eating beans rather than other foods. When you first try a meal heavy on beans, you should check your blood sugar an hour after you finish your meal, and then check it again in 30 minutes, and then again 30 minutes later (two hours after the meal). You will likely find that it keeps rising a bit in that second hour. But in most cases, if your portion of beans was moderate, your blood sugar should fall within acceptable levels.

Now by low-carb bread I don't mean any bread you find on your grocery-store shelf. Even the double-fiber breads are probably going to be too much for you when you add the beans. Remember this simple rule: "Don't allow two major sources of carbs in the same meal." Below is a simple recipe for a low-carb bread you can make in your microwave in 90 seconds. The bread's tiny amount of carbs—about 2 grams—will allow you to enjoy a generous portion of cooked beans on top without straining your pancreas or overloading your blood-sugar-processing system:

Bread in a Bowl

1. Melt 1 tablespoon butter in a bowl.
2. Add one egg to melted butter.
3. Mix in 2 tablespoons of flaxseed meal.
4. Mix in 1 tablespoon of soy flour.
5. Mix in small amount of baking powder.
6. Mix everything very thoroughly.
7. Mix in 1 packet of stevia.
8. Cook in the bowl in a microwave for 1 minute 30 seconds.

Now pour a generous portion of your cooked beans all over the bread and enjoy. When I first enjoyed this meal I could hardly wait to test my blood sugar an hour later to see if this was going to be an acceptable food. When the results were well within the limits I set for myself (145 mg/dl or lower) I knew I could start enjoying this as one of my go-to lunches. It was a great day for me! And when I found out that my wife could cook a mean lentil soup that also proved acceptable, I was doubly blessed!

While most beans are pretty close in terms of total carbs, there are significant differences in their percentage of fiber, and therefore the net grams of carbs. Below is a table of some of the common types of beans you will find on your grocer's shelves. You will notice that some are far lower in net carbs than others. (Pinto beans can vary a lot, depending on the brand you buy). Naturally you should gravitate to the beans that have the higher fiber and the lower net carbs. The values below are based on 1/4 cup of dried beans. You would do well to eat primarily those beans that have a net carb gram value in the single digits.

Type of beans	Total carbs	Fiber	Net carbs
Northern beans	22	13	9
Lima beans	22	7	15
Black beans	22	5	17
Chickpeas	21	6	15
Lentils	20	11	9
Light red kidney beans	21	5	16
Navy beans	21	9	12
Pinto beans	22	14	8
Small red beans	23	16	7

Strawberries—You Gotta Love 'Em

I am happy to announce some really great news: Strawberries are relatively low in carbohydrates! And what makes that such great news? Well, if I tell you that cucumbers are low in carbs, or that celery is low in carbs (which are both true), you will add that bit of knowledge to your knowledge base, but it probably won't make you leap for joy, because these foods are simply not that exciting. After all, whoever heard of celery shortcake or cucumber shortcake? But everyone has heard of strawberry shortcake!

I grew up loving this taste sensation and still do. But when I developed blood-sugar problems I figured I had to give it up. I was wrong! I can still enjoy strawberries, thanks to the wonderful news that *an average-sized strawberry has about one gram of net carbs*. This means I can enjoy a bowl of seven or eight strawberries and not do that much to my blood sugar. I can slice several of these babies and put them in a salad. I can slice up three or four and put them in my low-carb cereal. And I can add several to low-carb yogurt in my blender and make a delicious smoothie.

Not only are strawberries relatively low-carb and tasty; they are also nutritious. They can give oranges a run for their money when it comes to vitamin C (bet you didn't know that) and they contain all sorts of minerals, other vitamins, and antioxidants, which do the body good. And on top of all of this they come in a pretty red color. Who could ask for more?

But for me, the greatest and tastiest form of strawberries is in strawberry shortcake. And while this can be safe for the diabetic, the one thing you cannot do is use the little yellow, spongy shortcakes that you find in your local grocery store. Just one of those scrawny little cakes has between 17 and 20 grams of carbs with almost no fiber. We will have to come up with a low-carb version.

But low-carb does not mean bad-tasting! There are a number of low-carb shortcake recipes available. Some of the ones that come closest to the original yellow cakes are a bit complicated, and I don't like complicated. So I have come up with a few of my own that do the job nicely, as far as I'm concerned.

A simple way to have strawberry shortcake is to use any low-carb muffins you have on hand (recipe in chapter 16). Just split the muffin into two or three slices, add about four sliced and mashed strawberries, and spray a little whipped cream on top. Or you can take any low-carb muffin recipe, bake the batter in a pan rather than in a muffin tin, and then divide into individual sizes when it is done. Another option is to simply put strawberries on a couple of low-carb pancakes (recipe in chapter 19).

The only caveat concerning strawberries is that carbs will eventually add up, so you can't just fill a bowl with 20 or 30 of these babies and eat to your heart's content. And, of course, if you are allergic to them you need to avoid them altogether. But for most of us, strawberries can really add a little pizzazz to a low-carb diet.

Another idea for strawberry short-cake: you can take a slice of the low-carb bread made in your bread machine (see chapter 10), cut off the edges, and use that as the base of your shortcake. It has a spongy texture that will remind you a bit of the store-bought shortcakes, and by the time the strawberries and whipped cream are poured on it, it is pretty good.

Teatime

Teatime is associated with the British, and was traditionally served in the late afternoon with scones and jam, and sometimes various other sweet little cakes. The tea was usually served with milk and sugar, and the tea and pastries served as an antidote to the afternoon doldrums. Teatime also became a social affair, with ladies and gentlemen of means inviting other ladies and gentlemen of means over to their houses for "tea." From there it spread throughout the populace.

I have found that an altered form of teatime can be quite useful for those who struggle to keep their blood sugar under control. A few adjustments must be made. First of all, you will have to lose the scones and jam (of course). However there are all kinds of low-carb treats you can have with your tea that will barely budge your blood-sugar levels. Low-carb muffins are a great choice. My preferred food is one tiny sugar-free chocolate candy and some peanuts.

The tea can be however you like it, provided you don't load it with sugar. I enjoy my tea with heavy whipping cream and some stevia artificial sweetener. The combination of the tea and the little snack makes for a relaxing time.

Actually, the practice for me started when I missed my connecting flight in London while on my way to Kenya. The airline offered me a free stay at a very nice local hotel while I waited about 12 hours for the next flight. I knew I had to choose between fretting and worrying about being late for my scheduled meetings, or just relaxing and enjoying the free room. I chose the latter. After getting settled I put on some enjoyable music, made myself tea, and had a marvelous time of relaxation.

At this point you might be wondering, *What does this have to do with my blood-sugar problem?* Actually, it can be pretty helpful for you in this respect. First, between the low-carb snack and the tea with cream and stevia, there is very little to raise your blood sugar. Second, you will find it quite filling and satisfying, which relieves you from those between-meal hunger pains. And third, when you take this teatime around 4:30 or 5:00 p.m. and then eat a couple of hours later, you will not be nearly so likely to overeat at supper (or dinner, or whatever you like to call it).

Often your worst struggle with high-carb foods will come at the supper table. By having teatime a couple of hours before supper, you can be more moderate in your portion sizes at the supper table. You will not be nearly so likely to devour mounds of rice or that huge biscuit as you would have been. Beyond these reasons, there is some evidence that tea actually improves blood-sugar levels to some degree.

Of course working folks often don't have the luxury of taking time off their jobs to sip tea at 4:30, but you can always have it as soon as you get home, and then delay your meal for a while. And be sure to put on some relaxing music while you sip your tea. Utter a few thanksgivings to God in between sips. It is a great way to unwind and soothe the soul. And soothed souls are much more likely to be self-controlled than unsoothed ones!

Don't Be Gullible!

When I was in college I went with some buddies to a carnival. Toward the end of our time there, a man in a booth offered me some free ring tosses. I thought I had nothing to lose (little did I know!) and took him up on his offer. He handed me several rings and instructed me to toss them at the soda bottles he had placed in the center of his booth. After tossing them he congratulated me and began to add up my "points." According to him I had accumulated around 90 points and was nearly at the goal of 100, which would have enabled me to win a major prize. But of course I would need to pay for the next set of rings.

I figured if I had gotten up to 90 with the first tosses, I could surely rack up another 10 with this next round. Afterward I was up to something like 96—still not enough to win anything but very, very close to that magic goal of 100. On top of this the operator told me this qualified me to win a second prize once I reached the 100 points, and he brought out a portable television (a lot bigger deal in those days that it would be today). Of course I would have to purchase some more rings, and this time they would cost more. I think you can figure out where this is going (I only wish I had figured it out then!). Eventually he cleaned me out of all the money in my wallet, and I was still without a single prize.

As you walk through the grocery store, you should imagine slick carnival guys like this fellow calling out to you, "Come and buy! This food is just the ticket for a diabetic like you!" Of course these are not living and breathing people—they are brightly colored banners that shout at you, "Low-fat," "fat-free," "no sugar added," "gluten-free," and other such things. It's not hard to be awed by these important-sounding proclamations and buy the product.

We will consider some of these claims in a moment, but before we do let me give you the most basic and simple rule when deciding whether a food will work for you. *The bottom line is the number of grams of carbs (minus the fiber) in the portion size that you will eat.* When considering foods with claims of being natural, organic, fat-free, or anything else, your first response should be to go immediately to the nutrition information and find the net carbs. Anything approaching 30-plus grams of carbs in your real-life portion size is near to what you would get in a candy bar.

When your blood sugar is rising, it is responding to the carbs—period! Your body doesn't much care (blood-sugar-wise) whether those carbs came from raisins or a chocolate bar, whether from orange juice or from Coca-Cola, whether they originated from stone-ground wheat flour or the whitest white flour on the face of the planet. The total number of carbs you are ingesting is going to have a direct correlation to that discouraging high number that shows up on your blood-sugar monitor. Yes, complex carbohydrates may break down somewhat more slowly than simple carbs, but not that much more slowly. And you will still "pay the piper."

Let's consider some of the slogans you need to take with the proverbial grain of salt:

"Low-fat" or "fat-free"—Many years ago nutritionists and medical "experts" decided that a high-carb, low-fat diet was the sure way to stay healthy, lose weight, and get along with your mother-in-law. They pushed this diet rigorously and with all sincerity. Eat as much bread, rice, bagels, doughnuts, and Corn Flakes as you like. Just stay away from that dreadful meat, terrible cheese, those horrible fat-filled nuts, and those heart-clogging cholesterol-laden eggs! Americans naively assumed that since the experts said it, it must be so. The facts and the research did not bear this out, however. Not only did most not lose weight on such a diet, but diabetes has gone through the roof. Stuffing our mouths with starches and sugars while avoiding meat and eggs led to millions of people with worn-out pancreases and insulin-resistant bodies.

Keep this in mind: most of the time when manufacturers reduce fat in a product, it means they have made up for it by increasing the sugar. If you take away the natural taste produced by the fat, the food tends to be bland and tasteless. The only way you'll ever get anybody to eat it will be by ramping up the sugar. And sugar is far more your enemy than fat ever could be!

"Gluten-free"—Gluten-free foods are necessary for people who are allergic to gluten, but for ordinary people, they serve no purpose. Some have supposed that gluten-free foods are especially good for diabetics. They are not. "Gluten-free" sounds sort of impressive, but if you look at the net carbs, most of the foods that boast of this are higher in net carbs than the wheat-based products. Unless you are allergic to gluten, the last thing you need to worry about is whether your carbs are coming from gluten foods or some other source. Carbs are carbs.

"No sugar added"—Once I enjoyed some "no sugar added" ice cream without checking the net carbs. I didn't realize that even without the added sugar, the ice cream was a significant source of carbs. A very high blood-sugar reading afterward convinced me of the error of my ways, and it motivated me to be more careful to check the carbs on foods rather than trusting the boasts on the package. Often you can find desserts such as pies and cakes that say "no sugar added." What people fail to realize is that a pie or cake contains a tremendous amount of starch. That starch will turn to sugar in your body with blazing speed. A food does not have to taste sugary to be a source of sugar. "No sugar added" is better than "sugar added" (a label I've never seen)—but in itself it is not enough. Check the net carbs!

"Cholesterol-free"—This may sound impressive, but in truth any food derived from any plant can boast of this. Doughnuts are cholesterol-free. Trix cereal is cholesterol-free. Almost every candy bar is cholesterol-free. You could kill yourself in a year's time eating cholesterol-free foods. If I had to choose between a cholesterol-laden egg or a cholesterol-free doughnut, it would be a no-brainer. The egg is better for us in every possible way.

The Inuit people, who traditionally lived on diets of fish and seal meat almost exclusively—foods high in fat and protein, loaded with cholesterol, and nearly totally carb-less—have been found to have far less heart disease and diabetes than the doughnut-stuffing, Cap'n Crunch–eating, Dr. Pepper–guzzling Americans. So don't be too impressed with the "cholesterol-free" boast proudly displayed on some food package at your local grocery store. Any old bag of potato chips could say that!

Working Fruit into Your Diet

When you grew up you probably heard the refrain many times: "Eat your fruits and vegetables." There was pretty good logic in such advice. Fruits and vegetables have loads of vitamins in them—far more than you will find in meats, breads, or rice. "Fruits and vegetables" are said together so often that it almost seems as though they are one and the same. But for the diabetic they most certainly are not.

Fruits are loaded with vitamins and they taste so good! But we all know the reason for that—they have a lot of natural sugar. It certainly is not necessary to eliminate them from our diets. In fact they should be a part of everyone's diet, diabetic or otherwise. But those who struggle with high blood sugar have to be more discriminating than those who don't. One aspect of this discrimination is to lean more toward the low-sugar fruits, like melons and berries. Another aspect is to eat them in meals where they will not "pile on" with other higher carb foods and do a number on your blood sugar.

Being able to instantly identify the high-carb foods and keep them within healthy boundaries is vital. When you look over the various foods set out on your table your eyes should be able to quickly distinguish the potential troublemakers. Bread, rice, pasta, potatoes, corn—these are some of the basic high-carb foods you will want to greatly limit. A simple rule I have mentioned before is that no meal should contain two generous portions of these high-carb foods. If you are going to have bread, don't have a potato also. If you want to indulge in corn on the cob, don't have the mac and cheese as well.

The ultimate goal is to keep your blood sugar from peaking any higher than about 145 (140 is better). If it takes pills to help you do this, use the pills. If it takes insulin, so be it. But you need to avoid the physical destruction that comes, albeit gradually, to men and women when their blood sugar is consistently too high, day after day, and year after year.

Because most fruits fall into the category of high-carb foods, they need to be eaten in meals where there are no other major sources of carbs. For most of us this means breakfast and lunch. At supper we usually end up eating bread or rice or some other higher-carb food that will lead us into trouble if we have, say, a bowl of grapes as well. For breakfast and lunch it is a fairly easy thing to craft meals that are quite low in carbs. Eggs, sausage, and a low-carb muffin will provide you very few carbs at breakfast. The same is true with low-carb pancakes and sausage, or a low-carb bagel half topped with an egg and slice of ham. With a little effort, it won't take you too long to find breakfasts that are going to keep your pancreas and your blood-sugar monitor happy. In such meals,

Fruits are so bursting with health benefits and vitamins that it is worth taking the necessary precautions and doing a little testing. You'll discover how many of them you can have, and in what sizes and types. And because there are so many excellent low-carb breads, muffins, and other foods, it is possible to eat meals that have very few non-fruit carbs and thus enable yourself to add some delicious and nutritious fruit to your diet without doing any damage.

most folks can add a peach, or half of a banana or apple, or the fruit of your choice, and still stay within a desirable range when their blood sugar peaks.

Notice the word *half*. Some fruits are simply too high in sugar and carbs for most of us to be able to eat a whole one, especially when they are of a large size. A large banana is probably going to have almost 30 grams of carbs—too many to be getting from one small food item at one sitting. On the other hand a small banana may only have 21 net carbs, which might be okay for some but not others. As we have been saying all along, let your blood-sugar monitor be your guide.

Lunches can also be created to be very low in carbs and thus make room for fruit in them. Some examples might be a garden salad or some high-fiber beans (see chapter 29) over a very low-carb bread. In such cases you buy yourself the luxury of enjoying an orange or tangerine, a peach, a bowl of berries, or a slice of watermelon.

Some fruits are clearly less problematic than others. A cup of papaya has less than half the carbs and sugar of a cup of mango. A medium peach has about half the carbs and sugar of a medium apple. A cup of raspberries has about one-twentieth of the carbs of a cup of seedless raisins! So as you add fruit to your meal, do it wisely and discerningly. Be aware of the sugar content of the particular fruit you are eating, and the size as well. And when you first experiment with fruit, be sure to check your blood-sugar peaks and see how your body is reacting.

The good news is that many type 2 diabetics can eat fruit with their meals and keep their blood sugar under control without the need for medication or insulin. Type 1 diabetics can certainly eat fruit and keep their blood sugar in bounds as well, but there will be the need for the proper amount of insulin. The one thing no diabetic or even prediabetic should do is eat as much fruit as they want as often as they want. Exercise some moderation and self-control, and your body will thank you for it.

Think Outside the Box

People are notoriously creatures of habit and culture, and the older we get the more we tend to plant ourselves in routines and habits that rarely vary. There is a certain amount of security and comfort in this. Doing as we have always done and living as we have always lived seems safe. It has worked for us thus far—why change?

But when it comes to runaway blood sugar, your lifestyle and routines clearly haven't worked very well for you thus far, since you are reading this book. "When it ain't broke, don't fix it," but when it is totally broken down and you are on the verge of self-destruction it's time to make some serious changes. And this will involve thinking outside the box, doing new things, eating new foods, and adopting new habits and patterns.

Be willing to be different! Do things in a way you haven't before. Do things that others don't, for the sake of your health. Here are a few simple examples to get you started, but don't stop with these.

The hamburger. Let's start with this most American of all foods. The burger itself is no problem for diabetics. No carbs worth mentioning. The ketchup will add a few, but you can go a bit light with it and be fine. The cheese and lettuce—again no problem. No, the only problem with the hamburger is that fat and sassy bun. That's where you are going to get most of your carbs, and that is what will produce those depressingly high numbers on your blood-sugar monitor. American traditions tell us exactly how a hamburger bun should look and what texture it should have. But here's a news flash: the hamburger bun's attributes weren't given by God to Moses on Mount Sinai! We can do all sorts of things to improve the hamburger, blood-sugar-wise.

For example, you can eat a hamburger on a low-carb waffle (see chapter 19). Yes, it will seem outlandish at first, but you will find that it's actually pretty good. Or you can buy the round flat buns at the store that have about 8 net grams of carbs each and probably still keep your blood sugar in bounds. Or you can make all sorts of other substitutions. The point is, you will not be arrested by the hamburger police for saying no to that round plump bun saturated with blood-sugar-raising carbs!

Strawberry shortcake is something that most Americans are accustomed to eating with strawberries piled inside those cute, spongy cakes that are hollowed out in the center. It hurts our sensibilities to eat strawberries on a square of bread or on something that isn't yellow and spongy.

But who says you can't enjoy strawberries and whipped cream on some other type of bread—especially some form that won't send your blood sugar through the roof? Most low-carb muffin mixes (as in chapter 16) baked in a small square pan can make a great-tasting "shortcake" that can be divided into quarters. No, they don't look so cute, but when they are drenched with mashed juicy strawberries and topped with whipped cream, they do the job wonderfully.

> You can use low-carb waffles (see chapter 19) to **make your own version of the Egg McMuffin**. Two of the low-carb waffles will have around 6 grams of carbs. The two halves of an English muffin, however, will have around 27 grams of carbs. The savings here are tremendous and are well worth eating a little "outside the box."

Bringing your own snacks with you is another "out of the box" behavior. But it works great for filler purposes. For example, when people go to Starbucks or other coffee places they often like to have a little snack with their coffee. But nearly all snacks sold at coffeehouses are little more than loads of sugar combined with lots of starch—a diabetic's nightmare.

Of course you can just have the coffee, but sometimes I bring my own snack to go with my sugar-free, half-and-half French vanilla latte. My snack of choice is usually a handful of peanuts and a small, sugar-free chocolate candy (Russell Stover coconut, to be precise). Yes, it may well be that a few people have seen me pull the peanuts out of my pocket and wondered what I was doing. But who cares? If I want to enjoy my coffee with a low-carb snack, I'll pay the price of looking a bit odd to one or two people who sit nearby. I sometimes bring a low-carb snack with me into McDonald's as well, when I want a hamburger and need to replace the typical accompanying fries. Of course I could always get a salad, but sometimes I prefer my own substitution. When I am wearing a sport jacket with pockets I sometimes bring low-carb muffins into restaurants. (Women have it easier, and with a large purse can smuggle in entire dinners!)

What we are saying here is pretty simple, but it needs to be said. People with blood-sugar problems cannot live and eat and do things the way others live and eat and do. It is nowhere written in stone that you must complete the latter portion of your life in the same fashion as you did the former portion. Indeed, once you begin to take your blood sugar seriously, there is no way you can possibly do that. It is time to think outside the box.

Using Your Freezer

When it comes to establishing disciplines in our lives, I am a firm believer in making things as easy as possible. The harder you make it to keep up with your new lifestyle, the higher the chances you will fail.

It would be so wonderful if all the grocery stores had low-carb food options right alongside the regular foods. In the candy-bar rack you would find regular and low-carb candy bars. In the bread section you could choose between normal and low-carb breads. Alas, it isn't so. Most grocery stores sell a few token low-carb or sugar-free items, but with many foods your choice is either high-carb or forget it.

If you have lots of money this isn't too much of a problem. You can order all kinds of low-carb foods, from doughnuts to barbecue sauce, from various low-carb websites. If you are willing to double your food bill, you can stay low-carb and steer clear of baking low-carb breads, pancakes, brownies, pies, and so forth. But for most of us this is not an option. We are going to have to do some cooking.

I have a few rules in this area. I rarely tackle complicated recipes that use more than a dozen ingredients or call for strange things such as cleaned squid or exotic spices I cannot pronounce. I get intimidated by recipes that tell you to fold something into something (folding is for clothes, not foods). Another rule is, whenever possible I like to make a large recipe and keep the leftovers in my freezer. It generally doesn't take much more time to make a dozen muffins than it does six. Why spend all that time messing up your kitchen for six muffins that will be gone pretty soon? Double the recipe, put six of them in the freezer, and bring them out when the first six are gone. Or you can make six muffins and then put the rest of the mix in a square pan. When it has baked you can divide it into portions for strawberry shortcake.

I love to treat myself to a really good low-carb dessert from time to time. I used to feel I had to eat a piece of pie or whatever it was every night so it wouldn't spoil by the time I finished it (since I was the only one eating low-carb). It was nice enjoying a dessert every night, but it tends to put on the pounds. Low-carb desserts are not low-calorie desserts, and moderation is required. Then I realized that I could keep a couple of pieces in the refrigerator, divide the rest into pieces, and freeze them individually. Then on Saturday evenings, while watching a film noir movie from the forties or fifties, I could bring out one of those bad boys, make some coffee, and have my own little low-carb classic-movie party. Try this with my cheesecake recipe in chapter 15. And for the movie I recommend *Laura* (from 1944) or almost any Humphrey Bogart movie.

Many low-carbers make an occasional trip to a special low-carb shop, but in most cases we don't live very close to one. We're not going to be making a lengthy trip to the low-carb store every week, so it makes sense to **buy the food or snacks in large amounts and freeze some of them.**

You can keep strawberries, blueberries, blackberries, and nearly every other kind of berries in the freezer, then bring them out to put on low-carb pancakes, waffles, and so forth.

The idea of using your freezer isn't new, profound, or brilliant. But it is smart in its own simple way. And the easier you can make a low-carb lifestyle, the more likely you will keep with it. So use your freezer. Make it easy on yourself.

The Power of the Scale

When I was a wild and reckless college kid, someone at our dorm got a call saying that a railroad company was paying students to come and clean up the mess that had been created by a train accident. I decided to join some of my friends who were going there to make a little extra money.

When we arrived on the scene of the accident, boxes were everywhere. We pitched in quickly and began loading everything onto a truck. But the sight of some of those things was too tempting for most of us. I am ashamed to say that I, along with most of my buddies, began helping myself to some of the smaller items and stuffing my pockets. We thought we were making a real haul until it was announced that when we were paid, we would be searched. That put a new light on things, and soon the air was filled with boxes and all sorts of treasures being thrown into the bushes as we divested ourselves of our loot. So much for our dreams of riches!

The power of accountability is truly amazing. But when it comes to your health, no one is going to hold you accountable but you. There are no sugar police to ticket you when you eat that third doughnut. You will not go to jail when you give your kids a breakfast of Pop-Tarts and Dr. Pepper. And no one will haul you into court when you become nearly as wide as you are tall. In America you can eat yourself to death pretty much undisturbed if you desire.

What this means is that you must take the initiative and hold yourself accountable. But this must be done in specifics, not just by a vague notion that you shouldn't "eat too much" or have "too much sugar." When it comes to obesity the evidence could not be more solid. As your weight increases, so does the likelihood that diabetes is going to come knocking on your door. Around 80 percent of type 2 diabetics are obese. What's encouraging is that often when obese people lose weight the severity of their diabetes lessens—and sometimes disappears altogether.

So how do you hold yourself accountable? Just as checking your blood sugar as it peaks after a particular meal holds you accountable for that meal, so weighing yourself daily on an accurate scale holds you accountable for staying at the proper weight. Facing the truth has a sobering effect. Humans have a remarkable ability of self-deception. We can delude ourselves into thinking we are nice when we are nasty, we may convince ourselves we sing beautifully when we croak like a frog, and sometimes we persuade ourselves, the mirror notwithstanding, that we are not really overweight—just "pleasingly plump."

The scale will not be impressed. It does not play favorites, nor will it go easy on you so as not to hurt your feelings. It will faithfully tell you exactly what you weigh every time you step onto it (if you don't buy the cheapest one possible). When I first started testing my blood sugar, there was nothing more disappointing to me than high numbers. On the other hand, low numbers made me absolutely euphoric. When I ate several slices of thin crust pizza and a salad and then tested at around 120 an hour later, I felt like I had climbed Mount Everest.

> Every pound you shed as you get to your desired weight is **making it easier for your body to process sugar** and decreasing the severity of your diabetes. If you are still in the prediabetic stage, your lessened weight is making it more and more likely that you will never cross that terrible border.

A scale can have that same effect. First, decide what is the ideal weight for you. Then start adjusting the intake of your food to get to that goal. (Don't get radical or extreme—take your time!) Weigh yourself every morning before breakfast. Your scale will either encourage you or rebuke you. And as you hold yourself accountable through the scale, you will find an extra portion of that vital and mysterious ingredient called motivation.

Allow your scale to hold you accountable. By sticking to a low-carb diet and weighing yourself daily, you are well on your way to getting to and maintaining your proper weight. You can do it! And that will have amazing benefits in your struggle with high blood sugar.

Give It a Rest!

One of the major rhythms of life is the pattern of growing weary and then being refreshed. The obvious example of this is our need for sleep. Most humans spend around 16 hours of their days awake and 8 hours asleep. Of course God didn't have to make us this way. He could have made us untiring creatures who never needed sleep at all. How much more productive we could be if we never slept! How many more books could be written, business deals transacted, and inventions created if nobody ever slept!

Our wise Creator did not see fit to make us thus. Somewhere in the evening we find ourselves running down. Our eyes become heavy, our concentration weakens, our productivity plummets, and even our desire for food gives way to the demands of our body that we lie on a comfortable bed, close our eyes, and lose consciousness for a period of six to eight hours (often more if you are a teenager). By morning, after breakfast and a cup of coffee, we are refreshed, alert, and ready to face another day.

The topic of rest has to do with a key question: What makes a person a diabetic? In type 1 diabetics the pancreas is simply unable to produce insulin. In type 2 diabetics things are a little more complicated. In many, and probably most, cases a vicious cycle has done the work. As people age their bodies often become less efficient in processing insulin. The pancreas says, "No problem—I'll simply produce more insulin and all will be well." As this "insulin resistance" increases, the pancreas gamely determines to keep up with the need, and after a while we are walking around with bodies flooded with insulin (a very unhealthy situation).

Even though our blood-sugar levels may not (yet) indicate there is a problem, the enormous load of insulin surging through our bloodstream is doing a number on us. The more insulin is produced, the more insulin-resistant we become; the more insulin-resistant we become, the more insulin must be produced. Our pancreas is working far harder than it was ever intended to work, and the insulin receptors in our cells are becoming impotent from the floods of insulin they are constantly forced to deal with. After a while the entire process starts to shut down. Another one bites the dust.

Incessant and addictive eating of breads, doughnuts, pasta, cakes, Cokes, fruit juices, and coconut cream pies is literally destroying our pancreases and our delicate blood-sugar-processing mechanisms. What should last us for 90 years is worn-out and almost useless at 45.

Pancreases, like people, are not made to be working nonstop and beyond their capacity. Your car may run just fine putting the pedal to the metal occasionally, but drive like that everywhere you go and you'll soon be looking for another car.

But there is good news here. Research and experience have shown that our body can often regain much of its effectiveness in processing sugar when we stop the constant abuse. The answer to this dilemma is rest. Your damaged and exhausted pancreas and insulin receptor cells need some quiet time to heal.

In a sense this is what is at the heart of this book. By adopting the three key ingredients of blood-sugar management—reducing carbs, exercising, and getting to the proper weight—you are taking an enormous strain off the blood-sugar mechanisms of your body. The beta cells of the pancreas can actually replenish themselves to some degree, and insulin resistance can be significantly lessened. No, you'll probably never be able to go back to the days of your youth when you could eat a huge plate of french fries and a big bowl of ice cream, drown them with a large Coke, and have blood sugar under 100 in an hour's time. But you may well be able to get that blood sugar down to a normal range and keep it there for the rest of your days—and that's not too bad! (In fact it's great!)

In addition to a basic low-carb diet, one of the healthiest things you can do is go on a limited fast. Now relax—I'm not talking about going without food for several days. But it can be very beneficial and healing to the body to give your pancreas a real break by going a few days without eating any major-carb foods. This is particularly helpful when you are first trying to get your blood sugar under control.

What this means is that you set a time of a few days to a couple of weeks during which you eat primarily low-carb vegetables, low-carb breads (or no bread at all), and proteins. No rice, no potatoes, no "normal bread," no sugary anything, and no fruit. Dr. Atkins was essentially recommending this when he urged his dieters to do the "phase one" eating plan. The South Beach diet also includes this regimen, calling it "pancreas rest and insulin receptor resensitization protocol."

Your beleaguered pancreas will hardly know what's going on when suddenly he has so little work to do. Healing and refreshing, the natural result of rest, are made possible and even, to a degree, likely. People whose fasting blood-sugar levels are 130 or more would do well to consider a two-week rest such as this. And then, every few months, take a three- or five-day "fast" just to do your pancreas a favor, and to say, "I'm sorry for all those years I've mistreated you."

As you learn more about low-carb foods, you will be able to craft many meals that would fit within such a fast. Here is one example of a Sabbath rest for your pancreas:

1. *Breakfast*: Eggs, sausage, and a low-carb muffin (see chapter 16)

2. *Lunch*: Low-carb bread covered with the highest fiber beans (cooked) you can find, plus an avocado

3. *"Tea-time snack"*: A small handful of peanuts and a cup of tea with heavy whipping cream and one packet of stevia.

4. *Supper*: A salad made up of lettuce, slices of green pepper, broccoli, and cucumbers with a low-carb dressing such as ranch or Italian; baked chicken breast, green beans, and a low-carb slice of bread (see chapter 10)

Meals like these will do very little to raise most people's blood-sugar levels. Of course if you are just starting to take blood sugar seriously and your fasting blood sugar is at 150 mg/dl, don't expect to see a post-meal peak of 125. But once you get that fasting blood sugar down into a reasonable range, you will be thrilled to discover that your blood-sugar peaks are ridiculously low! And when you go back to a more normal (albeit still low-carb) diet, you may find that your blood-sugar control is better than ever.

Sugar in Disguise

Because diabetes is all about high blood sugar, most folks normally think about controlling their intake of sweets when they decide to do something about their diet. No more ice cream or chocolate pudding. No more candy bars or milk shakes. "Those things are sweet—they must be bad for me." Their thinking is right as far as it goes, but it doesn't go far enough. They assume that by controlling and limiting the sweet things that go into their mouth, they are doing about all they need to. Wrong!

There are all sorts of nonsweet things that can be just as much a problem. These are "sweets in disguise." Rice does not taste sweet, nor do potatoes, or rolls, or bagels, or spaghetti noodles. So they must be okay—right? Wrong.

There are *two* types of foods that wreak havoc on our blood-sugar levels—the sugars *and* the starches. Sugary foods like Frosted Flakes and doughnuts are easy to identify as offenders. Your taste buds will immediately inform you that there is some serious sugar going on with these foods. But when we taste a large bowlful of bland rice there is no such warning. The starches are in effect entering your body incognito. However, those startches will almost immediately be converted into sugar once they hit your digestive system. And once they do, your body won't know the difference! They will be every bit as damaging as that candy bar or Pepsi.

To complicate the problem many health professionals have made far too much of "healthy whole-grain" foods. They act as though anything that is whole grain should be given a free pass. They imply that your body will hardly know you have ingested any carbs. But your body will indeed know! And your blood-sugar monitor will tell the tale when you test your spike after eating. To illustrate this, let me pose this question: Which would be better for you—a large bowl of Frosted Flakes fortified with all sorts of vitamins and minerals, or a large bowl of Frosted Flakes without fortification? Of course everybody would say the fortified flakes would be much healthier for us. But what in the world would a diabetic be doing eating Frosted Flakes in the first place, fortified or unfortified?

Some folks can eat a breakfast of a large bowl of bran cereal with a couple of slices of whole-wheat toast, and congratulate themselves for eating a "healthy" meal. Everything was whole grain and nothing tasted the least bit sweet. But if they check their blood sugar about an hour after the meal they will be dismayed to find that their blood-sugar levels have ascended into the heavens. After eating, their digestive juices made short work of the bran and bread, and with blazing speed converted them into sugars. Their pancreas uttered a groan—"Here we go again"—and tried its best to keep up with all that sugar. But simply couldn't do it. They might as well have eaten a doughnut and drunk a soda.

I am not saying you cannot ever eat bread or rice, but I am saying you need to be careful about portion sizes of all starches. They can bite you. Remember that it is carbohydrates that raise your blood sugar, and they come in many and varied forms. Some taste very sweet and some not at all, but if they are carbs (except for fiber carbs) they are dangerous little guys. Be careful and be temperate!

Blood-Sugar Targets

One of the sad realities of our time is that millions of Americans know that they are diabetic or prediabetic but have no idea what their blood-sugar levels should be. If you don't know what target to shoot for, you are not likely to hit it! Compounding the problem is the fact that there are different voices telling you different things. And doubly compounding it is the fact that some of these voices suddenly change their tune and tell you something different than they did previously.

The American Diabetes Association is a perfect example of this. For many years they declared that you are a true diabetic if your fasting blood sugar is 140 mg/dl or above. Then in the 1990s they changed their mind and reduced that number to 126. They state that if you get your blood sugar under control your fasting blood sugar should be no higher than 130 and your post-meal peaks no higher than 180. This is the target they suggest for diabetics.

However, the American Association of Clinical Endocrinologists suggests that organ damage and various diabetic complications occur when blood sugar of 140 or more lingers for several hours per day. What this means is that you may be following the ADA guidelines and feeling you have your diabetes totally under control—while your organs are being slowly destroyed by blood-sugar levels in the 150s, 160s, and 170s.

Unfortunately, the evidence is not complete, and each one of us will have to determine our targets according to the guidelines we deem reasonable. Of course you should be in consultation with your doctor on this. But allow me to point out what seems pretty obvious to me. Considering the tremendous damage high blood sugar can do to your body, if you are going to err it would be better to err on the side of caution. Let's say you give up a few extra foods and spend a couple of hours in the kitchen each week baking low-carb breads, muffins, and waffles just to ensure that your blood-sugar peaks stay under 140. Then 20 years later you hear a definitive report that you would have been just fine with blood-sugar peaks of 170. Well, you won't have lost all that much. But if you play it as close to the edge as you can, allowing blood-sugar peaks in the 180s and 190s, and then in 20 years end up blind with only one leg, you will have lost bigtime. There are times to take risks, but in most areas of life, a conservative approach will save you all kinds of problems.

Are there any dangers from becoming too fanatical about your diet? There are, but only the truly hard-core will ever face them. The primary danger from eating very few carbs is for those who determine to live on meat and cheese, and more meat and more cheese. These folks are getting very few vitamins and too much protein. This is far from an ideal diet, for a diabetic or anybody else. There is no reason you cannot eat vegetables and lots of them (with certain exceptions). And there are fruits that you should be able to fit into your low-carb diet without a problem. Also, don't forget to take a good multivitamin.

In my case, I have set my goal to keep my post-meal peaks under 140. I'm playing it safe. I like my fasting blood sugar to be under 100, but sometimes it gets a bit higher than that. The post-meal peaks are really more important than the fasting blood sugar, because if your post-meal peaks are decent, your fasting blood sugar will almost always follow suit. If you are keeping your post-meal peaks under 140 or 145, it will be nearly impossible for you to have fasting blood sugar over 120, and in most cases it will be significantly lower than that.

Read and research all you can, and talk to your doctor. In the end it is your life, and you will need to make the decisions that are going to affect you years down the road.

Glycemic Index Pros and Cons

As we note elsewhere, the glycemic index is an indicator of how quickly the carbs in various foods break down into sugar in your body. Foods like white bread and mashed potatoes break down lightning-fast, and are therefore given a high glycemic number (70 or above). Most (but not all) vegetables and beans are going to have a low number (50 or below), as they digest much more slowly in the stomach. Nuts are especially low on this scale.

Diabetics are nearly universally advised to eat foods on the low end of the glycemic index. The slower your foods break down in your stomach, the more gradual the rise in your blood sugar. Your pancreas may have to work longer to deal with these slowly dissolving foods, but at least it is not overwhelmed by the intense, sudden overload of sugars you get when you eat a meal of potatoes, white rice, and a Moon Pie.

This wisdom is good, as far as it goes, but there is something you need to keep in mind. Allow me to use the following illustration:

The vast majority of ordinary Americans cannot possibly afford to pay cash for a house. If it were a matter of saving the entire amount before buying and moving into a house of their own, almost nobody would own a house. But banks have come up with a marvelous idea called a mortgage. While you could never pay $150,000 in cash for a house, you might be able to come up with $1300 per month for the next 30 years. And so you sign a contract, proudly move into your new house, and begin to live. While you have made the process manageable, you should not think that you have in any way "gotten away" with something. When the 30 years is up you will have paid every penny you owe for that house, plus interest.

Suppose a man barely making more than the minimum wage goes to a banker, wanting a loan for a 10-million-dollar house. When the banker protests that his wages could never justify such a loan, the man indignantly declares, "Do you think I'm a fool? I'm not planning to pay the whole amount up front. I want a 30-year loan for this house!" Breaking the enormous cost of the house into 360 payments, this silly man has decided he can handle the 10-million-dollar price. But he most definitely cannot!

So it is with the glycemic index and diabetes. By all means, gravitate toward the lower-glycemic-index foods. But don't think that just because a food is lower on the scale, it is okay to eat as much as you want. Barley is a good example of this. Pearl barley has a GI (glycemic index) of only 22—very low on the scale. But it is by no means low in carbs. A serving has 44 grams of carbs. When you deduct the 6 grams of fiber you come out with 38 grams of carbs that your body will have to process—sooner or later. Yes, it helps that it doesn't dump those carbs on you all at once, but they don't just disappear. On the other hand, watermelon is high on the glycemic index because its sugars go into your bloodstream quickly. That sounds terrible. But it doesn't tell the whole story, because watermelon is (as its name suggests) mostly water, and doesn't have that much sugar or carbs. It really isn't a bad food to eat, as long as you are moderate in your portion size.

What I am saying is, "low glycemic" is not a magic bullet. As a diabetic, you cannot eat as many carbs as you once could, and the ultimate standard for the safety of a food is how many carbs it is forcing you to deal with (minus the fiber carbs). This is not to suggest that the glycemic index is unimportant. It can be a very helpful tool in enabling you to choose foods that will not overload your system and create havoc. Every diabetic and prediabetic should know about this index and use it to make wise food choices.

> **If you are taking insulin,** this adds a new and complex factor to your situation, and you may need to eat more often. Work on this with your doctor and monitor your blood sugar frequently.

Along the same lines, one of the standard pieces of advice to diabetics is to eat many smaller meals throughout the day rather than three large ones. Same concept as the mortgage. Stretch out your payments. And if you are determined to eat a lot of high-carb foods, this is precisely what you should do. But if you are eating low-carb at each meal, it is normally not necessary to eat a bunch of small meals throughout the day. For example, if you eat a big breakfast of eggs and bacon, with one low-carb muffin, your blood sugar will barely budge. And since it doesn't skyrocket upward, you don't have to worry about crashing mid-morning and then needing some more food to keep things balanced, nor do you need to split your eggs into two meals to be kind to your pancreas. A big breakfast of four eggs and three sausages is not going to require much more insulin than a smaller breakfast of one egg and half a sausage.

It is only when you eat higher-carb meals that you have a definite need to break those meals up into five or six per day. This will keep your pancreas and bloodstream from being overloaded, but it will also guarantee that your pancreas is working nearly nonstop throughout the day. On the other hand, when you allow four or five hours between low-carb meals, your pancreas gets a two- or three-hour rest. And a rested pancreas is a happy pancreas!

Not Bad Is Pretty Good

If you are to successfully tame the beast of diabetes, there is no getting around it. You are going to have to make some substitutions. There are a number of foods that cannot be eaten in their normal form, but can be made acceptable through certain alterations or substitutions. Some of these substitutions taste nearly as good as the original—but some do not. Here is where a little maturity and self-control becomes necessary.

If you are willing to change your diet only if you can find something that tastes every bit as good as the original, you will never make it. Happily, some substitutions get pretty close. Low-carb pancakes (chapter 19) taste just about as good as what you get at IHOP—in fact, better in my opinion. And chocolate-drizzled cheesecake (chapter 15) can put any regular dessert to shame. Low-carb ice cream comes pretty close as well.

But others fall a bit short. Perhaps in years to come there will be near equality in taste between high-carb foods and their low-carb substitutes, but probably not for a good while. So you have a choice: you can fuss and complain that these substitutions don't taste as good and refuse to eat them. If you do this, you will either have to go back to the high-carb foods you love and see your blood sugar skyrocket out of control, or limit your diet severely.

Now I'm no martyr. I don't like pain, and I don't like things I don't like (to state the obvious!). Shortly after trying to go low-carb I tried some low-carb pasta that tasted just horrible. That was the last time I ever bought such nasty stuff. While on the Internet I learned about shirataki noodles, which have virtually no carbs (they're made out of the tubers of an Asian plant). I got excited and immediately bought several bags full, sure I had discovered the pasta I could eat for the rest of my days. But when I tried them I nearly gagged. The problem really wasn't the flavor—they hardly have a flavor. It was the texture. They have a gelatinous, rubbery texture that is downright unpalatable to many Americans. It was work to eat each bite. If that's what it takes to eat low-carb pasta—no thanks!

So I have my standards. But in many of the substitutions we can make, the choice is not between great-tasting and nasty; it is between really good and pretty good. And *pretty good* I can live with. In conquering diabetes our great need is motivation. You don't have to read much to quickly learn what you need to do to protect yourself (reduced carb diet, exercise, maintain the proper weight). These things are affirmed by nearly everybody in nearly every diabetes book on this planet. The game is won or lost by motivation.

If you are determined that the only low-carb bread you can accept must taste exactly like the white bread you always had your sandwiches on when you were a child, you're not going to find it. If you insist that your low-carb muffins must taste every bit as great as the high-carb version, **it's probably not going to happen.** If your strawberry shortcake must taste every bit as light and sweet, and look just like those cute little shortcakes you used to enjoy, you'd better forget about strawberry shortcake.

This is why I push blood-sugar monitoring so strongly. If you eat a high-carb meal and don't test your post-meal peak, you can easily delude yourself into thinking you didn't do so badly. Perhaps your blood sugar didn't rise too much. You took it a little easy with those mashed potatoes, and at least you didn't have a second piece of chocolate cake. And you could have easily eaten two of those rolls, but you limited yourself to one.

If you do not test your post-meal peak, you can go on pretending that all is well. But when you stick yourself and hold that drop of blood against the test strip, and then discover that your blood sugar has risen over 220, you have confirmed once again that your blood sugar really does have a direct correspondence to the amount of carbs you take in. The disappointment that follows a high reading is good for you! It will motivate you to do better the next time around. You can't do much about the present state of things (other than take insulin). But you can make sure that next time you take a large salad and skip the mashed potatoes, that you eat a low-carb muffin and skip the roll.

If you are diligent you can find all sorts of substitutions for many foods that will enable you to leave the table full and that actually taste pretty good. No, many of them won't be quite *as* good as the original, but when you consider the blessing of getting a 135 post-meal reading rather than a 220, it's well worth sacrificing a bit of extra flavor. Doing this for a meal is good, and doing it for the rest of your life is great! And if you do, chances are that the "rest of your life" may well be extended far beyond what it would otherwise amount to.

When it comes to your health and diet, *not bad is pretty good*.

The Good Thing About Diabetes

Strange title, isn't it? Well, in truth there *is* one good thing about diabetes. Let me explain.

When you get cancer or leukemia or any number of other diseases, there is precious little you can do other than go to the doctor and submit to whatever medicine or surgery they suggest. Then you hope they're skilled enough, or the medicine is effective enough, or you are lucky enough. That's pretty much it—doctors and hope.

But with type 2 diabetes the situation is vastly different. By all means go to the doctor and cooperate with him or her in their attempts to help you. But know that you have a tremendous say in how badly this disease will affect you. And it is quite possible that having this disease could well result in your living longer than you might have otherwise, if you get serious about your diet and health.

In many ways I don't like to think of diabetes as a disease. If you are a type 2 diabetic, what has happened is that your body has become less efficient at processing sugar, for one reason or another. In many cases you have simply become insulin-resistant. (Your pancreas works fine at this point, but your body is no longer efficient at processing sugar.) This is not like some cancer that springs out of the blue, or pneumonia, or smallpox, typhoid, or influenza. This is more like the fact that you have to wear reading glasses in your forties, which was totally unnecessary in your twenties. Or like the fact that jogging causes all kinds of pain and stiffness for you in middle age, whereas in your youth you could run ten miles and feel just fine. The hard reality is simple but stark: our bodies don't work as well in our latter years as they did when we were younger.

The answer to this is equally simple: we learn to accommodate to these changes. We buy a pair of reading glasses, we quit jogging and start walking, we have sex twice a week rather than five times a week as when we were first married. We adapt.

When it comes to diabetes there are definite adjustments that *must* be made. A little stiffness of the joints you may be able to put up with, but high blood sugar you must not accept. It will hurt you, it will maim you, it may blind you, and it could lop years or even decades off your life. Once you discover that your blood sugar has jumped well out of the normal range, you are going to have to get it under control quickly and keep it that way for the rest of your years. If you do so, no problem. You have a great chance of living out your years and dying "in a good old age" (to use a biblical term). But if you don't you are in serious trouble.

When my blood sugar started running amok and I was researching diabetes, I ran across a great account in a book called *Protein Power*.[10] It thrilled me and gave me great hope for my situation. The book's authors, Michael and Mary Eades, tell of a doctor, Kerin O'Dea, who was working with and studying the health issues of Australian aborigines. She located a group of them who had migrated to the U.S. and become diabetics, and convinced them to return to their home and previous lifestyle for a seven-week period. In essence they went from American couch potatoes to their former "hunter-gatherer" lifestyle, where they hunted animals and ate various vegetables and other foods growing in the wild. During these seven weeks these diabetic men were eating primarily proteins and fats with few carbohydrates.

> If I were to be checked by a doctor today, I would be told I do not have diabetes. My fasting blood sugar and daily average blood sugar are in the normal range. Yet I am convinced that if I ate like many Americans eat, I could easily be a raging diabetic and be experiencing all sorts of health issues by now. I don't like to think of myself as a diabetic; **I prefer to say I have passed up a marvelous chance to become a diabetic.**

So what happened? At the end of the seven weeks these men, who had been classified as diabetics, all saw their blood sugar fall from an average of 210 mg/dl to 118 mg/dl. So were they diabetics or not? It all depended on where they lived—or to be more accurate, on how they lived and what they ate.

The point of all this is simply to tell you that you have a huge say in how far your diabetes will go. If you are prediabetic or have already been told you are diabetic, you will in all likelihood always be susceptible to blood-sugar problems. You will never get to the place where you can have a huge ice-cream sundae with no worries. I have fully accepted that. But by being wise and a bit conservative in your diet and lifestyle, you can overcome this obstacle.

The ball is in your court.

Pros and Cons of Insulin

Insulin is the one word that is most closely associated with diabetes. The standard idea is that if you have diabetes, you don't produce enough insulin. You will need to take a pill to stimulate more production of insulin or else take insulin shots that make up for the lack of insulin produced by your pancreas. Insulin is the good guy; a little is good and more is better. If you can just get enough insulin into your system, all will be well.

There's a lot of falsehood in the above statements, mixed with some truth. First, the truth: the type 1 diabetic is certainly suffering from a lack of insulin and will need to take insulin shots to make up for it. For one reason or another their pancreas has quit producing insulin, and high blood sugar is the inevitable result. Insulin is a powerful hormone and is the means by which our metabolic system moves sugar from the blood into our cells, providing us energy. Sugars are not supposed to hang around long in our blood; they are normally quickly dispatched by small doses of insulin, produced in and released by the pancreas.

So, yes—insulin is vitally important. Without it, either self-produced or injected, we would quickly die. But while in its proper measure it is a lifesaver, in massive amounts it is a nightmare. Michael and Mary Dan Eades say it beautifully in their book *Protein Power*:

> In the appropriate amount insulin keeps the metabolic system humming along smoothly with everything in balance; in great excess it becomes a rogue hormone ranging throughout the body, wreaking metabolic havoc and leaving a trail of chaos and disease in its wake.[11]

You might be thinking, *That may be so, but it certainly has nothing to do with me. As a diabetic I am dealing with too little insulin, not too much of it.* This may or may not be true. But many, if not most, type 2 diabetics are in trouble due to insulin resistance. Your body doesn't process insulin nearly as efficiently as it used to. It requires far too much insulin to keep up with your blood sugar. The fact is, you may have considerably more insulin filling your bloodstream today than you did ten years ago, but it is still not enough to deal with your inefficient insulin-processing ability. Thus in the case of many early-stage diabetics, they have a threefold problem: 1) They process insulin poorly. 2) Their pancreas is forced to put out huge amounts of insulin, and that excess insulin is causing all sorts of other problems, such as restricted arteries and high blood pressure. 3) Their pancreas is being worn out long before its time and will eventually give out altogether.

Both diabetes and heart disease are often results of hyperinsulinemia (a condition in which the bloodstream is constantly saturated with high blood sugar and too much insulin), many Americans who have diabetes often suffer from high blood pressure as well. The same high-carb, overweight, couch-potato lifestyle that makes diabetes a likelihood also carries high blood pressure and heart disease in its wake.

Nor does it follow that once your pancreas goes and you can no longer produce any significant insulin, this issue no longer relates to you. Even if you must take insulin shots, you have a significant say in how much insulin you will need to take. Stay slim, eat a low-carb diet, and exercise regularly, and you will require far less insulin than if you reverse these things. The person who is 60 pounds overweight and constantly eats pies, doughnuts, and pasta is fooling themselves if they think they can take a quick insulin shot, and all will be well. Lack of self-control is forcing them to take insulin in levels that are far too high. Sure, the insulin can

> As an unwanted bonus, **bodies that are daily saturated with insulin almost always produce too much cholesterol.** This explains the puzzling phenomenon that occurs in so many case histories of men and women who have gone to a low-carb diet, learned to eat meats, cheese, eggs, and fats without guilt, and found their cholesterol levels actually *decreasing*. It makes no sense until you realize that low-carb results in reduced insulin production, and that a high-carb diet that constantly results in excess insulin production is a major culprit in high cholesterol.

combat the blood sugar, and keep the numbers at a reasonable level, but while doing that it is producing untold damage to other areas of the person's overall health.

Of course diabetes is a complex disease that can result from many causes. We cannot suggest that hyperinsulinemia is the only reason people get diabetes. Insulin resistance and hyperinsulinemia go hand in hand, and trying to figure out which came first is like the chicken-or-the-egg debate. Regardless of the first cause, there is no question that having your bloodstream constantly overloaded with insulin is not healthy. On the other hand, we must have insulin to remain alive, so if your doctor prescribes injections for you, take them gladly.

Every meal you eat is making requirements on your pancreas, calling for it to produce precise amounts of insulin. A meal of spaghetti and French bread, followed by a large slice of apple pie with ice cream, is calling for a deluge. A garden salad with an avocado calls for a tiny squirt. By choosing what goes and does not go into your mouth, you are choosing whether your body, flooded with sugar, will spend the next few hours overloaded with insulin acting as a "rogue hormone"—or whether the resulting blood sugar will be quickly dispatched by a small amount of insulin, doing the job for which it was created and quickly disappearing.

Low-Carb Isn't Really Low-Carb

Throughout this book I have been emphasizing the need for a low-carb diet. I know this sounds pretty strange, but in this chapter I want to contradict myself. In truth, the low-carb diet I am advocating isn't really low-carb at all. Let me explain.

The term *low-carb* makes it sound like you are on some type of bizarre diet far removed from normal eating. You feel like you are being forced by your blood-sugar problems to eat like an alien from another planet. It seems that what you are doing is not natural, not normal, and runs counter to humanity's eating habits from the dawn of civilization.

Wrong, wrong, wrong! The truth is that the way most Americans eat today is what is strange and bizarre. It is they that are out of step, not you. Consider the common soda (take your pick: Pepsi, Coca-Cola, Dr. Pepper, 7-Up, you name it). Until recently you drank sodas all throughout your life. Your momma drank sodas. Your momma's momma drank sodas. What could be more natural and more American than "the pause that refreshes," slurping down a good old 16-ounce Coca-Cola (with its 54 grams of high-fructose corn syrup)?

However, your short lifetime and the life of your parents and grandparents represent a tiny drop of the history of men and women on this planet. The colas were first created in the 1880s and didn't become commonplace until the twentieth century. This means that for thousands of years of man's recorded history, there were no sodas. The surpassing drink of choice (and necessity) was, you guessed it, water. This same idea holds true for Twinkies, Trix cereal, candy bars, rocky road ice cream, cinnamon rolls, white bread, white rice, and scores of other nasty, colon-clogging, blood-sugar-raising, insulin-demanding foods that we often consider perfectly normal and natural. Although most of you cannot remember a time when these things didn't beckon to you from the grocery-store shelves, they are absolute newcomers to the scene of human existence.

Of course various sweet confections have been baked for many centuries, but these were primarily the food of the royalty and the rich (who suffered for their indulgence more than the poor folks who envied them). Poor to middle-class people ate rough whole-grain bread, meat (when they could get it), vegetables, and fruits when they were in season. Not only that, but if you had to eat the portion size they lived on from day to day, you would think yourself starving. They never sat down at an IHOP restaurant and ate a huge stack of white-flour pancakes smothered with sugary syrup. Had they tasted a cola they would probably have spit it out; it would have tasted sickeningly sweet to them, at least at first.

They had their health issues of course. Without antibiotics, modern medicine, and skilled surgeons many of them died prematurely. But if they did manage to live to old age they rarely suffered from heart disease or diabetes. They might be killed by a plague or an infection, but few died from skyrocketing blood sugar. In essence most of these folks were on a "low-carb" diet. They ingested far fewer carbs and sugar than the average American today, got far more exercise (mainly through work), and were generally considerably slimmer. The diet you call "low-carb" was normal for them. The lifestyle you might consider a burden was for them regular living.

At this point you may be asking, "What's the point? You are just talking semantics here. I still have to cut out sweets, exercise regularly, and watch my weight." Yes, you do, but the point is an important one. As long as you consider your diet and lifestyle some kind of abnormal one—some sort of cosmic punishment you don't deserve—you will have a hard time embracing these changes for the rest of your days. You will look enviously at your friend who eats everything they want and never worries about it, and wonder, *Why me?* The reality is that they are the odd one, not you. So the next time you pass on the dessert and drink water rather than soda, and are tempted to feel sorry for yourself— don't. You are not some miserable, unlucky person being forced to make terrible sacrifices and live abnormally just to survive. You're just doing the reasonable thing. You are living as you should have lived all along. It just took you a while to wise up, right?

> It's not really the case that you are on a low-carb diet. It is that **most Americans are on a high-carb diet.** No, let me take that back—most Americans are on a soaring, towering, health-destroying, pancreas-killing, life-shortening, sugar-gorging, stratospheric-carb diet.

Counteracting the Sedentary Life

In earlier times most people were busy and active throughout their days. If you could go back in a time machine to the 1500s and tell a typical laborer about today's jobs, where you sit at a desk and tap on buttons with your fingers and read things off a flat screen all day long, they would think you were crazy. But if they could believe you they would certainly be jealous. It would sound too good to be true—to engage in "work" that involved so little physical exertion.

In America we have become a nation of sitters. We sit while we work, sit while we eat, and sit while we drive to and from work and eating. And when we go home we sit some more as we watch television and surf the Internet for hours. In our guilt (and obesity) we may try to exercise a bit to make up for our sedentary lifestyles, but most folks fail to make this a lifetime habit. And usually the ones who do manage to exercise regularly are the ones who are doing it for their looks rather than their health.

Of course you could quit your high-paying job and become a migrant laborer, but for most of us that is impractical and not very appealing. The other choice is to counteract our many, many hours of sitting with a 30- to 40-minute exercise routine that we are willing to do as long as our health allows it. (And by starting early in life, we make it more likely that our health will allow it for a good, long time!)

The good news is that you don't have to exercise a huge amount of time to make up for all that sitting. If we had to exercise one hour to make up for every hour we sit, we'd all be in trouble. We don't. Research has shown that if we can exercise 30 to 40 minutes a day for around four or five days each week, we will improve our health immensely—and this includes our blood sugar. But let me depart from blood sugar for a moment and share with you an experience I had with my blood pressure. After having borderline, slightly elevated blood pressure for years, finally my doctor put me on a low-dosage medication to bring it down. I faithfully took the little pills, and to my wonder, they did the job beautifully. I went from around 138/90 to an average of 120/78 very quickly. I stayed at that level, frequently monitoring my blood pressure.

Then I went on a trip to Nigeria. I didn't take my blood-pressure monitor with me, so when I returned a couple of weeks later, I discovered that my blood pressure had gone back up to its former, higher level. While in Nigeria I hadn't exercised at all, and I now suspected that this might have something to do with the higher blood pressure. When I returned home, the treadmill at our small apartment fitness center was not working, so I went for walks instead of my usual routine. This brought my blood pressure down a bit but not as before.

After going to the doctor I was given a second pill to take. I was not eager to be taking two pills, and it so happened that the treadmill was fixed the next day, so I decided to hold off on the second pill until I could do my normal routine on the treadmill. Getting back on the treadmill forced me to work a bit harder (my walks tend to be pretty leisurely), and sure enough, within a couple of days I was having excellent blood pressure readings with only the first pill. This encouraged me so much that I stepped up the degree of difficulty on the treadmill, and started getting blood pressure readings even better (107/76). I never did take the second pill. After a while I was able to get off all blood-pressure medication.

The experts tell us **that exercise should be of sufficient intensity to get our heart rate up, but not too high.** Most recommend that you should get your heart rate to around 75 percent of its maximum. The Mayo Clinic has a website where you can type in your age, and it will tell you the heart-rate range you should target. Basically what all this heart-rate business means is that your exercise should get you sweating a bit and breathing somewhat more heavily than you normally do, but not gasping for air and feeling like you're going to faint.

The moral of the story is a simple one. It's something that doctors and health experts have been telling us all along—exercise really does make a difference. It also affects your blood sugar. An article in the journal of the

American Medical Association cited a study showing that the rate that diabetes normally develops in women was cut in half for those who walk regularly. I have noticed that when I go several days without exercise my fasting blood sugar starts drifting upward.

I am not talking about checking your blood sugar before you exercise, and then checking it afterward and seeing a dramatic decrease. This can happen, but also your blood sugar can increase a bit, as a result of the body sensing a need for energy and producing additional glucose. This is particularly an issue with very strenuous exercise. But in the long run, the exercise will go a long way in decreasing your average blood-sugar levels. Your metabolism will become more efficient, your circulation greatly improved, and you will be healthier when you make exercise a normal part of most of your days (at least four times each week, at most six).

There is a price to be paid for all our sitting, computer work, and TV watching. We can either pay for it with heart disease, obesity, and diabetes, or pay for it with about two to two and a half hours of moderately vigorous exercise weekly. Choose the latter.

Do-It-Yourself Sweetening

Those rare individuals who manage to save money and live on less than their income become experts at what my mom used to call cutting corners. They find all sorts of ways to save a dollar here, two dollars there, and so forth. These are the folks who don't sweat it when their washer goes out, or their air-conditioner quits working in the middle of July, or their tooth starts aching. They have disciplined themselves to save on the small everyday items, and so they have the resources for emergencies.

We need to be just as frugal in saving carbs as in saving dollars. Yes, it will help tremendously to cut out the big-purchase items, like refusing that sugar-drenched French silk pie or not emulating your buddy when he orders a giant-sized soda to wash down his large order of french fries. When you have begun routinely saying no to such carb atrocities, you are on the road to blood-sugar health. But you have not arrived until you have learned to spare yourself carbs in lesser ways as well.

One of the ways you can do this is to avoid buying things that have been pre-sweetened. Food suppliers are fully aware that in most cases the public prefers sweet to not sweet. There is no law that says that ketchup must be sweet, but who can imagine it without some sweetness? Pickle relish does come in non-sweet varieties, but many people would almost gag if they made their tuna-salad sandwiches without sweetened relish.

Some people like their strawberries sweetened, and you can buy frozen strawberries that have extra sugar added in. This is hardly necessary, but if you really want some extra-sweet strawberries, don't go out and buy the sweetened ones. Buy a package that has no sugar added and sweeten them yourself with your preferred non-sugar sweetener.

One simple solution is to always buy the non-sweet versions wherever possible. (In the case of ketchup, you could substitute tomato paste.) But by the time most of us become insulin-resistant, we have been using sweet condiments and sauces for four or five decades, and going cold-turkey is an appalling thought. Happily it is not necessary. One secret to saving carbs in smaller ways is to buy various products in the unsweetened version and then sweeten them yourself with a sugar-free sweetener. Here are some examples:

Teriyaki sauce: I love chicken teriyaki, but for a diabetic it requires some modifications. First, that bed of rice that the vegetables and chicken rest on must be brown rice, and it must be about half of what most people prefer. Turn the white to brown, cut the normal portion in half, and you are in business. Well, almost in business. The other thing is to do away with that sweet sauce most of us prefer. Go and check out all the various teriyaki sauces on the grocer's shelf and buy one with the least number of sugar/carbs. Then, when you are about to pour some over your teriyaki, put the necessary portion in a bowl (I usually dilute it with water to cut down on the salt) and mix in a little stevia, Splenda, or other artificial sweetener. It should only take one packet. Voilà, you have a sweet teriyaki sauce that does nothing to raise your blood sugar. Then drench your teriyaki with it and enjoy your meal. Your "savings" aren't tremendous, but in combination with other smart choices, they can make a real difference.

Barbecue sauce: Barbecue sauces didn't use to contain that much sugar, but over the years the popular ones have gotten sweeter and sweeter. To keep your carb count down, go out and buy the least sugary barbecue sauce available and do the same with it as is described with the teriyaki sauce.

I know this isn't profound, but it works! You can do this with spaghetti sauce, if you like a sweetened version (Prego brand is notorious for their sweetened spaghetti sauce), and pickle relish. Buy the blandest pickle relish on the shelf, and mix in one packet of stevia or Splenda with the other ingredients the next time you make a couple of sandwiches, and you'll have your sweet tuna-salad sandwich without the sugar carbs.

What we are talking about here is a heightened "sugar-consciousness."

Being aware of even those smaller sugar-contributing items will pay dividends in the form of lower numbers on your blood-sugar monitor and your A1C tests. More importantly, they will help in the battle to keep the blood that flows through your body in a healthy, low-sugar state, so that it enhances rather than destroys your long-term prospects for health and longevity.

Work Your Way Down

The post-meal blood-sugar reading (usually one to one and a half hours after your last bite of food) really is the ultimate gauge of your success in keeping your blood sugars under control. If you have set a target of 140 or below and are hitting it 90 percent of the time, your fasting blood sugar will almost always be in a decent range, as will your A1C score. Even more important, you will be doing a world of good for your body and making it unlikely you will suffer from diabetic complications, regardless of whether you are classified "prediabetic," "diabetic," or "hyper-super-mega diabetic."

This is great to contemplate, but it can be daunting when you first give serious thought to blood sugar and discover that your blood sugar never drops below, say, 165 mg/dl. How in the world can you shoot for a 140 or below post-meal reading when your fasting blood sugar is well beyond that? The answer is that you can't—at least not immediately. If 165 is your baseline before eating, and then you eat a meal, don't expect that your blood sugar will drop down to 140 an hour later. It will in fact rise. How discouraging is that?

The good news is that most type 2 diabetics can get their baseline blood sugar into a decent range with a little work. Your fasting blood sugar is not written in stone and impossible to change. In truth, fasting blood sugar is fluid; it is never static. It is always increasing or decreasing a bit, and in most cases you should be able to start it going downward with a little knowledge and effort.

The philosophy that will win the day here is what I call "calling out the reserves." This is a military concept—it simply means that you hit the enemy with all you have. No troops left in the rear for later actions. Everything and everyone you have available are thrown into the fray. Obviously you will only do this if you really want to win the battle, but we are assuming that you very much do.

You begin by taking assessment of yourself on the three different fronts of the diabetes conflict: *weight, exercise,* and *diet.*

Weight. You need to get your weight down to a reasonable level. You will never know just how much territory you can take back if you stay overweight. Start by severely limiting snacks, doing away with second portions at any meal, and weighing yourself daily to check your progress.

Exercise. Insulin resistance, that inability of the cells to efficiently process carbs/sugars, is normally at the heart of the type 2 diabetic's problems. You'll probably never totally eliminate this and get back to your teenage days, but you can make a huge dent in your insulin resistance by doing certain things. And exercise is one of those things! You exercise four to five times weekly in order to make yourself metabolically fit, increase your circulation, and enhance the efficiency of your body's carb processing. This is something every diabetic should be doing.

> **If your blood sugars are hovering around 160 or above** many hours after you have eaten, or in the morning after you have slept through the night, you need to take exercise very seriously. The person who has a baseline blood sugar of 160-plus is essentially doing harm to every organ in their body 24 hours a day. You may not feel anything or have any symptoms for a decade or more, but sooner or later it will catch up to you.

Carb intake. Finally, and most important, you are going to need to *seriously* cut your carb intake for a couple of months. The Atkins diet talks about an "induction phase" in which you pare down your carbs to the bare minimum. This may be exactly what you need, but for a different reason. Most people who are excited about Atkins have been attracted to it for the purpose of weight loss. In your case you have a far greater motivation for going low-carb: your life. For the next month or maybe two you are going to need to live on salads, various vegetables (no potatoes, corn, beets, or carrots), meats (no bread coatings), one low-carb bread item daily, and small amounts of nuts. Things that should not be a problem later on, such as many fruits, beans, and smaller portions of brown rice, should be avoided during this period.

You will almost surely lose some weight doing this, and unless you are a type 1 diabetic or approaching this state, you should see your fasting (baseline) blood sugar decreasing gradually but steadily. This is vitally important. The best way to measure success in the blood-sugar battle is to be able to see your post-meal blood sugars peak below the levels which can be harmful (140 to 180 depending upon whom you read—I like 140). But if they are already higher than your target before you ever put that first bite in your mouth, you have no chance of succeeding in this. By taking the steps outlined above you have an excellent chance of getting your baseline blood sugar into the 100 to 120 range, which allows for it to rise after a meal and still be in a decent range.

Ultimately you have to determine what is acceptable and what is not. Some people can live with a fasting blood sugar of 180 and not feel too bad about it. Their post-meal peaks will always take them well above 200. Because they accept the unacceptable they are doing great damage to their body hour by hour and day by day. Take your fasting blood sugar seriously. Most type 2 diabetics can get it into a healthy range with diet, exercise, and weight control. A one- to two-month "induction phase" dietary regimen is sometimes the kick start they need to get their numbers down. If none of this works, you will need to talk to your doctor about oral medication or insulin shots. But whatever you do, don't accept the unacceptable!

Types of Blood-Sugar Tests

Diabetes and testing go together. And you live in an opportune time. For most of recorded history there were no tests available at all. In the early nineteenth century chemical tests were developed to measure the presence of sugar in the urine. This gave an indication of diabetes but such a test was normally only used after people had developed severe symptoms of the disease and were pretty much beyond all help. In those days you had to go to the doctor to get the test; there were no "home tests." In the 1960s home tests for blood sugar in the urine became available. In the 1970s blood-glucose meters were developed. Today the blood-glucose meter has become far less expensive and more reliable. There is no good reason for the diabetic or prediabetic not to own one and use it frequently.

Actually, there are several different tests that are useful for diabetics. You would be wise to make use of all of them. Let me give four of the most important, noting some of the pros and cons.

The fasting blood-sugar test. This can be done at the doctor's office, or you can do this yourself at home with your own blood-sugar monitor. The fasting blood-sugar test is done in the morning after you have gone all night without eating or drinking anything but water. What you are measuring here is your baseline blood sugar—what your levels revert to once digestion is accomplished, your pancreas has done its part, and there are no more carbs in your system that haven't been processed.

In someone who is healthy and free from diabetic tendencies, the number should be in the 80s (mg/dl). However you can be considerably higher than that and still not be considered diabetic. Not so long ago your fasting blood sugar had to hit 141 mg/dl before you were officially labeled diabetic. In 1998 they changed their minds and declared that 126 mg/dl or above made you a diabetic. There have also been several revisions of what they considered the upper limit of normal, and currently they consider normal to be anything below 100.

The fasting blood-sugar test is great at identifying people who are diabetic or getting close to it. You cannot fool this test. If you have a major problem in this area, it will surely reveal it. The one negative aspect of the test is that, although it reveals much, it doesn't quite reveal all. The one category that escapes undetected are the folks whose pancreas is still managing to keep the numbers reasonable, but their insulin resistance is so high that this organ is pumping its little guts out to get the job done. This is an unsustainable task, and sooner or later the pancreas will hold up the white flag of surrender, and the numbers will soar.

There are folks who are going through each day eating far too many carbs and forcing their pancreases to put out way too much insulin. Their bodies are becoming walking time bombs, filled to the gills with insulin, which is doing them tremendous damage in itself—even though their numbers don't reflect it yet. The doctor checks their blood sugar in the morning; it reads 98, and he tells them they are fine. In fact, they are not fine.

The post-meal test. This test is a great addition to the fasting blood-sugar test. You do it one to two hours after a meal, and can determine just how radically your body is reacting to the carbs you just ingested. Of course this test will vary tremendously with the type of meal that was eaten. In the initial, discovery phase, this is the one time it might be good to overdo it a bit on carbs. If you can eat a spaghetti dinner, have a couple of rolls along with your spaghetti, and then an hour and a half later find that your blood sugar hasn't risen higher than 125 or so, you are probably in pretty good shape.

There will be some folks who have good fasting blood-sugar numbers and yet do awful on this test. What this normally means is that your pancreas is working pretty well. It will eventually dump lots of insulin in your bloodstream and get the job done. In three to four hours you may even find that your blood sugar is quite low (sometimes way too low!). Such sugar swings are bringing you good news and bad news. The good news is that your pancreas is working just fine. The bad news is that you are becoming seriously insulin-resistant. The worse news is that your pancreas and your metabolism will never be able to keep this up. You are a prime candidate for diabetes.

The A1C test. This test is normally done by a doctor, although there are now some kits you can buy: you take a blood sample, send it to a lab, and get your results in the mail in a couple of weeks. The A1C uses the condition of certain of your red blood cells to measure your average blood sugar over the last three months. The values of this test come in percentages, rather than mg/dl. A percentage of 4 to 5 is normal, 6 to 6.5 percent is problematic, and above 6.5 percent definitely indicates diabetes.

This test is superior to the fasting blood-sugar test in that it gives you a blood-sugar average. It will not be fooled by random factors that could make one particular fasting blood-sugar test not truly representative. The major negative to this test is that, like the fasting blood-sugar test, it does not reflect increasing insulin resistance until that resistance gets to the point where it is keeping your blood sugars high constantly. If you are having highs and lows, causing your body to be saturated daily with far too much insulin, this test will not know it. It may well show that you are in the "normal" range, and you may go home feeling elated, not realizing that big problems lie just around the bend.

The glucose-tolerance test. In this test you are required to fast for 8 to 10 hours and are then given a very sweet drink of pure glucose. Your blood is then checked every hour for the next several hours. This test is expensive, time-consuming, and a hassle. It is also very, very good at determining just how well your body processes carbs and sugar. Even if your fasting test and A1C test indicate that you are perfectly normal, if in fact you are becoming insulin-resistant and are losing the ability to handle carbs, this test will reveal it. The test is exactly what it says it is: a glucose-tolerance test. How well does your body tolerate sugar? How quickly does your metabolism get things back under control once you ingest a significant amount of glucose?

It is in fact a great test. The problem is, because of the cost and the time involved, doctors don't recommend it often and patients rarely ask for it. By the time a doctor may decide to use it, the patient probably already has such significant symptoms of blood-sugar issues that they hardly need the doctor to tell them they have a problem. If this test were given routinely to every person reaching 40 years of age, and if they could be sufficiently motivated into taking the necessary actions when it reveals they are becoming insulin-resistant, it would save untold misery for millions.

Of course the "poor man's" glucose-tolerance test is simply to use your blood-sugar monitor an hour or two after meals for a number of different meals. If, no matter what you eat, your blood sugar never rises above 140 mg/dl, you are in pretty good shape. But if you find it soaring into the 180s or above 200 you know you have some work to do. Time to see your doctor, cut down on the carbs, get to the proper weight, and start a regular exercise program.

These four tests are of great value in discovering where you are and what steps you need to take in the battle against diabetes. A person who is overweight is probably never going to lose weight without a scale. And a diabetic or prediabetic is likewise not likely to make any progress in getting their blood sugar under control if they simply make a few minor adjustments and "take it by faith" that they are getting the job done. You must measure yourself and take the tests—again and again and again. It is a very small price to pay for a healthy, happy second half of your life.

49

. . . .

Thoughts on Soup

When I first decided to get really serious about watching my carbs I gave up soup altogether. That was then, this is now. Today, I enjoy many different soups, but mostly of my own creation (actually, my wife's, with a little input from me). Soup can be problematic for carb-watchers. One of the reasons for this is that soup cannot simply taste like vegetables dropped into a pot of water. For soup to be soup it has to have some sort of thickening agent. Traditionally this has been white flour, which jacks up the carb count. On top of that, many soups contain noodles, which increases the carbs further still. Others contain rice, which does the same. Many canned soups have added significant amounts of sugar to jazz them up.

Another factor is that almost nobody can eat soup by itself for a meal. The traditional companion to a bowl of soup is a sandwich, which means two slices of bread to add to the carb count. Remember the old Campbell's Soup commercial, "Soup and sandwich…go together"? (You have to be ancient to remember this—but strangely I do!) Some people add insult to injury by breaking up soda crackers (about as pure a carb source as you'll find) and putting them in their soup.

If you look at many of the soups on your grocery store shelves you'll find that the carb counts don't seem too bad. Some say 14 grams, some are as low as 10. But check out the serving size. Nearly all list serving sizes that wouldn't satisfy a scrawny church mouse. If you have any kind of appetite at all, you can pretty much figure on doubling the carb count that they give.

Besides the carbs, **most soups contain way too much sodium,** which won't directly affect your blood sugar, but will drive your blood pressure up. All in all, much of the canned soup you find at the store is junk. You can make a lot better choices.

This doesn't mean you have to give up on soup—not at all. There are two choices in the soup department for carb-watchers. First, you can check out some of the soups specifically touted as being healthy. Check the nutrition information to see if their idea of "healthy" means reduced sodium only, or also reduced carbs. But remember that with nearly all store-bought soups, you'll have to be very moderate in your portion size.

Another choice is simply to make your own soup. Here is your chance to eat a large bowl of soup and still do very little to your blood sugar. It's not at all likely that anyone will put a gun to your head and force you to add noodles or rice, or use white flour to thicken it. To my mind home-made is by far the best choice. One simple way to do this is go on the Internet and type these words into your favorite search engine: "low-carb soup recipes." You'll soon have enough recipes to last you for a dozen lifetimes.

Some of the basic rules in making your own soup are these:

1. Never use flour as a thickening agent. Instead, experiment with some of these:

    - Add heavy whipped cream for an interesting and tasty thickener.

    - Remove some of the vegetables from the soup and puree them in the blender. Then add them back to the soup. Voilà!—your soup has gone from watery to thick.

    - One simple way to make soup thicker is simply to cook it longer. Over time two things happen: the vegetables in the soup break down more and mix with the water, and you lose more water through evaporation, making the soup thicker.

    - Try adding a small amount of olive oil or vegetable oil to give the soup a richer and thicker taste.

    - Beans in bean soups break down enough to make their own thickening agent. The longer the beans are cooked or boiled, the more the content of the beans ends up in the soup.

    - Spaghetti sauce can be used sometimes, but don't feel obligated to empty the entire can into the soup. Use just enough to get the right consistency. Check the labels and make sure to use one that is on the low side in carbs—some spaghetti sauces have a significant amount of added sugar.

2. No rice or noodles in the soup.

3. No corn or potatoes in the soup.

With a little research and experimentation you can quickly come up with some great low-carb soup recipes. For people who don't like to cook, remember this. Although making soup seems like a significant time expenditure, if you make a fairly big pot of it, you can save it and have soup for the next week or more. You can even freeze some of it and bring it out a month later. What this means is that you have a very quick and easy lunch for quite a few days, so in the end you save time.

As we said elsewhere, soup practically begs for something else to be eaten along with it. Almost nobody would want a meal of soup alone. Salads work fine here, as do low-carb breads and muffins. An avocado is filling and adds few carbs to the mix. A piece of celery filled with peanut butter will do the job nicely. I sometimes have a low-carb tortilla with my soup. (No, I don't try to pour the soup in the tortilla—I roll it up and eat it like a piece of bread between sips of soup.)

Since most of the vegetables in soup end up surrendering their unique flavor and blending with the whole, vegetable soup is a great way to get some of those veggies that you don't especially like on their own. Chop up some spinach and okra and throw them in the soup. My wife introduced me to okra soup and to my amazement I loved it! And after I eat a big bowl of it, my blood sugar hardly budges.

Another soup I highly recommend is lentil soup. Lentils have a lot of fiber, more than most beans, and are a great choice for people wanting to keep their post-meal blood sugar at a reasonable level. A large bowl may end up giving you too many carbs, but a small- to medium-sized bowl will be no problem to most type 2's, provided you don't eat some other significant source of carbs.

When it comes to soup, the diabetic must learn to think outside the box. There are endless possibilities that will be blood-sugar-friendly if you take a little time to experiment and research.

Benedicta's Okra and Spinach Soup

My wife grew up in Africa, and this is pretty much a typical African soup, with a few American adaptations. Even if you are not a big okra fan, you will probably like this. In Africa she used palm oil, but since that is not plentiful in America, you can substitute olive oil. Use a large pot for this; it will make enough for a good-sized family with some to spare. For a smaller amount cut the ingredients in half.

Ingredients:

3 pieces of boneless, skinless chicken breasts
1/2 small to medium onion
1/2 can (12 ounces) of spaghetti sauce (cans are often found in 24- to 26-ounce sizes)
28-ounce bag of frozen okra
10-ounce bag of spinach (Walmart sells spinach in a 10-ounce bag; if you buy in a bunch, 2 bunches should be about right)
6 ounces olive oil
1 chicken bouillon cube
1-1/2 cups water

Instructions:

1. Fry or bake the three chicken breasts and then cut in small pieces to be added to the soup later.

2. Chop up the spinach into small pieces to be added to the soup later.

3. Place the frozen okra in a food processor (do it in 2 or more batches) and chop it up fairly fine. This will be added to the soup later.

Benedicta with her okra soup

4. Chop up the 1/2 onion into small pieces.

5. Place the onion pieces in a pan with the olive oil and heat to a boil.

6. Keep the oil at a low boil for four to five minutes to soften the onion.

7. Mix 1/2 a standard can of Hunt's pasta sauce or about 12 oz. of any lower-carb spaghetti sauce in with the oil and onions, and cook at a medium to medium-high heat for four minutes.

8. Raise the heat back a little below high, add in the chopped okra, the chicken pieces, and one chicken bouillon cube, and mix thoroughly while continuing to cook for another 8 minutes.

9. Add the chopped spinach and the water, mixing well, and cook for another five minutes. Keep the heat a little below high. Stir well so that the spinach mixes completely into the soup.

This soup has no major source of carbs, it is jam-packed with nutritious okra and spinach, and because these vegetables are not cooked very long, they retain most of their vitamins. It is very easy on your blood sugar. On top of that, it tastes terrific! Africans eat it in a thicker version than this. To thicken it, use less water, or if you desire it thinner, increase the amount of water added. If the soup is a bit bland for you, you can add some garlic as needed to give it a little more pizzazz.

Insulin Shots

People are diabetic for two basic reasons: 1) their pancreas no longer produces sufficient insulin to process the carbs they are ingesting, or 2) their body has become insulin-resistant and can no longer process those carbs even though the pancreas is still able to produce what should be a sufficient amount of insulin. When many people think about diabetes they think about using hypodermic needles to give themselves insulin shots—and they shudder. To many, this is the worst sentence imaginable.

Many will resist the idea of insulin shots literally to the death. They will put off going to the doctor for fear he is going to hand them a hypodermic kit and tell them to "have at it." Others will plead with their doctor to give them a chance to try any and every other possible alternative to see if they can get by without the shots. Some would rather see blood-sugar levels of 300 mg/dl than deal with those nasty needles.

To be blunt, this is a really bad idea. If you can escape the need to take insulin shots through diet, exercise, and weight control, by all means do it. It would be foolish not to. But there are times when insulin shots can become most useful, and you would be crazy not to take advantage of them. Here are a couple of scenarios:

The type 1 diabetic. This person's pancreas has retired. It produces absolutely no insulin, which means that their blood sugar will rise precipitously with nearly every meal. In this case insulin shots are a must. There are no ifs, ands, or buts. If you are in this situation you need to be working with your doctor continually to ensure you are taking the right amount of insulin at the right times. One thing to keep in mind: the amount of insulin you need per meal can be dramatically changed. For example, if you have been eating the typical high-carb American diet and suddenly decide to reduce your carbs significantly, you will need less insulin.

Generally speaking, the fewer carbohydrates in your meals, the easier it will be to calculate precisely how much insulin to take before your meal. Some type 1 diabetics also fall into the category of being insulin-resistant. In a sense they are a "double diabetic." Even with liberal insulin shots their bodies don't handle the sugar at all well, and they find it almost impossible to keep their blood sugar in a reasonable range. They end up with lots and lots of insulin filling their blood almost continually, and still it cannot keep up. In such a case they are doing double damage to their bodies. The elevated blood sugar is daily doing a number on their organs, and the high dosages of insulin are doing significant harm of their own. The answer is not to give up on taking insulin. It is to radically reduce the carbs in your diet, get to a decent weight, and exercise until you reduce your insulin resistance. Then you can start using more reasonable dosages of insulin.

> Think about **the meal-to-meal differences in insulin requirements.** A ham-and-eggs breakfast will require a far lower dosage of insulin than a lasagna dinner with rolls and tapioca pudding. Too little insulin and your blood sugar will be off to the races; too much and it will drop out of sight, and you will be in a hypoglycemic state in no time.

"Nearly type 1" diabetics. As admirable as it is to be able to control your diabetes with diet, weight control, and exercise, there are some, even those who are not totally type 1, who may not be able to do it. We like to divide diabetics into neat type 1 and 2 categories, but some folks are "nearly type 1" diabetics. Their pancreas still has some function, but it is not nearly adequate to control their blood sugar, even with all their best efforts. Sometimes even pills don't get the job done. This does not mean you give up on your low-carb diet and start injecting yourself with huge measures of insulin while whistling "Que Sera, Sera." Stay low-carb, keep lean, and exercise—plus take the shots as directed by your physician. Remember, the goal is to keep your blood sugar as close as possible to normal. If it requires insulin shots to do this, take the shots!

Pancreas relief. When you first discover you have diabetes, it is highly likely that you have been struggling with high blood sugar for a good long while. If your pancreas is still working, it is probably severely strained, and it is likely that it has lost some of its function. Some of the beta cells in it may have died. One of the principles of God and nature is the principle of rest. We were never made to be continually overtaxed—either in mind or body. When we are pushed to the limit far beyond our endurance, some pretty terrible consequences can follow. The best prescription in such a situation is rest. Allow time and rest to bring healing to that which has been abused.

There are times when doctors will recommend that you start taking insulin shots for this very purpose. The insulin coming into your body through the shots will say to your worn-out pancreas: "Take it easy, big guy. I'll handle things for a while." Your pancreas will gamely give a nod of thanks and take some time off for healing and recuperation. This is not a bad thing! It is no admission of failure, and it does not place a label on your back telling the world that you are a loser. In truth, you may well turn out quite the winner. Your pancreas may heal considerably over time, and when it is its turn to take over again (with a much lower-carb diet on your part) you may find that it works better than it has in years.

Earlier I talked about resisting insulin shots to the death. This may be precisely what you are doing if your body is producing little insulin and your blood sugar is far too high. This is definitely an area in which you need to see a good doctor and allow him or her to guide you. If it turns out you need the shots the rest of your life, there are a whole lot of worse things—like not having a rest of your life!

Richard Bernstein

In the world of sports there are certain individuals who achieve permanent and universal fame for their achievements. In baseball a list of these athletes would have to include such men as Babe Ruth, Willie Mays, Ty Cobb, and Hank Aaron. In the world of diabetes doctors and experts there is no hall of fame. But if there were one, there is no doubt in my mind about the one man who should be the first candidate for admission. His name is Dr. Richard Bernstein, and his story is amazing.

Richard developed type 1 diabetes at age 12 back in 1946. In those ancient days, ignorance reigned among the diabetes "experts." They did know enough to prescribe insulin shots, without which he would soon have died. But they also put him on the absolutely disastrous low-fat, high-carbohydrate diet that reigned in those days (and in some quarters still does today)—about the worst thing they could have done. Richard, knowing no better, followed their advice dutifully. As the years went by he grew up, married, and had children. He gained a degree in engineering and seemed to be living the American dream. But his body was falling apart from diabetic complications.

His feet became deformed, his vision began to fail, his shoulders were frequently frozen, he was losing feeling in his feet, the hair on his lower legs disappeared (indicating peripheral vascular disease), he suffered night blindness, developed cataracts, and felt like an old man. He states, "I had three small children…and with good reason was certain I wouldn't live to see them grown."[12]

Bernstein's life began to turn around when he saw an ad in a medical magazine, which was promoting a machine for doctors and hospitals that would read blood-sugar levels in one minute using only a drop of blood. Richard immediately knew he had to get this device. It was expensive—it cost $650, equivalent to several thousand dollars today. Second, it wasn't even sold to ordinary folks. You had to be a doctor to order it. Bernstein's wife happened to be a doctor, and he had her order it for him.

With the new device he started measuring his blood sugar throughout the day and found it swung up and down wildly. Sometimes it would rise as high as 400 mg/dl; yet it could sink as low as 40 mg/dl after a large injection of insulin. He went from one insulin injection per day (the standard treatment in those barbaric days) to two and began to cut down on the carbs after noticing that the more carbs ingested, the higher the blood sugar. This helped stabilize the blood sugar a bit, but his diabetic complications were still increasing. Clearly there had to be something more he could do.

Richard began to research the medical literature to see if he could find articles giving a plan that would turn things around for him. At first he was looking primarily for some sort of exercise plan, thinking some research somewhere would show him just what type of exercises he could do to get his diabetes under control. But he could find no such research. What he did find, however, were animal studies that indicated that the closer you could come to bringing a diabetic animal's blood sugar to that of a non-diabetic, the more effectively you could stop and even reverse the deleterious effects of the diabetes.

Excited about this new information, he talked to his doctor about it, who wasn't the least impressed. He told him that humans weren't animals and besides that, it was impossible to normalize a diabetic's blood sugar. Bernstein wasn't buying it. He immediately began to do everything he knew to get his blood sugar normal. Being a type 1 this meant taking insulin for sure, but instead of just taking one or two shots per day, he began to take smaller and smaller doses, meant to deal with the precise number of carbs that entered his

At the time of this writing Dr. Bernstein is in his late seventies and is still healthy and active. Considering the primitive state of the field of diabetes research in his early days, he should be long dead by now. Because of the discoveries he made, he has no doubt added decades to his life, with great health thrown in for good measure. On top of that he has helped thousands to learn the simple lesson he discovered: **get your blood-sugar levels under control and you'll be free from the ill effects of diabetes.**

mouth for a particular meal. He spent the next year checking his blood sugar five to eight times a day. In short he became what many would call fanatical about keeping his blood sugar in the normal range around the clock. No highs, no lows, just the type of levels a normal person would have. He found that it was a lot easier to do this with low-carb meals, and refused to eat anything that might create too much of a bounce.

Amazing things began to happen. He started to gain weight (previously he hadn't been able to get above 115 pounds), most of his diabetic complications disappeared (a few were irreversible), and he felt like a new man. Bernstein writes, "I had taught myself how to make my blood-sugar levels whatever I wanted them to be and was no longer on the roller coaster. Things were under my control."[13] He had truly gained a new lease on life. Naturally he wanted to share his secret with the world, but the doctors and the medical journals wanted no part of his success story. They had already decided they knew what was best for diabetics, and they were not about to allow this engineer to tell them any different.

Finally in frustration Richard Bernstein went to medical school to become a doctor, figuring "if you can't beat 'em, join 'em." In a few years he had his medical degree, founded a practice to help diabetics, and wrote his first book. Today this pioneer in the field of diabetes is looked upon by many as the premier expert on the subject of diabetes. *Dr. Bernstein's Diabetes Solution* is perhaps the definitive book on the subject. The only problem with the approach he recommends in the book is that it is so strict that few would be willing to follow it. Nevertheless, you can learn a great deal from it.

Those who read Dr. Bernstein's books will quickly recognize that he emphasizes "tight control," and I really mean "*tight* control." His plan calls for a radical doing away with nearly all starches and sugars. It is so radical that most of the people who end up following his plan to the letter are the type 1's and those type 2's who are in such terrible shape they know that only a draconian solution will save them. For many of you it may not be necessary to be so drastic in your diet. But there are some basic principles you can learn from Bernstein's life and writings that will do you a world of good:

1. *Wild blood-sugar swings are going to kill you if you do not*

get them under control. When your blood-sugar levels are swinging wildly throughout the day they are doing untold damage. The sooner you learn this the better off you'll be. Some folks are like the ostriches, sticking their head in the sand, rarely monitoring their blood sugar, paying little attention to their diet, and being overweight to boot. "If I pretend I don't have diabetes I'll have no problems." Wrong, wrong, wrong!

2. *You can make a difference—you really can take control of your blood sugar.* The tools are available. The knowledge is available. The only question is one of motivation.

3. *The closer you get to keeping your blood sugar in the normal range (80 to 130 mg/dl), the more likely you are to live your life to the full and die "old and full of years."* Whatever it takes to keep those numbers down, whatever sacrifices must be made, they are well worth the enormous benefits and health that result. One major qualifier to this is that diabetics who inject insulin cannot merely take more and more insulin while they stuff themselves with starches and sugars, and expect good results. Insulin injections are most effective when combined with a low-carb diet.

4. *For diabetics, a low-carb diet is a major tool in getting your blood sugar under control.* If you think you can slay this beast without significantly reducing your intake of starches, sugars, and total carbs, you're living in a fantasy world. Toss that potato, pitch that pasta, sneer at that Snickers bar, and pass on that ice-cream-covered piece of apple pie. You have a life to live.

5. *Monitor your blood sugar.* For those who are challenged in comprehending messages, let me say it again: *"Monitor your blood sugar!"* And do it again and again and again. Stay on top of things and make adjustments as needed. What you might have been able to get away with ten years ago will not work now. Your glucose monitor is your buddy. Be prepared for a lifelong relationship.

6. *Work with a doctor who knows what he is doing.* Even today some diabetes doctors are nearly clueless. They offer little hope and routinely prescribe the same patently destructive low-fat, relatively high-carb diet that got you into this mess in the first place. Many feel it is enough to encourage you to trade in your white bread for "healthy whole-grain bread." They are seemingly ignorant that whole-grain bread will raise your blood sugar nearly as fast and just as high as the white stuff. Not all doctors are created equal, so do your homework, read experts like Dr. Bernstein, and make sure you entrust your health to a physician who truly knows his stuff.

Belly Fat

In my mid-teens I was one skinny kid. It used to bother me to be so thin, but nothing I did seemed to help me gain weight. My finicky appetite didn't help matters. Finally, around the age of 16 I got desperate. I started eating a fourth meal in the evenings, made up of things I liked that were high in calories. I would indulge in huge bowls of ice cream or sometimes eat two or three slices of bread covered liberally with peanut butter. Lo and behold, I started gaining weight. My body shape wasn't very impressive, however. I was still pretty scrawny in my arms and legs, but I had developed a nice plump belly. Realizing that this wasn't working, I began to lift weights and started looking a little better.

I didn't realize it at the time, but the tendency to accumulate fat around the belly is a strong indicator of potential problems with diabetes in later life. Slim-legged people with big stomachs are a walking diabetic time bomb. Obesity itself is a huge risk factor in developing diabetes, but when the fat goes straight to the stomach, it is the worst of all scenarios. Dr. Gerald Bernstein, director of the diabetes-management program at the Gerald J. Friedman Diabetes Institute at Beth Israel Medical Center in New York City observes,

> When those fat cells go in and around your belly, not down in your buttocks or your hips, but when it's around the belly…that fat in and of itself works to block the action of insulin, which is necessary to lower the blood sugar.[14]

Beyond that, fat cells are terribly inefficient at processing insulin to start with; muscle does a far better job. The more fat you accumulate, the more insulin-resistant you tend to become. In your youth you may be able to get away with being overweight and still have normal blood-sugar levels. But as you age and your metabolism slows down, all that fat will catch up with you. The bottom line is this: people who struggle with high blood sugar cannot afford to be overweight. If you are serious about getting your blood sugar under control you must take the necessary steps to get to a proper weight. If when you turn sideways and look at yourself in the mirror you discover a blob of flesh hanging out over your waist, you must deal with this.

That's the bad news; here's the good news: Our bodies are remarkably responsive to diet and exercise. And here's better news: we're not talking about turning you into some obsessed, sweaty gym freak, or putting you on concentration-camp rations. The first thing to know (and rejoice in) is that doing stomach crunches and sit-ups won't get rid of your belly fat anyway, so you can breathe easy. It is a myth that if you target an area of your body for strenuous exercise (spot exercise), you will get rid of all the fat buildup around that area. You will not. Thus, the answer to a large stomach is not sit-ups. They can be useful in toning, but they are not compulsory.

The beautiful thing about push-ups is that you don't have to go to a gym, and you don't need fancy equipment or weights of any kind. All you need is your body and a convenient floor—something most of us should be able to come up with!

What is it then? First and foremost, it is getting to the right weight for your height. This is something that should happen pretty naturally when you get serious about a low-carb diet. It is possible to eat low-carb and still be overweight, but it is not easy and it is not normal.

Second, anaerobic exercise (lifting weights, doing push-ups, and so forth) will build muscle, and every pound of your flesh that is converted to muscle is one less pound that will sit around as useless fat. You don't have to look like a weight lifter to be sure, but being relatively toned is a worthy goal. The great news is that you can achieve this with very little effort. Three or four sets of push-ups per day for three days out of the week will do wonders in this area. Add to this by investing in a pair of dumbbells, and you should have all you need to turn things around.

In years gone by aerobic exercise was more highly recommended by the experts for diabetics than anaerobic. But today opinions have changed, and nearly everyone is recognizing that a toned, lean body is a tremendous asset in the war against high blood sugar. Don't give up on your walking, jogging, or swimming, but make sure to pump a little iron or do those push-ups!

Exercise by itself, however, is not likely to get rid of all your belly fat. You are almost certainly going to have to drop some pounds as well. Lose enough weight and you'll lose that fat. There is absolutely no way a large stomach can maintain itself if you stop feeding it all those extra calories. And once the fat goes, you'll be amazed at how your insulin resistance will be diminished. Some experts estimate that as much as 90 percent of type 2 diabetes (particularly in America) is related to obesity and belly fat.

So…get your weight and your belly under control, and watch your blood-sugar numbers improve dramatically!

Two or Three Witnesses

As you search for answers to your problems with high blood sugar, it shouldn't take long to figure out the steps you'll need to take. Reducing carbs, exercise, and getting to the proper weight are agreed upon by all but the flakes and nuts. No, the problem isn't really figuring out what to do; it lies in making the tough choices and sticking with them day after day, month after month, and year after year.

What this means is that anything we can do that will help us with motivation is of tremendous value. And there are some things you can do. One of the best things is to do exactly what you are doing right now—read some good books that inform you and inspire you to take the necessary steps to get your blood sugar under control. But don't just depend only on this book you are now reading. There are some great books available that can be potent weapons in your battle against blood-sugar problems.

One of the Bible's principles says, "By the mouth of two or three witnesses let every word be established." Anything God seems to feel is worth saying, He says it more than once. This is why there are four Gospels— Matthew, Mark, Luke, and John—in the New Testament, not just one. God is so determined that you learn of His Son Jesus Christ that He says it four times over. There is something in the human psyche that needs to hear things repeated and restated in various forms for us to really get it. The business world knows this well. This is why you see commercials played over and over again, and sometimes you see the same commercial several times during a one-hour program. Companies know that if you don't get it the first or the tenth time, you may well by the twentieth or thirtieth.

So what does this have to do with diabetes? We can use this principle for our good by exposing our minds to the facts we so greatly need to hear and heed again and again. Because there aren't many videos on the subject of blood sugar or 30-second ads telling you to watch those carbs, what this comes down to is reading some great books about diabetes, insulin resistance, a low-carb diet, and the like. Add some Internet research and reading, and as you read and embrace the facts, a little something called motivation will magically appear in your life. You will find yourself not just knowing the right things to do, but actually wanting to *do* the right things. Here is where the battle is won.

Allow me to recommend some of the books I consider top-notch in the area of diabetes and the control of blood sugar:

- *Protein Power* by Michael and Mary Dan Eades.[15] This book is well written, insightful, and provides all kinds of great information and studies to utterly debunk the low-fat, high-carb diet that the "experts" have been pushing for years, to the destruction of so many Americans. You've got to read this book.

- *Dr. Atkins' New Diet Revolution* by Robert C. Atkins.[16] This book has been a huge bestseller. Although its primary purpose is to help people lose weight, it is of tremendous value to people like you who need some good information about blood sugar, insulin resistance, hyperinsulinism, and the dangers of high-carb diets.

- *Beat Diabetes!* by Margaret Blackstone.[17] The author of this book is not a doctor but rather a woman who ended up with severe diabetes. She was determined to "beat diabetes" by lifestyle change rather than taking shots, and she managed to do it. She got pretty fanatical about doing all the right things, and her life serves as a tremendous inspiration to all.

- *Dr. Bernstein's Diabetes Solution* by Richard Bernstein.[18] As mentioned in chapter 51, Dr. Bernstein is one of the world's foremost authorities on diabetes, and it is worth reading anything he has to say. Some of this book relates to type 1 diabetes, which the type 2's may not find relevant, but there is a lot of great information here. The book is worth the price just to read his own personal story in the first chapter—titled "My First Fifty Years as a Diabetic." Dr. Bernstein should have died decades ago, but instead found a way to dramatically increase his years and the quality of his health through tight, precise control of his blood sugar.

- *Overcoming Runaway Blood Sugar* by Dennis Pollock.[19] If the name sounds familiar, that is because it is mine. This was my first blood-sugar book, and it sold so many copies it amazed both me and my publisher. Like the one you are reading, it is geared to providing the basic facts you need in a language ordinary folks can appreciate.

I don't agree with every point made by each of these authors (other than me); nor do they agree with each other on everything. But they do agree on the basics you need to know and embrace if you are to see those numbers on your glucose monitor come down to a reasonable range.

One word of caution: A major weakness with some books on diabetes is that they are far too mild in the diets they recommend. If you were a firefighter attempting to put out a blazing forest fire, you couldn't just stand at the edge and hurl teaspoons of water at the flames. Huge fires call for drastic intervention, and some of the information you will come across doesn't go nearly far enough. Some will suggest that if you turn in your white bread for whole-wheat bread and your candy bars for bananas, all will be well. Most of us are going to have to go a lot further than that. I have looked at some of the diabetic meals in the backs of some of these books and magazines, and they sometimes total enough carbs to choke the proverbial (diabetic) horse.

The list in this chapter is certainly not exhaustive. But these books would make a great start in your quest for information and inspiration. And yes, choose the books you read wisely. But by all means read. By the mouth of many witnesses let a lifetime of good health, smart choices, and iron resolve be established in you.

Fat—Not the Monster
You've Been Told

For decades most voices in the medical and nutrition worlds have been warning you about the terrible dangers of fat. Cheeseburgers are a heart attack on a bun. Steaks are a heart attack without the bun. Fat is evil, carbs are good. Wise, healthy, hip folks eat carbs; ignorant, overweight, uneducated slobs eat fat. Fat will kill you in your forties; carbs, lots of carbs, and nearly nothing but carbs will keep you alive into your nineties. Never tire of eating your bagels, crackers, rice, bread, and Cap'n Crunch cereal. Eat them morning, noon, and night. As for fatty foods, maybe you can treat yourself to a small steak once a year, perhaps on your birthday.

There is but one little, bitty problem with this advice. *There are virtually no studies or research that bears this out.* When Robert Atkins first became prominent in advocating a low-carb diet that allowed significant fat, most doctors and nutritionists were either horrified or scornful. Everyone "knew" that the high-carb, low-fat diet was best. But to the world's astonishment unexpected things happened to those brave souls who adopted his diet. First, they lost weight, significantly more weight than they had been able to on the traditional low-fat diet. When the evidence of this became so preponderant that it could no longer be denied, they argued, "Okay, maybe you can lose weight on this diet, but it will kill you. It will drive your cholesterol into the stratosphere, and you'll soon keel over of a massive heart attack."

But a strange thing, indeed an unbelievable thing, began to happen to these low-carb, don't-worry-about-the-fat dieters. Their blood profiles actually improved. Their good-cholesterol-to-bad-cholesterol ratio improved, their triglycerides took a nosedive, and their blood-sugar levels improved dramatically. Slowly, ever so slowly, some in the medical field began to modify their views and allow that perhaps low-carb, higher-fat eating might not be the bogeyman it was initially thought.

Nina Teicholz has written a great article about fat. She begins,

> Suppose you were forced to live on a diet of red meat and whole milk. A diet that, all told, was at least 60 percent fat—about half of it saturated. If your first thoughts are of statins and stents, you may want to consider the curious case of the Masai, a nomadic tribe in Kenya and Tanzania.[20]

Teicholz goes on to tell the story. In the 1960s, a Vanderbilt University scientist, George Mann, MD, found that Masai men consumed this very diet (supplemented with blood from the cattle they herded). Yet these nomads, who were also very lean, had some of the lowest levels of cholesterol ever measured *and were virtually free of* heart disease.

Scientists, confused by the finding, argued that the tribe must have certain genetic protections against developing high cholesterol. But when British researchers monitored a group of Masai men who moved to Nairobi and began consuming a more modern diet, they discovered that the men's cholesterol subsequently skyrocketed.

On a personal note, some years ago I was having lunch with a Kenyan man, when we somehow got onto the subject of the Masai people. He told me he knew a doctor who had told him how amazed he was when he went to do an autopsy on someone from the Masai tribe (who eat meat and milk almost exclusively). This doctor told him the veins and arteries of the Masai were always clean and youthful, not clogged or hardened like those of other Kenyans who had eaten a more traditional diet. **The Masai, the Inuit Eskimos, and other groups that almost exclusively eat meat live with virtually no diabetes and heart disease.** This is a paradox that the low-fat, high-carb promoters have never been able to explain.

There are three major elements to the food we eat: carbohydrates, fat, and protein. There are not ten, or fifteen, or twenty—there are three. What this means is, if you drop one of these, you will almost surely increase the other two. If you do without carbs you will end up eating more fat and protein. If you do without fat, you will end up eating more carbs and protein. And if you are told that carbs are the healthiest thing going, and that fat is an evil monster that will immediately clog and harden your arteries, you will surely end up precisely where America is today—obese, with high cholesterol, and with record numbers of people experiencing heart problems and diabetes.

The greatest enemy to our health in these matters turns out not to be fat, but excess insulin. The result of a high-carb diet will always be that we fill our bloodstreams with high levels of insulin. A little insulin is a very good thing, but massive amounts of insulin circulating through our bodies and bloodstream day and night year after year is a very, very bad thing.

Is there research to support the idea that fat isn't the bad guy we once thought? There is indeed. Allison Boomer writes,

> For the past 40 years, well-meaning specialists have told Americans that eating saturated fat is bad for heart health. It now appears that conventional wisdom is on shaky ground. Last month's American Journal of Clinical Nutrition published a landmark study from the Harvard School of Public Health and the Children's Hospital Oakland Research Institute that has turned current fat recommendations upside down. The verdict from the study is that *"there is no significant evidence for concluding that dietary saturated fat is associated with an increased risk for heart disease."* Equally important, we are learning that *restricting fat intake is not without serious health consequences, such as escalating rates of obesity and diabetes.* The report evaluates dietary data from a total of 347,747 subjects from eight countries in 21 studies, over 25 years.[21]

In *The Harvard School of Public Health* newsletter we read,

> "Low-fat," "reduced fat," or "fat-free" processed foods are not necessarily "healthy," nor is it automatically healthier to

follow a low-fat diet. One problem with a generic lower-fat diet is that it prompts most people to stop eating fats that are good for the heart along with those that are bad for it. And low-fat diets are often higher in refined carbohydrates and starches from foods like white rice, white bread, potatoes, and sugary drinks. Similarly, when food manufacturers take out fat, they often replace it with carbohydrates from sugar, refined grains, or starch. Our bodies digest these refined carbohydrates and starches very quickly, causing blood sugar and insulin levels to spike and then dip, which in turn leads to hunger, overeating, and weight gain. Over time, eating lots of "fast carbs" can raise the risk of heart disease and diabetes as much as—or more than— eating too much saturated fat.[22]

The truth is this: you're going to have to eat something. If you're scared to death of fat, you'll end up eating too many carbs, which is the absolute worst thing a diabetic or prediabetic can do. Nor is it healthy to live on pure protein. The good news is that study after study has shown that fat is not the monster you've been told it is. Indeed, most people who go from low-fat, high-carb eating to a low-carb diet that ups the proteins and fats nearly always show significantly improved blood profiles and dramatically reduced blood-sugar levels.

Thoughts on Calories

Nutritionist Dr. Jonny Bowden is quoted in a WebMD article about the concept of counting calories:

> People haven't been counting calories forever (though some days it may feel as if *you* have). The idea became popular around the turn of the twentieth century, according to Jonny Bowden, PhD, CNS, a board-certified nutritionist and author of *Unbiased Truth About What You Should Eat and Why.* At that time, scientist Wilbur Atwater noticed that if you put food in a machine, called a "bomb calorimeter," and burned it, you could measure the ash and heat to find out how much "energy" was released and therefore how much "energy" was in the food. The idea caught on, and people began counting calories—that is, calculating exactly how many calories were consumed when eating particular foods, and "burned" when engaging in different activities. "A spate of diet books in the early part of the century popularized the notion that it's all about the calories—and it's been with us ever since," Bowden tells WebMD. [23]

Knowledge about calories can be a useful tool in losing weight, which in turn can be a great help in getting your blood sugar under control. As valuable as it is to limit carbs and choose low-carb foods over their sugary, high-carb cousins, we cannot be so naïve as to think that calories are irrelevant. Many foods advertised as low-carb are in fact high-calorie. One of the reasons that people who go on low-carb diets lose so much weight initially is that, at first, they hardly know what they can eat. They have a big list of no-no's, but a tiny list of yes-yes's. So naturally their calorie intake drops drastically and they end up losing weight fast.

If they stay low-carb very long they will, out of sheer desperation, begin to discover all sorts of low-carbs foods that will broaden their diet and even taste great. Nothing wrong with that. But sometimes in their newfound enthusiasm for their discovery of many great-tasting low-carb foods, they go hog wild (figuratively, and perhaps sometimes literally) and begin to overeat. The idea is, "It's low-carb, so I don't need to worry about calories or weight gain." Wrong. Weight gain will always occur when your calories ingested exceed your calories burned. In such a situation, you have two choices: burn more calories or ingest less.

If you find your weight falls easily into the normal range by eating a low-carb diet without ever counting calories, great! Keep on doing what you're doing. But if you are still struggling with weight and find that excess pounds refuse to depart, it may be time to consider the calories you are taking in each day. Read the labels of the foods you are buying at the store. Check the calories *and* the portion size, and make sure you are staying in your target range.

> Thomas Giesecke, MD, writes, "For weight loss to occur, total calories ingested must be exceeded by total calories expended. Reduced total calories a day form the basis for diabetic diets with carb counting being integral to that." This is a simple law of nature that cannot be circumvented or overcome.

On certain commercials for weight-loss programs, individuals boast about how they lost weight and were still able to eat pizza, desserts, various sweets, and so forth. They are technically right. You can lose weight eating a diet of ice cream and pizza if you keep your portions small enough. Conversely, you can become overweight eating salads and brown rice— if you eat them in monstrous amounts. Said differently, 100 calories of pizza will have the same effect on your weight as 100 calories of cucumbers, just like a ten-pound bag of feathers will weigh exactly the same as a ten-pound bag of marbles.

But although you can theoretically manage to lose weight eating all sorts of sugary foods, almost nobody would. You wouldn't be able to limit yourself to the small portion sizes you would need to eat in order to keep your intake calories at a level where they would not exceed the calories you burn. Also, you would be losing the game nutritionally. And of course eating sugary foods would make your blood-sugar levels jump all over the place.

In short, there are many tools at your disposal in your quest to overcome high blood sugar. Being cognizant of the calories in the foods you eat may well be a tremendous help in shedding that excess weight which can greatly improve your blood-sugar levels. The simple rule about calories is this:

1. Eat *more* calories than you burn—gain weight.

2. Eat *fewer* calories than you burn—lose weight.

3. Eat about *the same amount* of calories as you burn—maintain weight.

It's not rocket science, but we do need to be reminded of this sometimes!

Vicious and Blessed Cycles

Vicious cycles can be hard to escape. Consider the following:

Susan has gained a lot of weight. She doesn't find herself very attractive when she looks at herself in the mirror, which makes her depressed. As a result she tries to cheer herself up with the one thing that never fails to give her a boost: food. As she indulges in ice cream and doughnuts she gains more weight, which makes her more miserable. She makes ice cream and doughnuts the standard therapy for her depression and becomes heavier still. The more weight she gains, the more depressed she becomes. The more depressed she becomes, the more she eats. The more she eats, the more weight she gains…I'm sure you get the idea. She is caught in a vicious cycle.

On the other hand there are *blessed* cycles. (Most folks call these *virtuous* cycles, but I like the word *blessed*!) Let's say that Susan is able to cut down on her eating and loses a few pounds. She starts feeling really good about herself, which results in her not having the psychological need to snack so much. You can see where this is going.

Diabetes and insulin resistance are all about a vicious cycle. Nowhere is the term "spiraling out of control" more appropriate than when a person with normal blood-sugar levels suddenly starts seeing their numbers rise higher and higher. What is happening here?

Insulin resistance—the body's inability to process insulin efficiently, which results in the pancreas being forced to produce more and more insulin to barely handle what it used to process with ease—will almost never remain static. The more insulin-resistant you become, the more your exhausted pancreas will dump prodigious amounts of insulin into your bloodstream. As noted elsewhere in this book, this in itself is a dangerous situation, even if your blood-sugar levels could somehow remain fairly normal (and they will for a while). But it will not last.

And there is another factor involved in this vicious cycle that makes it even more dangerous. Not only do high levels of insulin increase insulin resistance, but they also play a role in your body's gaining weight more easily. So the more your blood sugar rises, the more insulin resistance increases and the more weight you tend to gain—which heightens insulin resistance all the more. And all of this means your poor old pancreas must work all the harder to keep up. And it will at some point throw up the white flag of surrender. Then your blood-sugar levels will go up and up and up, and you will become a raging, full-scale, hard-core diabetic. This can happen with dizzying speed once your insulin resistance hits the "critical threshold."

The longer your body remains saturated with insulin, sometimes three, four, or five times the normal levels, the more immune your cells will be toward that insulin. In *Beat Diabetes!*, Margaret Blackstone writes,

> If you begin to overload your system with carbohydrates, your pancreas will respond by producing more insulin to cope with processing the carbohydrates. If you overload your system for years with carbs, your pancreas becomes stuck in an insulin overproduction mode. Concomitantly, your body becomes used to excessive amounts of insulin— you might even say inured—and more and more insulin becomes necessary to do the job of regulating blood glucose. Your cells become resistant to insulin. Whereas before the receptors on the cells needed only a small amount of insulin to keep blood sugar in the normal range, now they need more and more. The situation becomes chronic, and insulin resistance or hyperinsulinemia ensues. In much the same way as an alcoholic views liquor, your metabolism's relationship with insulin becomes one of too much is not enough. Eventually all the insulin in the world can't handle regulating glucose.[24]

There is, however, a possibility—even a likelihood—of halting and even reversing this cycle. You probably have already figured it out. When you stop overdosing on the carbs, your pancreas stops flooding your system with massive doses of insulin. Your receptor cells, the ones responsible for converting glucose into energy, begin to "perk up." They can actually recover much of their lost ability over time and become fairly efficient in processing carbohydrates again. In time you may well find that you can eat the same exact meal that used to cause your blood sugar to rise to 185, and discover that it now rises to a much more manageable 142. Same food, but a more efficient metabolism. You have entered the zone of the "blessed cycle." Stay there!

In short, do anything you can do to decrease insulin resistance so you can get off this terrible loop of ever-increasing blood sugar and demands for more and more insulin. Your primary weapon in this battle is to significantly reduce carb intake, not just for a time but for the rest of your days. Yes, there are other things you can do, but nothing works so well as carb reduction. Beyond that, exercise regularly as your doctor allows and get your weight to the proper level.

What a simple and yet awesome thought it is that we can do something about our diabetes! In so many diseases and physical afflictions we have only two things to do: 1) go to the doctor and 2) hope everything works out. But with runaway blood sugar we can have a *huge* say in determining the outcome. Will this thing spoil our remaining years and eventually kill us, or will it be converted from a fearful monster into a little harmless puppy that can do little more than occasionally yap at our heels and remind us of its presence?

Doctors—the Good, the Bad, and the Uninformed

When I first discovered I had serious blood-sugar issues I went into a research mode, reading all I could about diabetes and doing Internet searches using the phrase "reverse diabetes." For a while things just seemed to get worse and worse. Finally I did what I should have done much sooner—I went to the doctor. But not having health insurance I went to a general practitioner rather than one specializing in diabetes, trying to save money. This doctor was nice and I'm sure she was well intentioned, but she didn't seem to have a clue about what was really going on. She took out a list of questions and started asking me one after another, marking my answers. My fasting blood sugar was still in the normal range at that time, so this was the only other thing she knew to do.

I told her of my ups and downs and how I would have the hypoglycemic episodes, one of which caused me to pass out after church on Sunday morning. She told me to eat more protein, which was helpful, but seemed nearly as clueless as I was about the cause of my problems. I have often thought of how much more help I could be to someone in a similar situation who came to me now and told me their symptoms, knowing what I know today. (I know, I'm not a doctor, but one can fantasize!) First, I would immediately insist they purchase a blood-sugar monitor and start monitoring their blood sugar like crazy. I would have them keep a journal of their numbers, both fasting blood sugar and post-meal blood sugar, writing down what was eaten at each meal. Then I would have them come back in a few weeks to look at the results together. But this doctor did none of this.

Many years later I was at a general practitioner's office again, though for a different reason. By then I had long since figured out the things I am sharing in this book, and my blood sugar was under control. As we talked she mentioned how good bananas were in providing potassium. I told her that I rarely ate bananas because of my blood-sugar problems, and I mentioned that a large banana had as much sugar as a candy bar. She looked at me quizzically and said, "Really?" It had never dawned on me that a doctor wouldn't know this, but here was living proof.

The point here is that doctors are not always the all-knowing, all-wise repositories of knowledge and truth that we sometimes think they are. This is not to suggest we can do without them—far from it. But we must remember that just like there are better and worse plumbers, and good and bad teachers, architects, and police officers, so there are some doctors who are far more knowledgeable and helpful than others. And in the area of diabetes it is critical that you get excellent medical advice and help. You cannot afford to settle for a mediocre doctor or worse. If you were going to have heart surgery you would want someone who is world-class. You should be no less discriminating about the physician who provides you diabetes counsel and monitors your progress. Get the best you can.

If you encounter a dinosaur, run for your life and don't look back! By "dinosaur," I mean a doctor of the old-school type who still clings to the disastrous 1950s idea that diabetics need a high-carb, low-fat diet. There aren't too many of them still around, but there are probably a few.

You want a doctor who takes a positive, proactive approach to combating diabetes. Some doctors have decided that diabetes is going to get you eventually and there is not that much you can do but keep your blood-sugar levels from the uppermost limits. As long as you keep it under 190 or so, they are happy. Find a doctor who will work with you to help you bring your blood-sugar levels as close as is reasonably possible to a normal person's.

Remember that it is your life and your health that you are dealing with. It is not your doctor who will suffer from eye problems, kidney failure, and leg amputations if you don't bring that blood sugar under control—it is you! You have every right to look for the best, and if the first doctor you go to doesn't meet your standards, go to another. Don't quit searching until you find someone who knows what they are doing, and makes it clear that they are eager to work with you. If at all possible find one who specializes in diabetes. And by all means get a doctor who has a positive attitude and encourages you to believe that you can win.

Don't stop until you have found a doctor you can trust. The saying goes, "The man who represents himself in court has a fool for a client." Likewise the diabetic or prediabetic who tries to doctor himself...well, you get the idea!

Beware (Some) Diabetic Recipes

We sometimes see booklets in the stores that give a few suggestions for diabetics and then pack in recipes for all kinds of delicious foods "safe for diabetics." Far too often readers assume that *safe* really means *safe*, and get excited about this new collection of recipes to try. They follow the "experts," but sadly it is often the blind leading the blind.

In researching this book I picked up a couple of booklets like this, one by *Prevention Guide* and the other by *Reader's Digest*. The *Prevention* booklet proudly sports the headline, "Reverse Diabetes Naturally" (with a tantalizing piece of chocolate cake on the cover), and the *Reader's Digest* booklet leads with "Foods That Fight Diabetes." Not to be too much of a Scrooge, I will admit that some of the recipes they give could be useful and are well worth trying. But others are terrible. This is pretty much par for the course in most diabetic recipe books. Don't believe everything you read.

The problem with many of these recipe books is that they start with all the wrong assumptions. They aren't worried about what will send your blood sugar soaring; they are simply following a worn-out, patently false theory that says as long as you are eating whole-grain, low-fat foods, you are fine. Never mind that you are loading your body with carbs that will turn to sugar almost immediately. At least those carbs are coming from healthy, low-fat, whole-grain foods, and everybody knows that these are good for you—right? Wrong!

As an example, the *Reader's Digest* booklet contains a recipe for "Chicken and Broccoli Chapatis." At the top of the recipe it gives you what I suppose is their justification for calling this a food for diabetics: "Chapatis arc Indian breads made from whole-wheat flour and water, then baked on a dry griddle without any fat…" The accompanying picture looks delicious, for sure. And most of the ingredients are fine. But the "whole wheat,

cooked without any fat" chapati is a nightmare for diabetics and brings
the carb count up to 65 grams per serving. This is horrendous, and the
Reader's Digest folks ought to be prosecuted for attempted murder. (Okay,
I'm kidding, but surely they are committing some crime! Where are the
low-carb police when you need them?)

Worse still is the "Rigatoni with Broccoli Rabe" recipe, which comes
in at a whopping 98 grams of carbs per serving. If that doesn't drive your
blood sugar above 200 (and some of you closer to 300), nothing will.
They also have a homemade hamburger (combining lean ground beef with turkey) recipe, which they justify because "our beef and bird version cuts saturated fat and has just a third of the usual calories." They insist that you use whole-grain buns. Again we see the "carbs don't really count as long as they come from whole-grain products" mentality. In terms of nutrition, whole grain is preferable to white, but in terms of diabetes and blood sugar, a carb is a carb is a carb. If you don't believe that, just ask your blood-sugar monitor.

> **There are a number of low-carb desserts you can enjoy,** but cake is not one of them. Don't try to find a chocolate cake that has a few less calories than the regular one—give up on chocolate cake altogether. Even if the recipe doesn't call for a single teaspoon of added sugar, those flour carbs are going to turn into sugar with lightning speed once they hit your stomach.

The *Prevention* booklet is not quite so over the top, but some of its recipes are still far too high in carbs. The chocolate cake shown on the cover is titled "Double-Dipper Chocolate Delight." I suppose they justify putting it in a booklet that says, "Outsmart Diabetes" because they call for whole-grain pastry flour rather than white, and use sugar-free chocolate fudge frosting rather than regular. A single slice of this cake still comes out at 40 grams of carbs per serving—better than most chocolate cakes, but still far too high. Add this 40-carb-gram dessert on top of their "whole wheat penne with shrimp" meal, containing 50 grams, and you are sending shock waves throughout your body, metabolically speaking.

Diabetes is nothing to play around with. You have to trim your carbohydrate intake *significantly*. Changing from white flour to whole-grain may impress others, but it will not impress your weakened pancreas or your worn-out receptor cells, which have grown insulin-resistant.

And switching from regular pasta to whole-wheat pasta will show almost no difference on your blood-sugar monitor.

So be a little cautious, and remember that not all that glitters is gold, and not all recipes printed in a diabetic cookbook are fit for consumption by a diabetic.

Can Diabetes Be Cured?

When I first started experiencing blood sugar run amok, I soon knew I was facing the same beast that had taken both of the legs of my mother and brought her to an early death. I began to read and research like crazy. I was not looking for merely something to make me feel a little more normal; I wanted a complete cure. In my Internet searches I used phrases like "cure for diabetes" and "reverse diabetes," hoping I could find something that would make all this go away like some bad dream. I wanted to be so completely over this mess that I could eat a huge bowl of ice cream and my blood sugar would remain rock-steady. It didn't happen.

As you look through the nearly infinite number of books, booklets, and articles on diabetes, you will indeed find quite a few with titles like "Reversing Diabetes," "Cure for Diabetes," and so forth. Is this even possible? Once you are diabetic or prediabetic, can you ever be so completely recovered that you will never have to worry about diabetes the rest of your life?

The answer is yes…and no. First I have to confess my own complete conviction that with God all things are possible. So I would never tell anyone that any disease cannot be completely cured. But short of a divine miracle, we need to qualify ourselves when we speak of cures for diabetes or permanent reversal. Type 1 diabetics, whose pancreases produce no (or very little) insulin, will need to inject themselves with insulin for the rest of their days. There are no if's, and's, or but's about this.

However, they have a huge say as to how much insulin they will require. By strictly limiting carbs and keeping trim they can require far less insulin than otherwise (doing their bodies a tremendous favor), have far fewer hypoglycemic episodes, and experience few or no diabetic complications. In other words, apart from the fact that they will need to administer insulin to themselves, they can live normal lives, and die "old, and full of days."

Many, if not most, type 2 diabetics have the possibility of getting to the point of requiring no oral agents or insulin, and getting their blood-sugar levels to the point where a doctor would tell them they are not diabetic. Margaret Blackstone, author of the book *Beat Diabetes!*, is a great case in point. When she was first diagnosed as diabetic she was told she might be close to being a type 1. Her blood sugar was all over the chart, and her doctor wanted to start her on insulin injections. She convinced him to give her a week to get things under control and went on a crash low-carb diet, carefully counting her carbs and setting 30 grams as her total daily limit. She writes, "What I couldn't eat could fill a book."[25] To her great joy, she saw her blood-sugar levels drop to nearly normal in a very short time. Within a week she was seeing blood sugar consistently between 77 and 115. Such is the power of the low-carb diet.

There are thousands and tens of thousands of similar testimonies, including mine. By carefully controlling the number of carbs that pass through their lips daily, keeping at a reasonable weight, and exercising moderately four or five times a week, many type 2's will be able to bring their blood-sugar levels to resemble those of a "normal person."

Let's say you're a type 2 diabetic who has been carefully controlling your carbs, your weight, and the amount of exercise you get. You go to a doctor unfamiliar with your history and have him check you for diabetes. He will tell you with all confidence you are not diabetic! Your fasting blood sugar will be normal, your A1C test will be fine, and even your post-meal blood-sugar levels will be excellent. If you still said something like, "Doc, I'm worried I might be diabetic," he would assure you, **"You don't need to worry about that. Your tests show you're doing fine."** And he would be right, except for his ignorance of what you need to do to keep those blood-sugar levels low.

In practical terms it is quite possible and even likely that most type 2 diabetics (especially those who figure out what to do early in the game and have the courage to do it) should be able to live a normal life, maintain normal blood-sugar levels, and escape those terrible and fearful "diabetic complications." However, if your idea of "reversing diabetes" or being cured from it means you think you'll be able to go back to eating and living like you did when you were 20, guzzling king-sized soft drinks, scarfing down ice-cream sundaes, enjoying candy bars whenever you feel like it, and never exercising, you are living in a dream world. The diabetes you think you overcame will soon be back, and with a vengeance!

The reality is this: apart from a miracle, you will never be able to go back again. You will need to check carbohydrate grams on food products, say no to apple pie and ice cream, mashed potatoes, and french fries, test your blood sugar, and stay reasonably slim all the rest of your days if you want those low blood-sugar levels and the incredible benefits that they produce. But this should not be a discouraging thought; it should be exhilarating to know that you have a huge say in your own health and well-being, both now and decades down the road. By the grace of God, you can do it!

As the Years Roll By

Many years ago I bought one of the worst cars ever sold—a Yugo. It looked great but was built cheaply. It was always needing repairs. Finally a woman did me a favor and ran into the back of me one day, effectively totaling the car. I was determined to get a reliable vehicle this time around and bought a Toyota van. It wasn't new—we weren't rich enough for that—but it looked almost new and was the best vehicle I had ever owned up to that time. As it sat in our driveway, sleek and shiny, I was admiring my latest wheels, when a sad thought occurred to me: this was the best this van was ever going to look. No matter how well I cared for it, the years would bring on dents and dullness, and eventually engine problems and the car graveyard.

That is pretty much the state of the human body when we are 25 or so. It will never look better or work so efficiently. As you pass through your thirties, forties, and above, your body will grow increasingly less efficient and, sadly, less attractive. Some of us break down sooner than others, but we will all break down. We will run more slowly, see less sharply, hear less acutely, gain weight more easily, and lose weight with more difficulty— and (speaking to the point of this book) we will process carbohydrates and sugar less effectively.

Specifically, your metabolism will slow down, your pancreas will produce less insulin, and your body will require significantly more insulin to handle sugar than in the "good old days." You will likely lose muscle mass, become more flabby, and be less physically active than in your teens and twenties. Some people can handle all this and still maintain respectable blood-sugar levels. Since you are reading this book, chances are you cannot. Like millions of others your blood-sugar levels have been rising, and your poor, tired pancreas has been gamely wearing itself out, trying to keep up.

It is helpful to take inventory of what you can do and what you cannot do. Certainly you cannot turn back the clock. You will never get your 25-year-old body back. What you can do, however, is be far more conscientious about your health and eating habits than you were in your youth. This can go a long way in making up for a body that experienced its best days a couple of decades ago.

A 55-year-old woman who eats wisely (keeping carbs low and vegetables high), exercises regularly, and stays on the slim side is in many respects in a better position than her 25-year-old neighbor who does the reverse. The young woman is in the process of destroying her body. Yes, she may look better, run faster, be wrinkle-free, and push more pounds at the health club. But her foolish disregard for her health is steadily bringing about deterioration of health and body. She is slowly and surely destroying herself, day by day and meal by meal. On the other hand, the 55-year-old is on pace for a long and healthy life. She may well be nearly as healthy—metabolically speaking—15 years from now as she is presently.

> **Your exercise may need some alterations.** Older legs and knees can't handle the pounding they could in their youthful days. In most cases exercise sessions will need to be a bit longer than before, but less intense. Brisk walks will often be the best choice for us as we age. Swimming is also a nice low-impact exercise.

The key is to stay on target. Once you have determined your upper blood-sugar limit, do whatever it takes to keep within that boundary. As you get older you may find you can't tolerate the same portion of rice you could before and still maintain your goal. Before, you could eat a fistful of rice with a particular meal and keep under 150 mg/dl at your post-meal reading. Now you find that the same portion drives your blood sugar into the 170 range. The answer is obvious: cut back on the rice and make up for it with a larger helping of green beans (or broccoli, salad, or cauliflower). You may need to drop a few more pounds. Your body may not be able to tolerate sugar-alcohols as before. In short, there will probably be some adjustments you will need to make.

Don't ever stop checking your blood sugar. For those who are able to keep their blood sugar down without medication or injected insulin, there is a tendency to stop checking yourself once you have determined what works for you and what does not. You discover the safe meals and the dangerous ones. You have tested a particular meal five or six times and found that your blood sugar always behaves itself with that meal. So why keep testing?

It may not be necessary to test after every meal all the time in such cases, but changing and aging bodies require constant monitoring. In addition we are often trying new variations to our diets. We can sometimes be surprised when certain meals, which we feel confident will go easy on our blood sugar, give us a nasty surprise. So keep on testing. The little money you invest in test strips is one of the smartest expenditures you can make.

The great news is that with a little common sense, a moderate and informed lifestyle, and the grace of God you should be able to live out your years without those terrible diabetic complications. The information you need is readily available. Hopefully this book has provided a little of the inspiration. Now go out and make your life worth living!

List of Recipes in This Book

There are myriads of low-carb recipe books around, but it was not my intention to write one. However, in sharing some basic secrets and tips on the low-carb lifestyle, I couldn't resist sharing a few of the recipes that have become my old friends. To me, these recipes and the foods they produce are nearly indispensable. They help keep me from feeling so much like a martyr as I routinely say no again and again to foods that most Americans would never dream of sacrificing.

Most of the recipes relate to the bread family. Bread is especially problematic for the diabetic, since 1) most of us feel a meal is incomplete without it, and 2) it is becoming almost impossible to find low-carb bread items or even mixes in the grocery stores these days.

These few recipes can give you something to start with, as you begin to make the dietary transformation you know is necessary.

List of Carbohydrate Charts in This Book

Notes

1. Harvard Health Publications, "Eating nuts promotes cardiovascular health," May 2005, www .health.harvard.edu/press_releases/benefits_eating_nuts.

2. Mayo Clinic, "Nuts and Your Heart: Eating Nuts for Heart Health," www.mayoclinic.com/ health/nuts/HB00085.

3. Jenny Ruhl, *Blood Sugar 101—What They Don't Tell You About Diabetes* (Turners Falls, MA: Technion Books, 2008).

4. Ruhl, p. 51.

5. Ruhl, p. 51.

6. Laura Dolson, "Is Whole Wheat Bread a Good Choice on a Low-Carb Diet?" http://lowcarb diets.about.com/od/nutrition/a/wholewheatbread.htm.

7. CBS News, "Juice As Bad As Soda, Docs Say," February 11, 2009, www. cbsnews.com/2100-204_162-673229.html.

8. Abstract: Manisha Chandalia et al., "Beneficial effects of high dietary fiber intake in patients with type 2 diabetes mellitus," *The New England Journal of Medicine*, May 11, 2000, 1392-1398; abstract from PubMed.gov, www.ncbi.nlm.nih.gov/pubmed/10805824.

9. Laura Dolson, "Flax Seed—the low-carb whole grain," About.com, November 16, 2010, http:// lowcarbdiets.about.com/od/whattoeat/a/flaxinfo.htm.

10. Michael Eades and Mary Dan Eades, *Protein Power* (New York: Bantam Books, 1999).

11. Eades, p. 24.

12. Richard Bernstein, *Dr. Bernstein's Diabetes Solution* (New York: Little Brown & Company, 1997), xvii.

13. Richard Bernstein, p. xx.

14. Gerald Bernstein, as quoted in Health.com, "Why Getting Rid of Belly Fat May Lower Type 2 Diabetes Risk," Health.com, www.health.com/health/condition-article/0,,20188164,00.html.

15. Eades.

16. Dr. Robert Atkins, *Dr. Atkins' New Diet Revolution* (New York: Avon Books, 1992).

17. Margaret Blackstone, *Beat Diabetes!* (Avon, MA: Adams Media Corporation, 2000).

18. Richard Bernstein.

19. Dennis Pollock, *Overcoming Runaway Blood Sugar* (Eugene, OR: Harvest House Publishers, 2006).

20. Nina Teicholz, "What if bad fat is actually good for you?" MensHealth.com, www.menshealth .com/health/saturated-fat.

21. Allison Boomer, "What does saturated fat cause?" *Boston Globe*, February 24, 2010, emphasis (italics) added.

22. Harvard School of Public Health Newsletter, "Fats and Cholesterol: Out with the Bad, In with the Good," accessed December 26, 2012, at www.hsph.harvard.edu/nutritionsource/what-should-you-eat/fats-full-story/index.html.

23. Jenny Stamos Kovacs, "The Do's and Don'ts of Counting Calories," *WebMD*, www.webmd .com/diet/features/dos-donts-counting-calories.

24. Blackstone, p. 34.

25. Blackstone, p. 19.

About Dennis Pollock and
Spirit of Grace Ministries

Dennis Pollock is the founder and president of Spirit of Grace Ministries. His primary work in this ministry is to write and record devotional biblical teachings and to hold missions conferences and evangelistic outreaches in Africa. You can learn more about his ministry by visiting the website: **www.spiritofgrace.org.**

Dennis's experience with runaway blood sugar has led him to become a part-time health advocate, but his primary passion has always been to teach the Bible and lift up Jesus Christ. He has felt called to write some 1250 devotional teachings and record them, and is busy continually producing new teachings. A catalog of the teachings currently available is online, and this list is growing every month. You can find the current list by going to the Spirit of Grace website (spiritofgrace.org) and clicking on the "1250 Catalog" icon. Here you can read titles and descriptions of all the teachings available and order CDs or download the teachings as mp3 audio files (includes a written version).

The ministry sends out a newsletter, which includes a major teaching article, on a monthly basis. This newsletter is available in either regular or e-mail version. There is no cost for the newsletter—just e-mail or write Spirit of Grace Ministries and give your physical or e-mail address, and you can begin receiving these uplifting articles, plus the latest news about the ministry.

Dennis would love to hear from you! Feel free to e-mail him and share your journey with blood-sugar issues or your journey with the Lord Jesus. Send your e-mails to grace@spiritofgrace.org. Also, if your church or organization would like Dennis to come and teach on a biblical theme (and perhaps give a workshop on diabetes), feel free to e-mail him with your request and the time of the year you are interested in. Some of the themes Dennis teaches on include "The Ways of God," "The Abiding Life," "The Making of a Man or Woman of God," "The Holy Spirit in the Old Testament," "The Tough Questions of the Bible," and "Making Wise Decisions," along with many more.

Spirit of Grace Ministries
PO Box 2068
McKinney, TX 75070
Website: www.spiritofgrace.org
E-mail: grace@spiritofgrace.org